Penguin Books

Overcoming Computer Illiteracy

Ray Curnow was born in Aberavon, South Wales, in 1928. He first became involved with computers in 1945, as an undergraduate at Imperial College, London, where he worked on several of the first university-industrial joint ventures in computer development. After graduating in mathematics and statistics, he worked for a number of companies developing computer applications and for several computer manufacturers, including I.B.M., I.C.T. and Sperry-Rand-Univac. In 1967 he joined the Science Policy Research Unit, University of Sussex, where he specialized in the study of high technology and its applications. In 1978 he co-authored a major study for the U.K. Government on the impact of microelectronic technology, later published as *The Future with Microelectronics*. He left SPRU in 1979 to set up an independent consultancy, Probit Consultancies, which advises companies and government organizations concerning the impact of information technology and other new technologies upon their operations and their markets. Ray Curnow acted as adviser to the British Broadcasting Corporation on a number of recent television series on computing, microelectronics and their applications, including 'The Computer Programme'. He is a Visiting Professor in the Department of Systems Science at City University, London.

Susan Curran was born in Aylesbury in 1952, and grew up mainly in Sheffield. She read English at the University of Sussex, graduating in 1973. She then worked in insurance until 1979 when she joined her husband, Ray Curnow, in setting up Probit. She has since specialized in writing for lay audiences on computing and allied subjects; her books include *New Technology and Insurance, Office Automation* (with Horace Mitchell) and *Micro Man* (with Gordon Pask).

Susan Curran and Ray Curnow have collaborated on one earlier book, *The Silicon Factor*. They live in Norwich and have two sons.

Overcoming Computer Illiteracy
A friendly introduction to computers

Susan Curran and Ray Curnow

Penguin Books

Penguin Books Ltd, Harmondsworth, Middlesex, England
Penguin Books, 40 West 23rd Street, New York, New York 10010, U.S.A.
Penguin Books Australia Ltd, Ringwood, Victoria, Australia
Penguin Books Canada Ltd, 2801 John Street, Markham, Ontario, Canada L3R 1B4
Penguin Books (N.Z.) Ltd, 182–190 Wairau Road, Auckland 10, New Zealand

First published in Great Britain in simultaneous hardcover and paperback editions
by Allen Lane and Penguin Books under the title *The Penguin Computing Book* 1983
First published in the United States of America by Penguin Books 1984

Printed and bound in Great Britain by William Clowes Limited, Beccles and London

Filmset in Univers

For Rufus

Contents

List of Figures

List of Tables

Preface

This is a book about computing; it is only secondarily a book about computers.

Our aim is to show what computing means, what can be achieved through it, and how the application of technology to computing has enabled its meaning and its achievements to be expanded. We start with a basic look at how symbols can be manipulated; next, we propose, through a look at early computers, to consider the technology of modern computers and some of the peripheral devices used with them. We look at some simple programs for modern computers, then outline some applications that are too complex for us to show how they are programmed in detail. The book ends with a section on the most complex of all computer applications: the search for 'artificial intelligence'. Obviously, we cannot discuss every aspect of computing *en route*, but we hope to provide enough detail to enable a reader who is new to the field to understand how the very complex applications with which the book ends depend upon the basic principles with which it began.

This book is intended to be comprehensible to people who have little or no prior knowledge of computing. We do not take for granted any familiarity either with mathematics (which we have tried to avoid throughout) or with the principles of electronics. We do not assume that readers will have used a computer or will have access to a computer. Therefore, this book is not a guide to programming or operating any specific computer — though we do, inevitably, introduce some specific computers as examples when we come to consider computer system architecture and programming, and we do discuss some aspects of choosing and using a computer.

Stress is laid on the wide range of applications of computing and computers; we have devoted very little space to commercial data processing. However, this does not mean that the book is specifically about home or personal computers; we discuss larger computer systems and their applications, too. We do not, however, discuss (except in passing) the economics of the computer industry, or the economic implications of the use of computers.

How to Use this Book

The book is written as a narrative, and it will make most sense to a reader who starts at the beginning and works his way through it. The sections on the development of the computer, for instance, are not included purely for historical interest: they are intended to expand our thesis on what computing is all about, making use of historical examples. Similarly, the section on machine code programming is an important preface to the later section on programming in high-level languages; the latter will make more sense to a reader who has absorbed the former. However, we have tried as far as possible to make individual chapters comprehensible on their own, and we include cross-references from one chapter to another, as a guide to readers who do not wish to work right through the book. Many of the chapters in Part Three, on aspects of modern computer technology, and in Part Five, on larger-scale computer applications, *are* virtually self-contained, and may be used for reference without reading the rest of the book.

We have tried to cover a wide selection of aspects of computing that will be of interest to the general reader: to the reader who uses, or expects to use, computers on a casual basis; to the reader thinking of buying a personal computer; and to the reader who wants to gain a general overview of the field before considering a career in some aspect or other of computing. Initially, you will probably be uncertain how relevant some of the sections – particularly the more technical ones – may be to your own planned involvement with computing. However, we do urge you to persevere with them. They are designed to build up a good general level of 'computer literacy': of understanding just what computing is about, what comprises a modern computer, and what computers can do. Once you have read this book, we hope you will be able, say, to read through one of the more demanding computer journals (such as *Byte*) and make sense of its contents; or to make an informed evaluation of the respective merits of competing computer systems on offer; or to judge whether any specific application might reasonably be performed on a computer. We believe that a basic degree of familiarity with every field that we cover is essential to the acquisition of such understanding.

In short, if your interest in computing is a general one, then we hope to satisfy your curiosity and provide you with a good, broad grounding. If your interest is more specific, this book should provide a solid framework on which you will be able to build up more detailed knowledge in those areas that particularly concern you. After reading this book, for instance, you may like to go on to a book about programming a computer in a specific language . . . to a book that deals with microelectronic technology in more depth . . . or to a book that goes into greater detail in a particular field of application for computers. We offer some suggestions in the Select Bibliography at the end of the book.

Acknowledgements

Inevitably, we are not experts in the whole of the field we cover in this book; we have tried to make up for the gaps in our own knowledge by calling liberally on that of friends and colleagues. Particular thanks are due to the following:

Ian Haddon, who read through much of the first three sections of the book, and made many valuable comments;

Larry Rowe, Brian Ashton and their colleagues at LJ Electronics Ltd. Larry patiently explained many points about machine code programming and lent us the EMMA microcomputer system that we use as an example in Chapters 22 and 24. He also read and commented on drafts of these two chapters;

John Sayer and his colleagues at Tandy U.K. who lent us the TRS-80 Model II small business computer system that we use as an example in Chapters 23 and 26, and elsewhere in the book. We wrote much of the manuscript on the system, using Tandy's SCRIPSIT word-processing package. John also checked the sections of the book that deal specifically with the system;

Roger Mortimore, Mike Moore and their colleagues at Edenwade Ltd. They discussed and demonstrated their system at great length for us, commented on our draft of Chapter 29, and provided the material for Figures 82–85;

Dr Brian Golding, who researched the section on the U.K. Meteorological Office, and commented on our draft of Chapter 30;

Lewis Paterson, who helped to modify the ELIZA program we use as an example in Chapter 34;

And finally, special thanks are offered to Susan's parents, Maureen and Norman Griffin, who helped to keep us sane as the deadline approached.

Of course, the responsibility for any errors or shortcomings remains ours alone.

Susan Curran and Ray Curnow,
Norwich, U.K.
October 1982

Part One: Manipulating Symbols

What do computers do? That is a question which can be answered in at least two ways. Computers have an endless list of applications: specific tasks to which they are applied, in all kinds of fields. But they have a very small number of functions, that is, of basic abilities that they use in carrying out their tasks.

We shall tackle the problem of explaining what computers do by looking first, and very briefly, at some of their applications. We shall then try to distil out of these the common functions of computers that underlie them. Later in the book, we shall come back to look in much greater detail at present-day computer applications.

You probably already know that computers can be used to:

calculate: They perform the calculations that underlie weather prediction. They calculate the flight paths of spacecraft. They tot up gas and electricity bills.

store information: Computers keep track of files of financial information in most large companies and many small ones. They handle airlines' flight reservations. They hold information on criminals and suspects; on diaries and agendas; on recipes and birthday dates. They even hold the information needed to reproduce a particular picture, or play back a piece of music.

communicate: Networks of computers can shuffle information from place to place, from person to person. Computers are found in telephone exchanges and in satellites; running printers and controlling video screens.

control: Computers supervise the sequence of operations in automatic washing machines. They control the browning level to produce a perfect piece of toast. They keep industrial processes within safe limits; they keep petrol consumption in cars to an economic minimum.

Calculate, store information, communicate, control: these are all functions of computers. But are there other functions, underlying still other applications? Basically, the answer is no. Take any computer application, from the very simplest (adding 2 to 3, controlling a timeswitch) to the apparently very complicated ('writing' a novel, 'talking' to a psychiatric patient), and you will find that it can be broken down into some combination of calculating, storing information, communicating and controlling.

Let us put this a little more formally, and attempt to define the functions of a computer:

A computer is a device that stores and manipulates data, that can control other devices as a result of its manipulation and storage of data, and that can communicate with other computers, with other types of device, and with human beings.

This is one definition of a computer, but of course there are many more. We will quote some of them:

'machine which "memorizes", sifts, analyses and correlates data, and produces selective information as required'   (*Penguin English Dictionary*)

'Any machine which can accept data in a prescribed form, process the data and supply the results of the processing in a specified format as information or as signals to control automatically some further machine or process.'   (A. Chandor, *A Dictionary of Computers*)

'A computer is a machine for storing, processing and displaying information'   (C. D. Renmore, *Silicon Chips and You*)

The emphasis varies, but they all convey the same general idea. Computers store and handle data, control, and communicate. We will be looking at each of these aspects of computer capability in turn, and at how they are interrelated. In this first section, we shall look first at how the computer stores data, then at how it manipulates it.

1. In Theory: Aspects of Data

What is 'data'? We shall not offer another assortment of definitions here, but will just say for now that data are known facts. 'Data' is often confused with 'information'; it is perhaps fair to say that data *becomes* information when it is communicated.

Computers can handle data in many forms, and in only one form. That is not the contradiction it at first seems to be. For computer input devices (the devices responsible for reading data into the computer) have been developed to accept data in a wide variety of forms: numbers, letters and symbols, entered in a number of different ways: lines drawn by a light pen, sounds, data on the state of a device or process that the computer is controlling, and many more. One function of the input devices is to convert this rich assortment of data into one standard format, which is the format that most — admittedly not all: we shall look at some exceptions later — computers use for manipulation and storage.

Later in this chapter, we shall look in greater detail at this business of converting, or coding, data to suit the computer. For now, though, we shall concentrate on the form of data that the computer generally handles.

On and Off

In Figure 1 we show a number of ways of conveying a piece of information . . . of indicating a fact . . . of providing a datum. What do they tell us? You will probably agree that it depends very much upon the context. A light burning in the bedroom may mean 'Ah, Dad is just going to bed', or 'Oh dear, the baby's woken up again', or 'Help, we have a burglar!'. A gate left open may mean that the postman has called, or the dog escaped. In a different context, though, those pieces of data may convey quite different information to us, or even little or no information.

Whatever their significance, though, it is clear that each example provides one datum. 'Yes/no', 'on/off', 'open/closed', even 'hole/no hole': they are all two-state situations. And, by definition, they must provide that datum all of the time. To see the switch up may not convey any information about the process the switch controls, but it is still a fact that the switch is up. We may not know if the abacus bead on the left counts as 1, and that on the right as 0, or vice versa: but the fact remains as to where the bead is. Similarly with the piece of paper: if we know that it could have been punched with just one hole, then the absence of the hole provides us with a datum just as surely as its presence would. If we know that it could have been punched with, say, eighty holes, then the blank piece of paper still contains eighty data-carrying units.

Close analogies with all these ways of representing data can be found in the workings of a computer. And it is in combining pieces of data, indicated in this simple two-state way, that we build up the representation of much more complex forms of data inside the computer.

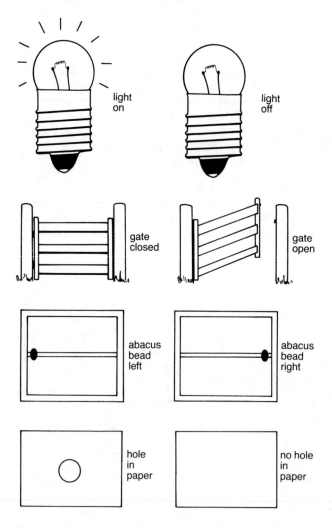

Figure 1: Some ways of conveying information

Building up the Bits

If one switch/lamp/hole provides us with one datum, how much data can we obtain from two switches/lamps/holes? In one sense, two pieces – but, in another, four! Figure 2 should make this clear.

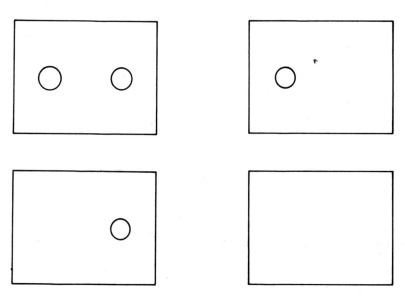

Figure 2: A two-position punched card can convey any of four alternative pieces of data

In Figure 2 there are two information-providing units: the left position on the paper, and the right position. But in combination, they can provide four different alternatives, which we might code, for instance, as A, B, C, D; or as 1, 2, 3, 4; or even as red/yellow/green/blue. And from three switches/ bulbs/holes, we can obtain no fewer than eight alternative codes, or eight coded pieces of data. We show how below, but this time we shall change our units. Instead of holes or no holes, we will use 1s and 0s to provide the two-state alternative:

```
0 0 0
0 0 1
0 1 0
0 1 1
1 0 0
1 0 1
1 1 0
1 1 1
```

To put it in mathematical terms, one digit provides us with 2^1, or two alternatives. Two digits can provide 2^2, or four alternatives. Three digits provide 2^3, or eight alternatives, and so on. By the time we reach eight digits, we will be able to code 2^8, or 256 facts! In other words, by indicating combinations of 1s and 0s in eight different positions, or by switching eight different switches in combinations of 'up' and 'down', we could represent the numbers 0 to 255 inclusive; or all the characters on a typewriter keyboard, upper and lower case (with plenty of room to spare); or 256 different musical pitches; or 256 different shades of the colour spectrum.

And that is how the computer stores and manipulates its data. As an example we shall take a widely used coding method for representing letters and standard characters in binary: that is, in combinations of 1s and 0s, our two-state character code. The ASCII Character Code is listed in Table 1.

You will see that the 1s and 0s are used in a systematic way: given the codes for 'S' and 'U', you would not find it difficult to guess the code for 'T'. This is deliberate: as the code is similar in construction to the way the computer represents numbers — and manipulates them — it means that the computer can easily sort words into alphabetical order.

You will doubtless have noticed that only seven digits are used in this code. In fact, the computer generally works with blocks of eight digits but, in the ASCII code, the left-hand digit is kept spare; it can then be used to provide a simple checking device. The computer counts the number of 1s and 0s in each group of code, and uses the eighth digit to make the numbers even: adding a 0 if there are, say, four 1s and three 0s, and a 1 if there are four 0s and three 1s. This 'parity' digit is then used as a check to help ensure that, when the code is transmitted from computer to computer, it is received accurately. (It is not a foolproof check, of course: it would not, for instance, pick up the transposition of two digits. But in most cases errors will only affect a single digit.)

Bits, Bytes and Words

It is time, at this point, to introduce some of the computer jargon for the codes and digits we have been talking about.

Each digit — that is, each two-state alternative, 1 or 0, open or closed, or whatever — is known as a bit. 'Bit' stands for binary digit, but it also means one single bit of data.

Combinations of eight bits — in other words, our eight-character code that can represent any one of 256 pieces of data — are known as bytes.

The combination of bits with which the computer is designed to work is known as its word length. If the computer works with combinations of eight bits, then its word length will be one byte. Many small computers use this word length; larger computers may handle 16-bit or 32-bit words. In some

Character symbolized	Code	Character symbolized	Code
A	1000001	!	0100001
B	1000010	"	0100010
C	1000011	#	0100011
D	1000100	$	0100100
E	1000101	%	0100101
F	1000110	&	0100110
G	1000111	'	0100111
H	1001000	(	0101000
I	1001001	)	0101001
J	1001010	*	0101010
K	1001011	+	0101011
L	1001100	'	0101100
M	1001101	—	0101101
N	1001110	.	0101110
O	1001111	/	0101111
P	1010000	0	0110000
Q	1010001	1	0110001
R	1010010	2	0110010
S	1010011	3	0110011
T	1010100	4	0110100
U	1010101	5	0110101
V	1010110	6	0110110
W	1010111	7	0110111
X	1011000	8	0111000
Y	1011001	9	0111001
Z	1011010	:	0111010
[	1011011	;	0111011
\	1011100	<	0111100
]	1011101	=	0111101
↑	1011110	>	0111110
←	1011111	?	0111111
SPACE	0100000	@	1000000
CAR RET	0001101	RUBOUT	1111111
LINE FEED	0001010		

Table 1: The ASCII Character Code

machines, the word length can vary according to the requirements of the codes used. Of course, a one-byte word in the ASCII code is not the same as a word in English. A one-byte word would contain only one letter of an English word, and several computer words would be needed to store the whole alphabetical word.

We shall try to clarify this concept with an example, using five bytes, or five one-byte computer words, to code one English word using the ASCII code (We also include the parity bits):

```
01000111
11010010
11000101
11000101
01001110
```

You probably found you had to double-check the code list, before you were satisfied that the word was GREEN. It is certainly a difficulty of ASCII, and of other binary codes, that they are exhausting for humans to work with; and you might well feel that you could never learn by heart what the code for, say, 'G' was, though you might be able to work it out systematically without using the code list. To encode the whole of this chapter in ASCII would obviously take ages.

Fortunately, the codes are something we rarely need to concern ourselves with in entering information into a computer. We just type GREEN on the keyboard (assuming that our computer has a keyboard input device), and the computer will translate that extremely rapidly into the code above.

Numbers and Characters

You may have already realized one difficulty in this neat system. Of course, the computer could use the 256 alternatives of an eight-digit binary code to stand for letters, or for numbers, or for some other set of data. But if it uses the entire set of alternatives to stand for characters and symbols using a code like ASCII, surely it cannot also use it to stand for numbers? How would it know which it was dealing with?

In fact we do indeed use the same standard eight bits of binary information to stand for numbers, for characters, for instructions to the computer, or for whatever we like. But we make sure that the computer has a way of telling what sort of code or numbering system it is dealing with in each case. As a much simplified example, the computer might associate with each word a separate piece of coded data that would tell it whether the original code stood for numbers, characters or some other kind of data. If the computer worked with a fixed one-byte word length, this would in fact necessitate its using two bytes to store one piece of data: one byte would contain the code that actually stood for the datum, the second byte the information as to whether the code was being used to stand for numbers or characters. We look at some alternative ways of designating the meaning of a string of binary code in greater detail later in the book.

We shall leave ASCII for now and go on to look at how the same coded digits are used to portray numbers.

Binary Numbering

Our conventional manual counting system is based on decimals: on powers of ten. We count up to 9 (a total of 10 digits, if you include 0) and then represent the next number in our counting system by 'carrying 1' and returning the first counter to 0.

Take the number 12939, for instance. There are two 9s in the number, but they symbolize quite different amounts. The 9 in the right-hand column actually stands in decimal for 9×10^0, or simply 9. The 9 in the third column from the right stands for 9×10^2, or 900. And the 3 between the 9s is in fact 3×10^1, or 30. We take the system so much for granted that we are not caused any confusion when the same digits appear repeatedly in a long number: we simply accept that their value differs, according to their position in the number.

Binary arithmetic works in just the same way, but there are two vital differences. First, we have only two digits to play with, 0 and 1. And second, we base the positioning of the digits on powers not of ten, but of two. In other words, in binary we count 0, 1 as in decimal; but then we run out of digits, and have to 'carry 1'. So the number after 1 is not 2, but 10 – which stands in binary not for 'ten' in decimal, but for 'two' in decimal.

Take a look at a longer binary number:

01000111

(87654321)

(Underneath, we have numbered the columns of the number, for convenience.) The digit in column 1 is a 1, and it stands for 1×2^0, or 1. In column 2 is another 1, but this stands for 1×2^1, or 2. The 1 in column 3 stands for 1×2^2, or 4. And the only other 'significant' digit is the 1 in column 7, which stands for 1×2^6, or 64. All the 0s, needless to say, stand for zero, just as the 0s do in a decimal number. So converting our binary number into its decimal equivalent, we have:

1×2^0	1
1×2^1	2
1×2^2	4
0×2^3	0
0×2^4	0
0×2^5	0
1×2^6	64
0×2^7	0
	—
	71

You may have noticed that 01000111 is also the code which in ASCII stands for G. However, in binary arithmetic – when the computer is told that it means a number, not an ASCII character – it stands for 71.

Obviously 71 is not the largest number we can represent in eight binary digits. The largest would of course be 11111111, which (work it out for yourself) represents 255 in decimal. *Not* 256: there are 256 different numbers that can be represented by the eight digits, but that means numbers 0 to 255 inclusive!

You will remember from page 24 that the eight bits in a byte can code 2^8, or 256 alternatives. But the eighth bit itself codes not the number 256, but 2^7, or 128. Similarly, seven bits could code 2^7 alternatives, but a 1 in the seventh position stands for 2^6, or 64. This is an important distinction.

Numbers as Characters

Let us add up one more binary number, 00110011:

1×2^0	1
1×2^1	2
1×2^4	16
1×2^5	32
	—
	51

We have chosen this example because it also appears in the ASCII code, complete with the correct parity digit. What does it represent in ASCII? Check, and you will see that it stands for '3'. But in binary arithmetic, it stands for decimal 51!

We need to make a clear distinction here between numbers and characters: and 3 could be either. If we want to use 3 as a number — that is, to carry out arithmetical operations using it — we must be careful to ensure that the computer has stored 'binary arithmetic 3', or 00000011. As a number, 3 is part of the decimal numbering system (or, indeed, of any other numbering system with a base of four or more) and, as such, it can be manipulated according to the rules of arithmetic. As a character, 3 is simply a sign with a fixed meaning, like 'A', '2', '+' or ';'. We cannot manipulate it mathematically, though we may want to store it, reproduce it, or reorganize a group of characters containing it. If we want to use 3 as a character, the computer will work with 00110011, or the same as binary arithmetic 51. Obviously it can't carry out any arithmetic, or it would come up with a hopelessly wrong answer. But it could, for instance, include 'ASCII 3' in a file containing names and addresses. If we were entering something like:

> Mrs J. Smith
> 3 Wells Close
> Canterbury

we would tell the computer to encode all these characters using ASCII or a similar code. We would not want to switch codes just for the 3, and as there would be no reason to carry out any arithmetic using the 3, no confusion could arise.

Binary Arithmetic

Of course, binary numbering can be used for arithmetic in just the same way that decimal can. It appears cumbersome to us, but it suits the computer very well: fortunately, we rarely — if ever — have to imitate the computer and calculate using binary. We shall next look at a couple of simple examples, though, just to show how it is done.

Adding. Let us add the two numbers we have already looked at:

```
01000111
00110011
--------
01111010
```

As you see, the procedure is just the same as in decimal. In column 1, we add our two 1s, run out of digits and 'carry 1' to column 2, returning column 1 to 0. Then, in column 2, we carry 1 and have 1 left over to retain in the column. We carry 1 from column 3, too . . . and the rest is plain sailing. If you translate the answer into decimal, you will find that it is what you would expect: 122.

Subtracting. We shall use the same two numbers:

```
01000111
00110011
--------
00010100
```

Columns 1 to 4 are straightforward. Look at what we do in column 5, though. To subtract 1 from 0, we have to 'borrow' 10 (2, that is) from column 6. Subtracting 1 from binary 10 leaves us with 1. Then in column 6, we 'borrow 10' again. 1 has been used in column 5, so 1 is left (remember, $1 + 1 = 10$) to subtract the 1 from, leaving 0. And nothing is left, either, to column 7. Check the answer; again, it is just what it would be in decimal: 20.

Binary can, of course, be used for much more complicated arithmetic. This is not a maths textbook, though, and we will not burden you with more elaborate examples. It is perhaps worthwhile to point out at this stage that it is by no means impossible to represent, and calculate using, numbers larger than 255 using one-byte words. A larger number has to be spread over several words, and the computer needs a special system for 'carrying' digits from the left-hand column of one word to the right-hand column of the next.

It may not need a special system for 'borrowing' digits in the reverse direction, for the simple reason that subtraction in the computer is often not carried out as we did it above. Instead, a neat system called 'two's complement' is used. The number to be subtracted is translated into a 'complementary' number — which is in effect its negative — and then the two numbers are added together, instead of being subtracted. You might think of it as adding 71 and (−51) together.

How do we get (−51)? We simply change all the 1s in the binary number equivalent to 51 to 0s, and vice versa, and then add 1 to the result. We shall do that, and then add 71 and (−51):

```
  01000111
  11001101
```
(1)00010100

Changing the digits in 00110011 gives us 11001100, and we add 1 to this to give us 11001101, which we used above. And then adding this to 01000111 gives us exactly the same as our earlier answer: 00010100. You will notice that we also have a carry 1 on the left. We knock that off, as a way of compensating for the 1 we added originally. If you find this a little unnatural, you may like to compare it with the way we add up the time on a clock face. Nine o'clock plus six hours equals three o'clock: an improbable sum on the face of it, but one we understand and take for granted.

Other Number Codes

Though modern computer users rarely actually have to calculate using binary, they do have to enter the binary numbers into the computer, so that it can calculate using them. On sophisticated computers, this is no problem. The keyboard has decimal number keys, and the operator just types in, say, 12345 × 6789. The computer then does the work of translating this input into the binary code it will use for the calculation.

Of course, the operator has to tell the computer whether he (or she, of course) is entering numbers or characters. There are several ways in which this is done. Sometimes the computer may interpret all decimal digits as numbers unless it is told to store them as characters, by a prior code. Enclosing them (and all other characters) in quotation marks is one way of telling the computer this. By the latter convention; 123 would be a number, "123" a string of characters.

Some computer systems have a full alpha/numeric keyboard − like a typewriter keyboard − which includes the digits 0 to 9 as characters, and a separate calculator-style keypad, which repeats the same digits, but this time as numbers. Such a repetition may be purely for operator convenience, though, and have no significance to the computer.

On more crude computer systems, though, such facilities may not be provided. Instead, the programmer actually inputs the binary numbers. To make the task easier, a number of 'intermediate' codes have been developed.

Introducing yet more codes may not strike you as a step towards simplification! In fact, however, programmers find it very worthwhile. After all, it is not easy to convert long binary numbers into their decimal equivalents, or back again. It *is* relatively easy to convert binary numbers into octal.

What is octal? It is a numbering system using base eight. In other words, it contains eight characters, 0 to 7 inclusive. It works just like the binary or decimal numbering systems; but it has the special advantage that each digit in an octal number corresponds to a group of three digits in a binary number. (Remember that three binary digits also provide 2^3, or eight alternatives.) So the octal numbers 0 to 7 can be interchanged with the binary numbers 000 to 111, as follows:

Octal	Binary		
0	000	4	100
1	001	5	101
2	010	6	110
3	011	7	111

And longer binary and octal numbers can be converted into each other in the same way. 010111001 in binary, for instance, can be broken into groups of three digits – 010, 111, 001 – and translated into the octal number 271. Of course, 271 in octal is not the same as 271 in decimal! So a programmer who uses this route to convert a decimal number into binary must first convert the decimal number into octal (easier – but not all that much easier – than converting it directly into binary), and then convert the octal number into binary.

It may seem cumbersome, but programmers who work at this level do generally find it worthwhile. After all, it is quite feasible for a programmer to learn the octal/binary conversion chart, while you will surely agree that it would be quite a feat to learn the decimal/binary conversion chart, even as far as 256.

Converting decimal into octal is straightforward enough, and is largely a matter of dividing by eights. However, we shall not look at any examples here; for there is yet another code to be introduced.

One disadvantage of octal is that its digital correspondence with binary is three to one, while the computer generally works with binary numbers in groups of eight digits. Largely as a result of this, many programmers prefer to use a numbering system which has a four-to-one correspondence with binary. This is the hexadecimal, or base-16 system.

Hexadecimal ('hex' for short) needs sixteen characters, six more than in decimal. To make up its set, it borrows the first six letters of the alphabet. That makes the hex/binary conversion chart look like this:

Hexadecimal	Binary		
0	0000	8	1000
1	0001	9	1001
2	0010	A	1010
3	0011	B	1011
4	0100	C	1100
5	0101	D	1101
6	0110	E	1110
7	0111	F	1111

Table 2: The Hexadecimal to Binary Conversion Chart

It is important to remember that, in hex, 'B' (for instance) is not simply a character. It is a number, or one character in a number. So B4 is a number in hex, equivalent to 180 in decimal ((11 × 16) +4) or 10110100 in binary. And of course, it is quite possible to perform arithmetical operations in hex. At first it may seem very strange to confront a sum like D2 + 3F but, in principle, it is no different from, say, 2 + 2.

The hexadecimal/binary chart is twice as long as the octal/binary one. This, together with the awkwardness of the concept of using letters as numbers, means that some programmers prefer to use octal. As both are basically aids to the computer programmer, not codes required by the computer itself, it is a matter of choice which (if either) the programmer uses.

We will be putting these tools to use in Chapter 24, when we come to look at programming a computer.

2. In Practice: An Introduction to Electronics

Now we have seen something of the theory of how data are stored and manipulated in the form of 1s and 0s inside the computer, we need to look at the technology in which these 1s and 0s are represented. In modern computers, that is almost always electronic technology. In this chapter, therefore, we are offering a brief introduction to electronics: what its basic principles are and how it is used in computing.

If you already understand the basics of electronics, you may prefer to move on to page 41, on which we start to consider the use of electronic components to form logic gates; or on to Part Two of the book, which starts on page 49.

What is electronics? It is the science and technology concerned with the behaviour of electrons: subatomic particles that can, under certain circumstances, move from atom to atom and thus produce an electrical current.

Electronic devices work both through the movement of electrons around an electrical circuit, and through their static pattern, in the absence of a connecting circuit. In order to understand the behaviour of electrons, we must first look very briefly at the structure of the atoms of which they form a part.

The Atom

As we understand it today, the atom consists of three major types of particle:
(1) one or more neutrons, central particles that are electrically neutral;
(2) one or more protons, central particles that are electrically charged positive;
(3) the same number of electrons as of protons. Electrons are electrically charged negative, with a charge equal (and opposite) to that of a proton.

Figure 3 is a simplified schematic of the structure of an atom of silicon. It has fourteen protons, and fourteen electrons (some silicon atoms have fifteen or sixteen) arranged in concentric 'shells' around the nucleus of the protons and the neutrons. Each electron has an amount of energy that is broadly related to the diameter of its 'orbit': its movement around the nucleus. This energy, that keeps the electrons orbiting in an attempt to 'take off' from the atom, is counterbalanced by the 'pull' (similar to gravitational pull) that attracts the negatively charged electrons to the positively charged protons. The electrons in the outermost shell are known as 'valent' electrons: they may become detached from the atom, and thus turn into 'free' electrons. The 'valency' of silicon (which in this case, though not in all, equals the number of electrons in its outer shell) is 4.

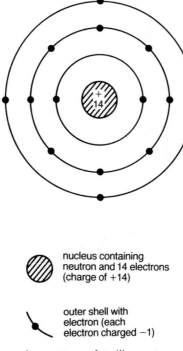

nucleus containing
neutron and 14 electrons
(charge of +14)

outer shell with
electron (each
electron charged −1)

Figure 3: The electronic structure of a silicon atom

An atom or group of atoms that loses an electron can be thought of as acquiring a 'hole' into which another electron may fit. Electrically, it becomes positively charged; electrons will tend to be attracted to it. An atom or group of atoms that gains an extra electron is negatively charged; it will tend to repel electrons.

In some elements, the valent electrons have an energy level that enables them to free themselves from the nucleus very easily. The substance is thus well equipped with free electrons that can be attracted towards a positive electrical charge or away from a negative one. Put another way, the substance is a good conductor of electrical current. In other substances, the electrons are tightly bound to the atomic structure, and it may be virtually impossible to give them sufficient energy to free them from it. In these substances, there are no free electrons to respond to electrical stimuli; the substance will tend to act as an insulator, preventing the flow of current. Yet other substances come midway between conductors and insulators: they do not normally have free electrons, and thus do not permit the flow of current. However, the addition of energy (perhaps through the addition of heat) to the valent electrons will free some of them and so improve the conductivity of the substance. Such substances are known as semiconductors.

It is important to distinguish the conductivity of a substance from its electrical charge. The conductivity is related to the number of *free* electrons. In a good conductor of electricity, there will be many free electrons, but there may be no more electrons *in total* than there are protons; the charge of the substance will then be zero. Charge, on the other hand, is related to the *disparity* between the number of electrons and of protons. A highly charged substance need not be a particularly good conductor of electricity: it may retain its charge indefinitely unless given an external stimulus to release it.

Doped Silicon

When atoms of different elements are combined (perhaps in molecules, perhaps more loosely) to form a complex substance, then the situation of the valent electrons (that is, their role in the structure of the substance) becomes more complex. According to the way in which the atoms, and particularly the valent electrons, fit together, the new substance may be extremely stable in structure or it may be rather unstable. And there may be more, or fewer, free electrons than are found in the pure elements.

Let us consider what happens when a sliver of silicon is 'doped': another substance is added to it to form, not a new molecular compound, but an impure version of silicon. The impurities that are commonly added are three-valency elements, such as boron or indium, or five-valency elements, such as phosphorus or antimony.

The silicon doped with a five-valency element acquires an awkward 'extra' electron (see Figure 4a). It is a relatively stable substance, but it has a negative electrical charge; under suitable circumstances, it will dispose of the extra electron to leave a network of four-valency atoms. The silicon doped with a three-valency element acquires a 'hole' where another electron could fit (see Figure 4b). As a result, this (also relatively stable) substance has a positive electrical charge; under suitable circumstances it will acquire an extra electron to fit into the hole.

Pure silicon can. act as a semiconductor. At 0 °K, absolute zero, its electrons are all tightly bound and it does not transmit current. At room temperature and higher temperatures, the bonds are weakened, and some current can be transmitted. However, the doped versions of silicon act as much better semiconductors. The instability of their electron pattern means that, in suitable circumstances, electrons will move freely. We shall next look briefly at the circumstances in which this happens. First, though, we must consider the nature of electrical current and of electrical circuits.

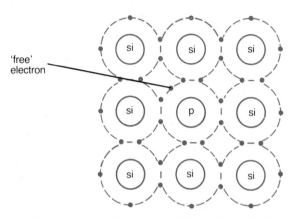

'free' electron

(a) Silicon doped with an atom of phosphorus (valency of 5)

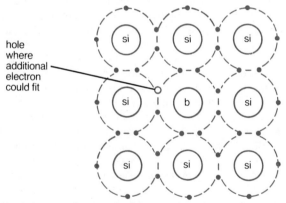

hole where additional electron could fit

(b) Silicon doped with an atom of boron (valency of 3)

○ nucleus and inner shell(s) of atom:
si = silicon
p = phosphorus
b = boron

outer shell with valent and potentially 'free' electrons

Figure 4: Simplified atomic structure of doped silicon

The Flow of Current through a Circuit

What *is* an electronic circuit? And what actually happens when current 'flows' around it?

An electronic — or electrical, for that matter — circuit must have two basic constituents:

(1) there is a positive electrical charge and a negative electrical charge. In other words, there is a *reason* (in subatomic terms) for electrons to flow in a definite direction around the circuit: from the negatively charged area (too many electrons) to the positively charged area (too few electrons). The 'push' that this differential charge gives to the circuit (or to a portion of it) is known as its voltage. The voltage could be provided by a battery, or by some other means of generating electricity.

(2) there is potentially a connecting circuit of conductive material between the positive pole and the negative pole: of wires, or of traces of conductive material on a circuit board; and of components through which current will flow in at least some circumstances. The pattern of wires will normally be fixed. However, the path that the current takes around the circuit (or, indeed, whether current flows at all) can be regulated by changes in the states of the components. Different types of electronic component form different types of 'gate', that will allow current to flow in some circumstances and prevent current from flowing in others. Semiconductive materials are one type of gate. We shall later go on to look at some gates in greater detail.

When the circuit is closed — that is, when it is possible for current to flow around it — how do the electrons move? One electron is hardly likely to move right around the circuit. Instead, there is a 'wavefront' movement in which each electron 'pushes' the next one a little further along. The speed of the wavefront — this is what we normally mean when we speak of the speed of the current — is the same as the speed of light. The speed of each individual electron is much less.

When we use the presence or absence of a current or charge to denote the 1s and 0s of a binary code then, we do not think in terms of each electron as a 1 or a 0, present or absent. We think in terms of:

(1) the flow of an electrical current of a given voltage through a fixed portion of the circuit at a given time as being the equivalent of a 1 in binary code, and the absence of that current, or the flow of a much weaker current, as a 0.

(2) the presence or absence of a particular electrical charge in a specific component or set of components as being the equivalent of a binary 1 or 0 respectively.

In Chapter 7 we shall look at ways in which data are stored electronically. For the moment, we are concentrating on the dynamics of manipulation. Depending on the way in which the circuit is set up, the current that we interpret as being equivalent to coded 1s and 0s can be manipulated to enable us to carry out simple logical and arithmetical operations — adding two numbers together, or comparing two patterns of binary code to see if they are the same, for instance.

Combining electrical conductors and insulators, positively and negatively charged materials, in different ways can produce a wide variety of different effects. For our purposes, we need to examine only two of these effects: the ability to produce a gate, or valve, that enables current to travel in one direction around a circuit, but not in the opposite direction; and the ability to amplify current, or to produce a large output current from a small input current. We shall look at one simple way in which each of these effects can be achieved, using solid-state devices (that is, devices with no moving parts) containing doped silicon. There are many other ways in which the same effects, and variations upon them, can be obtained: using different materials, or linking the circuit in different ways. Not all of them employ solid-state devices. However, the methods we shall outline are very commonly used today in making the digital circuits of computers.

The Diode

A diode is a device that permits current to flow in one direction only around a circuit. When it is used in an a.c. (alternating current) circuit (one in which current switches rapidly from one direction of flow to the other, and back again), it acts as a rectifier, producing d.c., or direct current.

A simple diode can be formed from a wafer consisting of a layer of positively doped silicon (silicon with 'holes' that attract electrons) and a layer of negatively doped silicon (with surplus free electrons). Figure 5 shows a very simple electronic circuit containing such a device.

The battery produces an electrical charge that, if the circuit is complete, will lead to the flow of current from the negative pole to the positive pole: clockwise in Figure 5a, counter-clockwise in Figure 5b. In Figure 5a, however, the positive pole of the battery attracts the free electrons in the negative part of the diode, and the negative pole of the battery attracts the holes in the positive part of the diode. The junction between the positive and negative layers of the diode is stripped of both free electrons and holes into which they might be attracted, and no current flows across it. In Figure 5b, the attraction between the electrons in the negative substance and the holes in the positive substance is reinforced, not counteracted, by the force exerted by the battery. The electrons flow towards the junction, where some of them combine with the holes in the positive substance; meanwhile, new holes are formed at the positive end of the diode, and new electrons are injected into its negative end. Current will continue to flow as long as the circuit is complete.

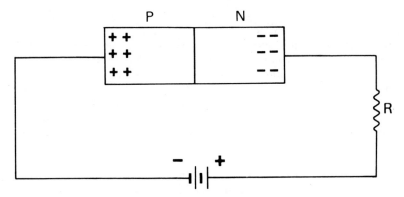

(a) Set positive/negative in the circuit: no current flows

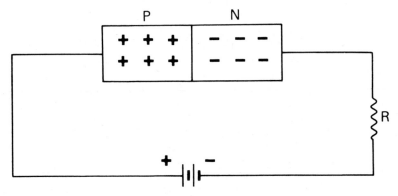

(b) Set negative/positive in the circuit: current will flow

ǀǀ¦ǀ	Battery (or other source of electrical charge)
⟩R	Resistor (necessary to limit flow of current)
+ +	Positively doped silicon (holes attract electrons)
— —	Negatively doped silicon (free electrons available)

Figure 5: The semiconductor diode

Transistors

The fundamental difference between electronic circuits and electrical circuits is that the former make use of amplifying devices: devices that can increase the flow of current to a sufficient extent that they turn the virtual absence of a current (or the size of a current that counts as a binary 0) into the presence of a current that can be interpreted as a binary 1. Valves, or vacuum tubes, can do this. So can the solid-state devices known as transistors: and it is with transistors that we must now concern ourselves.

The bipolar transistor consists of three layers of doped silicon. The emitter layer is very heavily doped; the central base layer is lightly and oppositely doped; and the third, collector layer is lightly doped in the same direction as the emitter. We shall look at a negative-positive-negative (N-P-N) transistor, but positive-negative-positive (P-N-P) transistors work similarly if the current is adjusted appropriately.

Figure 6 shows the transistor linked into a circuit in which current flows from point x into the base, and out from the collector towards point y. At the top of the picture is a strong, positively charged source, z, providing a positive pull that reinforces the current flow. The resistors in the circuit ensure that the current flows, not towards z, but in the direction of y.

The charge at z attracts free electrons from the transistor. The emitter is well supplied with free electrons, and its supply is effectively topped up by its earth connection, e. However, the base region, though comparatively thin and lightly doped, forms an obstacle that the emitter electrons have to surmount before they can flow towards y. The light doping of the base means that free electrons are comparatively unlikely to fill the holes in the base; instead, they will, under suitable circumstances, flow directly into the collector and from there towards y.

The current that flows in from x effectively controls the gate formed by the base. As a negative current (with free electrons), it can neutralize the positive charge of the base and thus increase the flow of electrons from the emitter. The flow of current out of the transistor is proportional to the size of the current entering at the base. It may be much greater than the initial current: a typical transistor, for instance, could amplify the current (between x and y) 100 times. A very small current that represents a binary 0 can therefore be amplified into a current interpreted as a binary 1.

These simple solid-state devices, and others like them, can be combined to make up much more complex devices. We must now look at three configurations that together give the computer the rudiments of an ability to carry out logical and arithmetical manipulations.

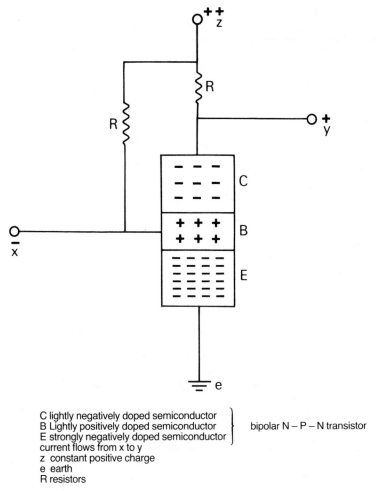

C lightly negatively doped semiconductor
B Lightly positively doped semiconductor } bipolar N – P – N transistor
E strongly negatively doped semiconductor
current flows from x to y
z constant positive charge
e earth
R resistors

Figure 6: A bipolar N–P–N transistor

Logic Gates

The three configurations are together known as logic gates: the AND gate, the OR gate, and the NOT gate. Together, they comprise the entire manipulative repertoire of the computer; and, together with the devices to store electrical charge that we shall consider in Chapter 7, and with resistors to control the path of, and quantity of, current flowing, they are the basic components of digital electronic circuits.

The AND gate

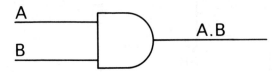

Figure 7: The symbol for an AND gate

This is the symbol for an AND gate. The gate will output a binary 1 if, and only if, all its inputs are equal to 1. If any input is equal to 0 – and there may be more than the two inputs shown above – then the output will be 0.

We can express this in the form of a 'truth table', showing the output for various combinations of the inputs A, B and C:

A	B	C	A, B and C
0	0	0	0
0	0	1	0
0	1	0	0
0	1	1	0
1	0	0	0
1	0	1	0
1	1	0	0
1	1	1	1

In terms of an electrical circuit, the AND gate can be thought of as a series of switches or gates. Every gate must be open, or every switch closed, before the current will flow from x to y.

Figure 8: Circuit showing gates in series

The OR gate

The OR gate has this symbol:

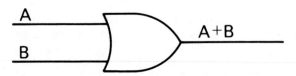

Figure 9: The symbol for an OR gate

It will output a binary 1 if any one of its inputs — and again, there may be more than two of them — is equal to 1. If no input is a 1, it will output a 0.
Here is the truth table for a three-input OR gate:

A	B	C	A or B or C
0	0	0	0
0	0	1	1
0	1	0	1
0	1	1	1
1	0	0	1
1	0	1	1
1	1	0	1
1	1	1	1

In circuit terms, the OR gate can be thought of as a set of gates or switches in parallel, rather than in series. If any gate is open, or any switch closed, then the current will flow from x to y.

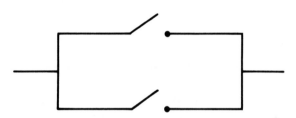

Figure 10: Circuit showing gates in parallel

There is also a variation on the OR gate, the Exclusive OR gate. This is a two-input gate. It will output a 1 only if exactly one input is a 1. If no input or two inputs are 1s, it will output a 0.

The NOT gate

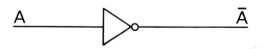

Figure 11: The symbol for a NOT gate

This is the symbol for the NOT gate. It will invert its output: producing a binary 0 if the (single) input was a 1, and amplifying an input of 0 into a 1.

The truth table for a NOT gate is very short:

A	Not A (or $\bar{A}$)
0	1
1	0

Of course, circuits are often needed to cope with more elaborate logical situations: to determine if exactly two out of three inputs were 1s, for instance. It is possible to compile logic circuits to express these situations out of combinations of AND, OR and NOT gates.

Adder Circuits

Adding two numbers together in binary, and allowing for carrying digits over, is just such a complex situation. And it is possible to combine AND, OR and NOT gates to make an 'adder' circuit. We shall next look at how a simple one is built up.

First, we must construct a truth table for adding two binary digits together, adding in a 'carry 1' if necessary, and producing both a sum (1 or 0) and a carry digit (1) if necessary. Here it is:

A	B	C^1	S	C^2
0	0	0	0	0
0	0	1	1	0
0	1	0	1	0
0	1	1	0	1
1	0	0	1	0
1	0	1	0	1
1	1	0	0	1
1	1	1	1	1

'C^1' is the carry forward from the previous addition, 'C^2' the carry forward from this sum.

How do we construct a circuit for this situation? Well, we need a positive (that is, a 1) SUM output if:
(1) all three inputs are 1;
(2) only one input is a 1.
Clearly, (1) will require a three-input AND gate.

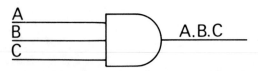

Figure 12: A three-input AND gate

(2) is a little more difficult. We can handle it by taking each input in turn and putting the other two inputs through NOT gates. Then we combine the three through an AND gate; only if exactly one original input signal was positive will we get a positive output. Finally, we take our three intermediate outputs through an OR gate, and if any one is positive we will have a positive SUM output. Figure 13 shows the circuit needed.

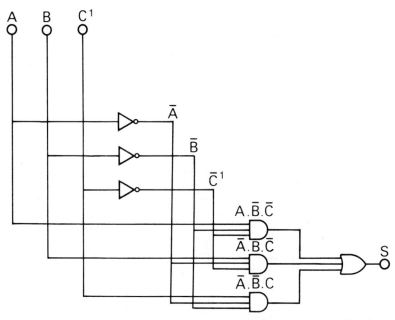

Figure 13: Part of logic circuit for summing two numbers

Let's make that clearer by taking a line of the truth table from which we want a 1 SUM output, and applying this process to it:

When   A   B   C
        1   0   0
Then: A $\bar{B}$ $\bar{C}$
        1   1   1 = AND 1 ⎫
        $\bar{A}$ $\bar{B}$ C
        0   1   0 = AND 0 ⎬ = OR 1
        $\bar{A}$ B $\bar{C}$
        0   0   1 = AND 0 ⎭

and a line of the truth table from which we want an 0 sum output:

When   A   B   C
        0   1   1
Then: A   B $\bar{C}$

$$\left.\begin{array}{ccc} 0 & 0 & 0 = \text{AND } 0 \\ \bar{A} & \bar{B} & C \\ 1 & 0 & 1 = \text{AND } 0 \\ \bar{A} & B & \bar{C} \\ 1 & 1 & 0 = \text{AND } 0 \end{array}\right\} \begin{array}{c} \\ \\ = \text{OR } 0 \\ \\ \end{array}$$

Since either (1) or (2) will mean a positive SUM, we must then combine the two via yet another OR gate.

We will need a positive CARRY output if:

(3) any two inputs are 1;

(4) all three inputs are 1.

And we can do this by putting AND and OR gates together, as in Figure 14.

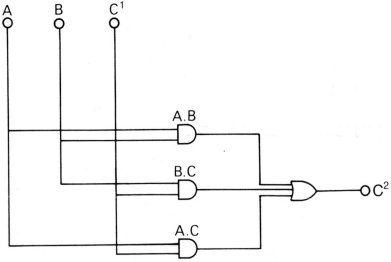

Figure 14: CARRY circuit

Let's test it again, with a line from the truth table from which we want a positive output:

When   A   B   C

          1   1   0

Then: $\left.\begin{array}{l} \text{A AND B} = 1 \\ \text{A AND C} = 0 \\ \text{B AND C} = 0 \end{array}\right\} = \text{OR } 1$

and one from which we don't:

When   A   B   C

          0   0   1

Then: $\left.\begin{array}{l} \text{A AND B} = 0 \\ \text{A AND C} = 0 \\ \text{B AND C} = 0 \end{array}\right\} = \text{OR } 0$

Finally, we can combine our CARRY circuit and our SUM circuit to make the complete adder circuit, shown in Figure 15.

Of course, this adder circuit is only a very small building block in making a complete arithmetic/logic unit: it adds only two digits, not even two complete one-byte binary numbers, let alone doing anything more complicated. But understanding how it is made up does give us some idea of how simple electronic components can be built up into circuits that can carry out more complex operations.

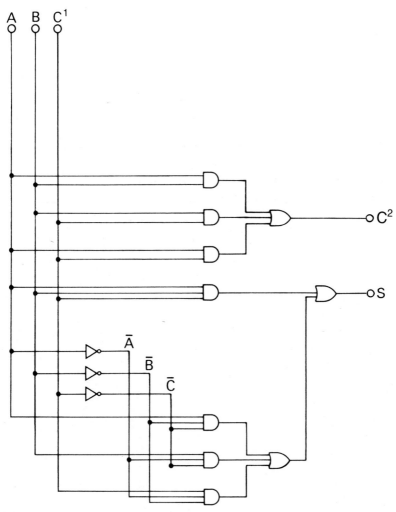

Figure 15: Circuit for adding two binary digits (with carry forward)

Part Two: Development of the Computer – An Historical Perspective

In Part One we looked at the principles of how data can be stored and manipulated in a digital (and, in particular, in a binary) form; we began to look at how these general principles are realized in electronic circuits. In Part Two, we shall go backwards in time to look at some aspects of the historical development of computer technology.

Our survey will be divided into four sections; they overlap historically, but trace different sides of the computer story. First, we shall look at techniques of digital calculation, from the abacus to the modern 'pocket' (or even smaller) calculator. Next, we shall explore the divergence between calculators and computers, starting with the development of the concept of the stored program. Then, we shall look at the alternative analog technique for dealing with data that does not fit easily into a digital format. Finally, we shall examine the transition from massive 'mainframe' computers to the minicomputers and microcomputers that dominate the computer market today.

Though we shall use an historical framework in this part of the book, our primary objective will not be to produce a history of computers: rather, it is to explain how the concepts behind computing, and the technology of computers themselves, have developed. The examples we introduce are intended to bring out conceptual, rather than historical, points: to computer historians, we must apologize for the absence of some well-known figures. It is always difficult to discover to which individual particular ideas should be attributed: even those who were there at the time cannot always be certain to whom the credit was due! To the best of our knowledge, our attributions are accurate, but we cannot claim more for them than that.

3. Digital Calculation

Let's begin with that simplest of all mechanical aids to calculation, the abacus.

The Abacus

There are many different designs of abacus, but they all use the same basic techniques. We shall first explore the techniques, then go on to look at some of their more common realizations.

The abacus uses beads to represent the digits to be manipulated. We must be careful in making this statement, though. The number of beads on the abacus does not vary, in all but the most primitive versions, so it is not strictly true to say that the mere presence of a bead signifies the presence of a digit. And the colour of the beads doesn't vary, nor does their internal state, so it is not as if we could say that a black bead represents a 1, and a white bead a 0. What *is* significant is the position of the beads. In effect, we take the beads into account only if they are placed in a defined area of the abacus: against the left-hand side, or against a beam that runs across the centre, for instance. Beads not in this significant area are really just storage; they are not directly implicated in the calculation, but are held in reserve in case they may be required at some future stage.

Position is relevant in a second dimension, too. The different wires, or strings, of the abacus represent different digital positions in the number being stored or manipulated. Just as a 1 in an eight-digit binary number will take a different value, depending on the column in which it appears, so a bead on an abacus will have a different value, according to the wire on which it is located. What exactly that value is will depend not only on the location of the wire but also upon the numbering system being used. There is no reason why the abacus cannot be used for calculations in base two (binary), base ten (decimal), base sixteen (hexadecimal), or any other system for which it has sufficient beads to be manipulated. There is equally no reason why the same abacus cannot be used for calculations in a number of different base systems.

What can the abacus be used for, then? It can certainly, and very simply, be used for adding two numbers together. This is done just as it is on paper: column by column, starting with the least significant digit, and carrying a digit where necessary. It can be used for subtraction, in much the same way. And it can be used for multiplication, achieved by repeated addition, and for division, achieved by repeated subtraction. It has in some historical periods been used for more complex mathematical operations, but these require additional refinements.

Types of Abacus

The most primitive types of abacus that seem to have been used in Ancient Greece, in Egypt, and in Mexico and Peru consisted simply of heaps of pebbles or clay beads, laid out in grooves (cut in wood or gouged in sand) or threaded on to open wires. Later types enclosed the beads, and the wires on which they were threaded, in a wooden framework.

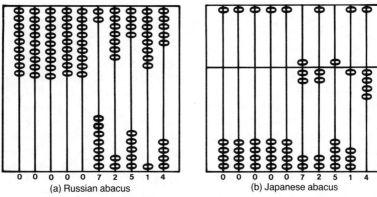

(a) Russian abacus	(b) Japanese abacus

Figure 16: Types of abacus

The simplest of these later types was probably developed in Russia. It consisted of a set of simple wires, on to each of which nine or ten (a little thought shows that the tenth bead is redundant in decimal calculations) beads were threaded. Beads moved to one side were counted, those to the other side ignored. Thus the abacus in Figure 16a reads 72514. A later refinement led to the introduction of a central beam, with one or two beads on one side of it, and four or five on the other. (Again, the second and fifth beads are not necessary in decimal calculations.) In this system, a bead on the 1 or 2 side (often known as 'heaven') counted as 5 in decimal, while beads on the other ('earth') side counted as 1 only. The version shown in Figure 16b therefore reads 72514, too. This more sophisticated version could do no more elaborate arithmetic, but it was easier to manipulate quickly and to read numbers off.

Mechanical Calculators

How are numbers represented in mechanical calculators? Very often they are communicated to and from the operator in the form of arabic notation (that is, the figures 1, 2, 3 . . .). However, they also need to be represented physically in order that arithmetical operations may be performed.

A common method is to inscribe the numbers 0 to 9 (or an appropriate set of numbers, if a numbering system with a base other than ten is being used) at regular intervals around the circumference of a gear wheel. One position on the wheel (at the top, say) then represents the significant digit, just as one position on the abacus represented the significant quantity. A display window may be provided at this point, while the rest of the wheel is hidden from view. Moving the gear wheel will of course alter this digit.

Gears in the ratio of 1 to 10 (or the appropriate base number ratio) can then be linked together to create a mechanical 'carry' operation. The linkage might consist of direct gearing shafts, or of a 'stripped gear' arrangement like that shown in Figure 17.

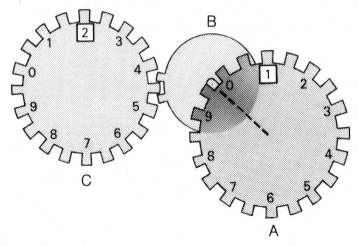

Figure 17: Stripped gear arrangement for producing a mechanical 'carry'

In Figure 17, the two wheels C (tens) and A (units) read the number 21. Wheels A and B are joined on a common shaft, so B rotates as A does. Each time wheel A makes a complete revolution, the two teeth on wheel B move wheel C, with which it is engaged, along by the space of two teeth, or (since it has twenty teeth) one-tenth of a revolution. If we add 12 to wheel A, by turning it 24 teeth (12 numbers), then this will take the number at the top of wheel A from 1 to 3. At the same time, wheel C will be moved along by the space of one number, and the number at the top of wheel C will become 3. The two wheels now display the answer to 21 plus 12, 33.

Mechanical calculators working on these principles can be thought of as having two 'registers', that combine written numbers with physical representations of the quantity they symbolize, either on gear wheels or using some similar method, such as notches on a shaft. In a very simple system, to add two numbers together the operator would enter the first number to register A, then enter the second number to register B, which is connected to register A via a ratchet mechanism of some kind. Entering the second number would change the total registered on A to the sum of the two numbers.

A more practical and extensible system designates one register as the 'setting' register and the other as the 'result' register. The first number is entered to the setting register and simultaneously (again, via a ratchet mechanism) to the result register. The two registers are then disengaged while the setting register is returned to 0. The ratchet is re-engaged, the second number is entered, and the result of the addition appears in the result register.

Subtraction can of course be achieved in a similar fashion, by reversing the rotation of the registers. Multiplication and division can also be achieved once again, simply by repeated addition or subtraction. More sophisticated machines, however, mechanize these latter operations too.

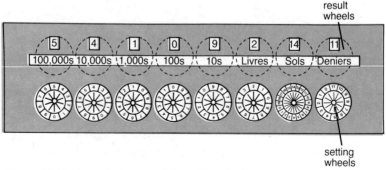

Figure 18: Layout of the top of Pascal's calculator

In 1642, a French mathematician and philosopher, Blaise Pascal, produced a mechanical calculator based on these principles. Figure 18 shows the top of Pascal's small (approximately 14″ × 5″ × 4″ (36 cm × 13 cm × 10 cm)) machine, with a set of setting wheels (cogs moved by a stylus) at the bottom, and a set of result wheels at the top. The number of cogs on the setting wheels varies, for this was designed to add the French currency units of Pascal's time, the *livre* and the smaller units of a *sol* (one-twentieth of a livre) and a *denier* (one-twelfth of a sol). The 'carry' on Pascal's machine was achieved by a ratchet device, and subtraction was done by a two's complement system like that we discussed on page 29.

It was not Pascal, but Gottfried Wilhelm von Leibniz, who went on in the 1690s to mechanize the operation of multiplication. On Pascal's machine, a number had to be re-entered to the machine repeatedly and added to the running total, in order to carry out multiplication. On Leibniz's, it was possible to enter the number once only, and then the turn of a crank would add it to the total the required number of times.

Leibniz's major innovation was the stepped roll, a cylinder with nine cogs of varying lengths that represented the digits 1 to 9 (see Figure 19). This could be engaged with another roll, or with a gear wheel, at varying points along its length, and thus move it differentially. Later designers went on to refine these basic constituents of the mechanical technology still further, and finally to electrify the operation of the machine. However, the mechanical desk calculators (both manually and electrically operated) that were in common use until the middle of this century — when they began to be replaced by electronic versions — had much in common with Leibniz's designs.

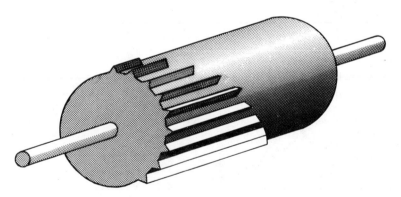

Figure 19: The stepped roll arrangement used in Leibniz's calculator

The Difference Engine

Mechanizing addition and subtraction, multiplication and division is all very well. But much mathematical calculation demands the use of more complex functions. Analysing polynomial expressions, for instance, cannot obviously be done merely by repeated addition and subtraction. Pascal's and Leibniz's machines (and their modern successors) would seem to be no use at all for such tasks.

But, in fact, polynomial expressions *can* be analysed by addition and subtraction. The realization of how this could be done, and be mechanized, was made largely by Charles Babbage, an English mathematician of eclectic tastes. He conceived his method of differencing, and the idea of a 'difference engine' to perform it, in 1812. And in 1822 his seminal paper, 'On the Theoretical Principles of the Machinery for Calculating Tables', was published.

Difference Tables

Let us take a simple polynomial equation, $y = x^2 2x + 3$. Successive integer (whole-number) values of x will give us different values of y, and we can tabulate these values for, say, $x = 0$ to $x = 6$:

x	y
0	3
1	6
2	11
3	18
4	27
5	38
6	51

What happens if we then calculate the *differences* between the successive values of y, by subtracting the y corresponding to $x = 1$ from the y corresponding to $x = 2$, and so on? And then calculate the differences between those differences? We can produce a table of successive differences that will eventually end with the production of a constant difference – at a level determined by the highest power in the equation. The highest power in our equation is x^2; to equalize the differences of successive values of the expression, we shall simply need to calculate two levels of differences:

x	y	first difference	second difference
			(2)
		(1)	(2)
0	3	3	2
1	6	5	2
2	11	7	2
3	18	9	2
4	27	11	2
5	38	13	
6	51		

(The numbers in brackets are extrapolations backwards of the table.)

How can we then mechanize this operation? Once we have calculated the differences back to a constant level, we can then work backwards *from* the differences, to produce successive values of y. For this example, we would need to set up three registers, which we will call 'A', 'B' and 'C'. 'A' would contain a value of y; 'B', the first difference, working backwards; and

'C', the second difference, again working backwards. For instance, if 'A' contained 11, then 'B' would contain 5, and 'C' 2. Then we would add the number in 'C' to the number in 'B', and the result to the number in 'A':

$$C + B + A = 2 + 5 + 11 = 18$$

Result: the next integer value of y. And we can repeat the process, incrementing the value in 'B' and 'A' each time, to produce successive values of y.

If our equation contained higher powers, we would of course need to use more registers, but there is nothing in principle to stop us calculating values of expressions with any number of powers in them by this method.

Babbage developed his idea of the difference engine into a detailed design, using mechanical registers and mechanical devices for adding the contents of one register to that of another in a fixed cycle. He succeeded in building a small version, but the technology of his day was not equal to the task of producing the full-scale version he had planned, and its only realization appeared in a description in the *Edinburgh Review*, published in 1834.

This description caught the eye of a Swedish engineer, Per Georg Scheutz; with his son Edvard, he went on to design a difference engine using slightly different mechanical principles. This version did work and was successfully demonstrated in 1843. It spawned a modest industry of successors, and mechanical difference engines continued to be used for calculating tables up to the early years of this century.

Punched Card Machines

In Chapter 1 we mentioned briefly that the presence or absence of holes in a fixed position on a piece of card could form the basis of a binary code. Punched-card techniques for storing and manipulating information were first developed in the eighteenth century. Initially they were used, not for computing, but for manipulating the pattern shafts on looms for fancy weaving. This technique was pioneered by Bouchon and Falcon, and brought to commercial realization by Joseph Marie Jacquard at the end of the century.

Charles Babbage was the first to realize that the same techniques could be applied in calculating machines. Once again, however, he never succeeded in producing fully functional machines employing the techniques, and it was not until the late nineteenth century that Herman Hollerith, a German-American working for the U.S. Bureau of the Census, succeeded in developing commercial machines using punched-card storage of information.

Hollerith's aim was to mechanize the sorting of data from the population censuses taken every ten years. In consequence, he developed a simple code in which 240 squares on a rectangular card represented questions posed in the census. A hole punched in a square represented the answer, 'yes'; and a blank square was a 'no'. Later cards were developed with not just 240 but with 960 information-carrying positions, arranged in 80 columns and 12 rows. A typical card is shown in Figure 20. These cards could then be coded in any of the following ways:

(1) The card could record decimal numbers. One hole was punched in each column, in the row corresponding to the number. Ten eight-digit numbers, or one 80-digit number, could thus be recorded on each card.

(2) The card could record binary numbers. A hole represents a 1, the absence of a hole a 0, so 960 binary digits (or 80 one-byte binary numbers, using only eight rows in each column) could be stored on the card.

(3) The card could record alpha/numeric information, using codes like the ASCII code we listed on page 25.

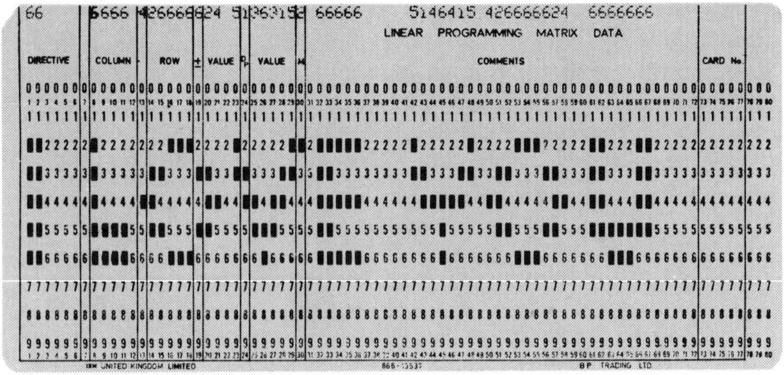

Figure 20: A typical punched card

As punched-card technology developed, conventions grew up concerning the ways in which information was to be stored: the top two rows, for instance, are commonly reserved for special instructions, while the actual data is recorded on the remaining ten rows.

Manipulation of Punched Cards

Punched cards themselves are a remarkably passive medium: acceptable for the storage of information, but not obviously suited to its manipulation. How were the holes on the cards transformed into electro-mechanical (or, later, electronic) activity?

The holes were normally 'read' by electrical means. The cards were placed, one by one, in the path of a series of electrical circuits, one for each location on the card to be read. (Normally, one row was read at a time.) A hole in the card would permit the completion of a circuit: by a brush touching a metal plate, or a pin contacting a terminal, or by a photo-electric cell; and the resulting impulse would register in the circuits of the machine. The absence of a hole would mean that the circuit could not be completed, and no impulse would be registered.

Hollerith's initial machine was designed primarily for sorting and counting the cards. The electrical impulses produced via the holes in the cards were used to power a mechanism that directed the cards differentially into a set of sorting pockets where they could be counted, and then perhaps re-entered into the machine for further sorting according to different criteria. Later, the techniques of punched-card manipulation were refined further, and these early machines fathered several generations of collation and computation machines.

Collators were used for selecting, matching and merging sets of cards, while tabulators handled the addition and subtraction of numerical data on the cards, and the printing-out of the results. In the latter type of machines, the data on the cards were transferred to sets of electro-mechanical registers, or accumulators, upon which the arithmetical operations could be carried out in a way similar to that used by the calculating machines described earlier. Special refinements in the reading mechanism handled niceties, such as the layout of the results and the printing of sub-totals at regular intervals.

These machines were extremely effective for use in data-processing situations, where a great volume of data had to be processed in routine and relatively simple ways. A sizeable industry based on punched-card office machinery grew up, and Hollerith's own company was later incorporated into the developing I.B.M. empire. The machines were widely used during the period from the end of the First World War to the late 1960s, when improvements in electronic computer technology made them obsolescent. Many commercial machines could read cards at up to 400 per minute and manipulate them at comparable speeds. They were also used for some scientific and technical calculations, but they were less well suited to the more intensive computation demanded in these fields, and were rapidly superseded by newer designs of machine.

The punched cards themselves survived for a little longer, as a very common form of computer input. They had obvious disadvantages: punching the cards and verifying their correctness were dull and time-consuming jobs; and not being able to read data easily straight off the cards (though a transcript could, of course, be written in the margin) was clearly a drawback. However, they were cheap and comparatively durable, and data on them did not decay when the cards were stored.

Punched cards could also serve as 'unit records', since the 80-column cards could often carry the complete data and alpha/numeric description or record of a single transaction. They could therefore be filed for manual reference, as well as being machine readable.

Data and Instructions

In Chapter 1, we spent some time looking at what 'data' are. To recapitulate, we described data as 'known facts'. When we come to consider calculating machines, 'data' becomes something more precise: the data we use in an operation are the known facts *we want to manipulate*.

But what of the manipulation we want to do? When we write '4 + 6 − 8', then in one sense all these symbols are 'data'. They could all be coded in ASCII or a similar code, and be input to an electronic computer. They could be stored by the computer, sorted with other strings of symbols, and be output again. In another sense, however, there is a vital difference between the 4, 6 and 8 on the one hand, and the + and the − on the other. If we plan, not merely to store and recall those symbols, but to carry out an arithmetical operation, then the 4, 6 and 8 become the data on which we wish to perform the operation, while the + and the − become the *instructions* that tell us what to do with those data. In other words, symbols like ' +' and ' −', or even words like ADD and SUBTRACT, can in some circumstances *be* data. In other circumstances, though, they become instructions that tell the computer, calculator or human being what to do with the data.

Let's take an example. On an electronic typewriter, you may press the keys in the order, '4 + 6 − 8 ='. The output – the message that appears on the piece of paper in the machine – will read '4 + 6 − 8 ='. But try keying that same set of symbols into a pocket calculator. The output won't be the symbols as you input them: rather, it will be the answer to the equation, 2. The typewriter treated all its input as data; the calculator treats some of it as data and some as instructions. There is a major difference between what these two electronic machines actually *do* when the symbol ' =', for example, is keyed into them.

Data are passive facts. A punched card can contain data. It just sits there until someone or something does something to it. Instructions are active; they are what prompts the doing. And ADD, when it leads to the actual operation of adding two numbers together being carried out, is an instruction. It does not matter whether the instruction is input by turning a crank handle, by keying ' +', or by keying ADD. If it leads to action on data, it is an instruction.

Of course, when we type ADD as data on a typewriter, something *happens*. The machine has inbuilt 'instructions' that tell it what to do with the data. But when we type ADD as an instruction into a computer, then the machine doesn't just follow its inbuilt rules. It responds to our input *as* an instruction.

Entering Data and Instructions

In Pascal's calculating machine, entering the data and the instructions was a fairly transparent business. To input a number as data, you literally turned a cogwheel by an amount directly corresponding to the size of the number. To input an 'add' or a 'subtract' instruction, you turned a handle and initiated the action represented by the instruction. The operations triggered by pressing keys are less obvious though, particularly when this same input medium is used both for instructions and for data.

Keyboard input of data started back in the mechanical era when many commercial calculators had keyboards, each key being marked with a number. Pressing the key triggered a series of rods and levers, and this in turn led to the registering of the number inside the machine. Keyboard input of instructions as well as data had to wait for the electrification of calculating machines. To implement an 'add' instruction on a mechanical calculator requires quite a lot of force, especially if there are many digits with carries to be allowed for. It is not easy to provide such force via a key mechanism. The principle behind key input of instructions, however, is the same as that used for data. Pressing an instruction key similarly triggers a series of rods and levers, and they in turn activate the 'add' sequence of movements inside the machine.

In that era, of course, a key represented *either* data *or* instruction input, but not both. Today, many computer keyboards have keys that can be interpreted as providing either kind of input, depending on the circumstances in which they are used.

In an electronic calculator, the principles employed for input are much the same. The keys or touchpads with numbers on them are the medium for data input. The keys with operators on them (+, −, log, =, CL, or whatever else appears on the keyboard) are the medium for instruction input. Both data input and instruction input are converted into a series of electronic pulses, conveying the message in binary coded form. The machine's built-in instructions cause it to convey data input to a register, where it is stored until required. Instruction input triggers a sequence of electronic activity (routeing the contents of two registers through an adder circuit like that we drew up on page 47, for instance), which has the effect of implementing the instruction.

Electrical Relays

During the Second World War, heavy demands were created for rapid and accurate calculation. Calculating bomb and shell trajectories was a highly complex task. Punched-card machinery could not cope with it, and the result was a drive towards the development of more efficient calculating machines. The type that emerged first replaced the gear and ratchet mechanisms of the earlier generation with electrical relays.

A relay is a simple electro-mechanical device that relies upon the magnetizing effect of electric current. Figure 21 shows its general construction. The iron core of the solenoid (the device at the bottom of the illustration) is magnetized when current flows through the coil of wire surrounding it. The magnetic force it exerts attracts the switch (or armature) at the top of the figure. It closes, and current flows through the circuit. When the current in the coil is switched off, the core is demagnetized and no longer attracts the armature. Spring tension causes the switch to open. The circuit is interrupted, and current ceases to flow in it.

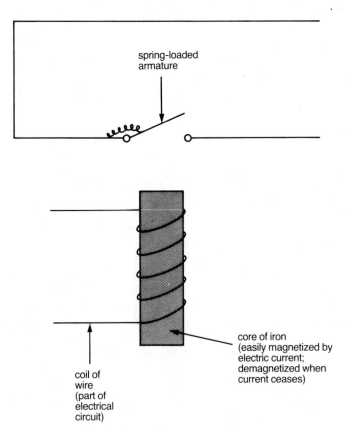

Figure 21 : An electro-mechanical relay

Relays had already been in use for twenty years in the telephone industry, where indeed they still provide the basic form of switching mechanism today (though they are now slowly being supplanted by more modern technology); their applicability to data processing had not previously been noticed, though. In fact, the implication of electrical and, later, electronic switching devices for data processing was to be enormous, as we have already begun to see. In the first relay calculators, however, the relays themselves did not store binary data. They simply provided a clutch mechanism that could couple and uncouple registers according to the demands of the calculation. In other words, the information they carried was not data, but instructions that caused particular operations to be performed.

ASCC

The Automatic Sequence Controlled Calculator, or ASCC, was perhaps the best known of these relay machines. It was designed by Howard H. Aiken of Harvard University, in collaboration with I.B.M., and completed in 1944.

The registers in the ASCC consisted of sets of wheels on which decimal numbers were stored. There were 72 such registers, each consisting of 24 wheels (to hold 23 digits and one sign, + or −). Each register was fitted with an adding mechanism, so that its contents could be added to or subtracted from those of another register, without first copying them into an arithmetic unit. There was a separate unit that handled multiplication and division, and there were facilities for some more complex mathematical operations to be performed. One specific area held up to 60 constants, on registers consisting not of wheels but of switches that were set by hand before the calculation commenced.

Electrical contacts fitted to each counter wheel gave an electrical indication of its position, and these electrical signals could be connected to the relay-based clutch mechanism. The wheels of one register could thus be rotated by varying amounts that depended on the numbers stored in another register.

ASCC used punched-card input for data, and it also took its instructions from punched patterns — but these were on paper tape, not cards. Each instruction consisted of 24 binary digits, and might specify either the operation to be carried out or the location in the machine of data to be operated on.

ASCC was an incredibly complex machine. It contained over 750,000 parts; it worked at what today seems an extremely slow pace. Adding two numbers took three-tenths of a second, and division up to twelve seconds. Work it did, though, and it continued in use for fifteen years.

Electro-mechanical relay calculators were much faster than previous mechanical calculators of the same complexity, and the new technology enabled machines to be constructed of greater complexity than any previously built. The output from these machines was often in the form of light-bulbs that lit up to represent a significant digit (that is, a 1 rather than a 0). However, the relay calculators were by no means perfect. They were bulky and consumed a great deal of power. The search continued for a more convenient way of switching electrical current, and shortly afterwards it proved successful.

Valves

The thermionic valve, or vacuum tube, was the first *electronic* device: that is to say, it could act as an amplifier of electrical current. In construction it was much like a filament light-bulb (as you can see from Figure 22a). The filament and its surrounding cathode are encircled by a metal plate, and these three elements are then enclosed in a vacuum-filled metal or glass case.

There are two circuits in Figure 22b, which shows how the vacuum tube diode works. The first applies a voltage to the filament wire, which acts as a heater. Its heat liberates valent electrons in the cathode, which is a good conductor of electricity. The second circuit connects the cathode and the plate in series.

When a negative voltage is applied to the plate and a positive voltage to the cathode, this reinforces the electron flow triggered by the heater. The electrons are pulled across the vacuum to the plate, and current flows in the circuit. When the circuit is connected in the reverse direction, the electrons are not attracted towards, but are repelled by, the plate. No current flows.

This diode acts, therefore, as a rectifier of alternating current into direct current. Vacuum-tube technology can also be used to make triodes; they amplify current in the same way as does the semiconductor transistor we looked at on page 41.

As a form of on/off switch, valves can act as binary information carrying and storage devices; and they were used in the first valve-based calculator, ENIAC, to transmit and store both instructions and data.

ENIAC

ENIAC (the Electronic Numerical Integrator and Calculator) was completed in 1946, but it too owed its birth to wartime calculation needs: though it was a general-purpose machine, its prime function was to calculate bomb and shell trajectories. It was designed by J. P. Eckert and J. W. Mauchly, of the Moore School of Electrical Engineering at the University of Pennsylvania.

In ENIAC, all operations (apart from the input and output of information) were handled electronically, by circuits that incorporated no less than

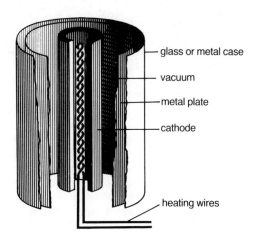

glass or metal case

vacuum

metal plate

cathode

heating wires

(a) Construction

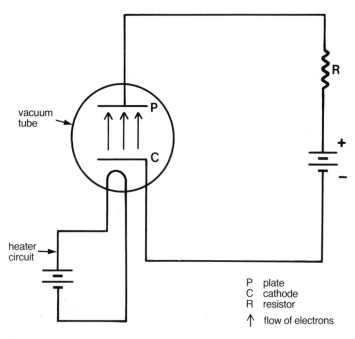

vacuum tube

R

P

C

+

−

heater circuit

P   plate
C   cathode
R   resistor
↑   flow of electrons

(b) Operation in a circuit

Figure 22: The vacuum tube diode

18,000 valves. It was a massive machine, taking up a floor space of around 2,150 square feet.

At the heart of ENIAC was an electrical pulse generator that supplied a continuous stream of pulses to all parts of the machine. One pulse occurred every ten microseconds – in other words, there were 100,000 pulses every second. These pulses were then converted by electronic circuits into sets of standard waveforms, that could be used to represent coded instructions or data. Each of these waveforms also represented the opportunity to carry out a different stage of the calculation. They were repeated at intervals of 200 microseconds; and in consequence, the speed of ENIAC's calculations was about 1,000 times greater than that of a relay machine like the ASCC.

ENIAC did *not* use binary coding of information. Instead, numbers were stored in decimal form, on a device called a ring counter. This was a circuit linking ten valves, one to represent each of the numbers from 0 to 9. Only the valve corresponding to the number actually being represented by the circuit was 'on' at any one time. When a pulse was received by the circuit, this valve would be switched off, and the next one on. To transmit data, the circuit would emit a number of pulses corresponding to the number of the 'on' valve.

There were twenty registers, each consisting of ten ring counters and a 'sign' device. Each could act as an accumulator: that is, it could be linked to other registers and perform addition and subtraction operations, as could the registers in the ASCC. Transmission of a number from one register to another was via a group of eleven wires, representing the ten digits and the sign of the number.

Like the ASCC, ENIAC made use of punched-card information and of switches for the input of special data and instructions. Its sequence of calculations was predetermined, not by the input of a continuous series of instructions during operation, but by setting a series of connections in the machine before it began a calculation. In this way, it could 'store' up to 300 separate instructions in the pattern of its circuitry.

ENIAC and ASCC, and the other large-scale machines of their era, were influential in the later development of both calculators and computers. However, they did not have a great impact upon the general design of contemporary calculating machines. The technology of both of them was cumbersome, and neither could easily be translated into the format of desk machines. In the years immediately following the Second World War, small-scale calculation continued to be carried out on manually operated mechanical calculators, or on newly electrified versions with electrical motors powering the same type of component arrangement. Only a very few of the large relay and valve machines were in use, while many thousands of these more traditional designs were still being produced.

Semiconductor Technology

As well as being bulky, valves were energy-intensive and unreliable. The heat of their operation made the filament brittle, and eventually it would break. Finding and replacing a burnt-out valve from among ENIAC's 18,000 was quite a feat.

Fortunately, the valve was soon superseded by the semiconductor technology we looked at in Chapter 2 (pages 38 to 41. The transistor was invented by a team from Bell Laboratories, John Bardeen, Walter Brattain and William Shockley, in 1948, and even at the start it was both faster and smaller than the valve. Early difficulties in mastering the mass-production techniques demanded by transistors delayed their impact upon calculating technology, but by the late 1950s these had been overcome. The first transistorized desk calculator was made in 1963 by the British Bell Punch Company. Transistorized computers, the offspring of ENIAC along a different path of development, had appeared a little earlier.

These first electronic calculators contained a number of transistors, resistors and other separate electronic components, laid out on a circuit board and wired together. Later technology enabled several components, and the wires connecting them, to be manufactured in a single operation, and on a single 'chip' of material — often of silicon. These integrated circuits were in turn superseded by the arrival of Large Scale Integration (LSI), in which hundreds of components could be crammed on to a single chip, and then by Very Large Scale Integration (VLSI), and finally by Ultra Large Scale Integration (ULSI). Today's technology is at a stage where literally thousands of components can be incorporated into a chip only about a $\frac{1}{4}''$ (6 mm) square; and Japanese manufacturers are now talking about million component chips. We shall look in much greater detail at the technology of silicon chips, and their newer rivals, in Chapter 20.

The techniques by which numbers are stored and instructions implemented electronically in modern calculators are identical to those used in modern computers. Indeed, calculators and computers are by no means entirely separate stables of devices: there is a spectrum of machines providing a range of facilities from the simplest four-function calculator to the most complex and powerful computer. Where is the dividing line? We shall attempt to answer that question in the next chapter; we shall also look at aspects of the technology common to both calculators and computers later in the book. We conclude this section by taking a brief look at the development of modern calculators for the desk, the pocket and those with even more scaled-down applications.

Modern Electronic Calculators

In the early 1960s, desk versions of electronic calculators began to appear for common use. They generally had keyboards for input of both instructions and data, and a display area that employed 'Nixie tubes'. Each of these tubes is a series of circuits of small wires, each following the outline of a numeral. When current flows through one of the circuits, the numeral glows. An alternative output technology, the light-emitting diode, consists of arrays of chemical semiconductor materials that glow when a current is applied to them. When lit up, different patterns of the diodes in the array make up the outline of the different numerals. Today, yet another output technology has been developed: the liquid crystal. We look in detail at both light-emitting diodes and liquid crystals in Chapter 19.

Of course, many of these desk calculators also incorporated a printer for hard-copy output of the calculation; today, some smaller calculators also boast this feature. Printer technology too has developed, and we take a further look at it in Chapter 16.

Initially, these calculators had only four arithmetical functions: $+$, $-$, $\times$ and $./.$, just like their mechanical predecessors. They also had keys for clearing the display and their registers, and for instructing them to execute their operations ($=$, for instance). As the number of components that could be fitted into the calculators grew and the cost of the circuits fell, these functions were extended. Today, many calculators of all sizes boast one or more additional 'memory' registers and more complex arithmetical functions such as log, sin. and x^2. The range of additional functions is often tailored to specific professional requirements: there are calculators aimed at engineers, architects, scientists, and so on. The principle behind all of them is the same, though: by pressing the key, the operator sets off a different predetermined set of operations in the circuits of the machine (a sequence which may be extremely complicated, in some cases). Even higher up the hierarchy come programmable calculators that have much in common with computers proper.

Instead of a keyboard input panel, some cheaper calculators use a touchpad system: there are no keys to press, but a continuous plastic surface printed with rectangles labelled with numbers and instruction codes. Beneath each of these is a pad of touch-sensitive material that acts as a form of electronic switch. Touching the pad activates an electronic impulse, which then acts in the same way as the impulse triggered by a key.

Inside a Modern Electronic Calculator

Figure 23 shows a typical slimline modern electronic pocket calculator, the Sharp ELSI MATE E1-8130. As you can see from the drawing of the casing,

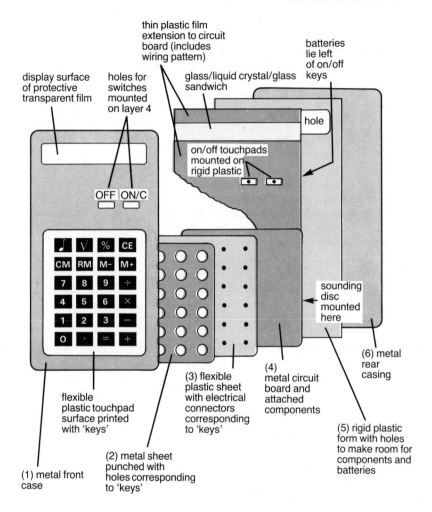

thin plastic film
extension to circuit
board (includes
wiring pattern)

batteries
lie left
of on/off
keys

display surface
of protective
transparent film

holes for
switches
mounted
on layer 4

glass/liquid crystal/glass
sandwich

hole

on/off touchpads
mounted on
rigid plastic

OFF ON/C

sounding
disc
mounted
here

(6) metal
rear
casing

flexible
plastic touchpad
surface printed
with 'keys'

(3) flexible
plastic sheet
with electrical
connectors
corresponding
to 'keys'

(4)
metal circuit
board and
attached
components

(5) rigid plastic
form with holes
to make room for
components and
batteries

(2) metal sheet
punched with
holes corresponding
to 'keys'

(1) metal front
case

(total thickness when assembled approx. $\frac{2}{10}''$ (0.5cm)

Figure 23: Construction of a typical modern pocket calculator (roughly to scale)

it has an 'on/constant' switch, an 'off' switch, and a touchpad with a simple selection of numeric and function keys.

What is inside the case? Immediately under the flexible plastic surface of the touchpad is a rigid metal grid, with holes corresponding to each key. Under that is a flexible plastic sheet with an array of electrical contact pads

– again, one for each key. When the key is pressed, the contact pad presses against part of an electronic circuit, printed on the obverse of a two-sided circuit board.

On the reverse side of the circuit board is a less regular circuit wiring pattern, with a small selection of components soldered on to it. The main component is the microprocessor chip (just under $\frac{1}{2}''$ (12 mm) square), that contains all the arithmetic/logic circuitry, in its plastic casing. Metal pins protrude from each side of the casing to connect it to the board circuit.

And what else? At the top is the circuitry and hardware of the liquid crystal display: a wafer-thin layer of liquid crystal sandwiched between two thin sheets of glass. It traces out a total of eight digits, a memory/error indicator, and a picture of a musical note, to show if the 'bleeper' (the calculator makes a noise when a key is pressed, unless silenced by pressing the appropriate key) is on. The bleeper itself is a simple metal disc, fastened to the plastic casing that completes the calculator 'sandwich'; it is vibrated by a contact pin and held in contact with the circuit board by a simple spring. Two long-life batteries, each just under $\frac{1}{2}''$ (12 mm) in diameter and about 1/10″ (2 mm) thick – and that's the lot. Retail price in 1983 of machines like this: well under £5. We have come a long way since Pascal's day!

4. The Stored-Program Concept

When was the first computer built? Which machine *was* the first computer? These are not easy questions to answer. Claims to be the first computer have been advanced on behalf of at least a dozen machines. Some of them are machines that became widely known only many years after they were constructed: 'kitchen-sink' machines, cobbled together from bits and pieces, like George Stibitz's 'Model K' ('K' stood for 'kitchen table'), and Konrad Zuse's Z1; or machines constructed in conditions of wartime secrecy, and not declassified until many years later, like the British 'Colossus' code-breaking machines. As more has become known about them, these machines have superseded some earlier and better-known claimants to the title. Others are machines that were definitely the first, as far as we know, to embody particular advances in technology. The trouble is, few people agree just *which* advance was the vital one that turned the calculator into a computer.

To some extent, the question is an academic one. The ASCC, the Z3, ENIAC, EDVAC and so on are all machines that have played a part in shaping modern computer technology; they are all worth learning about. However, it seems we must come down on one side or the other: and we therefore pronounce that, for our purposes, the difference between computers proper and mere calculators is that computers embody the stored-program concept.

What is the stored-program concept? That, again, is not as easy a question as might first seem. Let us go back a little way, and draw a distinction between general-purpose machines and special-purpose machines.

General-Purpose and Special-Purpose Machines

A special-purpose machine is just that: a machine designed for a special, specific purpose. A general-purpose machine is a machine *not* designed for a special purpose; in other words, one that can be adapted to carry out a number of different operations.

Of course, this too begs a question: how do we define a special purpose? Babbage's Difference Engine might, for instance, be described as a special-purpose machine in that it could only analyse polynomial expressions. But it was a general-purpose machine in that it did not merely calculate the values of, say, $x^2 + x - 6$ for integer values of x from 1 to 10. Instead, it could be set to calculate the value of *any* polynomial expression that fell within the boundaries of its calculating abilities.

The border between the special-purpose and the general-purpose machine becomes a little less fuzzy if we reintroduce our distinction between instructions and data – though that, again, has caused some controversies in its time. In effect, the Difference Engine had one sequence of instructions: to analyse any polynomial expression it was given, for a range of values that, again, were given in advance. But it could carry out those instructions on a wide variety of data: that is, on different expressions, and across different ranges of values.

In other words, the Difference Engine needed only one type of input: the data on which it was to carry out its fixed sequence of operations. It did not need to have instructions input into it. Its sequence of operations was determined by its hardware – by the way in which the machine itself was constructed – and by its simple, virtually unchanging operating instructions: first turn this handle, then that, and so on.

As a general rule, the more special-purpose a machine, the less instruction input it requires. The more general-purpose it becomes, the more its sequence of operations is likely to vary. As those operations start to vary, so they must be controlled: by operating instructions that are conveyed by the operator to the machinery, either before or during operation.

Instructions

How then can instructions be transferred from the operator – who presumably knows what he or she wants the machine to do – to the dumb machinery? Basically, there are three ways:

(1) The instructions can be embodied in the machine's hardware before the process of computation begins: by meshing or disconnecting gears, flicking switches on or off, replugging an electrical circuit so that the pattern of current flow is altered. This effectively creates a special-purpose machine out of the general-purpose machine, but one that can later be adapted into a different special-purpose machine, to carry out a different sequence of operations.

(2) The instructions can be performed by the operator, in the course of a computation, by physically initiating certain actions. For instance, the operator might turn a crank a set number of times, unplug and replug connections at a specific moment, or generally act in some way to adapt the hardware of the machine to suit the evolving requirements of the instruction series.

(3) The instructions can be automatically fed to the machine in advance: for instance, in code on a pack of punched cards, as in a Jacquard loom. As each instruction reaches the control unit of the machine, it is

'decoded' into a sequence of activities that then take place: circuits may be completed as the holes in the card cross them, or broken if there is no hole, latches may be triggered, and so on. Again, the instructions lead to physical changes in the hardware of the machine.

Three quite different methods . . . but all of them have the same aim: at any fixed moment in the computation, they ensure that the hardware of the machine — whether it be mechanical, electro-mechanical or electronic — functions in a specific way. The machine itself cannot *decide* what to do next: the instructions, translated eventually into a hardware configuration, ensure that it does what is required in order to achieve the specific purpose for which it is being used.

The Program

What is the difference between instructions and a program, then? In the specific sense in which we are using the word:

a program is a *sequence* of instructions — possibly a fixed sequence, possibly one in which later operations can be modified as a result of the outcome of earlier operations — that is *determined* before the start of the operation and *translated* into a series of actions performed by the hardware of the machine, in one of the three ways outlined above.

In this sense, every general-purpose machine is transformed into a special-purpose machine when it carries out a specific task. And the sequence of instructions by which it is so transformed is its program.

There are obvious advantages in simplifying the task of inputting the program to the machine. The machine may go through an elaborate sequence of hardware changes in the course of performing a computation. Each one of these must be initiated in some way: either as part of an independent sequence of actions that directly and inevitably leads to other actions (cogs that turn other cogs, currents that flip open circuit gates, and so on), or as a result of program input. To initiate each action by hand would be a time-consuming business, and be prone to error. But the amount of human intervention can be cut down in two ways:

(1) by building more special-purpose circuitry into the machine, so that a single instruction can trigger a more elaborate sequence of activity, and fewer instructions are needed in order to complete a computation;

(2) or by storing the program instructions on a medium such as punched cards or one of the more modern media examined later, and then inputting them to the machine automatically. The program can then be checked in advance, so that its operation is less likely to be ruined by an inadvertent slip in transmitting the instructions; and it can be read automatically into the machine more rapidly than a human being could convey it.

In tracing the evolution of the stored-program concept, we shall come across a variety of combinations of these two techniques later in this part of the book.

Storing the Program

To return to where we started: what do we mean by the *stored* program? Obviously, a program is *stored* if it is recorded permanently, or semi-permanently, in any medium: as a list of instructions on paper, or in a stack of punched cards. But when we talk of a stored-program computer, we mean a computer that actually stores the program inside itself, that is, in its hardware configuration. When the program is initiated, each of the stored, coded instructions is then accessed, decoded and translated into action, in the sequence determined by the program's structure.

To some extent, as we have seen, every computer and calculator does this. Indeed, special-purpose machines embody their instructions almost entirely in their hardware. So why did the concept of the stored program later become so important?

As we shall see when we come to consider programming techniques, for very many elaborate programs it is desirable to build in a degree of flexibility. The machine must not only carry out a fixed sequence of instructions; instead, the outcome of a particular operation may make it desirable for the sequence of later operations to be varied or even for the content of later instructions to be changed.

Let us offer a very simple example. Say we want to find the lowest integer that fulfils a specific condition: the lowest integer exactly divisible by both 3 and 14, for instance. The program we would devise would probably start with the lowest integer of all – 1 – and then proceed to test every integer in ascending order, until it met one that fulfilled our conditions. We could not say in advance how many numbers of the program we would have to test. But after each number was tested, we would want the computer to make its next sequence of operations conditional upon the result of the test. Our program instructions would be something like this:

If the number is divisible by 3 and 14, *then* output the number and end the program.

If not, then continue to test the next number.

We can offer many real-life examples in which the same procedure would come in handy. For instance:

if the water is hot enough, *then* turn off the heater; *if not*, continue to heat the water.

if it has been a dry day, *then* water the plants; *if not*, do not water plants.

if the burglar alarm is triggered, *then* sound alarm; *if not*, do not sound alarm.

In every one of these cases, the outcome of one operation (a test, an action, a calculation) will have an impact upon the way in which the rest of the program is executed. Of course, we *can* include such conditional branches (as they are called in programming) in written sequences of instructions, or in packs of punched cards that can be read in a variable sequence. But if our technology enables us to do so, then there is scope for using many more elaborate techniques for modifying the order or content of programs in operation: techniques that cannot be implemented using the simple technologies of pen and paper or punched cards.

They cannot be implemented practically in mechanical machines, either. But they *can* be implemented in electronic machines. Electronic technology, with its lack of moving parts, its speed of operation, and its wide variety of techniques for changing the path of current flow, is well adapted to the amendment of stored programs. And the pre-electronic development of the stored-program concept paved the way for the elaboration in program modification techniques that electronic technology made possible.

The Analytical Engine

Charles Babbage designed the first machine we know of that included all the functional elements of a modern computer, the Analytical Engine. It was *not* the first real computer, for two reasons: first, it did not embody the stored (variable) program concept; and second, it was never actually built. However, it is a good introduction to the developments in ideas and in technology that led to the modern computer.

What did the Analytical Engine – as Babbage designed it – consist of? It was a mechanical machine of incredible complexity and would have contained over 50,000 moving parts, even in its simplest incarnation. These were arranged to make up five major functional sections:

(1) input devices, that enabled numbers and operating instructions to be supplied to the machine, in a variable sequence.

(2) a store, that broadly corresponds to the modern computer memory. This could be preset with direct input, at the start of a computation. It contained intermediate results, and at the end of the computation it held the final results.

(3) a mill, or computing unit, that carried out addition, subtraction, multiplication and division – and, by extension, more elaborate mathematical operations that could be built up from these. The store itself could *not* perform arithmetical operations – not even simple addition, unlike the registers of the ASCC.

(4) a control unit that handled the sequencing of operations.

(5) output devices, for displaying the results.

These five elements can be discerned in any modern computer. Their interrelation is summarized in Figure 24.

The Analytical Engine was a general-purpose machine. Its hardware

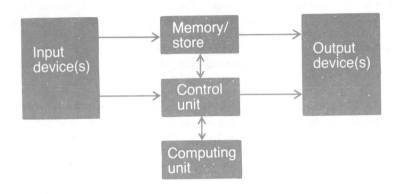

Figure 24: The elements of a computer system

would have embodied the instructions for carrying out the four basic arithmetic operations and some equally basic control operations; but the bulk of its instructions were to be supplied as input, in the form of punched cards. Babbage planned to use cards for a variety of purposes in the machine, and even included a design for a card-punching unit so that new cards could be created in the course of a computation. The cards triggered mechanical action by their connection with an array of levers. Where there was a hole in the card opposite a lever, the lever passed through the hole and was not moved; where there was no hole, the lever was triggered by the connection with the card.

Babbage envisaged that 'operation cards' – possibly colour-coded according to the type of operation (white for addition, yellow for subtraction, blue for multiplication and green for division) – would trigger the arithmetical operations. Special 'combinatorial' cards would contain instructions for the repetition of a sequence of operations, and would trigger the backing-up of the card input so that a series of operations could be repeated as often as specified. Another type of instruction, covering the transfer of data between the store and the mill, was to be handled by cards known as 'variable' cards. Yet more cards would store additional data, so that the operation of the machine would not be limited by the size of the store. Finally, punched cards were one of several output media Babbage planned to use.

The complexity of these arrangements meant that even a single operation required many instructions. To add two numbers together, for instance, the machine needed two operation cards, one to specify the sign of each number, and three variable cards: two to transfer the two numbers from the store to the mill, and a third to indicate where in the store the result was to be deposited. Multiplication and division would have required six cards each. However, for more elaborate computations these arrangements would doubtless have been worthwhile. The machine was to work to fifty significant places of accuracy — and dividing one 50-digit number by another would have been quite a task by hand.

Babbage's weakness was always in bringing his idea to fruition. His failure to construct working machines was undoubtedly due in part to the limited accuracy of precision-engineering techniques in his day; but a large part of the blame must be attributed to his own temperament. It seems that he was simply not prepared to compromise and devise a machine on a workable scale. He must have been far more excited by the idea that underlay his inventions than by the prospect of their realization in concrete form; and he undoubtedly had personality difficulties that discouraged many of his contemporaries from giving him their full support. Despite government funding for some of his endeavours, and Babbage's own persistence with the idea of the Analytical Engine for nearly forty years, from 1833 to his death in 1871, no functioning machine was ever constructed. Babbage's son Henry later succeeded in realizing parts of his design, but not in producing a full version.

The Uses of Computing Machinery

One difficulty in Babbage's era lay in envisaging the practical uses to which a machine like the Analytical Engine or its predecessor, the Difference Engine, might be put. It is hard not to sympathize with Sir Robert Peel, then Prime Minister, who remarked in 1842 that 'I should like a little previous consideration before I move in a thin house of country gentlemen a large vote for the creation of a wooden man to calculate tables for the formula, $x^2 + x + 41$' (the formula with which Babbage first worked on the Difference Engine). Peel himself was a competent mathematician by the standards of the day, but that evidently did not alter his judgement, and it was one which many of his better-informed contemporaries shared.

Of course there were fields in which an ability to perform complex mathematical calculations quickly and accurately would have been of great value. In general, however, the use of mathematical techniques in science and technology has gone hand in hand with — or even rather behind — the ability of calculating machines to perform such feats of calculation. Many fields of science, of social science, of economics and so on, had not reached a level of sophistication at which their laws were even expressible in algebraic terms. Until such expressions had been formulated, there was no need for an ability to manipulate the formulations mathematically. Conversely, the doubt that such formulations would be manipulable in any meaningful way would have led to a lack of urgency in making them in the first place.

There *were* areas in which the need was clear: in astronomy and, by extension, in navigation, for instance; in ballistic science, too. But there was as yet no demand for the use of computers by physicists, by electricians, by economists, by statisticians, and so on. Largely as a result, it was not until a century after Babbage first devised the Analytical Engine that interest in his ideas was fully revived; and by then, there was a much greater demand for devices capable of undertaking complex scientific and mathematical calculations. Again, it was led by the demand for accurate gunnery and ballistic tables, this time in the Second World War.

Lady Lovelace and the Computer Program

Though Babbage performed a great service to the future computer industry in simply designing his Analytical Engine, he failed, as we have seen, to make its relevance clear. In part, this omission was rectified by two commentators who together extended the ideas behind the Analytical Engine: an Italian engineer and mathematician, L. F. Menabrea, and his English translator, Ada Augusta, Countess of Lovelace.

Menabrea's paper on Babbage, 'Sketch of the Analytical Engine invented by Charles Babbage, Esq.', which was published in 1842, is valuable more for its clarity than because it contains any new ideas. Lady Lovelace's translation is far more important today. She added extensive notes to Menabrea's original; and in them she brought out a number of ideas that are seminal in the historical development of computing.

Perhaps the foremost of these is her development of the idea of computer programming. Babbage's outline of the Analytical Engine made it clear *how* the machine was to be programmed, by enumerating the functions of the various types of punched cards it was to use. Lady Lovelace went much further than Babbage in drawing up actual programs for the machine, specifying what data should be punched, on what types of card, and in what order the instructions were to be executed. Her most complex program was for the computation of 'Bernoulli numbers', a series of numbers with special properties in mathematical number theory; her notes contain a complete listing of the program steps. Since the machine was never built, of course, the program was never run!

Lady Lovelace's other major contribution was perhaps even more significant. Babbage and Menabrea both perceived the Analytical Engine primarily as a mathematical tool for carrying out mathematical operations. Mathematics is, of course, a tool in many practical activities, from bridge building to writing music, and the Engine would thus have found a range of practical uses. However, neither Babbage nor Menabrea (nor, it seems, any of their other contemporaries) perceived that direct uses other than the purely mathematical would be found for it. Lady Lovelace makes it clear that, as well as manipulating numbers and algebraic symbols, the machine could be used to manipulate other kinds of symbol and thus to perform the range of tasks we associate with computers today. Her words are prophetic of the structure of the modern computer industry:

> In enabling mechanism to combine together *general* symbols, in successions of unlimited variety and extent, a uniting link is established between the operations of matter and the abstract mental processes of the *most abstract* branch of mathematical science. A new, a vast, and a powerful language is developed for the future use of analysis, in which to wield its truths so that these may become of more speedy and accurate practical application for the purposes of mankind than the means hitherto in our possession have rendered possible.*

Lady Lovelace's paper even suggests that the Engine might be used to compose 'elaborate and scientific pieces of music, of any degree of complexity or extent'.†

Her paper makes it quite clear (far more so than Babbage did) that the program itself can be considered in isolation from the data upon which the operations are to be performed. In effect, Lady Lovelace's programs are algorithms: outlines of programs, waiting to be made concrete by the addition of data. We shall look in greater detail at the development of programming theory, from the first conception of the algorithm to the design of high-level languages, in Chapter 9.

Boolean Algebra

If Babbage can take credit for mapping out the general design of computers, a British contemporary of his, George Boole, can claim much of the credit for developing the theoretical principles on which they work. His work, too, was little appreciated in his day, and its true importance was only recognized a century later.

Boole's work centred on closing the gap between mathematics and logic, and his great creation was a simple system whereby logical reasoning could be expressed in algebraic form. It is largely as a result of this cross-connection that computers have come to be used in so wide a variety of applications today.

---

* From 'Notes by the Translator [Lady A. A. Lovelace] to "Sketch of the Analytical Engine invented by Charles Babbage, Esq." by L. F. Menabrea'. Note A. Reproduced in B. V. Bowden, *Faster than Thought*, Pitman, 1953.

† Ibid.

Boolean algebra is based on the idea of sets, that can be designated by algebraic symbols: thus x might represent the set of all dogs; y, the set of all cats; and z, the set of animals with red fur. The interrelationship between the contents of the three sets can then be expressed by equations similar to, but not identical with, the equations of conventional algebra.

Boole's two vital operands are '.' and '+'. The convention 'z . y' is used to make up the set of objects with the qualities designated by *both* z and y; so, in our case, 'z . y' means 'cats with red fur'. Similarly, '$x + y$' is used to make up the set of objects that fall into *either* the x class *or* the y class; so to us, '$x + y$' means 'dogs and cats'. And by extension of these simple rules, $z(x + y)$ means 'dogs and cats with red fur'.

The vital difference comes, though, when we take two sets with the *same* contents. The concept of $x . x$, or x^2, cannot mean any more than simply x – dogs is dogs; cats is cats. Thus in Boolean algebra:

$$x^2 = x . x = x$$

This *can* be true in conventional algebra: but it is only true when x is equal either to 1 or to 0. Hence the intimate relationship between Boolean algebra and binary arithmetic; both function in a very similar way, and the logic circuits we examined on pages 41 to 44 can be used to carry out the manipulations required by both.

Boole's ideas were expressed in two fundamental books: *The Mathematical Analysis of Logic*, published in 1848, and the larger *An Investigation of the Laws of Thought, on which are Founded the Mathematical Theories of Logic and Probabilities*, that followed in 1854.

Later Logicians

Symbolic logic has come a long way since Boole's day. Subsequent philosophers and mathematicians like Frege, Russell, Whitehead and Wittgenstein have produced far more complex logical languages than anything Boole attempted. However, their work extends rather than contradicts Boole's and is far less suited than his to automation. As a result, it is Boolean algebra that has remained at the heart of computer logic operations.

One successor to Boole must, however, be mentioned: W. S. Jevons who was responsible for propagating the idea of truth tables. You will recall that we introduced these in discussing the operation of logic gates. Jevons not only explored this concept, he also applied it to machines; and in one of his papers. 'The Mechanical Performance of Logical Inference' of 1869, he discussed a 'Logical Abacus' that he had built for performing logical manipulations. This could solve simple problems involving overlapping sets, with up to four different components to be interelated. An example might be:

Only members of the Supercomputer Club can operate the club machine

The club machine is a 'Maestro 20'
Only operators of 'Maestro 20s' can operate the improved 'Maestro 30'
I can operate the Maestro 30
Am I a member of the Supercomputer Club?

Following Jevons' machine, which was more interesting than practicable, a number of specialized 'logical machines' were built in the early days of computing: the Kalin—Burkhart logical machine, constructed at Harvard in 1947, and the 1950 Ferranti Logical Computer are two early examples. This rather esoteric field of endeavour was short-lived, however, as it began to be realized that digital computers operating in binary could be adapted to solve this kind of logical problem.

The Turing Machine

The Cambridge mathematician Alan Turing played a vital part in mapping out the conceptual basis of modern computers; perhaps his most important contribution was his demonstration that any problem (like the simple logical problem above) that could be solved on a special-purpose machine could also be solved (albeit perhaps at greater length) on a general-purpose machine.

Turing's famous paper, 'On Computable Numbers with an Application to the *Entscheidungsproblem*' of 1937, outlined a 'universal automaton', a general-purpose machine that could be programmed to solve finite mathematical and logical problems. The 'universal automaton' was not intended to be built, and it was not: not because it was horrendously complicated, like Babbage's machines, but because it was so simple. It consisted merely of an 'automaton', that could carry out the add/subtract/compare operations with which it functioned, and a storage/instruction medium, a tape of theoretically infinite capacity. The automaton could read data or instructions off the tape, then write them back on to it, working with only a small area of tape beneath its read/write head. And that was all. It is all, come to that, that any modern computer can do at heart; but, as we know today, that does not prevent the computer from engendering immense computing power.

Turing worked on a number of early computers and code-breaking machines (which had in some ways more in common with the logical machine tradition than with the arithmetical): among them, the famous 'Colossus' series of code-breakers and the ACE computers built at the National Physical Laboratory at Manchester, England, that were to be the basis of Ferranti's first commercial computers. He left another legacy to the computer fraternity: the 'Turing test' for determining whether a machine is intelligent. We shall re-encounter this when we come to look at artificial intelligence in Chapter 31.

The Delay Line

The delay line was a storage device used in the first generation of computers, two of which we shall now consider. It had obvious advantages in both cost and reliability over the vacuum-tube technology it partly superseded. However, it proved to be a dead-end in technological development, and its use was a short-lived phenomenon.

The type of delay line used in early computers consisted of a long tube filled with fluid – either mercury or a mixture of water and other substances to give suitable transmission properties (Alan Turing is claimed to have advocated gin as the ideal substance). At one end of the tube was an input device and at the other end an output device, crystals capable of transforming electrical signals into sonic signals – that is, into a pattern of wavelengths – and back again. The sonic waves travel through the fluid much more slowly (about 200,000 times more slowly) than the electrical signal travels through the wire; thus the tube 'delays' the signals and effectively stores them for a short period.

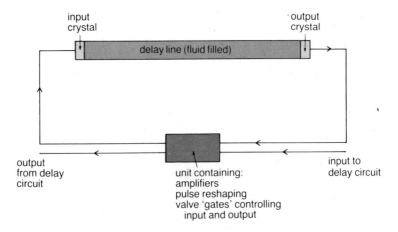

Figure 25: Delay line storage circuit

Delay lines can be built into a circuit, with a control unit containing amplifying valves and a device to reshape the waves and avoid corruption of the pattern of data, as shown in Figure 25. The circuit can contain a continuous series of binary bits of data, alternately in electronic pulse form and in sonic wave form, input at the input point and output at the output point when required, or cycled around the circuit indefinitely. A typical delay line was about five feet long. It held anything between 500 and 1,000 bits of information in series, with a maximum access time to the stored information depending on the length of time it took a signal to traverse the circuit – a few milliseconds. Only about ten vacuum tubes were required for the amplification unit, by contrast with the one tube per bit in pure vacuum tube storage.

EDVAC

EDVAC (the 'Electronic Discrete Variable Automatic Computer') is a particularly interesting early computer, not only because of the technological advances it embodied, but because the principles which underlay its design were exhaustively discussed in writing before it was completed. The series of papers by John von Neumann, John Mauchly, Arthur Burks, Herman Goldstine and others involved in the project at the Moore School of Electrical Engineering at the University of Pennsylvania outline many factors that influenced the later history of computer development.

Von Neumann's 1945 paper, 'First Draft of a Report on the EDVAC', outlines the functional parts of a computer in a way that is reminiscent of Babbage, though its identification of them is clearer than anything Babbage or his commentators provided. Von Neumann saw these as being:

(1) an arithmetic unit, to carry out a set of basic arithmetical operations.

(2) a central control unit, to sequence and decode instructions.

(3) an extensive memory. (A later paper by Burks, Goldstine and von Neumann envisaged a hierarchy of memories, some small and rapidly accessible, some larger and more slowly accessible.)

(4) input and output devices, divided into:

(a) a medium for recording input and output in a form compatible with the human user (for instance, in decimal rather than binary notation);

(b) a means of converting the humanly accessible input and output to and from the form required by the computer's own manipulative circuits.

Von Neumann also discussed the advantage of the binary and decimal systems, and concluded that the advantages of the binary system in manipulation justified the task of converting decimal data to and from binary. He considered the advantages of parallel processing (in which several units carry out arithmetic/logic operations simultaneously) as opposed to serial processing, and came down firmly in favour of the latter, less complex version. He also discussed the role of the clock and the need to synchronize operations (though he also recognized the possibility, later realized in practice, that asynchronous operation might in some circumstances have its uses).

The question of programming such a machine was discussed at greater length in John Mauchly's paper, 'Preparation of Problems for EDVAC-type Machines'. A number of ideas that, though they may have originated elsewhere, received a particularly clear exposition in this paper, are worth bringing out.

Mauchly was firmly against the concept of developing elaborate circuits for performing arithmetic/logic operations, such as finding square and cube roots, or logarithms. He believed that the basic 'instruction set' of hard-wired circuitry should be limited to fifteen or twenty basic operations at most (including transfer of information to and from the memory and the arithmetic unit), and that all more complex operations should be built up from these. Today it seems clear that it was primarily the technical limitations of the day, not philosophical considerations, that caused this viewpoint to find such favour.

However, Mauchly envisaged two alternative ways in which the production of elaborate instruction sequences might be simplified. The first was the provision of a library of subroutines, fixed sequences of instructions held perhaps in a medium such as magnetic tape and 'called up' by the program instructions when the operations they covered were to be performed. The second was the concept that lies at the core of this chapter: the concept of the variable stored program.

Mauchly had the following to say on the subject of the stored-program concept:

> ... instructions are stored in the internal memory in the same manner as are numerical quantities, and one set of instructions can be used to modify another set of instructions. This is directly related to the finite capability of the internal memory and the limited number of basic operations. Calculations can be performed at high speed only if instructions are supplied at high speed. Thus many instructions must be made quickly accessible. The total number of operations for which instructions must be provided will usually be exceedingly large, so that the instruction sequence would be far in excess of the internal memory capacity. However, such an instruction sequence is never a random sequence, and can usually be synthesized from subsequences which frequently recur.
>
> By providing the necessary subsequences, which may be utilized as often as desired, together with a master sequence directing the use of these subsequences, compact and easily set up instructions for very complex programs can be achieved. Even greater powers are conferred, however, by the ability to use one instruction to modify another. An unlimited number of different instructions may be generated within the machine by this process. One can, therefore, modify not only the numbers which are substituted into a process, but the process itself, in any desired systematic way. By use of this facility, an EDVAC-type machine can, with surprisingly few instructions, automatically carry out processes which would otherwise require an instruction sequence greatly exceeding its internal memory capacity.*

* J. W. Mauchly, 'Preparation of Problems for EDVAC-type Machines', Proceedings of a Symposium on Large-Scale Digital Calculating Machinery, 7–10 January 1947, in *Annals of the Computation Library of Harvard University*, Vol. 16, pp. 203–7. Reproduced in B. Randell (ed.) *The Origins of Digital Computers: Selected Papers*, Springer-Verlag, 1973.

After all the excitement caused by these discussions, the EDVAC project apparently ran out of steam. The personnel involved in the project changed, the design evolved considerably, and the eventual computer — using delay line technology to realize the basic ideas we have outlined, and taking the idea of serial operation so far (making use of the serial way in which delay lines store and transmit data) that each number was added together serially, digit by digit — was not completed until late 1951. In the meantime several other computers, including the British EDSAC, had beaten it in the race to produce a variable stored program computer.

EDSAC

EDSAC was built at Cambridge University by a team headed by Maurice Wilkes. It was first operated on 6 May 1949.

EDSAC, too, used delay lines or, rather, ultrasonic tanks, five feet long, as well as some smaller tanks. Each five-foot tank could hold 32 numbers of 17 binary digits (plus a sign digit); or the numbers could be amalgamated to give longer numbers of 35 binary digits (plus a sign). These tanks were used not only to store data but to make up the accumulator and multiplier registers, and for controlling the instruction sequence. A special tank (called the sequential control tank) handled the control of instructions, counting by increments of 1 as the numbered instructions were handled, or switching to a new sequence of numbers if a 'conditional' instruction, causing a break in the numerical sequence, was encountered.

EDSAC took the tube/tank technology even further than this: its display of stored information was by oscilloscope tubes.

It had only a short list of order (that is, of instruction) codes; it is worth repeating this in full (see Table 3) to give an idea of how the logical and arithmetical operations were built up.

Table 3: EDSAC's Order Codes

An	Add the number in storage location n into the accumulator.
Sn	Subtract the number in storage location n from the accumulator.
Hn	Transfer the number in storage location n into the multiplier register.
Vn	Multiply the number in storage location n by the number in the multiplier register, and add into the accumulator.
Tn	Transfer the contents of the accumulator to storage location n and clear the accumulator.
Un	Transfer the contents of the accumulator to storage location n and do not clear the accumulator.
Cn	Collate the number in storage location n with the number in the multiplier register; i.e. add a 'I' into the accumulator in digital positions where both numbers have a 'I', and a '0' in other digital positions.

$R2^{n-2}$ Shift the number in the accumulator n places to the right; i.e. multiply by 2^{-n}.

$L2^{n-2}$ Shift the number in the accumulator n places to the left; i.e. multiply it by 2^n.

En If the number in the accumulator is greater than or equal to zero, execute next the order which stands in storage location n; otherwise proceed serially.

Gn If the number in the accumulator is less than zero, execute next the order which stands in storage location n; otherwise proceed serially.

In Read the next row of holes on the tape and place the resulting five digits in the least significant places of storage location n.

On Print the character now set up on the teleprinter and set up on the teleprinter the character represented by the five most significant digits in storage location n.

Fn Place the five digits which represent the character next to be printed by the teleprinter in the five most significant places of storage location n.

X Round off the number in the accumulator to 16 binary digits.

Y Round off the number in the accumulator to 34 binary digits.

Z Stop the machine and ring the warning bell.

As is usual in mathematical and computing notation, 'n' is a variable; the address of any particular location would be provided at this point in each instruction. This will become clearer when we look at programming in Chapter 26.

It should be clear from this list of instructions that the input mechanism of EDSAC was itself controlled by program orders. As a result, the input mechanism could not be used to input those program orders: they had to be already in the machine before the input process started. Unless they *were* already in the machine, there would be no way of implementing the input procedure. The process of introducing initial instructions that are needed in this way is known as 'bootstrapping'.

To bootstrap EDSAC, a sequence of 'initial' orders was input directly to the machine, not by the usual input channels but by wiring the orders on to a set of rotary switches, and then transmitting them to the store by pressing a button. The initial orders then enabled a fixed pattern of subsequent orders – the pattern exemplified in the sequence above – to be input. In other words, the initial orders handled the conversion of the order instructions, in the sequence, first a letter indicating the function; then (if required) a number designating a storage location, in decimal form; then (again, if required) an S to indicate that the number was short (17 digits) or an L if it was long (35 digits), into a machine-usable form.

With EDSAC, we come to the end of this chapter of computer history: the stored-program computer had become a reality. But there was still some way to go before the laboratory models of the 1940s could be translated into operational commercial computers in the offices of the 1960s and 1970s, and now in homes and schools as well. We shall trace this evolution from experimental machines to their mass-produced successors in Chapter 6.

5. Analog and Digital

Measurement systems and counting systems are closely linked — but they are not the same. There is a significant difference between measuring how loud a noise is or how hot a liquid is, and counting how many sheep there are in a field or rooms in a house. Let us try to analyse that difference by looking in detail at counting, at measurement and at numbering — which is not quite one or the other.

Counting is what we do when we want to know *how many* individual objects come into a specific set — like the set of people with red hair in a room, or of pebbles on a tray. To do this, we use the series of integer numbers 1,2,3,4,5,6 and so on, or 0, 10, 11 and so on, or whatever we choose, according to the number base of the system we are employing. The decimal system, with base ten, is the one we are most used to in the modern world, and it is intuitively obvious that underlying its development was the use of our ten fingers as an aid to counting. However, one Red Indian tribe used the four spaces between the fingers of a hand as the basis of their numbering system, and counted in octal (base eight)! It makes no difference: counting is counting, whatever symbols we employ to stand for the growing number of integral units.

Today we use numbers other than integers, though: numbers like 7·3, or even 7·393412. These have no clear relation to the business of counting the number of people in a specific room at a given time. But they *do* come into focus when we think of working out the average number of people in a room, averaged perhaps over a period of time or over a number of different rooms.

With other types of phenomena, there are no integral units to be counted. Consider a saucepan of milk being heated on a stove: it will continuously increase its temperature, until the heat-gain and heat-loss from the pan are in equilibrium. Or think of the bending of a bimetallic strip, as it grows hotter: it does not move suddenly from 'straight' to 'bent'; it bends slowly and continuously.

To measure such phenomena, we use numbers: but we do not count, we *quantify*. And we quantify along a continuous scale that we mark out in suitable units — that need not be, and often are not, integers — for our own convenience, and not because the gradations necessarily represent specific points of recognizable change in the attribute we are measuring.

In other words, when we read the scale on the edge of a thermometer, it is we who approximate, saying at one moment that it reads 83°, and at the next 84°. If the scale were divided more finely, we might read off 83·1, then

83·2, and so on. Given a magnifying glass, we might come up with 83·14° as a reading. It makes no difference to the temperature of the milk which reading we take; it affects only the accuracy of our representation of the temperature.

Whenever we make such a measurement — converting the property we are interested in into a numerical representation — we are digitizing. Digits are numbers; digitizing is representing a property by the use of numbers on a scale. And the specific property of numbers is that they are individual and separable. There is a distance between them. The difference between 83·14° and 83·15° is not very great when we are concerned with how long the milk will take to boil (it might, of course, be very significant under different circumstances) — but it is still a difference. In order to bridge the gap between those two different numbers, however precisely we specify them, we must approximate. The numbers 2, 3 and 4 can correspond to the number of people in a room, using a precision with which 83° does not correspond, referring to the temperature of the milk. The first is a count; the second is an approximate measurement.

Properties — attributes of something — that change continuously, like temperature and pressure, we describe as being 'analog' in nature. We can use the terms 'analog' and 'digital' as broadly being opposites, but we must always remember that analog properties are capable of being *measured* digitally. Indeed, measuring an analog property *means* digitizing it, expressing it in numbers.

Do we always want (or, indeed, need) to make digital measurements? There are many circumstances when we want two different properties to vary proportionally, and there is no advantage in approximating one of them digitally and then calculating the variation of the other from the digital approximation. The process only introduces a needless degree of error. We would be much better off if we could link the two attributes directly, and make them interdependent.

Take the process control operation in a factory manufacturing a product with several raw ingredients. We want to regulate the flow of liquid B so that it continues to be exactly two-thirds the rate of flow of liquid A, but we do not particularly need a measurement of the rate of flow of either liquid. Take the intensive care unit of a hospital, where a patient's dose of a drug through a continuous drip needs to vary with his temperature or blood pressure. There is no need to keep measuring the temperature, though, if only we can link the change in the rate of flow of the drug with the change in temperature.

Historically, many mechanical devices have been developed to provide a form of action that varies exactly and continuously in response to changes in the attribute to which they are coupled. Much mechanical ingenuity has been expended on developing devices that can exaggerate the change in the attribute over particularly critical regions; shaped cams like the one shown in Figure 26 were often used for this purpose. If a mechanism was required, say, to close a valve when the substance flowing through it reached a precise temperature, then the final closing could be accelerated by a suitable design of cam that exaggerated the stimulus from the original source (here, the temperature). In these cases, the two movements (in the temperature and the valve-closing mechanism) are not proportional, but they continue to be analogically related.

Figure 26: A shaped cam

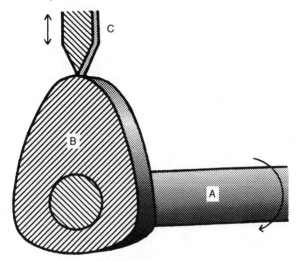

Shaft A turns cam B, which controls the movement of shaft C.

Table 4 gives some further examples of analog systems that convert some form of property, attribute or movement into some other form that is analogically related to it.

Table 4: Examples of Analog Systems

Thermometer: converts temperature into linear reading
Thermostat: converts a given temperature into mechanical movement (shutting off heating device)
Speedometer: converts horizontal movement into (e.g.) dial reading
Automatic lightmeter on camera: converts light intensity into aperture setting/ shutter speed
Sundial: converts movement of sun into reading on clock face

Analog Computing

You may protest (quite reasonably) that the simple ability to make an attribute change as another changes, either in direct proportion or by some more complex relation, does not have anything to do with computing. So what do we mean when we talk of analog computing?

There are many instances in which we habitually use digital approximations of analog properties, and then manipulate these approximations in order to calculate the required change in some other attribute. One familiar example is the business of integrating an equation, that is, providing a continuous representation of how y changes in relation to changes in x. The graphic representation of quadratic equations consists of a curve, of a shape that varies according to the type of the equation, but which will, by its very nature as a curve, be continuous. However, in order to calculate the route across the graph paper the curve will take, we normally have to work with the concept of infinitesimally small steps along the curve, steps that can be approximated by drawing straight lines tangentially to the curve.

Need we use the digital approximation at all, though? Early mechanical integrators were devices that used movement, not numerical methods, for obtaining the same curve as could have been obtained numerically – or an even more precise one. In the sense that they carried out an operation that would normally have demanded a fairly elaborate calculation, they can be thought of as 'analog computers'.

More generally, we use the term 'analog computers' to describe a machine in which at least part of the manipulation of qualities is handled by direct physical representation, and not numerically – even if numbers are used at some stage in the process (for reading off results, for instance). So analog computers do not necessarily carry out actual computation, in the numerical sense in which we normally mean it; but they *do* carry out the business of relating the change in one attribute to the change in another which, if it were carried out by other means, would demand computation.

The Slide Rule

For many years, until the development of the pocket calculator, a very ingenious aid to calculation that employed analog principles – the slide rule – was in common use. Figure 27 shows a simple slide rule. Note that each scale is numbered, but that the space devoted to each integer interval is not constant along the length of the rule, as it is with a conventional rule measuring centimetres or feet and inches. This very common form of slide rule uses a logarithmic scale.

Logarithms are numbers related to each other and to other numbers in such a way that to add the logarithms of two numbers produces the

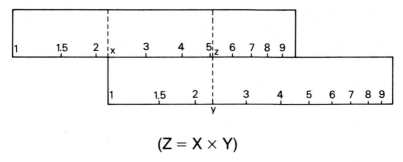

$$(Z = X \times Y)$$

Figure 27: A slide rule

logarithm of the number that forms the product of them. In mathematical terms:

log (A) + log (B) = log $(A \times B)$

The logarithms of individual numbers can of course be digitized; and logarithmic tables listing them were in common use until recently. But the representation of logarithms along a physical scale is an *analog* representation, as indeed is the representation of feet and inches. If we select two points on the scale, the relationship of the distances between them and the end of the scale will be a direct representation in physical terms of the logarithmic relationship between them in numerical terms.

The slide rules uses the manipulation of these different distances (and not the mathematical manipulation of the logarithms themselves) as a computation device for use in multiplying two numbers together, or dividing them. The rule is worked by sliding the upper rule along the lower until the left-hand end of the lower (its origin, marked 1 in the diagram) is level with a specific point, x, on the upper. This point x forms one of the numbers we are multiplying; the other number, y, is then located on the lower strip, and the number on the upper strip which is now level with y is read off. This number, z, is the product of x and y.

In order to read off the number, we have to digitize — and to approximate. The rule itself gives an exact representation, but we inevitably approximate both in positioning it and in reading off the result. So in the diagram, the product of x (2·3) and y (2·4) is *approximately* 5·5.

Of course, the digital approximation we can make from a 12″ (30 cm) slide rule is not very precise. The precision with which numbers could be read off was enhanced by the use of a magnifying glass, or of a cursor, a device that enabled the slide rule to be both set more precisely and read more precisely. Another type of slide rule allowed for much greater accuracy: it consisted of a series of sleeved cylinders that could be slid along one another. Each cylinder was printed with a very long logarithmic scale that curved in a slow helix around the cylinder. These sliding cylinders were capable of use with very high precision: it was possible to achieve six-figure accuracy for a single operation.

It is hard to find a slide rule around today, since they were cheap enough to be regarded, if not as throwaways, then as ephemera. But the highly precise cylindrical slide rules, beautifully engineered in precision metal with brass and mahogany mountings, are now museum pieces and command high prices. Twenty years ago, every scientist, engineer and high-school student had his or her own slide rule, and each research laboratory had access to a cylindrical version. Of course, it was possible instead to use the tables of logarithms, calculated and published by specialist organizations, but the more precise tables were voluminous, costly and more awkward to use than the simple analog calculator called a slide rule.

The Mechanical Integrator

The acts of integrating an equation (for instance, of determining the value of a mathematical function when its rate of change over time is known), and of differentiating an equation (or deriving, from the function's value, its rate of change over time) are closely linked. Both are at the heart of a wide range of computation problems: determining tidal movements, the trajectories of gun shells, the forces on an aeroplane wing, and so on. And a number of mechanical devices that used analogical principles for this purpose were invented in the nineteenth century.

One of the best known was a mechanical integrator invented by James Thomson and used by his brother, Lord Kelvin, the great English mathematical physicist. Its general construction is shown in Figure 28.

A is a flat disc that can be rotated on a shaft. On the surface of A is a sphere, B, that can be fixed at any position on A's diameter (the dotted line). The movement of B, when A is rotated, thus depends both on the speed of movement of A and on B's distance from the centre of A. B makes contact with C, a cylinder that can also be rotated; therefore, as A and C are rotated, the contact with B traces out a line on C's surface. By manipulating these various speeds of rotation, and the location of B, curves analogous to particular equations (and, in turn, to particular real properties) may be traced.

Many improvements to this general type of design were later made. Mechanical analog calculators, using some form of continuously varying gearing arrangement, were revived at various dates and a similar technology, making use of several devices coupled together in series, formed the basis of the extensive work done at the Massachusetts Institute of Technology by Vannevar Bush, prior to and at the beginning of the Second World War. Miniaturized versions of these mechanical devices, powered by electrical motors, formed the bomb-sights of many bombers of this period.

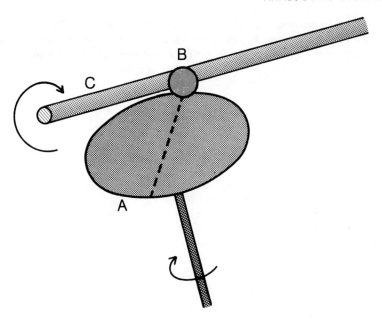

Figure 28: James Thomson's mechanical integrator

Electrical and Electronic Analog Devices

Developments in the technology of digital calculators and computers reduced the appeal of these analog versions, and the mechanical analog calculator fell into disuse after the creation of the digital ASCC (which we discussed on page 63). But for many years afterwards, an analog computing approach, based on the use of electrical current as an information-carrying medium, was used in the field of process control.

The voltage of an electrical current is itself continuously variable: when we describe it as being, say, 240 V, we are digitizing this analog quality and, indeed, approximating. When electrical current is used as the basis of a binary information system, we arbitrarily select two different areas of voltage: one low, to represent 0, and one higher, to represent 1. But when we use electrical current as an analog representation of a continuously variable quality, then we make full use of its own analog characteristics.

In electrical analog calculators or computers, the voltage represents the analog quality being measured: the temperature of a substance or its rate of flow, for instance. Then the electrical or electronic circuitry through which this current flows is designed to carry out the exact equivalent of the computations that a digital approach to the task would demand.

Analog computers are still used today, in fields where the special and direct physical relation between constituents of the computer and constituents of the process to which it is linked is particularly appropriate. This is true in some of the control devices of a motor car, and in some medical therapeutic control systems.

The Encroachment of Digital Computing

Digital computing is steadily gaining ground from the analog version, though. Why is this?

First, digital computation is generally faster than the analog systems that can be designed to carry out all but the very simplest manipulative tasks.

Secondly, digital information does not decay. As analog signals (sound waves, light waves, electrical current of a particular voltage) are transmitted, they tend to be affected by interference and to lose their clarity. A digital signal is confirmed as a 1 or an 0 every time it passes through an electronic component; and a strengthened and clarified signal continues through the circuit. With the aid of simple 'booster' devices to confirm the signal at regular intervals, digital signals can be sent extremely long distances with no loss of clarity.

Third, digital systems are becoming capable of more precision, and are thus eroding the major advantage of analog methods. The trend towards the use of longer 'words' in a computer – the eight-bit words of early microcomputers are giving way to 16-bit, and in turn to 32-bit units – lies behind this.

And finally, it is easy to carry all kinds of information in a coded binary digital form, and to switch from one storage or transmission medium to another when appropriate. Handling analog signals is a far more delicate business, and it is not easy, for example, to store an electrical impulse of a particular voltage.

Digital to Analog (and Analog to Digital) Conversion

The manipulation of analog properties is still important in many applications though, and analog signals – sound waves and radio waves, for instance – are still in common use as a means of communication. As a result, a number of devices have been constructed to convert analog signals to their digital equivalent.

How is this done? Let us take a simple example, using sound waves.

Figure 29a shows a pattern of complex harmonic sound waves, typical of those produced by musical instruments. It is made up of a set of related sine waves. (We look in a little more depth at waves and their measurements in Chapter 15.) How can this type of wave pattern (or any other sound wave) be recorded digitally? Conversion of the wave into a digital representation involves 'freezing' it at suitable time-intervals, and measuring its amplitude.

Figure 29: Analog to digital conversion of a waveform

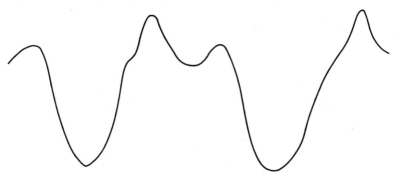

(a) Sound wave (pattern typical of a flute)

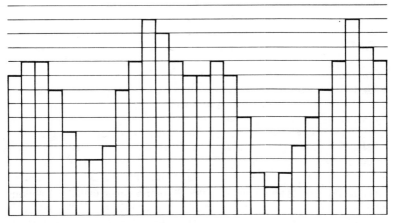

(b) Digital version of the same wave

The successive readings build up a picture of changes in the wave, just like a series of dots at specific points on a graph, making up the outline of a curve. Figure 29b indicates how this process works. Sixteen different amplitude levels (the vertical axis) are being recorded: the number that can be stored in four binary bits. The pattern that results is much 'choppier' than the original waveform; but increasing the number of amplitude levels, and the frequency of readings, can produce a very acceptable result. The wave can be 'ironed out' again if it is reconverted into analog form for later reproduction.

We look in greater detail at the business of sound digitization, and at the sampling levels required to give an adequate sound quality, in Chapter 18 (pages 220 to 227).

Analog to digital conversion, in order to enable analogical properties to be manipulated inside a computer, is now extremely common. The reverse, digital to analog conversion, is much less common. Analog output from a computer has some advantages, however. It is much easier for most people to read a graph than to read a table, to tell the time from a dial watch than to read off digital numerals correctly. However, many computer graphics, though they give the appearance of an analog display, are actually built up digitally.

One case where digital to analog conversion *is* used is in the communication of binary data. We look at this aspect further in Chapter 15.

Analog Calculators and Analog Computers

We have already looked at the difference between calculators and computers in the digital sense. What is the difference – if there is one – in analog devices?

We cannot trace an exact equivalent of the stored-program distinction that we used in describing how digital computing diverged from simple calculation. Analog devices do not carry instructions in the same medium as they do data, because instructions are not amenable to analog representation. Instead, the analog circuit is wired in a specific pattern to induce a set series of manipulative operations to take place, much as early digital computers like ENIAC (page 64) used to be set up manually. Early mechanical analog devices were of the special-purpose type: they were designed to carry out one specific kind of computation and could not be adapted to tackle different types of problem. The programs in electronic analog devices *can* be adapted, if their circuits are not hard-wired but are set up on a plug board (where wires can be unplugged and replugged into different sockets). However, it has never been usual to treat an analog computer as a general-purpose computer: their special advantages are fitted to extremely limited classes of computational problems. And, of course, pre-wired programs do not have the range of branching facilities that can be built into a digitally stored program.

Perhaps the greatest difference between various classes of analog devices lies in whether their input can vary in response to time (that is, vary over time in the course of a computation), or whether it is fixed at a particular level during a particular computation. As a result, it is common to describe devices with variable input as analog computers, and devices with fixed input as analog calculators. These classes present broad analogies with digital computers and calculators, but no more: after all, in the strict sense, the devices neither calculate nor compute.

Process control operations are a typical example of an application that does require variable input. In a continuous-process chemical or petro-chemical plant, for instance, the input of raw materials may show variations in quality as it is being monitored; the reactions themselves may require controlling within pre-defined limits; and the desired properties of the output may change over time. Many of the instruments that form part of the control apparatus measure analog qualities such as temperature, pressure, flow rates of gases and liquids, and so on. The input from these instruments, in an analog (electrical voltage) form, then passes to controllers that manipulate it and produce the required output signal. Each controller falls into one of three classes. They may produce a response proportional to the deviation from the norm; or a response proportional to an integral of the deviations; or a response proportional to the differential of the input signal. All these types of response signal can easily be produced by analog circuits; as a result, fully analog computers are well fitted to this type of operation. Today, though, these computers too are being superseded by digital computers taking advantage of the power of cheap microelectronics.

6. Coming up to Date: From Commercial Computers to Personal Computers

The experimental computers we examined at the end of Chapter 4, EDVAC and EDSAC, and the closely related ENIAC, belong to the late 1940s. By the very early 1950s, computers had moved into a new field: commerce and industry. The technology of the experimental computers was applied to the first commercial computers, and commercial computer applications began to take shape.

Perhaps the first commercial general-purpose computer was the Ferranti Mark 1 that went on sale in 1951 in the U.K. It was based on a Manchester University design, and was intended to carry out scientific and technical calculations in a business environment. The same year also saw the birth of the first office computer, the LEO (Lyons Electronic Office). Based on EDSAC, LEO was built by the J. Lyons catering company who set up a computing subsidiary that was eventually incorporated into the British computer giant I.C.L.

In the U.S., Eckert and Mauchly capitalized on their experience with ENIAC by launching a commercial computer company which eventually took shape as Univac. Their first UNIVAC (Universal Automatic Computer) machine was also launched in 1951. I.B.M., the firm that was to dominate the computer industry, was a little slower in getting its feet wet. Their first computer, the Model 701, was unveiled in 1953. This computer, too, was aimed at a technical market, and found early buyers in the major U.S. aircraft companies who used it for aircraft design calculations. U.S. office and commercial uses rapidly took shape, too: in 1952, American Airlines launched the first computerized ticket-reservation system, using 200 terminals in the New York area connected to a central computer, with a second computer standing by to cope with the all-too-frequent breakdowns.

This brief summary gives a rough indication as to where the computer industry has its roots. It was a hybrid of electronics firms, like the British Ferranti, Elliot and S.T.C., office-machinery firms like I.B.M. (itself descended from Hollerith's technology) and Burroughs, and academic and military expertise. Over the next twenty years, a series of amalgamations, with less committed firms dropping out and new arrivals, brought about an industry dominated at its upper end by I.B.M., but with a host of smaller firms playing their part in a field still characterized by rapidly developing technology.

The Technology of the First Commercial Computers

We have already outlined the fundamental features of the electronic technology used in these early machines, as indeed it still is, in a more compact form, in today's computers. We must look briefly, though, at two of the early memory media which vied with the delay line (see page 82) for use in these first commercial machines.

The magnetic drum: Magnetic storage media still dominate the computer mass storage market today. The first to be developed was the magnetic drum: a cylinder, typically about 9″ (22 cm) in diameter and 12″ (30 cm) long, coated with a layer of magnetizable material, usually iron oxide.

The direction of magnetization of a small area in a magnetic medium can be used as the basis of a binary code for storing data. Magnetization in one direction (say, north–south) is taken to represent a 1, and magnetization in the other direction (south–north) a 0. The direction of magnetization can be altered by a 'write' head that magnetizes the material in a direction depending upon the direction of the current it carries, and read by a 'read' head. (In some systems, the same head can be programmed to carry out both functions alternately.) As the magnetic medium is used in a simple two-state way, and not in the more complex fashion demanded by audio recording, no 'erase' head is required. The medium is non-volatile: unlike delay lines and many electronic storage media, it does not lose its data when the current is disconnected.

The drum was rotated at a fixed speed (typically about 2,000 r.p.m.) past a series of read/write heads (100 or more), each of which handled data on a specific circular track around its circumference. Access to the stored data was thus sequential: the head had to pass around the track until it reached the location of the particular data required. This meant that the typical access time to data was slow: about fifteen milliseconds, as compared to one-half a millisecond for a typical delay line store. However, the other advantages of the drum guaranteed that it would be widely used as a computer data storage medium where rapid access time was not all important.

Magnetic core memory: Magnetic core memory was invented by Jay Forrester of the Massachusetts Institute of Technology in the late 1940s. It remained the standard form of internal computer memory until the 1970s.

The memory was made up of an array of small doughnut-like circles of ferro-magnetic material, typically about 0·05″ (1.2 mm) in diameter and 0·015″ (0.36 mm) thick. Four wires were threaded through each core, to make the arrangement shown in Figure 30. Two of these wires were 'write' wires, that together (but not separately) produced a pulse of electricity sufficient completely to magnetize a ring in one direction or the other. One

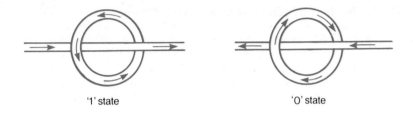

'1' state   '0' state

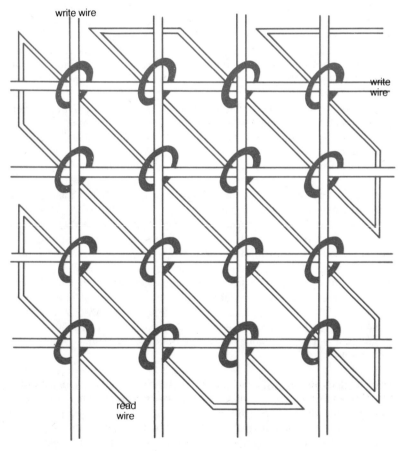

Simplified section of core array (does not show inhibit wires)

Figure 30: Magnetic core memory

direction of magnetism, again, represented a 1 and the other a 0. Thus, the two 'write' currents could individually designate, and write into, a single core without affecting the contents of the others in the array. A third wire provided a read signal, when used in conjunction with the write wires to designate the cell to be read. The read procedure destroyed the stored information, so the fourth 'inhibit' wire was a necessary part of the process of restoring the information (by writing the data back into the core) at the end of the read operation.

A Typical 1950s' Commercial Computer

·What was a commercial computer of the 1950s like? Typically, it might have consisted of the following configuration:

a large 'main' cabinet, that contained the electronic circuits at the heart of the computer, making up the arithmetic unit and the central control unit, and providing at least some working memory. These circuits consisted of thermionic valves, capacitors, resistors and their connecting wires. The circuits themselves were soldered together.

memory or storage space, in the form of delay lines or magnetic drums. These might be incorporated into the main cabinet, or contained in a separate unit.

a separate cabinet containing the power supply.

an input unit: typically, a punched-card or paper-tape reader. Before photo-electric sensing came into use in about 1956, this sensed the presence of holes electro-mechanically, and hence slowly: at around thirty characters per second (c.p.s.). Photo-electric sensing, by contrast, can reach speeds of 1,000 c.p.s. Typically, about 200 cards were read each minute, taking all 80 columns on the card simultaneously.

an output unit: typically, a punched-card or paper-tape punch. This worked at about half the speed of the input unit, at about 100 cards a minute.

a desk for the operator.

Computers in the 1960s

Following these initial forays into the commercial market, the computer industry developed rapidly. Table 5 gives some indication of how the usage of computers grew in this early period.

The growth of the industry was enhanced by the steady improvement in computer technology. On pages 64 to 67, we traced how the thermionic valve gave way to the transistor that was more compact and more reliable, and how the integrated circuit paved the way to large scale, very large scale and, today, ultra large scale integration. These technical developments, and other, less central improvements, were steadily incorporated into com-

Table 5: The Growth of Computer Usage before 1960

Figures on computer installations are hard to finalize, because: (1) definitions of computers vary; (2) sources do not always indicate the geographical area covered; (3) it is difficult to separate new or replacement systems from in-use systems. These are our own best estimates:

In 1953, there were approximately fifty computers in use in the U.S.A.; less than fifty others in the rest of the world

By 1959, there were about 4,000 computers in use in the U.S.A.; perhaps 600–900 in Western Europe (about 150 in the U.K.).

By 1960, the figures had shot up to 5,000–6,000 in the U.S.A.; about 1,500 in Western Europe as a whole; up to 2,000 more in the rest of the world.

For later comparison:

By 1970, there were probably over 100,000 computers in use worldwide.

The total number for 1983? Several million.

puters. By the 1960s, computers were beginning to be constructed according to a unit-assembly approach: by adding together a number of cabinets containing processing circuitry, memory or peripheral devices, until the required capacities were achieved. A large computer installation (and, in this period, most installations *were* physically large – though not particularly powerful by today's standards) might have consisted of fifteen or twenty cabinets, spaced out in an air-conditioned environment. Their contents were roughly as follows:

the main cabinet, containing the arithmetic/logic and associated circuits, in integrated-circuit form, and based on transistors and other solid-state electronic devices.

2–8 high-speed storage units, probably consisting of magnetic cores. The capacity of each would have been 4,000–8,000 words – but words were comparatively long, consisting of 32 or 48 bits.

2–20 (or even more) magnetic drums, to provide a supplementary memory with slower access but greater storage capacity than the core memory. Each drum would have held 8,000–32,000 of these long computer words.

up to 30 magnetic tape decks. Large reels of magnetic tape became very popular in this period as a secondary storage medium. (We shall discuss this in more detail in Chapter 7.) The tape could be read extremely rapidly (at up to 100,000 characters per second), but the strictly sequential access to stored data still involved up to several minutes' access time. By the mid-1960s, disc storage (see Chapter 7) with faster access was coming to rival the ubiquitous tape. However, tapes could be stored and replaced on the tape decks; these early discs were fixed in their drives, thus limiting their versatility.

one or more punched-card readers, operating at 400–800 cards per minute, and/or paper-tape readers, operating photo-electrically.

one or more card punches for card output, operating at 150–300 cards per
minute, and/or paper-tape punches.

one or more high-speed line printers for printed output (see Chapter 16),
printing entire lines of type typed simultaneously at up to 1,200 lines per
minute.

one or more teletypewriters, to provide communication between the
operators and the computer in a relatively convenient fashion, but on a
small scale.

and finally, desks and other facilities for the operators.

How 1960s' Computers were Used

Today, we are growing used to 'user friendly' home computers that almost
anyone can teach themselves to operate, and even program, with little
difficulty. In the 1960s, though, things were different. Preparing computer
input (that is, punching the cards or tape) and operating the computer
were full-time jobs, carried out by trained personnel. The operation of the
computer was much more opaque to the untrained observer than is that of
today's models; and the eventual users of the computer's services sub-
mitted input data and received output; but they may never even have seen
the machine itself. Instantaneous interaction with a computer via a terminal
was unheard of; typically it took days, rather than seconds, for the computer
department to turn around a processing request.

As a result, commercial computers were used almost exclusively for
routine applications involving large volumes of data. Table 6 summarizes
the most common applications during the period.

Table 6: Typical Computer Applications in the early 1960s

The following applications were performed on a representative sample of 100
commercially used computers in the U.K. Some computers were used for more than
one application:

Payroll	50
Stock control	35
Invoicing	20
Sales accounting and analysis	15
Costing	14
Production control	13
Operational research	12
Revenue accounting	9
Production scheduling	7
Budgetary control	5
Distribution of supplies	3

Source: S. H. Hollingdale and G. C. Toothill, *Electronic Computers*, Penguin Books, 1965.

One feature shared by almost all these applications is that the actual processing they required was relatively trivial. The real chore lay in handling the input and output, using comparatively cumbersome media, such as punched cards, paper tape and large volumes of poor print-quality printout.

In consequence of this trend towards high-volume, low-complexity applications, and of the comparative slowness in operation of peripheral devices, there was an apparent imbalance in the usage of the system. The processing circuitry worked increasingly rapidly, but how was it to be kept fully occupied when the workload was so heavily input/output oriented?

At this period, it was regarded as highly desirable to utilize the computer as intensively as possible. Computers were major capital investments for even very large firms (it was still out of the question for a small firm to buy its own computer), and their air-conditioned environments and battalions of operating personnel meant that they were expensive to run. In order to gain full value from the investment, operating procedures placed a heavy emphasis upon split-second timing of processing operations, and on twenty-four-hour utilization of the computer. The user's convenience came a poor second to the demands of the computer's tight schedule. As our brief rundown of the contents of the 1960s' installation has shown, it was common to have more than one input, and more than one output, medium to a single processing unit. The computer was then programmed to interleave the processing requirements generated by these peripheral devices and to handle more than one program at a time. (We look on pages 146 to 147 at operating systems, the software designed to handle the interleaving of processing demands from different sources.) In this way, a better balance of resource utilization could be achieved.

Batch Processing and Computer Bureaux

The common method of handling computer operations at this period was known as batch processing. Batch processing is still carried out today, but it is becoming less common.

What *is* batch processing? Basically, it is:

the handling of a 'batch' of computer input (for instance, a stack of forms containing file updates or accounting information) in one operation: first preparing them for input, then inputting them all.

the handling of input, processing and output as a single, continuous process.

Batch processing may be contrasted with interactive processing. In an interactive process, the operator feeds data to the computer, and receives requests for information and output, at points throughout the processing operation. In a batch process, there is *no* opportunity for user involvement between handing over the input and receiving the final output.

In an alternative definition, batch processing might be seen as the opposite of transaction processing. Transaction takes each individual transaction through the entire process – from input, through processing to output – before attacking the next transaction; batch processing involves first the input of an entire batch, then its processing, then its output. Each kind of processing might, in limited ways, be interactive.

Obviously batch processing makes it easier to control a tight processing schedule. Processing jobs are clearly defined (by a batch of input, and the associated processing requirements); they do not change as a result of interactive user responses, and the system need not wait for routine user input at points during the processing operation. This relatively simple method of user/computer interaction made practicable the multiprocessing (that is, interleaving processing operations on several programs) operating procedures that were common in the period, even though the art of programming was still in its infancy.

From the batch processing philosophy, it is easy to make another jump: to the computer bureau. Bureaux were extremely common in the 1960s and early 1970s; now they are becoming less so, or at any rate are evolving beyond recognition. The bureau owned (or, more frequently, leased) a computer, and sold processing time on it to user organizations.

Bureaux were popular for a variety of reasons.

(1) Only the largest companies could afford to buy their own computers. There were large computers and massive computers; there were no small, cheap, usable installations on the market. As a result, many smaller companies chose to use the bureau service for just one or two applications that took up a small fraction of the total available processing time on even the smallest computer.

(2) Computers were complex to program, maintain and operate. The bureaux had experts in all these fields to hand; user companies did not often have, or want, such expertise.

(3) Many bureaux sold access to popular programs (payroll packages, invoicing packages and so on) as part of their service. It would have been more expensive for an individual company to develop programs in-house for their exclusive use. The bureaux kept development costs down by spreading them across a number of users. There was as yet no organized market for the sale of software, other than as part of a software/hardware computing service.

(4) Even in-house processing was a slow business. Users were resigned to a lengthy wait for their output. Delivering the input to, and receiving the output from, a bureau using a well-organized messenger service added only a small percentage to the elapsed time. Later, bureaux provided terminals, connected to their computers via telecommunications lines, into which users of their service could input their own data. This innovation continued to make the time factor no bar to bureau development.

(5) Bureaux had, on the whole, a good reputation for preserving data security.

The Computer Market in the 1960s and early 1970s

Throughout this period, the world computer market was dominated by I.B.M. It is no exaggeration to say that I.B.M. defined what a computer was: its capacity, its software facilities, what it should be used for. And most rival computer companies built computers that did not contradict this I.B.M.-defined image.

In the early 1960s, commercially available computers were commonly divided into two types: 'scientific' and 'business' computers. The scientific type was epitomized by I.B.M.'s Model 7094, the business type by their 1401 range. (Of course, many special-purpose machines and analog computers that did not fit neatly into either camp were also available.) The differences between the two types were not great: scientific computers, for instance, worked with floating-point arithmetic, while business computers used the familiar fixed-point decimal system.

In 1964, I.B.M. chose to annihilate this division of the market into two separate sub-markets. Their System 360 was launched as an all-purpose computer. The 360 has been widely criticized as baroque in design, difficult to program, and all but impossible to use interactively. In many ways, it failed to capitalize upon the modest advances towards simplifying programming that had been made by other manufacturers. However, I.B.M.'s support organization and reputation were second to none, their user loyalty legendary; and the 360 became *the* model for computers for the next ten years.

Among other computers that had a significant commercial or technical impact at this period, we should mention the Burroughs 5000, with a much-praised, simple to use 'master control program' (M.C.P.), and Control Data's Cray machines, also launched in 1964. Their successors are the biggest of the big computers today.

The company that was to come to dominate the market for smaller computers, Digital Equipment Co. (D.E.C.), also got under way in the early 1960s. The early machines in their PDP (Programmed Data Processor) series were the first 'minicomputers' (see below). For instance the PDP5 (launched in 1963) was a fraction of the size of I.B.M.'s smallest machine, and cost under $30,000, at a time when most managers 'knew' that computers cost millions. Digital's machines were designed to appeal to technical people (engineers, laboratory staff and so on) rather than to businessmen, and they were very successful in this quite different market. In the lower price ranges, the technical people specified which machines they wanted to use, and their managers were not in a position to question the wisdom of their choice.

Mainframe Computers and Minicomputers

What is a minicomputer? Come to that, what is a mainframe computer? Or a microcomputer (which we shall come to shortly)? It is difficult to say, because these terms are used with varying definitions, and with varying degrees of precision, in different contexts. However, this is a brief definition.

The business computers that were what most people understood by the word 'computer' in the 1960s and early 1970s were 'mainframe' computers. This term was originally used to apply to the framework of the main computer cabinet in which the central processing unit circuits were mounted. Later, it came to be applied to all large computers constructed in the modular fashion, with a separate processor unit.

The smaller computers (D.E.C.'s models and their imitators) were not constructed modularly. All their processing and memory circuitry was normally encapsulated in one unit. This compactness, and their lower prices, earned them the 'mini' designation. Otherwise, minis were basically just small computers – by the standards of the period. Their circuitry was no different from that of a mainframe. They were not designed to handle multiple applications in parallel, as were most mainframes, and obviously they were less powerful (they had less processing and control circuitry, and less memory space). But the differences were of degree, not of kind.

Today, the term 'minicomputer' is used to apply to middle-sized, middle-range computers: small business computers and other computers that do not fit the 'microcomputer' designation. Minicomputers have not got bigger, of course: their processing power is now greater, but they have shrunk physically. But other, smaller computers have crept in below them in the size/power spectrum.

The Microprocessor

With the advent of large-scale integration, it became possible to place a larger and larger percentage of a computer's electronic circuitry on a smaller and smaller 'chip' of material. We shall discuss the manufacture of silicon chips in detail in Chapter 20.

Computers in the early 1970s, and many computers today, were constructed on a circuit-board basis. Their components were linked on a series of circuit boards, and these were themselves linked together by a bus network. Open a c.p.u. (central processing unit) cabinet, and you would have seen a serried range of circuit boards, each containing a wiring pattern, and a selection of components plugged into slots, with perhaps room for more boards to be added if the computer's capabilities were intended to be expandable. As chips were introduced, the chips themselves were plugged into holes on the circuit boards.

The early chips did not contain all the circuitry necessary to make up a central processing unit, let alone the necessary memory and peripheral handling circuits. Instead, a number of chips were linked together to provide the required capacity.

One method by which this was done is known as 'bit-slicing'. Each chip literally provides the circuitry for a number of bits (say, two) of the words the c.p.u. works with. So a 16-bit c.p.u. would contain eight c.p.u. chips, each with two bits of arithmetic/logic circuitry and a proportion of the necessary working registers. Yet another chip is used to control the co-operation of the components, and to hold data on the required instruction set.

As integration densities increased, so it became possible to provide more circuitry on a single chip: to provide, in effect, a 'processor on a chip'. This is the 'microprocessor'.

The first microprocessors had very small word lengths. Even one-bit microprocessors are useful for controlling the operation of simple machinery (coin-in-the-slot machines, for instance). Four-bit microprocessors are used in electronic calculators. Computers proper (machines programmable to an extent comparable with early commercial mainframes) require at least eight-bit words. Soon chips like the Intel 8080, that had this capability, were coming on to the market.

Since then, the trend in microprocessors has moved in two directions as the number of components that can be incorporated on a chip has steadily increased. First, the word length has continued to be extended, first to 16 bits, and now (just about) to 32 bits. Clearly, this is a step towards giving microprocessor-based computers the power of mainframes that have traditionally used long words. Second, the amount of peripheral circuitry and memory circuitry available on the same chip as a c.p.u. has increased. Some of today's chips can themselves be described as 'microcomputers': they contain all the circuitry necessary to create a fully functioning (if limited in memory space) computer.

The word 'microcomputer' is often used, however, to refer to complete systems – including input, output and additional memory devices – that are based around a microprocessor chip. Only some microcomputers use 'microcomputer' chips: in many there are a number of chips in addition to the microprocessor, providing essential additional control functions.

Many minicomputers, and virtually all mainframes, do not use microprocessor chips. There are a number of reasons for this; but perhaps the major one is that the technology used for very large scale integration is slower in circuit operation than that used for lower-scale integration. Minicomputers and mainframes can work faster by using TTL chips with less circuitry, rather than a fewer number of MOS chips. We discuss these different technologies, their advantages and disadvantages, in Chapter 20.

The Computer Kit

The Intel 8080 microprocessor chip was not a computer. It was not even designed with computers – in the conventional sense – in mind. But it *could* be built up, with additional circuitry to perform the functions it did not encompass, into a real computer. And in 1974, just that was done. The January 1975 issue of *Popular Electronics* (published in December 1974) carried the first advertisement for a computer kit. The Altair, based on the 8080 chip, was sold in kit form for just $420.

Of course, the machine that could be built for $420 was a good deal different in appearance from the commercial computers, even the minicomputers, then available. For a start, it was just a chunk of machinery. To program it, you had to bootstrap it slowly, feeding in programs using a set of toggle switches on the front panel. It had no systems software (see pages 142 to 143), no inbuilt language capability, no keyboard. Only electronics enthusiasts would have tackled the kit-building process. But at the heart of the Altair, there was real, powerful computer capability.

This first Altair machine heralded the beginning of the 'hobby' computer era: an era in which electronics enthusiasts could begin to get involved in computing on a small scale, without spending a fortune on hardware. The Altair advertisement resulted in 200 orders in the first day's mail. Soon, there were a number of other kit computers on the market, the first computer stores were appearing, and the first small computer systems magazine, *Byte*, had been published. By the end of 1976 there were at least 30,000 hobby computers around; 300 computer stores in the U.S.; and *Byte* had a circulation of 100,000. Small computers were here to stay.

The fascination of these hobby machines was literally a 'hobby' fascination: in building them, learning how they worked, and learning how to program simple applications in the time-consuming machine language that was all that could be used with the first models. They could certainly be used for simple applications: in fact, the EMMA machine that we shall be looking at in greater detail, and writing some simple programs for, later in the book is just like them. But there was no question of their being used for handling, say, the payroll in large companies. They didn't have the speed, the memory capacity or – most important – the ease of use necessary in such an environment. The gulf between them and even the smaller commercial computers, not so much in power as in usability (as well, of course, as in price) was massive.

And it soon began to be filled in. In 1977, Commodore introduced the 'PET' computer: a ready-assembled machine with keyboard, screen and a cassette drive to provide additional memory capacity, for just $650. The PET was the first of the personal computers, machines intended to be used by people with no electronics background, and sometimes no programming ability either. A library of ready-written programs was soon being developed, to enable users to start to put their machines to practical use (playing games, for instance, or keeping track of their bank balance) as simply as possible. The possibility of using them, after all, not fascination with the electronics, was what made most people buy personal computers. Some programs were distributed by the manufacturers; others by independent software suppliers; still others through the developing network of individual users who had written programs of their own. They were sold prerecorded on to the simple audio-type cassettes that these cheap machines used, or even just as listings of program statements on paper. (Every personal computer magazine — and soon there were dozens — carries program listings for an individual computer or for a variety of different ones.)

Today, the personal computer field is coming of age. It is increasingly professional in its organization, on both the software and hardware levels. There are computer stores in most towns in advanced industrial countries. A full range of machines is available, at prices starting at well under £100 in the U.K. or $200 in the U.S.A., up to thousands or even millions of dollars. Of course, to a large extent you get what you pay for: if not in raw power, then in peripherals, in software support, in maintenance support. But they are all computers, and all capable of performing the same basic functions. Later in this book we shall be looking at what some of the small, and some of the large, ones can be used for.

Speed and Reliability

Two major technological factors have affected both the design and the use of calculating and computing machines: their speed and their reliability. Clearly, the two are interconnected: there is no use in a computation taking so long that the machine is likely to break down while it is in progress. (This used to be a very real problem!) A look at the historical development of these two aspects of computer technology gives a more general indication as to how it was progressing, and how the potential uses of computing were growing in number from the early years onwards.

The speed at which mechanical difference engines could be operated was extremely modest. For simple calculations, they were no faster than hand calculation. Of course, the machines were both more reliable and less prone to tire than human beings, but their pace of operation was hardly prodigious, and certainly limited their attraction. The ASCC also performed very slowly by today's standards: it took around six seconds to do a multiplication operation, and twelve for division (a more complex operation). It was doubtless as a concomitant of this slow pace that it was designed so that every register, and not just the arithmetic unit, could perform simple arithmetical operations. This reduced the amount of data shuffling required before an operation could be performed.

The electronic ENIAC was a great deal faster. An addition or subtraction took only 200 milliseconds — that is, 1/5,000 second. Multiplication took fourteen times as long, and division rather longer; even so, these speeds were considerably greater than anything the designers of mechanical or electro-mechanical machines could have aspired to.

By contrast, modern computers can carry out millions of arithmetic operations a second. The fastest, such as the Cray 1 and the Cyber 205, can perform nearly 100 million every second. Today, we have a new measure of arithmetic speed: the 'megaflop', equal to a million arithmetic operations per second.

To put this into perspective, it has been estimated that (with no allowance for human error):

ASCC could do in a day what a human being computing similar problems could do in six months;

ENIAC could do in a day what a human being computing similar problems could do in six years;

a very fast modern computer could do in a day what a human being computing similar problems could do in 120,000 years.

Mechanical and electro-mechanical machines were, on the whole, very reliable. The price for electronic speed was at first a great deal less reliability. Each of ENIAC's 18,000 valves was liable to fail about once every 10,000 hours, so a breakdown might have been expected every hour or so. In fact, by running the valves at less than their rated voltage and never switching them off, failures were limited to one or two per week. It was clear, though, that to increase the capacity of a computer using ENIAC's technology would have rapidly led to unacceptably frequent breakdowns.

As ENIAC had a serious breakdown problem and no speed problem the prime motive in designing its circuitry was clearly to minimize the complexity and the number of components required, even at the expense of some speed. From ENIAC onwards – until recently – the parallel mode of operation that was adopted in the ASCC was largely replaced by a serial mode of operation. There was only one arithmetic/logic unit, and *all* computation was carried out there. This enabled the storage registers to be constructed as simply as possible.

The smaller number of valves associated with delay line storage meant that reliability increased, and computers with much greater storage capacity (and more circuitry) could be built. However, it was only when solid-state semiconductor devices took over from valves that the way was paved for the present explosion in computer capacity. Semiconductor devices operate faster than valves (just *how* fast, we shall discuss in Chapter 20), but their real gain is in reliability. Once in operation, they virtually never fail; and it is this reliability that has made it possible to construct computers with so many millions of components, in the confidence that, on the whole, they will work accurately and reliably.

Indeed, with the coming of discrete electronic components such as transistors, the reliability problem switched from the components themselves to the interconnections between them. The high degree of reliability of integrated circuits is based upon the fact that connections are formed by the same production process as are the individual components. An integrated circuit chip that checks out satisfactorily upon manufacture is likely to continue to perform satisfactorily for an indefinite period, provided its design parameters are not exceeded in use.

Indeed, the incredible degree of miniaturization exemplified by a modern silicon chip is a by-product of the search for reliability. It is easier to achieve a perfect circuit on a very small piece of silicon than on a large one, if the etching process to 'draw' the circuit can be done on a sufficiently small scale.

Part Three: Aspects of Modern Computer Technology

Our brief look at the historical development of computing has done much to outline what computers are and what they do. But we still have many gaps to fill in. In this long section, we shall be filling many of them.

Some of the chapters in Part Three are concerned with pure technological issues: with memory, with input and output handling, with peripheral devices such as printers, and so on. Some look at the development of software, and others in depth at the dividing line between software and hardware. And finally, as our knowledge of the technology of contemporary computers becomes more complete, we shall look at some of the factors that might affect your own choice of a computer, and in detail at two machines that represent different aspects of the small computer market.

Computer technology is not stable: it evolves almost daily. To provide an up-to-the minute picture, we shall be looking at some aspects of the technologies that may be incorporated in tomorrow's computers, as well as at what is being done today.

7. Storing Data: A Look at Memory Media

In looking at the developing history of computing, we have encountered many ways in which data and instructions can be stored. Let's recall some of them:

in the positioning of abacus beads;
on the wheels of a mechanical calculator;
on punched cards or punched paper tape;
in thermionic valves, and circuits based on them;
in delay lines;
on magnetic core store arrays;
on magnetic drums.

However, we have not yet looked in detail at the most common media used for internal computer storage of data and instructions, and as secondary storage, in today's generation of computers. This chapter will repair that gap.

Internal Memory

Today's computers generally store data in solid-state electronic circuits, packed tightly together on silicon chips. There are a number of circuit configurations that enable data to be written in, stored and read, and that can be rewritten with new data when the old are no longer needed. We will look at one of the simplest and most common, a form of 'flip-flop'.

The Flip-flop Circuit

A flip-flop is a simple device that:
(1) 'stores' a digit (1 or 0), in the sense that it can continue to output the same 1 or 0 signal while it is connected into an electronic circuit;
(2) can be triggered to store the opposite digit instead;
(3) 'flips' over from one stable state (an output of 1 or 0) to the other only at fixed time intervals.

We shall illustrate the action of the circuit in terms of the logic gates we described on pages 42 to 44. As you will recall, these gates are the basic building blocks of digital electronic circuits; they can be constructed out of simple solid-state electronic components.

Figure 31: Clocked flip-flop circuit

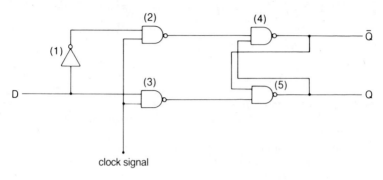

(a) Schematic of gate layout

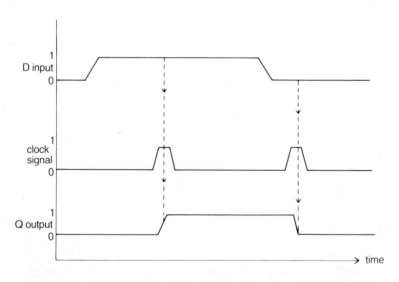

(b) Graph of timed section. Output signal Q varies as clock signal C
     samples data input D

On the left of Figure 31a, D is a data input signal, that can change from 1
to 0 and back again over time. The clock signal is a fixed pulse signal: it
normally signals a 0, but at regular intervals it changes briefly to a 1. Figure
31b indicates how the D and C signals might vary over a brief period of
time.

Gates 2, 3, 4 and 5 are all Not-AND (or NAND) gates; that is, they have the following input/output table:

Inputs		Outputs
0	0	1
0	1	1
1	0	1
1	1	0

As you see, if *either* input is 0, then the output will be 1. So when the clock signal is at 0, then gates 2 and 3 will both output a 1 signal, *whatever* the D input is.

When the clock impulse is at 1, then the gates will have the following outputs, depending upon the D input (which is inverted to $\bar{D}$, or not-D, for gate 2):

Gate 2		Gate 3	
Inputs	Ouputs	Inputs	Output
C	$\bar{D}$	C	D
1	1	0	1	0	1
1	0	1	1	1	0

In other words, the outputs of gates 2 and 3 may be:
(1) both 1, if the input from gate C is 0; or
(2) one 0 and one 1, if the input from gate C is 1.

They *cannot* both output 0s. If they did, it would confuse operations in the right-hand part of the logic circuit, as we shall see.

What happens to gates 4 and 5, then? They each have two inputs: their direct input from gate 2 (to gate 4) and gate 3 (to gate 5), *and* an input which is drawn from the output signal of the other gate (4 for 5, 5 for 4). Both gates again are NAND gates, so they will output a 1 unless both their inputs are 1 — in which case they will output a 0.

Let's look first at what happens when one input is a 0, and the other a 1. If one input to a gate (say, 4) is 0, then its output must be a 1, regardless of what its second input is. As a result, we can complete the logic table as follows:

Gate 4		Gate 5	
Inputs	Output	Inputs	Output
2	5	3	4
0	0	1	1	1	0

Whichever way round the 1 and 0 inputs are, the two outputs, Q and $\bar{Q}$ (not-Q) will be opposites.

What happens when both inputs from 2 and 3 are 1? The output signal from gate 4 or gate 5 could be either 1 (if only one input signal to 4 or 5 is a 1) or 0 (if both inputs are 1). Let us first assume that the existing output from gate 5 is a 1. This means that gate 5 had only one 1 input. Its input from gate 3 was a 1; so its input from gate 4 must have been 0. Fair enough: gate 4's inputs of 1 from gate 2 and 1 from gate 5 would indeed give it a 0 output. In effect, such a situation will lead to no change in the existing outputs of the two gates.

Disaster would strike, though, if the outputs from both gate 2 and gate 3 were 0. The inputs and outputs of gate 4 and gate 5 would be mutually inconsistent. That is why the circuit on the left-hand side of the diagram is deliberately designed to prevent this from happening.

Let us conclude this explanation by summarizing the results of all this activity. Line D provides a data signal, 1 or 0, at any moment. However, this signal will have no impact upon the output of gates 4 and 5 *unless* it coincides with a pulse (a 1 signal) from the clock input. In this case, the signal will pass through the gates in such a way that, whatever the previous output Q, the new output Q will be identical to the data D. The output Q̄ (not-Q) will always be the opposite of the output Q, and thus opposite to a data signal that has been accepted.

Dynamic Semiconductor Memory

The flip-flop provides a *static* form of memory cell; that is, it continues to hold its information as long as current flows through the circuit of which it forms a part. An alternative form of semiconductor memory does not have this characteristic. Instead, it needs to be 'refreshed' regularly: to have a 1 or 0 rewritten into it. We shall next look at this 'dynamic' form of memory cell, outlined in Figure 32.

The 'cell' is formed in the space between four wires: read and write wires, shown as running from left to right in the diagram, and data input and output wires, running from top to bottom. The wires only intersect at the marked junctions, a, b, c and d.

There are three transistors in the cell, but only one of them – the storage transistor, labelled S – actually stores the data: again, a single digit, 1 or 0. Its storage capacity is provided by a capacitor, C, that holds an electric charge (to represent a 1) or lacks charge (to represent a 0). When it is boosted by the circuit voltage, the capacity charge is turned into a current flow, as we saw when discussing transistors on pages 40 to 41.

Let us assume that we want to write a 1 into the cell. The write line at the bottom of the diagram and the input line on the left must both simultaneously produce a 1 level pulse of current for this to take place. The current on the write line creates a path across the write transistor (from b to e), and the current on the input line can then flow across the transistor, from a to e. This creates an electrical charge in the capacitor: by doing so, in effect, the read and input lines are writing a 1 bit into the cell. If a 1 is not written into the cell, it is assumed to contain a 0. If there is already a 1 charge on the capacitor, the write operation discharges it and returns it to 0, by a similar method.

To read the 1 – to output it – it is necessary to activate the read line at the top of the diagram. This creates a path across the read transistor, R, from c to f, and from f to d. The charge created at the read transistor turns the capacitor charge into current flow, and the 1 strength current flows through the transistor from f to d, and out on the output line.

Figure 32: Dynamic memory cell

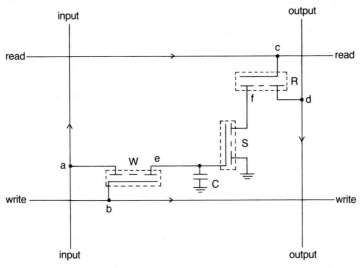

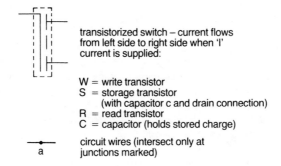

W = write transistor
S = storage transistor
    (with capacitor c and drain connection)
R = read transistor
C = capacitor (holds stored charge)

circuit wires (intersect only at junctions marked)
a

This type of storage circuit has several advantages over flip-flop storage circuits:
(1) they are much more compact, as they require fewer electronic components;
(2) as a result, they are cheaper to manufacture;
(3) and they consume very little power when they are not being written into or read from.

However, there is a disadvantage. Charge leaks steadily from the capacitor, and if the circuit is to retain its bit of data accurately the charge must be renewed regularly (about every 2 milliseconds, or 0·002 seconds). Special 'refresh' circuitry, rather than the data and read/write circuitry shown on the diagram, is normally used to perform this housekeeping task. The necessity for this reduces the advantage that dynamic memory circuits have over their static counterparts.

Of course, neither type of memory cell is normally found in isolation. They are grouped in series to represent the digits in an 8-bit (or 4-, 16- or 32-bit) binary number, or of an ASCII (or similar) coded alpha/numeric symbol. And these series of locations are then combined into arrays with many memory locations. Figure 33a illustrates a very small array with four rows, each containing four binary digits: 16 storage locations in all.

Addressing Storage Locations

In order to read information from, or write information to, a single memory cell or series of cells making up, say, one byte in the memory, it is necessary to label each cell or group of cells with an address. Like all other instructions and data inside the computer, the address will normally be in binary form, and will comprise a sequence of binary digits that uniquely identify the particular section of the store. Figure 33b indicates how a binary address, in the form of electronic pulses that represent the 1s and 0s, can be passed through circuitry that leads to the accessing of the particular memory location(s) it designates.

Our small array has only four different addresses, to identify each of the four rows of four locations, so the addresses consist of only two binary digits. The signals that indicate the address are passed through a series of NOT and AND gates, with the result that the required 'read' line carries a 1 output signal. These gates are designated as the 'address decoder'.

In a full-sized array, two different sets of decoder circuitry would be needed, one to identify the rows and the other to identify the columns. A positive signal along the wires indicating both the row and the column sections of a particular address would be needed, in order to activate the location for reading and writing operations.

The Size of Memory Arrays

This decoding arrangement does have an important influence upon the size of memory arrays found in computers, either on memory chips or in some other form. Typically, they come in multiples of 2^{10}, or 1,024. This unlikely number (to non-computer people) makes it easy to arrange the decoder circuitry efficiently.

The number 2^{10} is so familiar, in fact, that it has a special designation in computer jargon: 'K'. When you read or hear about '16K' or '32K' memories, what are actually being referred to are memories with $16 \times 1,024$ or $32 \times 1,024$ locations. Of course, 'K' (as 'kilo') is commonly used, not only in computer circles, to mean 1,000; sometimes this alternative use crops up in computing, too.

Figure 33: Array of semiconductor storage locations

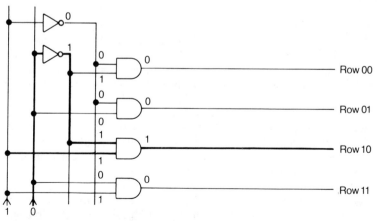

(a) Outline of the array structure

(b) Operation of the address decoder (heavy lines indicate the activation of row 10 by address signal 10)

Read Only Memory Media

The complexity of both flip-flop and dynamic storage is largely due to the ability of the storage locations to change their stored information in response to an input signal. However, it is not necessary for all the memory in a computer to possess this ability. The computer needs to store a great deal of unchanging information such as operating instructions and the ability to decode programming languages. This information can be stored in a different type of memory: read only memory, in contrast to the read/write memories we have just been discussing.

In fact, there are various degrees of 'writeability' in read/write memories. These are the most common types:

Simple ROM (Read Only Memory): means that a pattern of bits is fixed in the memory location array when it is being manufactured — a process we explore for semiconductor memory chips in Chapter 20 in depth. In the very simplest form, a connection between two crossed wires at a particular location indicates a 1, the absence of a connection a 0.

Programmable ROM (PROM): is also a permanently marked memory, but the pattern of bits is fixed in the array at a later stage: by the user or by the manufacturer of the computer in which it is to be used, rather than by the maker of the silicon chip. Usually, the full array is made with cross-connections in each memory location, and the user burns away the connections in some locations by passing through them a strong pulse of electrical current.

Erasable Programmable ROM (EPROM): is still more flexible. The user again programs the memory, but he can (with difficulty) erase the program and reprogram the array to a different pattern. However, the locations cannot be reprogrammed electrically while the memory is in normal use. The device has to be reprogrammed by special equipment, often using ultra-violet light.

Electrically Alterable ROM (EAROM): can be reprogrammed while it is still included in an electronic circuit. In effect, this memory is not really 'read only' at all but, in its operating characteristics, it has more in common with read only memories than with common read/write memory media.

Read only memory has one great advantage over many forms of read/write memory. The permanence of its means of storing data means that the data it contains are *not* lost when the circuit is not powered. By contrast, flip-flops and dynamic memory arrays lose their data if the power supply to them is disconnected.

Virtually all modern computers have some read only memory and some read/write memory, in one or other of the forms we have specified, permanently connected to their control and arithmetic units, and other internal parts. However, memory is expensive; addressing memory locations is a complicated business; and it is not practicable to store permanently in a computer all the application programs it will ever need to run. Such data (and instructions) that are sometimes, but not always, required by the computer are typically stored in a 'secondary' medium. This can then be coupled to the computer's circuits when it is required; it can also be stored separately when not required, without taking up any of the computer's information processing capacity.

Assessing Secondary Storage Media

What are the factors used to assess the relative merits of different storage media? They include the following:
(1) the size of the medium, in relation to the amount of data it can store;
(2) the reliability of it: can data become corrupted, does it degrade after long storage? Is the medium flammable or subject to some other form of interference (e.g. magnetic interference)?
(3) the cost of storing data;
(4) the cost, reliability and ease of use of the read/write mechanism that couples the storage medium to the computer;
(5) perhaps most important, the access time: the average time it take the computer to access a piece of data stored in a secondary medium that is coupled to it; and the maximum time it can take — even more critical in some circumstances.
The varying importance given to these different factors by different users, and for different applications, means that a wide variety of secondary storage media have been — and still are — used.

Random Access and Sequential Access

The borderline between random access memory media and sequential access media is just as blurred as that between read only and read/write memories. However, the distinction is very commonly used, so we shall consider it here.

Basically, a random access memory medium is one in which the read/write device can directly access any specific memory location, regardless of its physical location on/in the medium. It is not necessary to skim past other locations: the device goes directly to the required one. The array and decoder of Figure 33, and the larger real-life versions based on this technology, are random access arrangements: the address lines directly access the required data. True, in a two-dimensional array with both row and column decoders, the individual currents activating address lines may flow through other storage locations before reaching the required one; but the combination of signals accesses only the one location that is required.

By contrast, a sequential access medium is one in which the locations can be accessed only in a fixed sequence. To access a location towards the end of the sequence, it is first necessary to access all those earlier in the sequence. A piece of music recorded at the end of a cassette tape provides a good example: it is necessary to pass all the first part of the tape past the recording/playback head, either playing or fast-winding it, before a piece of music recorded at the end of the tape can be played.

The term 'random access memory' is commonly used to apply to internal read/write memories. A 'RAM', or a RAM chip, means a static or dynamic memory array of the type we have described, or some similar type. This term is used in contrast to ROM though it is not strictly its opposite, as we have seen: read only memories are in fact commonly random access.

Magnetic Tape

Large-sized magnetic tapes, similar in technology (but larger in size) to those used for recording music, were (together with punched cards) until recently one of the most common secondary memory media used with mainframe computers. They preceded, and have outlasted, the magnetic drums we discussed in Chapter 6. Today, they are increasingly being superseded by disc storage; but they are still in general use, and small cassette-type tapes are widely used as a cheap storage medium for home computers.

The tapes can easily be written on, erased and rewritten. A thin film of magnetizable material (iron oxide, or some similar magnetic oxide) that covers the tape's plastic backing is magnetized in either a north-south or a south-north direction, one direction representing a 0 and the other a 1, just as was done with the magnetic drums.

The tapes contain (typically) seven, eight or nine tracks of data across the $\frac{1}{2}''$ (1·3 cm) width of today's standard tape (earlier tapes were $\frac{3}{4}''$ (2 cm) or 1" (2·5 cm) wide). Each sequential portion of the tape can contain a coded digit on each track. As flaws in the tape or dust between the tape and its read/write head can prevent correct recording of the data, one track is often used as a parity device, to check accuracy in the way we described on page 24.

Tape storage has several major disadvantages. First, it is a relatively fragile medium: it is easily subject to interference from other sources of magnetism; the tape is breakable; and reading and writing from and to it can be affected by dust. As a result, if magnetic tapes are to be used intensively they have to be stored carefully and used in controlled environments. The technology is improving steadily, though: when tapes were first introduced, it was essential to use the highest-quality equipment; today, microcomputers can access data stored on ordinary cassette tapes and played back over even the cheapest cassette players.

A second disadvantage of magnetic tape is that it is a strictly sequential medium, and reading and writing are relatively slow operations. The access time for data stored at the end of the tape can be several minutes, in contrast to the fraction of a second it takes to access internal read/write memory. And a third disadvantage: although tapes can store a considerable quantity of data (a tape 2,400 feet long could today hold up to 6,250 bits per inch, or 125 million characters in all), the tapes are relatively cumbersome to store. Finally, on cassette systems without adequate means of indexing the tape, it can be extremely difficult to find where one program or sequence of data ends and another begins. Unfortunately, different types of processor, and sometimes different operating systems (see Chapter 9) use different labelling procedures to indicate the beginning and end – and this compounds the problem.

To enable ordinary audio cassette tapes and players to be used as a secondary storage medium for simple computer systems, these systems use a two-step encoding system for data. The data on the tape are held in magnetic form; but the computer 'writes' on to the tape in audio form. A 'bleep' at a fixed interval on the tape represents a 1, the absence of a bleep a 0. The player mechanism then records the bleeps on the tape in just the same way as it would record speech or music; but in this case it is using the potentially complex sound waves as a simple binary storage medium.

These disadvantages are largely avoided by the disc technology that is now taking over from tapes in all but very small-scale systems.

Disc Storage

Discs, like tapes, are magnetic data storage media: again, a thin film of magnetic oxide covers their aluminium or plastic core and can easily be magnetized or demagnetized in small sections. But accessing data on the disc is quite a different business from accessing data stored on tape. It might be compared to the difference between playing a track on a gramophone record and finding the corresponding track on a music cassette. Discs are much closer to being a true random access memory medium.

The discs are rotated in a disc drive unit, and the circular tracks of data stored on them (*not* one spiral track, as on a gramophone record) are read by one or more reading heads as the disc rotates. In some drive units there are multiple fixed read/write heads: one to access each track on the disc; in others, the single head can move from track to track. In each, however, the head can read data only when the disc is rotated so that the data are in the right position on the radius of the unit: thus access is not truly random but, rather, pseudo-random. Speeds of rotation are fast, however: often around

300–360 r.p.m. for floppy discs, and up to ten times faster for the hard versions.

Hard discs: A single hard disc is called a 'disc cartridge'. Often a group of discs is stacked together on a common spindle to form a 'disc pack'. A corresponding group of read/write heads move together, to access a 'stack' of tracks (a 'cylinder') all at once. A further trend has been towards the development of 'datapacks', in which the moving read/write heads are sealed inside the pack for extra security. The additional cost of these packs is offset by the lower cost of the drives needed to read them.

Both cartridges and disc packs can be replaceable inside the disc drive, so one drive can handle many discs of data, just as one tape reader can be used to read many different tapes. However, there is now an increasing trend towards the use of non-interchangeable discs in large installations. The great majority of fixed discs use moving-head access mechanisms, but there are also non-removable fixed-head discs. Non-interchangeability is not an undue disadvantage: in many computer installations it is necessary to keep large volumes of data permanently on-line (that is, immediately accessible by the central processor), and fixed-disc drive units are ideal for this purpose.

The storage capacity of discs varies widely, but it is considerable. Many single discs hold around 10–20 megabytes (a megabyte is a million bytes, or eight times as many bits) of information. Some disc packs can hold up to 500 megabytes. The very large capacity discs are always non-interchangeable and sealed: only with this technology can the highest data densities be achieved.

Floppy discs: Floppy discs function much like hard discs, but instead of being rigid they are made of flexible plastic. They are smaller and cheaper than hard discs: a floppy disc costs only a few pounds, and they can easily be sent by mail or filed in folders. A single-density, single-sided disc can hold around 250,000 characters of information, while double-density, double-sided versions can hold up to a million characters (or even more, on the latest models). Smaller 'mini-diskettes' hold fewer: typically around 90,000 characters.

Floppy discs are very commonly used with minicomputer and microcomputer installations. One difference between their mode of operation and that of hard discs is this: the read/write head does not actually touch the surface of the hard disc: it is suspended a fractional distance above it on a cushion of air. The read heads on floppy disc drives, by contrast, are brought directly into contact with the appropriate portion of the disc. As a result, floppy discs wear out faster and are not really suitable for storage of information that is kept constantly on-line and is frequently accessed by many different users. The floppy disc's useful life (which in practice is usually limited more by careless handling than by actual wearing-out of the tracks) is, however, quite

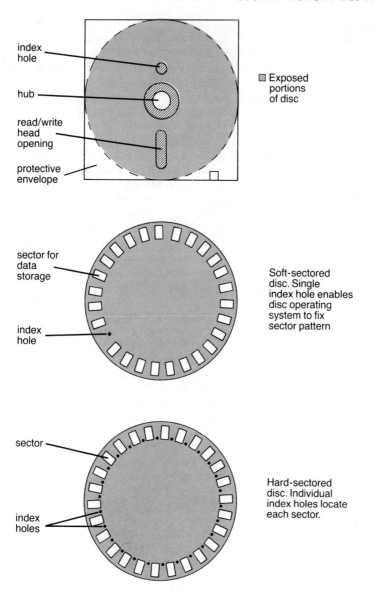

index hole

hub

read/write head opening

protective envelope

Exposed portions of disc

sector for data storage

index hole

Soft-sectored disc. Single index hole enables disc operating system to fix sector pattern

sector

index holes

Hard-sectored disc. Individual index holes locate each sector.

Figure 34: Floppy discs

adequate for the less intensive data access typical of small computer systems.

'Single-density' and 'double-density' are purely manufacturer-defined terms: usually double-density discs are later models in which the storage density has been much increased. Indeed, storage densities are increasing all the time: the figures we quote here, though accurate today, may well be outmoded before the book is even published.

'Single-sided' and 'double-sided' are self-explanatory terms. Double-sided discs may appear more desirable, as they can store more data in the same physical space, but they have two disadvantages: first, they require two read/write heads in the drive unit, and this makes the latter more expensive; second, the heads must be carefully aligned with each other, a complex task when such precise and small distances are involved.

One other set of terms used in connection with floppy discs requires mention: hard sectoring and soft sectoring. In hard-sectored discs, the fixed number of tracks on the disc is divided up into a fixed pattern of 'sectors' for arranging and indexing stored data. Soft-sectored discs, by contrast, are not sold ready divided into sectors. Instead, the disc operating system (the hardware/software system that handles data operations between the computer and the disc drive) 'formats' the discs, dividing them up as required by its programming. The characteristics of the operating system will determine which type of disc a particular computer system uses. Figure 34 gives a visual indication of the difference between these two types of floppy disc.

Neither hard nor soft discs are particularly robust as storage media go, though they can be handled with normal care and may be re-used a number of times. Like magnetic tape, discs are subject to accidental erasure of data if they come into contact with a strong source of magnetism; the data on them can also be corrupted by dust and fingerprints. However, they do have many advantages over rival media; though they are more expensive than tapes of comparable capacity, their faster access time makes them an attractive choice in many circumstances.

Bubble Memory

'Bubble' memory is the latest in a long line of devices that use electro-magnetic technology as the basis of a storage system. However, it has far more in common with silicon chips than with other magnetic storage devices, such as tape and discs.

The bubbles are actually magnetic domains, small cylindrical areas less than one-sixteenth the diameter of a human hair, that are located in a thin film of crystalline magnetic material about a $\frac{1}{4}''$ (6 mm) square. The polarity (the magnetic direction) of the bubbles is the opposite of that of the film so that the bubbles are created when a magnetic field is applied perpendicular to the surface of the film.

Magnetic driver coils move the bubbles around the chip, so the chip can actually be thought of as containing a long loop (or series of loops) of data, with a bubble in any particular location indicating a 1, and its absence a 0. Access to the data is strictly sequential but, as the bubbles move quickly, access is still relatively swift: faster than the pseudo-random access to data on a disc, though slower than access to semiconductor memory.

Bubble memory has three major advantages. It is rugged: the bubbles are not affected by shock or vibration, by humidity, temperature extremes or radiation — though, of course, they can be affected by magnetic interference. As a result, the devices are well suited to environments like portable computer terminals and even fighter-plane control systems. The memory is non-volatile: that is, the data are not lost when the power to the system is switched off. And storage capacities are high: a bubble the size of a typical silicon chip can contain up to one megabit (a million bits) of information.

However, difficulties have arisen both in developing cheap mass-production techniques that would enable bubble memories to compete in price with semiconductor memory chips, and in devising efficient logic circuits to interface the chip with the rest of the computer's circuitry. Much of the memory is manufactured in exactly the same way as is a conventional chip, using photolithographic techniques. However, the driver coils that move the bubbles around require a more old-fashioned, and less easily automated, production technique. As a result of these problems, the market for bubble memory has not yet taken off in the way some early commentators predicted it would. Bubble memory was invented in 1966, and was in commercial use by the mid-1970s, but it is still not a major mainstream technology.

Other Memory Media

What other memory media are used today? We must not forget that punched cards and paper tape are still used in some computer installations, and for some other commercial purposes (in some 'memory' typewriters, for instance). Though cumbersome, they are extremely rugged and reliable.

However, the major threat to the magnetic media today comes not from paper media but from optical media: videodiscs, holograms and so on. We shall explore this alternative type of memory technology in Chapter 19, while looking at all the various intersections of optical and electronic technology.

8. The Central Processing Unit at Work

In this chapter, we shall be looking at some functional aspects of modern computers – and, in particular, of computers based on microelectronic components. We shall be building on what we have learnt in the last chapter about internal memory construction, and looking at some working parts of the processor (or central processing unit) and at how it fits together with the memory and the input and output handling devices.

The features we look at in this chapter are common to the vast majority of general-purpose digital computers in operation today. Obviously, particular models vary in their design features, but they all cope with these basic functions, and most of them cope with them in very similar ways. It is irrelevant in this chapter, for instance, whether the computer has a microprocessor – a central processing unit on a single chip – or whether its central processor is made up of a number of components. Later in Part Three we shall go on to look at some specific computers, and examine how they put these principles into practice. Before we begin to look at individual functional components, let us briefly recap on what are the main constituent parts of a computer – not just a modern computer, but *any* computer from Babbage's day onwards. Every computer (whether it meets the stored-program qualification or not) has:

(1) a central processing unit (c.p.u.) that handles arithmetic/logic and control operations. This is sometimes known as the central processing unit, sometimes as the processor (or microprocessor, if it is contained on a single chip). In the Analytical Engine, you will recall, this comprised two separate units: the mill and the control unit. The successor to Babbage's mill is sometimes described separately as the arithmetic/logic unit: together with the control unit (or controller) and a few other bits and pieces, it makes up the modern c.p.u.

(2) memory locations: today, some read only memory and some read/write memory is the norm.

(3) at least one input device.

(4) at least one output device.

The Central Processing Unit

In this chapter, we shall be describing some parts of the central processing unit in detail, but not all of them: some we have already covered adequately, and some need no in-depth explanation. For completeness, then, we will include in this section a summary of the main constituent parts of the c.p.u. Any c.p.u. will need:

(1) an arithmetic/logic unit (a.l.u.), for carrying out arithmetic and logic operations. This will be made up of circuits like the adder circuit we looked at in Chapter 2, through which data can be passed in order to perform arithmetic/logic operations on them.

(2) a number of internal storage locations that, in the c.p.u., are normally known as registers. These are for handling the transfer of information to and from memory locations and the a.l.u., and for various other control functions that we shall look at later.

(3) a control unit, for handling the interpretation and performance of program instructions. This will include the ability to:
(a) obtain and 'decode' instructions: that is, to translate them into the required sequence of actions. This is done by the 'instruction decoder';
(b) obtain data stored in memory, with the help of the address decoder;
(c) handle the sequencing of competing instructions. On pages 170 to 171 we look at the 'interrupt' procedures used for this purpose;
(d) handle the synchronization of operations: the control unit will either incorporate a clock/timer or it will be able to read in signals from an external clock/timer;
(e) output signals that get the rest of the computer working. The input/output and memory devices, and the c.p.u.'s own internal registers, must be triggered to send and/or receive data or instructions; the a.l.u. must be triggered to perform the required manipulations.

(4) Internal communication lines, or buses, for linking these various parts to one another and to the rest of the computer.

Executing a Program

How does a c.p.u. go about carrying out a program that has been entered into the computer? It repeats the following sequence of operations, until the program is completed:
(1) identify the next instruction in the program, and read it from memory;
(2) identify the location in memory of, and read, any data specified by the instruction;
(3) execute the instruction;
(4) write the result into the desired memory location, or output device.
In order for the processor to perform this sequence of operations, it must use three of its basic abilities:
(1) it must use decoder circuitry, for interpreting instructions and translating them into action;

(2) the a.l.u. will be needed to execute the instructions;

(3) it will need to make use of the communications network that connects it with the memory, input and output devices.

We shall start to consider how this sequence is carried out in practice by looking at buses, the communication lines inside the c.p.u. and elsewhere inside the computer.

Buses

There are three basic types of bus. All three are found in any computer:

(1) a control bus that conveys control signals;

(2) an address bus, indicating the address of data to be read from, or written into, memory;

(3) a data bus, for the actual transfer of data.

The address bus is one-way: it conveys information *from* the processor *to* the other functional units. The data bus is two-way in operation: its bi-directional lines can be used for both read and write activities. The control bus has two sets of lines: one to sense input signals, and one to generate control signals.

Figure 35 gives a very simple indication of how the bus structure interconnects the basic components of a computer system.

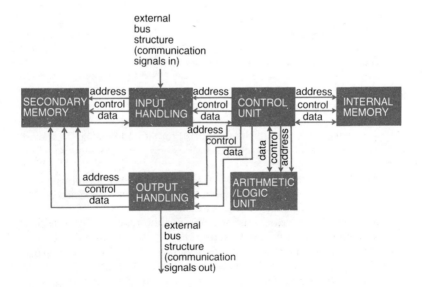

Figure 35: Simple schematic of a computer bus structure

The control bus: The control bus usually has 3–10 lines, each of which transports one bit of data at a time. It handles the following types of signal: *clock* impulses, to control the timing of system operations. The impulses may be generated within the c.p.u., or generated outside it and transmitted through it.

activating signals, such as 'memory enable' or 'memory read', that activate functional units and prepare them to send or receive data, and determine the direction in which the data lines are to operate.

interrupt signals, that handle the co-ordination of the activities of reading in input and carrying out processing. (We discuss these on pages 170 to 171.)

The address bus: Data being sent from or to a particular storage location, and the address of the location in question, are handled separately by the bus system. However, the strict timing control of operations ensures that the data and its address are kept together.

The address bus may have 4–32 lines, depending upon the number of memory locations it accesses. A 16-line bus could identify 2^{16}, or 65,536 memory locations; a 32-line bus, 2^{32} locations.

The data bus: This normally consists of four, eight or sixteen bi-directional lines, depending upon the capacity of the memory locations. The direction of data flow is determined by the control bus; the destination is determined by the address bus.

Registers

A register is a set of storage locations, made up of electronic components like those we considered on pages 115 to 128, into which changeable information can be written in digital electronic form. In other words, a register is fundamentally no different from a set of read/write memory locations. There *are* some important differences, though:

(1) A register is a location in the processor itself, not one of the array of addressed memory locations.

(2) The information in a register may be manipulable, in ways in which the information in memory locations is *not* manipulable. The manipulations that can be carried out range from simply incrementing or decrementing by 1 the number stored in the location, to a full assortment of arithmetic/logic operations, according to the function of the register and the design of the processor.

Like an addressed memory location, a register is of fixed capacity (often eight bits), but two registers can be used in conjunction if it is necessary to store a longer piece of data.

All c.p.u.'s contain a variety of registers in which data being manipulated, or data about program operation, can be stored. Some of these have very specific functions, and their circuitry is connected to the control circuitry in a way which recognizes this; others are multi-purpose.

These are the most common types of register found in modern processing units:

Data registers: These provide temporary storage locations for data awaiting manipulation, or awaiting transmission to an output device or to a memory location after manipulation. They can be more rapidly and easily accessed by the control unit than can normal RAM locations.

Sometimes data registers can be used to perform simple manipulations such as:

(1) incrementing or decrementing their contents;

(2) 'shifting' data a number of places to the left or the right (that is, multiplying or dividing a stored number by powers of 2);

(3) exchanging the contents of two registers.

The data can also be evaluated by the control circuits, according to criteria like:

(4) are the contents of a particular register zero, less than zero or greater than zero?

(5) are the number of bits of each state (1 or 0) in the register odd or even? (This is, as you will recall, the 'parity' or otherwise of the data.)

Data address registers: These are just the same as data registers, but they normally contain, not data, but an address in memory in which data is to be found. If the memory addresses are sixteen bits long, then two eight-bit data registers may be combined to provide a data address register. Sometimes data registers are used as required as data address registers; sometimes special registers are designated for this purpose. As well as functioning as data address registers, they can also function as instruction address registers, keeping track of where a particular program instruction (perhaps one that will be required once a program subroutine has been completed) is stored.

Stack pointers: A group of memory locations into which a sequence of data can be deposited is often referred to as a 'stack'. Stacks may consist of locations on a RAM chip, or of an area of memory locations specially set aside for the purpose in the c.p.u. The address in the stack in which data were last written, or from which they were last read, is designated by the stack pointer. Put another way, this is a specialized type of address register, that always has the ability to be incremented or decremented as locations are used in the course of a program.

Program counters: These hold the addresses of memory locations in which program instructions can be found. The program instructions are often stored location by location in the memory, and the counter is then incremented by ones as the instructions are performed. However, some instructions cause the program to 'jump' to a subroutine, or to branch out of sequence. In these cases, the data on the program counter will be changed accordingly. Any 'return address' that also needs to be recorded will be stored in the stack or in another general register.

Accumulators: These are manipulable registers, that enable a full range of arithmetic/logic operations (the exact operations will depend upon the processor's instruction set) to be carried out on their contents. Needless to say, they normally contain data, not instructions.

Flag status registers: 'Flags' are single bits that contain specific information such as:
(1) the parity (odd or even number of '1' bits) of a specific word;
(2) whether the result of a specific operation is equal to zero;
(3) whether the result of a specific operation is positive or negative;
(4) whether a 'carry' is generated in adding two long numbers (more than a register in length) together or performing some similar arithmetical operation; or whether an arithmetic operation has 'overflowed' beyond the capacity of the registers allocated for it.

These flags are 'set' when particular instructions are carried out. They are sometimes organized into a register known as the flag status register. There are rarely as many as eight status flags, so there will be spare bits if the register is eight bits in length. These may be used for other control functions.

Combining Registers and Buses

On pages 131 to 132, we identified the sequence of operations that the processor carries out in order to perform each program instruction. These are vital to understanding the operation of the c.p.u., so we repeat them here:
(1) identify the next instruction in the program, and read it from memory;
(2) identify the location in memory of, and read, any data specified by the instruction;
(3) execute the instruction;
(4) write the result into the desired memory location, or output device.

Now we are in a position to see how this ties in with the data held in the c.p.u.'s registers, and with the operation of the bus system. To carry out the instruction, the control unit will actually perform the following operations (they correspond to operations (1) to (4) above):
(1) The next instruction in the program is to be found in the memory location whose address is specified by the program counter. So to read it from memory, the control unit:
     (a) sends a 'read enable' signal down the control bus to memory;

(b) sends the contents of the program counter down the address bus to memory.

The instruction itself then travels along the data bus, from memory to the instruction decoder circuits of the central processing unit.

(2) The program instruction itself will consist of both:

(a) an arithmetic/logic operation (or other form of data manipulation) to be performed; and

(b) designation of the data on which the operation is to be performed. This data may already be present in the accumulator, or in another data register in the c.p.u. Alternatively, it may be necessary to retrieve it from memory. In this case, the instruction will either:

(c) indicate the actual address of the data; or

(d) indicate the data address register in which the address is to be found.

(We shall elaborate on the methods of addressing used in computers in Chapter 10.)

In either case, the control unit will:

(e) send a 'read enable' signal down the control bus to memory; and

(f) send the address of the location in which the data are stored down the address bus to memory.

The data will then travel along the data bus, from memory to the accumulator or to a designated register in the c.p.u.

(3) Once all the data are available, the timing signals activate the decoder and cause it to initiate the desired sequence of manipulative operations.

(4) Once the instruction has been completed, the central processing unit will output the following signals:

(a) a 'write enable' or similar signal along the control bus, to enable the result to be written into its designated destination;

(b) the address of the result's destination (that will have been determined as part of the instruction sequence) along the address bus;

(c) the data comprising the result itself, along the data bus.

And then, of course, the computer is ready to proceed with the next instruction.

9. A Matter of Definition: From Software to Hardware

A basic distinction that is often made in talking about computer systems is between their software – the instructions they are to carry out – and their hardware – the machinery itself. It is a useful distinction, but it is also a misleading one for, at a lower level, the distinction between the two becomes blurred, and finally disappears. In this chapter, we shall be tracing the linkages between software and hardware that make a hard-and-fast distinction between the two so impossible to define.

It is important to note that, because the distinction between software and hardware is fundamentally an artificial one, the terms 'software' and 'hardware' are used with a wide variety of emphases, depending upon where the dividing line is drawn. Many people use 'software' to refer to only a sub-section of the computer's range of instructions. Others have introduced additional terms such as 'intimate software' and 'firmware' to cover parts of this continuous spectrum. Though not strictly necessary, these terms can be useful, and we shall indicate the areas to which they can be applied.

Circuits with a Purpose

On page 47 we illustrated a simple 'adder' circuit, designed to add two numbers together. Is this software or is it hardware?

In a way, it is both. The concept of the circuit, as illustrated on that page, has no specific existence in terms of wires and transistors. It is merely a concept, a design; as such, it is software. But if this circuit were to be built, using the simple electronic components we discussed earlier in this book, then there would be no doubt that it was hardware.

But it is still hardware that *embodies* the concept of adding. If electronic impulses representing the two binary numbers are fed through that circuit, then there is no need to *tell* the circuit to add the numbers together. Adding is what the circuit simply does, by virtue of its configuration as a circuit; or, at any rate, it is the way in which we interpret what it does. The circuit has no choice: the codes representing the two numbers are transformed into a code representing their sum, simply by passing them through that particular circuit.

At this very basic level, *every* instruction we give to the computer is transformed into an inevitable series of circuit actions in just the same way. We do not mysteriously 'ask' or 'tell' the computer to add two numbers together. At some level, we physically trigger a sequence of movements –

initially perhaps of keys and switches, eventually of electronic pulses through a circuit – that leads to the physical process we interpret as 'adding' being carried out.

It is essential to remember this. An instruction in software form – an idea perhaps, or a note on a piece of paper – can only be implemented when it physically triggers a sequence of movements and, at the point where it does so, it ceases to be a (potential) instruction and becomes simply the sequence of inevitable movements, determined by the very nature of the electronic circuits, that performs the action in question.

Determined by the circuits *and* by their contents, that is: for there is obviously a difference between adding, say, 2 and 4 (or their binary equivalents) and adding 10 and 20. The sums are different, even though the basic process used to carry them out is the same. The sequence of electronic pulses is different.

Let us take another angle from which to explore the software/hardware distinction, and consider a flip-flop circuit that is storing a '1'. In hardware terms, the reality is the circuit and its electronic status. In software terms, its meaning as '1' is equally real, if less tangible.

General-Purpose and Special-Purpose Computers

We now digress slightly, and go back to the very similar distinction we drew, in Chapter 4, between general-purpose and special-purpose machines. A general-purpose computer is a computer that has to be given a program of instructions – that is, input other than the data on which it acts – before it can perform a sequence of operations. A special-purpose computer does not need any instructions. Its very circuitry determines which operations it will perform upon its data input.

But there is no fundamental difference between the circuitry of a general-purpose computer and that of a special-purpose computer. The actual operations they perform on their data are just the same. Similarly, read only (or special-purpose) memory cells are functionally no different from read/write (general-purpose) memory cells: both are devices used for storing a bit of data. In special-purpose devices, though, the program (or the data, in the case of memory cells) is permanently embodied in the hardware configuration. In general-purpose devices, the data or instructions must still be translated into terms of hardware status or activity; but their translation is done on a temporary, not a permanent, basis.

Types of Software

With this brief discussion as background, how might we define the word 'software'? Some definitions that have been put forward by computer experts may help to clarify our ideas:

'all programs which can be used on a particular computer system' (A. Chandor, *A Dictionary of Computers*)

'a set of computer programs, procedures and possibly associated documentation concerned with the operation of a data processing system' (Radio Shack, *Understanding Microprocessors*)

'a systematic collection of programmes and associated documentation concerning the use of a data processing system' (Robin Bradbeer, *The Personal Computer Book*)

What do these definitions have in common? The word 'program(me)', for a start. They do not speak of instructions: strictly speaking, programs consist only of *potential* instructions (together with data and associated material) until they are actually implemented. They do not mention data: and indeed, data (unless incorporated in a computer program) are not normally thought of as part of software.

They do not mention a medium. The medium in which the program is embodied is not the important thing about software: the important thing is the concept itself, not its realization. So, from another angle, we could offer our own, rather less conventional definition of software as:

Man's interpretation of the actual or potential activities of a computer system, in terms of arithmetic, logic and control operations (or combinations of these on a higher level).

In other words, software is not what the computer system does, or might do when the program is run; it is the user's conception of the *meaning* of what it does.

Nevertheless, most software *is* embodied in a physical medium. We can exemplify this statement by describing a spectrum of software incarnations, ranging from the totally insubstantial to the firmly, physically fixed:

(1) An idea in someone's head as to how a computer program might be planned to work — its algorithm, if you like.

(2) A listing of program steps, in a high- or low-level language, written out on paper.

(3) The same listing stored in a read/write memory medium, either in internal computer memory, or on a cassette tape or magnetic tape, or on a disc, or in some other temporary storage or communication medium.

(4) The same listing, permanently or semi-permanently stored in ROM or PROM (or EPROM) form.

It is this last, permanently embodied form of software that is sometimes known instead as 'firmware'.

What Software is Available?

That is perhaps a misleading question. It may be more illuminating to ask: What can we ask a computer system to do? And in what ways can we specify our instructions? We can then map out the field of available software as a continuous spectrum of different types of instructions, that are typically available in different physical manifestations: from those always embodied in the computer's microcircuit configuration to those always input to the system in application program form. Of course, this spectrum includes many instructions that may be available on several different physical or conceptual levels.

Basic Instructions

Every central processing unit contains circuits that enable it to carry out a range of basic operations. In other words, a single identifying trigger (and any necessary data) is all that is needed for these operations to be performed.

The range of basic operations is not standard: it is one of the distinguishing features of microprocessor chip design (and of the design of c.p.u.s not based on microprocessor chips). C.p.u.s designed for different computing purposes (arithmetic operations or communications handling, for instance) will boast different ranges of instructions. However, the following list should give a good idea of the field that is covered by these basic instructions. Some of these operations can be performed as a result of a single input by all c.p.u.s; others, by some but not all.

Arithmetic instructions:
Add two numbers together
Subtract one number from another
Find the absolute value (that is, regardless of sign, + or −) of a stored number
Negate a positive number
Multiply one number by another
Divide one number by another
Shift a stored number one place to the left or right in the storage register. (This is the equivalent of multiplying or dividing it by 2; it is also a preliminary to some comparison operations.)

Logic operations: Pass two or more numbers through the logic circuits
we looked at in Chapter 2, to determine if:
all inputs are equal to 1 (AND);
at least one input is equal to 1 (OR);

one and only one input is equal to 1 (EXCLUSIVE OR);
or to invert an input (NOT).

Data movement operations: Operations that are used to shift data
around from input devices to memory locations and processing registers,
between registers and memory, and to output devices.
They include, for instance:
initializing registers before beginning a program, by placing constant values
  into them;
receiving input and feeding it to memory locations;
fetching designated data from memory, and placing it in a register prior to
performing an arithmetic/logic operation on it.
   Sometimes these operations are broken down into three basic types:
   LOAD
   STORE
   MOVE.

Comparison operations: Unlike most arithmetic operations, these do
not alter the original numbers on which the operation is performed. They
consist of operations that ascertain if a number or piece of binary-coded
data (for example, letters coded in ASCII) is:
the same as another;
less than or equal to another, or to 0;
greater than or equal to another, or to 0.

Branching operations: These are operations that alter the sequence in
which instructions from a program are performed. In other words, they are
ways of manipulating the registers in which the addresses of program lines
are stored. There are three types of branching operation:
(1) Unconditional. At a certain point, the sequence of instructions
    followed simply deviates from the expected one.
(2) Conditional. An alternative sequence of instructions is followed if some
    particular condition is met (for instance, if a comparison operation
    indicates that two pieces of data are identical).
(3) Subroutine. The program deviates to a fixed and predesignated
    subroutine of operations, and then returns to continue with the original
    sequence.

Bootstrapping Instructions

What happens when you switch a computer on? How do you tell it what to
do?
   If it is a general-purpose computer (and from now on in Part Three, we

shall assume that it is), then it must be given instructions before it can proceed to do anything. But just *how* do we give it instructions? For instance, can we simply switch on a cassette player or disc drive, containing a cassette or disc with a series of instructions encoded on it, and expect the computer to absorb these instructions and act upon them? Or is something else needed first?

In reality, what we can do depends very much upon the computer's basic instruction set. Some computers have an extended set of basic instructions that enables them to draw data from an input device when a single instruction like LOAD is input. Others do not; they must be 'taught' to do so, via a simple program that uses only instructions included in their basic instruction set.

In other words, the instructions we are now talking about are just one step away from the most basic arithmetic/logic instructions that are embodied in the c.p.u. design. They are primarily instructions that simplify (in varying degrees) the input and output operations, and that enable these to be handled by a range of additional instruction codes that the computer is given the ability to act on.

Once the computer is given a very basic range of these operating instructions (either by a keyboard or in firmware form), then it can proceed to input programs containing more extensive operating instructions from a secondary storage medium (say, a disc or tape). In effect, we are teaching the computer to teach itself: it is this process that is known as 'bootstrapping'. The computer steadily pulls itself up by its own bootstraps: using a limited range of abilities to extend that range, using the extended range as a basis for further extending it, and so on.

Systems Software

Of course, these (perhaps very basic) operating routines are not the only 'housekeeping' instructions a computer can make use of – or needs. Even a simple computer will be more easy to operate if it is equipped with a range of instructions that enable the processor to handle automatically, for instance, the business of assigning suitable blocks of memory to hold incoming data, and keeping track of the addresses of each piece of data. (We look in depth at addressing practices in Chapter 10.) A complex mainframe, the hub of a system that has an elaborately structured database and a wide range of peripherals attached to it, will need far more extensive capabilities.

These housekeeping capabilities – capabilities that ease the problems of operating the computer, but do not actually constitute programs in the conventional, 'application' sense – are known as 'systems software'.

Monitors: A monitor is a simple set of systems software instructions taking up only a relatively small amount of memory space (typically from 256 bytes to 2,048 bytes, depending upon the capabilities it provides) of the type that would be useful in even the simplest microcomputer system. It is a very basic piece of systems software. Outlining the sort of capabilities provided by such a program (and we do loosely describe it as a program, though it is not one the computer 'runs' from beginning to end, as it might an application program) should give us an indication of the sort of area that systems software covers. A monitor might, for instance, enable the processor to:

examine the contents of individual memory locations, the addresses of which the operator specifies, display them on screen (or print them out if appropriate), and modify them if necessary, according to instructions input by the operator;

do the same with the contents of the various operating registers;

modify the way in which a program is run, perhaps beginning it at a specific point other than the start, for instance;

set 'breakpoints' in the program, at which it will stop running and control will revert to the monitor. This is an essential facility in 'debugging' (finding and correcting the errors in) an incorrect program;

fill sections of memory with specified binary patterns, before a program is run;

load sections of memory from a secondary storage device;

transfer or 'save' the contents of sections of memory on to a secondary storage device. (This protects against the accidental erasure of stored data.)

Computer Languages

Every time we 'teach' the computer to accept a 'compressed' instruction from us — say, LOAD telling the computer to input a specified set of program data — we are in effect teaching it a language. The computer's circuits perform the operation of loading: but they do so because our pressure on the LOAD key (or whatever we do to tell the computer: LOAD) is translated, by the various instructions that we have input (or that were originally incorporated) into the computer, into a set of electronic pulses that cause that operation to be carried out. The pulses are the immediate trigger of the operation; LOAD is merely our shorthand way of referring to (and, at a higher level, initiating) them.

Does a monitor program, or even a very short bootstrapping program, give the computer the ability to understand a computer language, then? In a very limited way, yes, it does. But we must elaborate on this statement by discussing what languages are, and how they are translated into the electronic pulses which *are* the computer's operation.

Machine code: Our way of designating the pulse pattern is itself a language. We call it machine code, or machine language: and we generally work with the digits 1 and 0 to represent the presence of a pulse or charge (1) or its absence (0).

By inputting the stream of pulse data directly (by switching switches, pressing keys, or inputting an equivalent binary-coded form of data from tape or disc, that the computer has the capability to transform into those basic pulses), we are in effect giving the computer instructions that it can implement directly. This is known as programming in machine code. (We shall look in greater depth at how it is done in Chapter 24.)

It is important to recognize that the precise pattern of pulses required to trigger a sequence of operations (that we interpret as being arithmetic/logic operations of the types we have already described) depends upon the exact layout of the c.p.u.'s circuits. So different designs of c.p.u. will demand different codes (different sequences of 1 and 0) to trigger the same sequence of operations. In other words, machine code is extremely machine-specific. It is *not* portable from machine to machine: a program written in this form will operate only on a machine it was written for, or on one absolutely identical in circuit layout.

Assembly language: Working with strings of 1s and 0s is exhausting and leads easily to errors. It is much more convenient to be able to use mnemonic codes (like ADD or LOAD) to stand for the basic instructions while actually writing the program. Before the program is run, the mnemonic codes must be converted to their binary equivalent. This equivalent is fixed: ADD will always be translated into the same sequence of 1s and 0s in a particular processor's machine code, and the same is true for every mnemonic used.

The business of translating each mnemonic into its binary equivalent *can* be done by hand. It is a dull and tiring task. It can also – since it is the purely mechanical operation of looking up the equivalent each time – be done by the computer itself if it is programmed to handle the task. A special set of systems software called an assembler does just this. It 'assembles' the input (in mnemonic form) into the binary pulse form the computer needs, before the program as a whole is run.

We shall see how assembly language works in Chapter 24, as an adjunct to our look at machine code programming.

High-level languages: High-level languages move the boundary between the programmer and the computer still further towards the programmer. The programmer's specification of what he wants the computer to do can be still briefer, and specialized software in the computer will translate his truncated instructions into the necessary physical activity.

High-level languages basically offer a repertoire of command words, each of which is the equivalent of a string of low-level instructions. Typically, the programmer need not concern himself with details like the assigning of memory locations that will be needed while the program is being run: all such 'housekeeping' is handled by the systems software. So a command in, say, BASIC (one of the most common languages) like:

LET A = 1

actually tells the computer to:

set up a variable location in memory (that is, a memory location whose contents can be changed in the course of the program running) and keep track of its address;

assign to it the 'name' A, which can be used by the programmer in referring to it (instead of its actual address, which he need not know);

enter the data, '1', into that location.

Each language has its own set of commands, depending on the purpose for which it has been designed. There are many dialects (developed variations) of some common languages, which again differ slightly in their command vocabulary. As well as offering a vocabulary of commands, the languages typically provide a range of facilities for handling the input and output of data, and for documenting application programs.

In Chapter 27, we shall look at the strong and weak points of the most common high-level languages, and in Chapter 26, at programming in the widely used BASIC.

High-level languages are not as machine specific as the low-level codes: the same languages are used by many different computer systems. However, programs written in a high-level language are not always easily 'portable' between machines. The following features are among those that may limit their portability:

(1) the exact 'dialect' the computer uses, determined by the software used to convert the high-level commands into actual hardware operations;

(2) the features of the rest of the systems software that affect how a program is executed;

(3) the amount of memory available on the system.

Compilers and interpreters: There are two types of software device used for translating high-level language commands into a form that the computer can deal with: compilers and interpreters.

Compilers work by quite literally 'translating' the program into machine code. Each high-level statement or command is converted into a corresponding series of machine-code instructions. Typically, the compiler works in conjunction with an array of special machine-code routines known as 'run-time routines': routines that comprise commonly encountered instruction sequences (such as complex mathematical operations) not directly covered by the c.p.u.'s basic instruction set. Instead of translating such sequences each time they are encountered in the program, the compiled program treats the run-time routines as a bank of subroutines on which it can call when necessary.

The entire program is compiled in this way before any of the instructions are actually executed. Once the compiling operation is complete, the program can then be run. Its running is controlled by yet another piece of systems software known as an 'executive program' that handles the flow of data and instructions, the calling-up of the run-time routines and so on.

Interpreters work quite differently. They take the high-level statements (a 'statement' is a small set of instructions and accompanying data, intended to be executed as a piece) one by one, and interpret them, again with the aid of machine-coded subroutines. Each statement is then executed before the interpreter moves on to the next statement.

Both types of program have advantages and disadvantages. Interpreters are generally easier for the programmer to handle. However, they operate much more slowly than compilers: depending on the nature of the program, up to ten times more slowly. If a program contains repetitious loops, for instance, in which the same operations are carried out repeatedly on different data, the compiler will need to translate the instructions in the loop only once. The interpreter translates them afresh, each time they are executed. In addition, interpreted programs generally take up more memory space than compiled programs. This can be an important drawback, particularly in small computer systems.

Operating Systems

We must also mention one other type of systems software: disc and cassette operating systems, and indeed operating systems for other peripherals.

Any peripheral device has its own way of formatting, coding and generally handling data (including stored program instructions). This method must be reasonably compatible with that used by the computer itself, but it need not (and often will not) be exactly the same: different devices have different characteristics, and hence different requirements for handling data. Conversion of data into and out of the various formats used by peripheral devices must itself be handled by microelectronic circuitry, or by software instructions that can be translated into circuit operations. Sometimes, all the necessary conversion is carried out by circuitry that is embodied in the peripheral device; sometimes it must be done by the computer. In either case, what is required is a software/firmware/hardware tool known as an 'operating system'.

Proprietary operating systems, designed and sold for use with a variety of different computers, may in fact include not only peripheral handling routines but also a range of other systems software: compilers and interpreters for various languages, machine-code routines to simplify computer operations, and so on. Among the best known of these are CP/M and Flex. These systems were developed to provide a standard for formatting and encoding data, for use on a range of computers using specified bus systems and chips. CP/M, for instance, is for use on computers based around Z80 or 8080 microprocessor chips, amongst others, and using S-100 buses. Flex works on SS-50 bus-based systems, using the 6800 chip and later derivatives. (We look at these standard hardware items in Chapter 14.) Both have routines for allocating file space, and for compressing and expanding nominated files on the disc when the original space allocation proves inadequate or inefficient.

Disc operating systems such as these take up a moderate amount of internal memory space and are designed to handle a fair amount of memory on disc. CP/M takes up around 4K of ROM and demands around 24K of RAM to handle its programs. It can – and needs to – handle at least 250K of disc memory space. Flex demands a minimum of 20K RAM and controls a dual disc drive with around 160K memory capacity.

The standardization at which such systems aim is intended to help improve the portability of software developed to work on the system. Some success has been achieved, but portability is a difficult issue, and problems can arise when trying to use software developed for one system on another, even when the same operating system is being used.

Applications Software

Applications software is what we generally think of as programs: listings of instructions and data in a computer language, input to the system and then run to make the system *do* something. It covers the sort of applications we look at later in this book: controlling machinery, performing calculations, handling files of business data and so on. In fact, any computer application at all demands a program in some form to control it.

There is of course a grey area in which applications software shades into systems software. Word processor packages, for instance, may enhance the computer's basic information-processing abilities in ways that seem to be system-based, rather than application-based: though word processing is often thought of as a computer application. (And, of course, word processors are themselves special-purpose computers, programmed by a mixture of hardware and software to perform this specialized range of tasks.) Database management systems are an essential tool in handling complex files of data, and this is often regarded as an application; at the same time, however, they are first cousins to disc operating systems that are thought of as systems software; and so on.

Particularly in this grey area of programs that can be used not only for outside applications but also as a systems tool by other, more specific application programs, some applications software is sold – as is so much systems software – in firmware form. Special ROM chips provide accounting packages, word processing packages, voice recognition circuitry and so on. As ROM technology develops, and the user market grows ever larger (for this technique is only practicable for programs designed to be sold in relatively large numbers), so this current tendency towards producing programs in the form of firmware, which is easier to handle and more compact than programs stored in disc or tape, may be expected to accelerate.

Intimate Software

Every commercially available computer system has some software capabilities incorporated into it: not just a basic set of instructions, but operating routines, compilers or interpreters, and other systems software tools. This software is sold as part of the computer system: it takes up part of the computer's internal memory capacity, and it cannot be removed. It is often referred to as 'intimate software'.

What distinguishes intimate software is not its function: it is just a subset (determined and selected by the computer manufacturer) of the potentially available systems software. It is not its physical form: it is generally found in ROM form; but plug-in ROM chips bought separately from the manufacturers of the computers into which they are to be plugged are not intimate software. It is simply the fact that intimate software is part of the basic computer system, and helps to determine the system's unique characteristics.

Subroutine Libraries

We have already mentioned that the computer's basic instruction set is effectively complemented by the presence in its intimate software of a library of subroutines. These can be called up by application programs just as if they were hardware programmed instructions.

What sort of instructions might a library of subroutines include? These are typical examples:

Algebraic functions: Square roots, logs, exponentials, trigonometric functions.

Matrix algebra: An assortment of ways of manipulating algebraic data, including routines for the solution of simultaneous equations.

Sorting routines: For putting arrays into alpha/numeric or some other defined order.

Input and output routines: Decimal to binary (and vice versa) conversion routines, facilities for reading characters from keyboards and to display screens.

Filing functions: (See the section on filing systems, below.)

Peripheral control: Routines for handling tapes, discs and data communications.

Operating routines: For controlling interrupts, etc.

System tests: Routines that generate warnings to the user if system malfunctions are detected.

Filing Systems

A filing system is a way of holding data in a permanent storage medium (that is, one whose contents are not lost when power is switched off, though they can be altered if necessary; typically, a secondary storage medium such as magnetic tape or a floppy disc) in an orderly way. The system itself is created and managed by software, though it will be dovetailed with hardware aspects of the storage medium itself (the sequence of data storage and retrieval, the length of any 'fields' or 'pages' of storage space in hardware terms, and so on).

What does the software do? Basically, it:

sets up the concept of 'files' or 'documents' (the term used depends upon the type of system), by allocating space in the system to them and defining their necessary attributes, and provides a means for the user to name them, and designate where they start and end;

supports the addition, retrieval and updating of stored material;

manages the efficient allocation of space in the storage medium;

may control access to file contents (for instance, by asking the user for a password);

supports the copying of filed data, for security purposes.

We will look at some aspects of file structure in Chapter 25.

Editing and Debugging Programs

Editing and debugging programs are sometimes differentiated from each other, but they perform a similar function: allowing the user to amend data held in the computer. The data may be routine file contents to be altered or may be a program listing that needs to be tested and amended where necessary ('debugged', in computer jargon) before it will run correctly.

If data are stored sequentially, or in a compressed array structure where every storage location is full, it is not easy to amend or add to the data efficiently while leaving other portions of the data sequence (the file, document or whatever) unchanged. Editing programs use a variety of methods to enable data to be changed safely (without losing the original version until its successor is safely stored) and economically (leaving a new version that makes equally efficient use of memory space). They may, for instance, copy the entire document to be edited (including the required changes, that would be entered interactively while the contents are on display) into a new set of storage locations, and then delete the previous version.

Word processing programs generally provide comprehensive editing routines. However, editing is also applicable to forms of stored data other than alpha/numeric characters: data on graphics, stored sounds, numerical data or whatever.

'Debugging' a new program is a particularly complex business; and if the program is long and involved in structure, it may be all but impossible to test its running exhaustively and guarantee its correctness. However, a variety of hardware and software devices have been developed as aids to programmers, to assist in the debugging operation.

We encountered some debugging facilities in describing the operation of a monitor program on pages 142 to 143. In effect, a monitor acts as (among other things) a debugging program. Other debugging tools include:

simulators that simulate the running of a program in a computer, but provide information (which the programmer would not receive during normal operation) on the computer activity that the program generates. Simulators for complex programs are slow and expensive to use: they may run up to 10,000 times slower than would the same program under normal operation. However, they can be invaluable in helping the programmer to track down obscure programming faults;

disassemblers that can convert a binary-coded program back into a mnemonic code, as an aid to analysing its contents;

logic analysers, hardware devices that simulate the movement of data in a c.p.u.'s registers.

The Development of Software

The first commercial computers, like their more experimental predecessors, were laborious to program. Each program step had to be written in machine code; the address in memory or working register in which each piece of data or instruction was to be stored had to be specified by the programmer. The detailed working-out demanded by these requirements made programming a difficult job and limited the complexity of programs that could be written.

Slowly, this state of affairs improved. The symbolic addressing techniques that we look at in detail in Chapter 10 made compiling a program a much simpler task. Concepts such as the use of a library of subroutines also made programming less laborious; steadily, the idea of high-level languages evolved. In parallel with language development came a slow development in systems software: not only in subroutines and addressing techniques, but in the general control of processing operations, eventually leading to the development of the first proprietary operating systems. Simultaneously, the hardware methods of inputting programs were also improved. The first programmers had to set registers and flick switches; their successors today simply type instructions on to a keyboard.

Perhaps the first commercial programmer was Grace Hopper. She was responsible for programming the experimental Mark 1 machine built at Harvard, and later worked on the Univac I and II, developing probably the first commercially oriented programming language, FLOW-MATIC. Early software development was, not surprisingly, extremely machine-specific: it was sponsored by individual manufacturers and was aimed at making the best possible use of the hardware features of their machines.

The development of FORTRAN, a programming language designed primarily for scientific applications, typified this approach. It was an I.B.M. development, begun in 1954. The development team, headed by John Backus, is reputed to have spent twenty-five man-years developing the first FORTRAN compiler. Typically of almost all software, it was delivered late, and with a number of bugs! The language was first put to use on the 704 machines in 1957.

Many industry commentators criticized the reliance upon manufacturer-developed software. They felt that a measure of standardization was desirable, and that languages should not be developed solely for use on one machine, or on one manufacturer's range. The next step, in consequence, was the setting-up of a plethora of organizations and committees aimed at developing common computer languages.

A.C.M., the Association for Computing Machinery, set up their committee in 1957 to work on a universal programming language that they hoped would avoid FORTRAN's failings. Their work led in 1958 to the first publication of an ALGOL standard; numerous revisions have followed. ALGOL was widely accepted in Europe, where there were a number of sizeable home-grown computer companies; in the U.S.A., I.B.M.'s predominance meant that FORTRAN was to remain pre-eminent.

FORTRAN and ALGOL were both unashamedly oriented towards science and mathematics. The developing commercial applications, dependent more on data shuffling than on number crunching, demanded a language with a different orientation. A meeting held at the Pentagon in 1959 led to the formation of a Conference on Data Systems Languages (CODASYL), and to the setting-up of committees with a brief to develop a hardware-independent business language. COBOL, the result, is still widely used today.

Once languages become accepted, inertia tends to lead to their continuing life. Programmers familiar with, say, COBOL may not wish to start afresh with a newer and better language; programs written in COBOL continue to be used and revised. The languages of this early period are still widely used today, even though many others have since been developed, either as attempts to improve upon the originals, or as special languages for specialist applications.

At this point, we should mention one other language: BASIC, developed at Dartmouth College, U.S., in the early 1960s. BASIC was specifically designed as a language for non-professional computer-users who wanted to be able to write simple programs quickly. It began as a short, simple language, but has been much developed and extended since: many of the extant versions are not notably simpler than other languages used by professional programmers. However, it has become *the* language of personal computing, supported by the vast majority of small computer manufacturers and used by millions of part-time programmers. Though many people claim that rival languages like Pascal have more to offer, the sheer volume of BASIC programmers and BASIC programs now available means that it will be difficult, if not impossible, to supplant it.

We provide a brief rundown of some of the main high-level languages and their distinguishing features on pages 344 to 345.

The Development of Systems Software

Much of the initial work on systems software, other than language compilers and interpreters, was also carried out by I.B.M. The work done for their series 702, 704 and 705 machines is typical of the first systems software developments. It included the development of: job sequencing facilities, and other basic routines found in monitor programs today; a library of subroutines; and better addressing techniques. By late 1956, I.B.M. had developed a full-scale operating system, albeit one that does not compare with the sophistication of today's offerings. SHARE Operating System (S.O.S.) was available on their 709 series.

In the late 1950s and early 1960s, provision of at least a basic range of systems software was normal with all commercial computers. The following facilities were typical:

a 'job monitor' program, to control the linkages between successive programs run on the same machine;

a low-level assembler, to 'assemble' mnemonic code into machine code;

a high-level language compiler, usually for FORTRAN, COBOL or ALGOL;

a load program, that often needed to be bootstrapped into the system by the operator;

and a library of subroutines and operating utilities (typically, these were held in tape form).

In Chapter 6 we traced how multi-user systems and multiprogramming became a major feature of computing in the 1960s. Multiprogramming demanded much more complex operating routines to handle the allocation of memory space and processing time to the different programs being interleaved. Perhaps the first operable system to do this was that designed for the ATLAS machine at Manchester University, England, in 1959.

An offshoot of the multiprogramming era provides the dominant content of operating systems today: routines for the handling of interrupts, and for switching between different input and output devices. These led, in turn, to the emergence of interactive programming techniques. Development of this area, and the improvement and extension of system monitoring facilities, were the prime areas for software development over the next few years. By the mid-1960s, the basic ingredients of today's systems software were all in place. Much refinement and improvement has been undertaken since, of course; but for the majority of routine commercial and personal computer applications, the software tools developed over the first ten years or so of commercial computing are those still in use today.

10. Techniques for Addressing Memory

In this chapter, we shall be building on our earlier description of how the c.p.u. handles control operations, by looking at how it keeps track of the addresses of program instructions, and particularly of data required by the program.

The operations that we discuss in this section are all operations that must be understood – and specified – by the machine code or assembly language programmer. When a computer is programmed in a high-level language, its systems software and operating system will handle many of the tasks of controlling the location of data and instructions. However, understanding how such control operations function on a machine-code level is essential to understanding the operation of the computer as a whole, and not just to learning machine-code programming.

There are a number of different modes of addressing, or ways in which the address of a location whose contents are required by the c.p.u., can be specified. Individual processors and computer systems do not utilize any of these uniquely; depending upon the requirements of the individual program, they will make use of several of them. Each mode has its own merits. However, not all c.p.u.'s have the facilities to use all the addressing modes we shall describe: they may lack either necessary registers, or necessary instructions in their basic set.

Programs in Memory

Of course, many programs operate in an interactive mode, with the computer requesting and receiving fresh input from the user in the course of the program execution. Control programs rely upon data from the processes they control, fed from sensors; and this again they receive in the course of program execution. In short, the program need not be self-contained; it spills out into data and instructions that are received from the outside world. For clarity, though, we shall talk in this section as if all the program instructions, and all the data that will be required in the course of its execution, have been stored in RAM before the program is run. The c.p.u. simply carries out the program instructions in the prescribed sequence, obtaining data and instructions from memory when it is instructed to do so. In principle, the procedures used for interacting with input and output devices, and secondary memory media, are no different from those we describe here, and the simple operations we describe can be extrapolated into the more complex operations handled by large-scale real-life computer systems, obtaining data and instructions from a variety of sources and perhaps running a number of programs simultaneously.

The program in memory (as we shall think of it) consists of a series of computer 'words' that the c.p.u. fetches: either in a sequence determined by the order of the addresses of the memory locations in which they are stored, or otherwise as it is instructed to do by previous instructions. The length of these words (usually 4-, 8-, 16- or possibly 32-bit) depends upon the computer architecture, and is fixed for any specific computer. The longer the word, the fewer different words are needed to encompass some complex instructions. There are a number of program instructions that *do* take up more than one 8-bit (or longer) word to specify. In this case, the control unit will fetch the first word and be instructed by that to fetch the next, and so on, until it has obtained the full instruction and can perform the required operation.

The control unit keeps track of where it is in running the program, by keeping track of the addresses of the words that comprise the program. This is done — as we mentioned earlier — by a special register in the c.p.u. known as a program counter. The program counter does not hold program instructions; it holds the addresses of the locations in memory (one at a time, of course) that hold the program instructions. If more than one 'current address' needs to be held (for instance, if control has been delegated to a subroutine, and the c.p.u. must keep track of its place in the subroutine, but must then be able to revert to the original point in the program), then an additional set of storage locations, the stack, controlled by the stack pointer, can be brought into play.

What do Program Instructions Consist of?

A 'program instruction' is a section of the program that comprises all the information the c.p.u. needs in order to be able to carry out an operation. 'Instruction' is the term normally applied to sections of machine-code programs; the building blocks of high-level language programs are 'statements' and may encompass more than one basic instruction. Each instruction will consist of:

one or more commands or instruction codes or operating codes (different phrases meaning much the same thing), that tell the c.p.u. exactly what operation it is required to perform;

any data that may be required by the operation;

or the address in memory, or specific register in the c.p.u. itself, in which any data required by the operation is to be found (the commands in the statement will include a command to fetch any data, not already located in the c.p.u., that is required by the operation).

All these various parts of the instruction are encoded in the same binary form; but the fixed structure of which the instruction is made will ensure that the c.p.u. interprets some coded digits as commands, some as data and some as addresses.

Let us make that a little clearer by looking at some typical program instructions.

Eight-bit (one-byte) instructions: instructions using one-byte-long words, but possibly more than one of them):

These might comprise:

(1) a single word that designates the operation to be carried out on data already available in the c.p.u.'s accumulator or registers. The 'operating code' will specify *what* the basic operation (arithmetic, logic, or data movement) is, *where* in the c.p.u. the data are to be found, and *where* the data that result are to be placed. So the code (one from a set of up to 256 that can be specified in that one byte of memory space) might say, for instance:

   (a) add the contents of register A to the accumulator; or

   (b) move the contents of register B to register A; or

   (c) divide the contents of the accumulator by the contents of register C, and leave the result in the accumulator.

(2) two words: one to designate the operation to be carried out (from the set of operating codes we have just mentioned) and one giving either:

   (a) a necessary piece of data; or

   (b) the address at which a necessary piece of data is to be found.

   The operating code itself will have to specify whether the second byte contains data or an address.

(3) three words: one for the operating code and either:

   (a) two addresses or pieces of data required (for instance, two numbers to be added together); or

   (b) a single address or piece of data that takes up two bytes to specify.

As you will realize, the 256 operating codes that can be specified in one byte do not seem so many, once all the permutations of locations available for data in the c.p.u., and of data/address formats, have been taken into account. Only a limited number of possible movements between data registers can be catered for in a single 256-code set in which every register specified demands a different code, for instance. A longer operating code permits more permutations to be incorporated into the set, and hence gives the c.p.u. greater power and flexibility. However, a longer code demands not an eight-bit, but a sixteen-bit formula.

Sixteen-bit (two-byte) instructions:

These might comprise:

(1) two different instructions that might both be included in a single sixteen-bit word, if they can be described succinctly. If this possibility

is to be allowed for, then one bit from the sixteen has to be used to designate the fact that the word is to be read in two halves.

(2) a one-word instruction, complete in itself, just as a one-byte instruction can be. The single word is unlikely to include data or an address; aspects of the operating code will take up its entire length. It *will* include details like:

(a) the type of operation to be performed;

(b) the addressing mode used (a matter we come to shortly);

(c) where the data (or data address) is to be found;

(d) where the data is to be deposited after the operation.

(3) a two- or three-word instruction, including data or addresses, as well as an operating code. The number of words required will depend on:

(a) the amount of data required by the operation (none, one or two pieces);

(b) the complexity of the addressing mode used to locate the data.

Table 7: Typical Program Instruction Formats

Eight-Bit Instructions

One word: Op. Code (8 binary digits)

Two words: (1) Op. Code (8 binary digits)
               (2) Operand or address of operand (8 binary digits)

Three words: (1) Op. Code (8 binary digits)
               (2) First operand or address of operand (8 binary digits)
               (3) Second operand or address of operand (8 binary digits)

Sixteen-Bit Instructions

One word:

Digits:	
0–2:	Op. Code
3:	Bit to divide word into two instructions or keep as one
4–5:	Addressing mode to locate destination of data (in one-word format, will be inherent or immediate)
6–9:	Actual data
10–11:	Addressing mode to locate source of data (inherent or immediate)
12–15:	Actual data

Two words:
Word 1 digits:

0–3:	As one-word above
4–5:	Addressing mode to locate destination of data
6–9:	Data or address
10–11:	Addressing mode to locate source of data
12–15:	Data or address
Word 2:	Source or destination data address (16 digits)

Three words:

Words 1 and 2:	As for two-word instructions
Word 3:	Second (source or destination) address

Table 7 should help to make this question of instruction formats a little clearer. A single c.p.u. may make use of several instruction formats for different purposes.

Now we must look at the various methods used to specify where data required by the c.p.u. for a processing operation are located.

Immediate Addressing

As we have just seen, some instruction formats make use of two or three words: one for the operating code, and the succeeding words for the necessary data. In effect, the operating code is announcing, 'The data are coming up next.' The program counter indicates the address of the data: nothing else is required in order to obtain it.

Immediate addressing may seem direct and simple, but it is also limited in its uses. The data are in effect part of the program itself: a constant, that cannot be changed by the outcome of program operations. It is often desirable to change data (while using their address in memory to preserve their identity), and immediate addressing is no use for this purpose. It *can* be used to set registers and memory locations to the required initial values — in others words, to initialize them — before a program is run.

Inherent or Register Addressing

Sometimes the entire address of the data is included in the program instruction; sometimes the instruction merely indicates how the address can be obtained. One addressing mode that uses the former approach is known as inherent or register addressing.

You will recall that when the data are located, not in memory, but in a register in the c.p.u. itself, it is possible to indicate their location as part of the operating code. In other words, the operating code will instruct the c.p.u., for example, to 'add the contents of register C to the accumulator'. The data are in register C; the code gives this address information in full.

Inherent addressing is so called because the address is inherent in the operating code itself. It is also known as register addressing, because this method of providing the address is only possible when the address is a register. There are not enough operating codes available for it to be possible for memory locations to be specified individually in them. However, it *is* possible to use a separate operating code to specify each of a small range of registers.

Direct Addressing

Direct addressing is another method of directly indicating the address of the data in the program instruction. This time, however, it is not incorporated in the operating code, but is provided in an additional word of the instruction, just as are the data in immediate addressing. Note the difference: in immediate addressing, the instruction contains the data, while in direct addressing, the instruction merely contains the address of the data.

Direct addressing is a slow process, for the c.p.u. has to:

read the first word of the instruction, that contains the operating code and an indication that direct addressing is being used;

read the second word, to obtain the address;

fetch the data from the address indicated in RAM.

These three separate operations may be contrasted with the single operation required by inherent addressing, or the two of immediate addressing.

However, direct addressing is useful, or even essential, in some circumstances. It is often used:

when no register is available to hold either the data or their address;

when a single variable is used only occasionally in the course of a long program;

as a means of changing the program counter contents when the program execution 'jumps' to a new point.

The efficiency of direct addressing can be enhanced if memory is organized in a way known as 'paging'. Only a specified section of a paged memory is available to the c.p.u. at any particular point in time, and the address need only be pinpointed from among this limited range. As a result, to specify the address might take up only one byte instead of two. Of course, if the address is *not* in this range, then difficulties arise! We return to look at the concept of paging in detail on page 161.

Register Indirect Addressing

With this type of addressing, the address of the data (in memory, not in a register) is contained not in the instruction but in a register which is designated in the instruction. The c.p.u. reads the (normally) single-word instruction, then fetches the data from the address held in the register designated.

Register indirect addressing may seem like a cumbersome process compared to the more direct ways of obtaining data, but in fact it is a very flexible and practicable method. It is particularly convenient when a long sequence of data needs to be obtained. The same instruction (for example, instructing the c.p.u. to perform a special operation on the data in the memory location specified in register C) can be repeated again and again, and the value in the register changed, perhaps simply by incrementing it, between each of the repetitions.

Indexed Addressing

This is a variation on register indirect addressing that is used only by some c.p.u.s. Again, it is particularly useful (and is indeed the simplest method of addressing, though slower in use than register indirect addressing) when large amounts of data are to be moved around in the computer's memory banks and registers.

Indexed addressing makes use of a special register known as the index register, that is used to hold a 'base value' from which the actual address of the data can be built up. The program instruction indicates how this base value is to be altered, usually by adding to it an 'offset' value that is given in the instruction. The code then obtained represents the address of the data.

Indexed addressing normally requires two words of program instruction: one to indicate the operation to be performed, and that indexed addressing is being used, and one to provide the offset value. A variation, auto-indexed addressing, provides instead for the index register to be incremented or decremented automatically each time an address is read from it.

Relative Addressing

Relative addressing is used primarily – as direct addressing sometimes is – for providing the address, not of data, but of instructions, when the program branches from the sequence laid down by its pattern in memory. It works rather like indexed addressing, in that an offset value is provided in the program instruction; but this time the value is added (or subtracted) not to the index register but to the program counter. The program counter then contains the address of the information to be accessed: this may be a new program instruction or may be a piece of data, stored among the program instructions, and referred to frequently in the course of a short sequence of instructions.

Relative addressing (which is not found in all c.p.u. instruction sets) is less efficient than immediate addressing, but is considerably more flexible. However, it can only be used to refer to a range, normally of 256 memory locations around that in which the program instruction last implemented was stored. If it is necessary to refer to a location outside this range, it becomes necessary to use the slower direct addressing or some other addressing mode.

Paging

Paging is the technique of dividing up the total memory space available to the c.p.u. into blocks, each containing a specific number of memory locations. The size of the block is normally a multiple of 256 bytes: many c.p.u.'s utilizing paging employ large 'pages' of anything up to 8K bytes each. This technique is particularly useful for some types of computer application in which data are handled in discrete blocks; it is essential to ensure that operations performed on one block of data do not accidentally corrupt another block. Word processing (where the printed pages provide a natural division) and file handling (where a number of files are separately manipulated in parallel) are obvious examples of such applications.

A true 'paged' system limits the c.p.u. to operation in only one page at a time. A specific operation is required to move the program counter on to a different page in memory; it does not 'carry' automatically across page boundaries. And a special addressing procedure has to be used if data stored in another page have to be accessed.

Many systems use aspects of the paging method without actually carrying the concept through to their architecture, as do true paged machines. As we saw, the relative addressing technique is limited to a range of locations around the program counter locations that form a kind of floating 'page' of data. However, this is only a pseudo-page: unlike a true page, it has no fixed boundaries.

Indirect Addressing

In order to access data stored on a page in memory other than that to which the program counter gives direct access, paged machines make use of a specialized addressing technique known as indirect addressing. In this technique, a specific series of locations in memory are first accessed, using one of the addressing modes we have already discussed. These locations contain, not data, but the full address (including the page designation) of the actual data required — which are stored on a different page. Only once this information has been obtained can the c.p.u. proceed to obtain the data proper.

Table 8 summarizes the features of the various addressing modes.

Table 8: Summary of Addressing Modes

Mode of addressing	Address found in	Data found in
auto-indexed	index register	memory
direct	program statement (second/third word)	memory

Mode of addressing	Address found in	Data found in
immediate	program counter	program statement (second/third word)
indexed	index register plus program statement	memory
indirect	memory	memory
inherent (register)	program statement (op. code)	register
register indirect	register	memory
relative	program counter plus program statement	memory

Stacking

What is a stack? It is a specially designated set of data storage locations, either in memory or in the c.p.u. itself (that is, a set of registers) that can be used for storing data or memory addresses in a particular ordered manner.

The 'stack' concept refers to the fact that the information is added to the stack one piece at a time, and that it is retrieved from the stack on a 'last in – first out' basis. In other words, information is 'pushed down' the stack so that there is always room for a new piece to be added to the top of the stack, or 'pulled up' it, one location after another, so that the next piece can be easily retrieved.

Stacks are commonly used for storing the addresses of program instructions during a 'nest' of subroutines: a subroutine that calls up another subroutine, and so on. The addresses in the stack, which are taken from and sent to the program counter at the appropriate points in the program, tell the c.p.u. where to obtain the next program instruction at the start or end of a particular set of subroutine operations.

The contents of the stack are kept track of by a special register, called a stack pointer. (We discussed this on page 134.) It normally contains the address of the currently available empty location in the stack: that is, the location to which the next piece of information to be added will be sent.

This brief summary of addressing modes and associated matters may seem confusing at this stage. However, its relevance will be clear when we come to look at programming in machine code, in which the programmer has to select and use an addressing mode for each instruction to be carried out. You may like to look ahead now to page 279 where we list the instruction codes for the 6502 microprocessor. You will see that the microprocessor's range of addressing modes is clearly reflected in its instruction set.

11. A Simple Microprocessor: The 6502

Now that we know a little more about the c.p.u. and how it works, let us put that knowledge to practice, and look at how one typical modern microprocessor is organized. Figure 36 is a schematic of the layout of the 6502, a microprocessor found in many recent models of microcomputer – including one that we shall be looking at later in this book.

The Arithmetic/Logic Unit

The 6502 is an eight-bit microprocessor: its arithmetic/logic unit works with eight bits, and most of its communications operations also work with eight bits. There is a 'carry' facility in the processor, so that longer numbers can be handled, and an overflow indicator, to show if an arithmetical operation has 'overflowed' the processing capacity of the arithmetic/logic unit (a.l.u.), giving a wrong answer.

As you can see from the diagram, the a.l.u. is directly connected to the accumulator, and can access registers and memory locations via the data bus.

The a.l.u. can perform the following arithmetic operations:

(1) adding the contents of a memory/register location to the accumulator, with a carry bit if required, in the lowest bit position (to allow for high precision arithmetic on long numbers). There are three basic ways in which arithmetic operations can be specified:

(a) all binary numbers may be considered as positive, giving a range of binary numbers to be handled in the a.l.u.'s eight bits of 0 to 255;

(b) binary numbers may be designated as either positive or negative. One of the eight bits must then be used as a 'sign' bit, so the effective range is −128 to +127;

(c) instead of true binary arithmetic, the a.l.u. can work in 'binary-coded decimal', in which each set of four bits is used to represent one decimal digit (0 to 9). So one eight-bit word can hold two decimal digits, making up one of the numbers, 0 to 99.

(2) subtracting the contents of a memory/register location from the accumulator, with a borrow bit.

And the following logical operations:

(3) AND the contents of a memory/register location with the contents of the accumulator. The result is placed in the accumulator; flags in the flag register are also set by the operation, as follows:

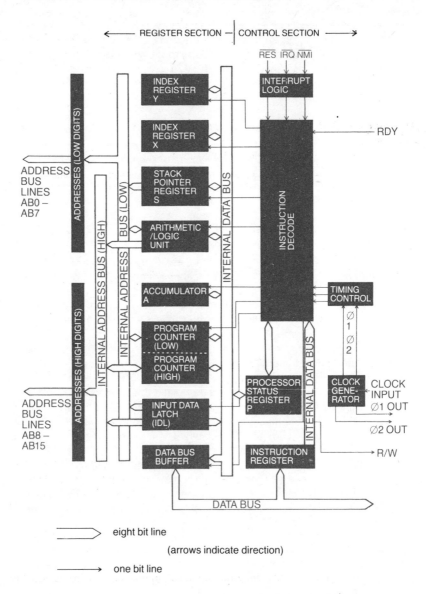

Figure 36: Internal architecture of the 6502 microprocessor

(a) if the result is zero, the zero flag is set;

(b) if the most significant bit of the result is 1, the negative flag is set.

(4) OR the contents of a memory/register location and the contents of the accumulator. This works similarly, but using an OR logic configuration.

(5) Exclusive OR the contents of a memory/register location and the contents of the accumulator. This works on a bit-by-bit basis, and the result is placed in the accumulator. It can be used as a step in complementing data (producing its opposite, as we saw on pages 29 to 30).

This is the sum total of the a.l.u.'s instruction set. Any other instructions that can be handled by the processor's internal instruction set need to be specified in terms of these basic building blocks, as we shall see later.

Registers

The 6502 has the following registers:

(1) Two index registers, known as 'X' and 'Y'. These are in effect flexible data/data address/index registers, as we shall see when we write some simple programs using this microprocessor, in Chapter 24. Control instructions enable the programmer to:

(a) increment or decrement their contents;

(b) compare their contents with those of a memory location;

(c) transfer the data they contain to and from the accumulator;

(d) load data from, or store data in, memory.

(2) A stack pointer. A fixed 'page' of 256 locations in the computer's RAM is designated as the stacking area; the stack pointer 'points' to the required address in this area. It is an eight-bit register that can, by this method, point to any of 256 pre-designated locations in the computer's memory.

(3) A program counter. This is a two-byte register, divided into two sections shown on the diagram as program counter (low), and program counter (high). This enables it to specify any one of 2^{16}, or 64K memory locations.

(4) The accumulator (A), another eight-bit register with a special set of instructions defining its potential uses.

(5) A flag status register (known for the 6502 as the 'processor status register', P). This has eight bits that are used as follows:

(a) a 'carry' flag (C);

(b) a 'zero' flag (Z), set when the result in the accumulator is equal to zero;

(c) an interrupt disable flag (I), that controls the interrupt operations;

(d) a decimal mode flag (D), that is set when the a.l.u. is used to perform binary-coded decimal, rather than true binary, operations.

(e) a 'break command' flag (B), that also reflects the activity involved in an interrupt sequence;

(f) a spare bit, for which the manufacturer has not designated any use;

(g) an overflow flag (V), that indicates whether a seven-bit signed number 'overflows' to affect the eighth, sign bit;

(h) a negative flag (N), that indicates, when signed numbers are being used, whether the result in the accumulator is negative or positive.

(6) Finally, an instruction register is used to hold instructions retrieved from memory, and input to the c.p.u. along the data bus.

Control Functions

You can see marked on Figure 36 the parts of the 6502 that handle the various control functions we discussed earlier. They are:

(1) Timing control. The 6502 has a built-in clock that receives signals from an outside periodic unit. It converts these into the timing signals the system requires, and sends them to the instruction decoder.

(2) The instruction decoder. This interprets instructions held in the instruction register, and (subject to timing and interrupt signals) transmits the appropriate signals to the a.l.u. and the working registers.

(3) The interrupt logic unit. Like the other control units, we shall not look at how this works in detail. (We do discuss further the outline of interrupt operations in Chapter 15 and in Chapter 24.) It does, of course, use the same basic electronic building blocks to provide it with a range of logical control operations.

A Bus Network

The network of data, address and control buses is also sketched out on the diagram.

12. Input and Output Handling

When we speak broadly of computer input or output devices, we are in fact speaking of two different classes of device. First, there are devices that are quite literally used to send data to the computer: keyboards, light pens, sensors and so on; and those used to receive data from it: printers, pen plotters, visual display screens and so on. Second, there are devices that handle the control operations associated with the input and output handling. Some pieces of equipment perform both these functions; others may handle one, but not the other.

We can break down this distinction between actual peripheral devices, performing the functions of input and output, and input/output (i/o) handling devices (that need not be peripheral devices) still further, and describe four quite separate functions involved in the input or output operation. I/o devices of both classes (considered together) serve to:

(1) receive data from the user, or from the system being controlled by the computer (input), or send data back to the user or system (output);

(2) convert those data into or out of a suitable form for storage and/or processing;

(3) hold the data, if necessary, until they can be handled by other computer resources (input) or by the output peripheral (output);

(4) make the data available for transmission to (input) or receive data transmitted by (output) other functional parts of the computer, as dictated by the system's control signals.

Devices that Obtain Data

A wide range of different devices are used to obtain data from various sources, and to make it available to both small and large computer systems. They include:

keyboard and touch-sensitive keypads, for inputting alpha/numeric data;

levers, knobs or joysticks, for the input of positional data (the desired movement 'left', 'right', 'up' or 'down' of a 'bat' in a video game, for instance);

electronic pads, on which can be written diagrams, signatures and so on;

light pens, for inputting two-dimensional visual data;

direct sensors, that relay information on the status of process variables: temperature, pressure, rate of flow of a substance, and so on;

special input devices that make use of the limited physical abilities of
    physically handicapped people;
voice input systems, 'trained' to interpret a limited vocabulary of command
    and data words.

Some of these devices demand initiation of the input by a human being;
others actively obtain the information when directed to do so by computer-
generated control signals. Whatever the type of device, though, it will act as
an 'interface' between the source of the data (the person or the process)
and the computer itself. In other words, it will have the ability itself, or be
connectable to a device that has the ability, to convert the input into a form
that the computer can handle. For digital computers, this will normally be a
binary coded electronic signal; for analog devices, the conversion may be
entirely different. We shall not consider analog devices further in this
chapter.

Devices that Output Data

Among the most common of these are:
printers (considered in Chapter 18);
visual display units (see pages 212 to 217);
actuators, that initiate physical actions (throwing switches, opening valves,
    etc.).

Devices that Convert Data

We cannot analyse all the processes necessary to convert all the possible
types of input data into a computer-compatible form, or to reconvert
computer-processed data into a humanly digestible form; but we shall look
briefly at some typical conversion processes.

Alpha/numeric data are normally converted either:
(a) into the equivalent binary numbers, ready for numerical processing; or
(b) into an alpha/numeric binary code like the ASCII code we looked at on
page 25.

Sensory input on a continuously variable property like temperature or
pressure is measured at regular intervals, effectively converting it from
analog to digital form. The digital measurements may be made in binary
form, or converted into binary for further processing.

Voice input or *handwritten input*, such as a signature for verification, is
analysed by measuring special characteristics that will help in identifying it.
A signature, for instance, will be recognized or rejected by assessing the
match, not between the stored and the newly input forms of particular
letters, but between the stored and input versions of features like: the area
covered; the number of up- and down-strokes made; the length of the line

of writing; the time taken to write it; the sequence in which 'i's are dotted, and 't's crossed.

Graphical input from an electronic pad can be analysed by breaking down the writing surface into a grid or array of separate segments, and storing data on what, if anything, is contained in each. We look at this process in more detail when we come to consider computer graphics on page 214.

Data intended for *printed output* must be converted into the characters used by the printer: selection of a number of dots from a matrix, or of a character on a daisy wheel print unit, for instance.

Data intended for *visual output* must be converted into on-screen symbols. We look at some of the processes involved in this in Chapter 17.

As well as simply coding input into binary form, or converting it from binary, an i/o device must perform three other conversion tasks:

(1) The input device must reorganize the data into binary 'words', of the length used by the processor (maybe 4, 8, 16 or 32 bits). Binary numbers that will not fit into a single computer word length, for instance, must either be rounded off or spread across a number of words that can be linked together (with 'carry' procedures for use during arithmetic operations, for example). Data derived from other types of input might also need to be stored in a number of locations, and these in turn linked together. Similarly, the output device must reorganize the data into the word length demanded by output channels.

(2) Much input comes — and, indeed, output goes — in serial form (one bit after another) rather than in parallel form (all the bits in a word of the length used in the system simultaneously). Serial transmission of data is less expensive than parallel transmission, so this is particularly true of data transmitted from other computers or electronic devices. If the computer handles data in a parallel form, then the i/o handling device must convert its serial i/o into the required format, storing the digits as they are received until a full word is obtained. Similarly, if the input is parallel but the number of data lines differs from that used in the computer, a conversion will need to be made. An output device will need to store subsequent bits of parallel words while the initial bits are sent serially.

(3) All operations within the computer are normally synchronized by a clock or timing signal. The input may not arrive at the time-intervals prescribed, and an input device must handle the task of synchronizing the data flow with the processing operations. Similarly, an output handling device may need to synchronize its output with the reception abilities of an output peripheral.

I/o devices are commonly categorized as being either synchronous or asynchronous. A synchronous device is one that works at the same clocked intervals as the c.p.u.: regulating its own timer so that it is synchronized with that of the c.p.u., or making use of the c.p.u.'s clock pulses. An asynchronous device may also work at clocked intervals, but these are *not* determined by the c.p.u., but by the device's own clock, or the clock of some external device.

Data Storage in I/o Devices

Some input handling devices always accept input, and output devices always output: they function in one direction only. Other devices can be programmed to handle either input or output. A special register within the device contains data as to which channels are acting as input channels, and which as output channels. (A 0 will designate one type of channel, and a 1 the other.)

Inevitably, the i/o handling system needs some additional storage capacity. It will need to store data, for instance:
(1) while serial data are being amassed into a group for parallel transmission;
(2) while data received between clock pulses are awaiting synchronous transmission;
(3) in a general 'buffer' until a destination for the data is made available;
(4) while waiting for the processor to interrupt processing activities and turn its attention (in other words, its control signals) to the input operation. We next look in a little more detail at this interrupt function.

Interrupt Procedures

The normal task of a c.p.u. is to process data, and usually it will proceed to carry out all the processing required by a particular program, in the order designated by the program instructions, until it has completed the task. When the processing task is interrupted so that the c.p.u. can handle new input, this is done by a special signal known as an 'interrupt signal'.

Interrupt signals may be handled in one of two ways:
(1) input may be 'looked for' only when the program instructions tell the computer to check to see if input is available, or at the end of a run;
(2) interrupt signals may be able to override the processing operation in predefined ways, allowing the processor to attend rapidly to randomly occurring or unexpected input.

The first, simple method is suitable for use in very simple computer systems. However, both efficient, accurate arithmetic in complex situations, and interactive operations, such as handling the flow of communications through a complex system, demand the provision of more complex interrupt structures. These may function on multiple levels, handling input of varying urgency in different ways.

An efficient interrupt signal demands a control structure that embodies both hardware and software elements, and co-ordinates the action of the c.p.u. with the actions of the input handling circuits.

Locating Input/Output Handling Circuitry

If an i/o handling system is very simple in operation — if the same input device is always used, for instance, and its technology is closely compatible with that of the computer's own processor — then it may be possible to incorporate all the necessary i/o handling circuitry into a small portion of a multi-function microprocessor chip. More complex i/o handling systems, however, take up entire chips by themselves. Among the general-purpose input and/or output chips to be found are the following types:

Programmable (or Parallel) Interface Adapters, or PIAs. These devices can be programmed to provide a variety of either input or output data channels.

Asynchronous or Synchronous Communications Interface Adapters (ACIAs and SCIAs). These devices are designed to handle remotely communicated i/o. They convert serial input or output to or from a parallel form, and handle the necessary timing operations.

Universal Asynchronous or Synchronous Receivers and Transmitters (UARTs and USRTs). These have similar functions.

There are also a number of special-purpose devices designed to interface the computer with specific types of input or output devices. These include:

hard or floppy disc controllers and tape controllers, that handle the tasks of writing data into, and reading data from, the external storage medium.

display controllers, that handle the business of creating and maintaining video displays.

keyboard decoders, that translate keyboard pressure into electronic signals, and printer controllers, that translate electronic signals into print impulses.

switching devices, to switch on and off actuators, and other controllers that handle input and output from and to mechanical or other peripheral devices.

Sometimes the circuitry that performs these functions (in integrated circuit or discrete component form) is found inside the computer system itself. Sometimes it is incorporated inside the peripheral device with which the system is being interfaced. If complex or programmable circuitry is incorporated in the peripheral device, then this is sometimes described as being *intelligent*. We talk, for instance, of 'intelligent terminals' and 'intelligent printers', and mean by this terminals or printers with this type of control circuitry incorporated in them.

13. Assessing Central Processing Units

If you are looking for a microcomputer to buy, you will see that the model of microprocessor chip is frequently mentioned as a selling point: invariably it is described as the best available! But what features distinguish one design of microprocessor chip from another? Should you be looking for a computer based around a particular chip, or is this a relatively minor feature, unlikely to affect your final choice of computer? In this chapter we shall look at some of the aspects of microprocessor design that affect a computer's performance. Many of these aspects also apply to central processing units that are not confined to a single chip.

Word Length

The word length, or bit length, of a c.p.u. is the number of bits of data it can handle in parallel. This is the normal size of registers in the arithmetic/logic unit: it is normally also the capacity of each memory location (or, rather, set of locations accessible by a single address code) in the computer. The longer the word length, the more information can be processed simultaneously, and the easier it is to program some applications.

Microprocessors typically handle bits one, four, eight or sixteen at a time. The 32-bit microprocessor is now a reality, too.

Very simple problems can be handled using single bit codes. Microprocessors designed on this basis are used in some simple control applications: for instance, to control slot machines. Basic arithmetic problems can be handled using four-bit codes. Many pocket calculators, and some pocket computers, use four-bit microprocessors. For the general-purpose range of operations typical of modern computers, an eight-bit or longer word length is normally essential.

Eight-bit chips have long been standard in microcomputers, but they are now being rivalled by a new generation of sixteen-bit chips. These are more powerful, but their power is not needed for all applications, and they have not yet acquired as much software support as some earlier popular eight-bit chips. As a result, eight-bit systems are still being introduced. Mainframe computers, as we saw in Chapter 6, typically use longer word lengths: 16 or 32 bits are typical.

The longer the word length, the more the accuracy with which the computer can handle arithmetic operations. The accuracy levels associated with various word lengths are approximately as follows:

4 bit: **6%**
8 bit: 0·**4%**
16 bit: 0·001%

If the c.p.u.'s word length is insufficient for a particular problem to be handled using single words, this can be overcome by using a number of words to store a single piece of data. However, doing this leads to increasing complexity in processing the data, and to a slower processing speed.

Some other aspects of word length need to be considered, as well as a.l.u. parallel processing capacity, and the size of the associated registers. The main ones are:

(1) the capacity of the addressing system. Longer addresses mean that more locations can be specified, and hence more data accessed. Systems with an address length of only eight bits are limited in their ability to handle large internal memories.

(2) the way in which data are transmitted: that is, the width of the data bus. A 16-bit word that will be treated as one unit by the a.l.u. might actually be transmitted in two chunks along an eight-channel bus.

Since some microprocessors have eight-bit capacity for some functions and sixteen-bit for others, we must be careful in talking about eight-bit or sixteen-bit chips. Many are in fact hybrids with aspects of both.

Speed

In some applications, the speed at which the c.p.u. works is all but irrelevant. Even 'slow' c.p.u.'s work fast enough to respond virtually immediately in an interactive mode, for instance. In others — for instance, controlling a system in which vital changes happen very rapidly, or undertaking complex scientific calculations — it is extremely important. What factors make one c.p.u. work more rapidly than another?

(1) The technology of the c.p.u.'s circuits, and their layout. As we shall see in Chapter 23, some of the technologies used in solid-state electronics produce faster-reacting circuits than others.

(2) The word length of the c.p.u., as we saw above. (A longer word means faster processing in almost all practical circumstances.)

(3) The nature of the basic instruction set, and whether operations are dealt with by a single instruction or by a series of instructions.

(4) General timing and control features.

(5) Interrupt procedures.

(6) The speed of access to the computer's memory, and input and output devices. Slow interfaces can slow down the processing of a program considerably.

There are a number of ways of assessing a c.p.u.'s operating speed. The length of its operating cycle (one fetch/decode/execute/store sequence) is one measure, but not always the most useful one. Many computer magazines rate computers according to the time they take to perform a series of test programs, that demand different operating characteristics.

Typical cycle speeds in microprocessor chips range from 1 megahertz (MHz), relatively slow by today's standards, to 4 or even 8 MHz. Many models of microprocessor can be operated at several different speeds: an external timing signal will determine what the actual speed of operation is in a particular computer system.

The Instruction Set

All arithmetic/logic operations carried out by a computer can be broken down into the simple add/subtract/compare operations we discussed in Chapter 1. However, from these can be built up the computer's more complex functions, such as:
x^2
sin, cos and other trigonometric functions
graphics abilities
elaborate functions for handling the movement of input and output data
any more complex logical and decision-making abilities.

Some microprocessors and c.p.u.'s have more comprehensive basic instruction sets than others. Some have better systems software support — simple subroutines available that build up the ease of programming, in the way we saw in Chapter 9 — than others. Some have sets better tailored to specific types of application than others.

Timing and Control

The timing features of a c.p.u. are important for two reasons: first, the c.p.u. must operate at a sufficient speed to handle the applications for which it is intended; second, the c.p.u.'s timing signals must be interfaced with the timing structure of peripheral devices — external memory devices, and input/output devices — that are used in conjunction with it. If this is not a straightforward process, then the additional circuits required to handle the interfacing may cause additional delays to the system operation.

Peripheral Features

(These are important in assessing microprocessor chips; they are not relevant to multi-component c.p.u.'s.)

Some microprocessors need to be used in conjunction with other chips that provide peripheral features such as input/output handling, interrupt facilities and timing signals. Others contain these circuits on the microprocessor chip itself. Some microprocessor chips contain ROM circuits (containing systems software: extensions to the instruction set, and so on), and/ or RAM circuits (for instance, an area of memory for use as a fixed-length stack). Whether these peripheral features on the microprocessor chip are desirable, or whether the system could better be built up from a range of chips, is a complex question that depends upon the precise circumstances under which the system is being designed and is to be operated.

Available Software

Systems software (including operating systems such as CP/M and Unix, and application programs designed to run with them) is intimately linked to particular models of chip or c.p.u. architectures. Obviously, popular models of chip, or popular mainframe computers, are better supplied with available software than are less well-known and less used ones. If you have located a specific program that you want to be able to run, or are updating an existing system with a range of applications programs currently in use, you will need to find a computer based around the right microprocessor chip, or one with a suitable architecture.

Common Chips

We have already looked in some detail at one particular microprocessor chip, the 6502. How does this compare with other chips in common use in small computers today?

In Table 9 we provide a brief rundown of the main characteristics of some well-known microprocessor chips. The list is not intended to be comprehensive, and inclusion or omission is no endorsement of a chip's desirability (or otherwise) for any particular application.

Chips designated by particular names are usually introduced by one manufacturer: but the names are then often adopted by other manufacturers who produce identical, or similar, chips. As a result, the manufacturers' names in the list are no more than guides. Chips bearing the same name by other manufacturers will normally share the characteristics given.

Table 9: Characteristics of Some Common Microprocessor Chips

Intel chips

8080   One of the first microprocessor chips, introduced in 1974, and linked with the development of the S-100 bus. Similar plug-compatible (that is, interchangeable) chips were subsequently introduced by other manufacturers. Now outmoded. Eight-bit. NMOS technology. 78 basic instructions. Execution time: 2 microseconds.

8085   A hybrid 8-bit chip: 8-bit addressing and data, but 16-bit internal architecture. Includes a wider range of peripherals than the 8080.

8086   A full 16-bit chip in the same family.

8088   A 16-bit chip similar to the 8086, but with an 8-bit data bus. Used in the I.B.M. and Sirius personal computers.

Zilog chips

Z80   A development from the 8080, and with an instruction set based on the 8080's: but more comprehensive and with better peripheral features. A very popular chip, used on the Sinclair ZX80 and ZX81, and with CP/M software. 8-bit. NMOS technology. 158 instructions. Execution time: 1.6 microseconds.

Z80A   A high-speed version of the Z80. 8-bit.

Z8000   An upgraded, 16-bit chip based on the Z80.

Motorola chips

6800   An early chip, with a comparatively weak instruction set. 8-bit. NMOS technology. 72 instructions. Execution time: 2 microseconds.

6809   An 8-bit successor to the 6800.

68000   The upgraded 16-bit version, available at up to 8 MHz.

Mostek chips

6502   A more flexible chip based on the 6800. Used by Commodore, Apple, Acorn, Atari, and many other manufacturers. A fast 8-bit chip.

Texas Instruments chips

9900   The latest in a long line, a 16-bit chip. Found (of course) in Texas microcomputers, but not widely adopted yet by other manufacturers. NMOS technology. 69 instructions. Execution time: 2.7 microseconds.

14. An Introduction to Standards

What is 'standard' about computers? All digital computers perform the same basic functions; but they do not have the same hardware to perform them. Several models may contain the same microprocessor or peripheral chip, but each will differ from the others in other respects. Each model of computer is unique in the precise combination of hardware (including both built-in hardware and expansion options) it offers. Indeed, that is how it should be.

Why do we need standardization, then? For three basic reasons:
(1) so different models of computer can use a common range of programs.
(2) so different models of computer can use a common range of peripherals (disc drives, discs, printers and so on).
(3) so different models of computer can communicate with each other, not only sending messages, but sending meaningful messages.

It is in these areas that the drive towards standardization has been concentrated. There are standard:

operating systems, that enable the same range of programs to be run on different computers using the same microprocessor chip;
hardware and software procedures for interfacing peripherals to computers;
rules for handling data traffic.

Of course, there are other standards, too. In fact, there are standards that are more or less acknowledged applying to just about every facet of computer design and operation. But in this chapter we shall be concentrating on interfacing standards: standards concerned with interfacing computers with one another and with other devices (primarily peripheral devices such as printers, monitors and secondary storage media). All three types of standard mentioned above have relevance to this topic.

Patterns of Traffic Flow

Many recognized standards apply to the design of the highways and traffic intersections along and across which data flow. The analogy with road traffic is a perfect one. Each and every computer, whether it be mass-manufactured, one of a short production series or hand-assembled, will have its own characteristic data traffic flow, covering all aspects of the coding and transmission of data. That traffic pattern may be a common one, or a rarer one, or a unique one. But clearly, the more common it is, the easier it will be to obtain software, to understand the operational manuals, to get service when things break down, and to obtain compatible peripheral devices: printers, monitors and so on.

Many methods for interfacing equipment are already defined primarily from the viewpoint of how electronic traffic is handled. The outstanding example is the public switched telephone network (P.S.T.N.); and the standards that it uses are particularly relevant to computer interfacing and communications in general. However, they are not the only relevant standards. There need not be – and there certainly is not – just *one* standard to which every machine must conform; but there are obvious advantages in there being no more than a manageable number.

This is the argument that lies behind the emergence of all the large standardization organizations. These range in a hierarchy (of increasing breadth of scope) from the nationally based professional organizations such as the I.E.E.E. (Institute of Electrical and Electronic Engineers) in the U.S. and the I.E.E. (Institute of Electrical Engineers) in the U.K., to the national standards bodies like the British Standards Institute, to the International Standards Organization (I.S.O.). Each takes prime responsibility for the development and enforcement of standards in defined geographical and functional areas.

Official and Unofficial Standards

There are both economic and marketing advantages to suppliers in encouraging standards, not least because governments procuring equipment will often stipulate that it must meet accepted standards. However, the structure of the computer hardware supply industry is such that two or three very large multinationals have such huge market shares that they can virtually dictate effective standards: other firms manufacture equipment that meets the standards they define.

This is not entirely a bad thing, although it may occasionally seem so to a user faced with a sudden change in commercially determined standards. The process of drawing up standards is inevitably a time-consuming one, increasingly so as the interaction between computing and communications grows, and it becomes necessary to co-ordinate standards between large bodies with a proprietorial or vested interest in preserving their own previous standards. There is frequently a conflict between innovatory change, that is often made economically feasible and technically desirable by advances in technology, and the process of standardization. Commercial standards with no legal force but wide industry support fill the gap before official standards are adopted.

If you are planning to purchase computer equipment, you should recognize that these effective standards are just as relevant to your choice as officially recognized standards. You will need to check where the equipment you select observes these, and be satisfied that you understand the implications if it fails to observe them.

The Limitations of Standards

Of course, the fact that a system observes a particular standard does not necessarily mean that it is compatible in every respect with other equipment that observes the same standard. Each standard only covers a few aspects of system operation; aspects *not* covered by the standard may well cause interfacing problems.

We may illustrate this by looking very briefly at the comparatively simple standards that cover the interfacing of cassette tape recorders with small computers. A number of standards, largely unofficial in status, have emerged: the Kansas City standard, CUTS (the Computer Users' Tape Standard), and KIM, for instance. However, the observance of these standards for writing data on to, or reading them from, cassettes does not necessarily mean that the resulting tapes can be used with other computer systems. For example, the language of the BASIC interpreter that the systems use may not be identical; the recorder-head alignments may differ, or there may be other small but real and irritating differences that are not covered by the standard.

These tape standards, however, are still not particularly widely used. The standards we will be looking at in more detail in the rest of this chapter *are* widely used. Understanding the sort of ground they cover should help you to understand their importance in the design of computers and related equipment.

Standard Bus Systems

In some microcomputers, the entire system – chips, peripheral circuitry and so on – is mounted on a single printed circuit board (P.C.B.). This is then, of course, normally enclosed in a display case that may incorporate the keyboard and/or other peripherals. In other systems, a number of circuit boards are used.

These circuit boards are linked together by a baseboard: another, long circuit board connecting sockets into which the individual P.C.B.'s can be plugged. And the baseboard is known as a 'bus'.

We encountered the word 'bus' in Chapter 8, when we used it to describe the power and data communication lines that link the components of the computer: lines both between chips and other components, and between components on a single chip. In this rather different use, the bus is the larger-scale connecting unit that links the major P.C.B.'s of the computer together, *and* provides connectors — ports — into which peripheral devices or communication lines can be plugged. When a computer is described as being bus-based, it normally means that it is designed according to this modular approach. (On the smaller scale, *all* computers, whether bus-based or single-board, have the type of buses we described in Chapter 8.)

The larger-scale buses, that we must now consider, are the subject of standards. The basic standards cover the number of lines/conductors and pins allowing connecting devices to be plugged into them that the bus contains, and the allocation of the lines/conductors and pins to different communication purposes. The S-100 bus has 100 lines, the SS-50 bus 50 lines, the SS-44 bus 44 lines, and so on.

Of course, this line/pin standardization is only one aspect of the bus construction — the most important, certainly, but not the only one. However, buses that follow the I.E.E.E. standard for pin allocations are to a reasonable extent interchangeable: equipment that works with one such bus will be fairly likely to work with others.

The I.E.E.E. Standard for the S-100 Bus: The original S-100 bus was developed for the Altair computer we mentioned in Chapter 6. Manufacturers of subsequent small computers created variations upon it; and finally the I.E.E.E. stepped in and drew up a standard that is widely acknowledged today.

What sort of uses are the bus lines/pins dedicated to? Basically, the range of uses makes up the three types of internal bus we described in Chapter 8: address, data and control buses. There are 24 lines dedicated to address functions, and 16 to data transfer. The remainder of the lines (excluding a few that have not been allocated to any set function) cover aspects of system control. The standard is designed so that 16-bit microprocessors can use the bus, and it allows up to sixteen of them to run simultaneously. In consequence, it has good interrupt handling capability! Of course, the actual description of the line functions includes details of power requirements and a number of other technical aspects that are beyond the scope of this book.

If you look through any personal computer magazine, you will see a number of advertisements for S-100 peripherals. These are hardware devices that are designed to plug into slots in a bus that uses this line/pin allocation.

From Buses to Interfaces

Bus systems work both inside and outside the computer system: they 'interface' with one another both the different parts of the computer system, and peripheral devices that are connected to the system. Another group of standards concentrates more fully on the communication aspects, including the interfacing of peripheral devices. It deals effectively with the designation of port functions and with associated control matters. Of course, every port, whatever its function, is a connection to a line inside the computer that is part of the computer's internal bus system; and these lines will have comparable designations. However, the communications-oriented standards concentrate on the external port functions, not on their internal ramifications.

The RS-232 Standard: The major standard in this group is the RS-232 standard: a standard developed by the Electronics Industry Association for the specification of interconnections between telecommunications equipment. As a result, it is particularly appropriate for the formatting and control of data to be sent comparatively long distances: from a terminal over public data lines to a host computer in another building or town, for instance. However, the RS-232 has also become a very widely used standard for the interconnection of computers and peripheral devices that stand right next to them.

RS-232 specifies 25 pin connections, providing two channels for the transmission of data. Data is transmitted along each channel in serial, rather than parallel, mode, as is most common in long-distance data communications. In consequence, there are not the 8 lines of a standard parallel data bus. Instead, there are just 2 lines: one for data to be sent in each direction. The other 13 lines of the first channel provide control signals, including handshaking protocols and power requirements. (These various functions will be clarified in the next chapter, on data communications.) The second channel, which has only 10 lines, works at slower speeds, and is rarely used for data communications purposes.

The RS-232 standard does not set down any fixed speed for communications. Instead, it offers a standard range of speeds, from very low to very high, from which a suitable speed can be selected for any fixed application.

Parallel communications standards: Though serial interfaces are most commonly used for long-distance communications, they are not always the most appropriate for interfacing peripherals to a computer system. It is normal to interface disc systems (either hard or floppy) using a parallel connector, and many printers also require parallel interfacing. As more data can be transmitted at a time, this reduces the need for buffer storage at either end, and increases the effective rate of data transfer.

Among the standards used for parallel interfacing of peripheral equipment is the Centronics standard, often used for interfacing printers.

The I.E.E.E. 488 (General-Purpose Interface Bus): The I.E.E.E. 488, or General-Purpose Interface Bus (G.P.I.B.) was developed by Hewlett Packard, primarily to handle the interconnection of a microprocessor with peripheral equipment it controls. A typical system using the G.P.I.B. might consist of one microprocessor-controller and up to fourteen devices being controlled. The standard is very precise in demanding the identification of peripherals as providing input, receiving output, or performing both functions.

The G.P.I.B. has only 16 lines: 8 data lines, and 8 control lines. Of the control lines, 3 handle the control of particular bytes of data: they are 'handshake' lines. The other 5 handle general control functions.

Using Standard Software

Of course, standards concerned with interfacing are only one small aspect of the standards developed to cover aspects of computer system operation. We shall end this chapter by outlining some of the other areas in which standardization is important, from the viewpoint of standardizing software.

If you are buying an application program for a small computer from a software house, what do you need to check in order to ensure that it will run on your computer system? At the very least, you need to check the following:

(1) What physical medium does it come in? If it is encoded on a floppy disc, for instance, then is it the same format (diameter? single sided or double sided? density?) as the floppy discs you use?

(2) How is the program data arranged on the medium? The disc operating system (if it is a floppy disc) defines the required format for data on the disc: is it formatted in a way that is compatible with your system?

(3) How is the data encoded? In ASCII, EBCDIC, or some other standard code? Is this the same code that your system uses?

(4) What operating system features does it make use of, and does your operating system supply them in a compatible way?

(5) What language and dialect is it written in, and is this dialect supported by your system?

In almost every one of these areas, a wide number of different systems are in use in the computer field today. Even in floppy discs, for instance (and they are only one secondary storage medium), there are an enormous number of different physical and data formats. Though some standardization in operating systems has been achieved (and the CP/M system in particular is very widely used in the microcomputer field), this is far from total, and is never likely to become so. ASCII has been widely adopted, but I.B.M. persist in using the EBCDIC code, and other data formats are used in many systems, even if they also support ASCII for communication purposes. And as we shall see, even 'standardized' high-level languages have many different dialects. As a result, there are formidable problems in making software 'portable', just as there are in making computers communicate with one another.

With the spread of computing on all levels down to the personal, and with the growth of information technology (including computing, telecommunications, the use of databanks, and so on) as a whole, the urge to standardize may grow greater. But at the same time, the investment in differing and incompatible systems will also grow greater. Can we expect to develop standard languages, operating systems, communications protocols? Do we want to, or is variety healthy and desirable? These are questions that will be mulled over for many years to come.

15. Data Communications

How are data sent from one computer, or input/output device used in conjunction with a computer, to another? Normally, they are sent in binary digits, since this is the form in which they will be used inside the communicating device. Sometimes they are converted into decimal digits, or even into an analog form that cannot easily be interpreted as containing either binary or decimal data. However, in looking at data communications in this chapter, we shall not be further concerned with these special cases.

However, whether the data are sent in digital or in analog form, the medium for communication is normally one that has analog characteristics: and, in particular, that has the shape of a waveform. It is the way in which waveforms in different media are analysed that enables us to interpret their information content as being binary digital, in some other digital form, or as being purely analog.

We shall look first at the basics of wave communications, then at specifically digital applications of this means of communication.

Figure 37: The form of sound, light and electro-magnetic waves

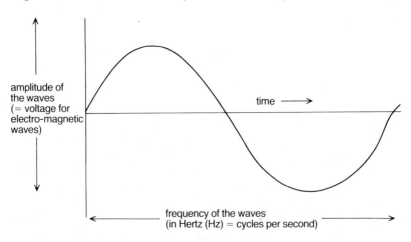

Waveforms

Sound waves (both inside and outside the audible spectrum) and light waves both have the same general form: the sine shape shown in Figure 37. So, too, do electro-magnetic waves. The fluctuations of alternating current (a.c.) from one direction of current flow to the other make up a waveform that can be used to transmit information just as do sound and light waves. Figure 37 can be interpreted as showing such an electro-magnetic signal. The upper half might represent positive voltage in a particular direction; the lower half, negative voltage in the same direction. The line across the centre represents zero voltage.

Communications media used in a digital manner often make use of a signal with an alternating waveform. The signal is then modified, and it is the modification, not the shape of the original signal, that constitutes the information content. The process of modifying the basic signal is known as modulation. There are four common methods of modulating wave signals:

Frequency modulation: The frequency of a wave is the number of cycles (zero to positive to negative and back to zero) that occur in a given time-interval: the usual frequency measurement is the Hertz (Hz), or number of cycles per second. This frequency can be altered, as shown in Figure 38b. For example, the frequency 'band' of 1,200 to 2,200 Hz may be used to carry a signal. A frequency of 1,200 Hz for a fixed period might then represent a binary 1, and a frequency of 2,200 Hz a binary 0.

Amplitude modulation: The peak-to-peak voltage of each wave is altered, as shown in Figure 38a, while the frequency of the signal remains unaltered. One signal amplitude will represent a 1, another a 0. Alternatively, several different amplitudes may be used. This enables the waveform to convey more than one binary digit of information at any one time. We shall look at this elaboration later.

Phase modulation: The direction of voltage of the signal may be altered so that, instead of continuing to complete a positive-zero-negative curve, it is switched to a positive-zero-positive pattern, or a negative-zero-negative pattern, as shown in Figure 38c. Each shift in the expected curve pattern represents the alternative data state: so that a continuous smooth curve might be interpreted as a series of binary 1s, and each shift in direction as a binary 0.

Pulse modulation: The data flow, in pulsed techniques, is divided not only into waves, but also into pulses that coincide with particular parts of the waveform. The pattern of pulses can then be adapted to the pattern of data being sent. There are a number of ways of doing this, and they are summarized in Figure 38d (i–iii).

Figure 38: Types of modulation of waveforms

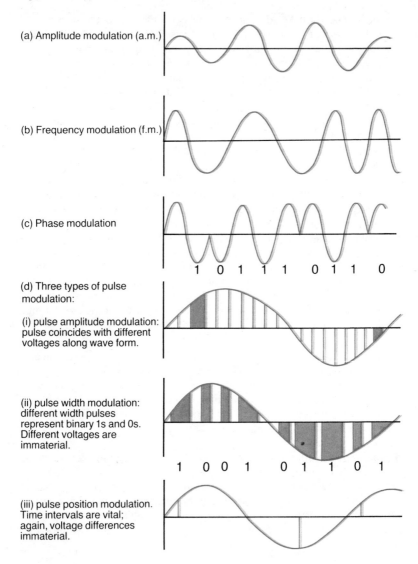

(a) Amplitude modulation (a.m.)

(b) Frequency modulation (f.m.)

(c) Phase modulation

(d) Three types of pulse modulation:

(i) pulse amplitude modulation: pulse coincides with different voltages along wave form.

(ii) pulse width modulation: different width pulses represent binary 1s and 0s. Different voltages are immaterial.

(iii) pulse position modulation. Time intervals are vital; again, voltage differences immaterial.

Wave Measurements

Sine waves can be generated with frequencies from a few Hz up to several trillion Hz. Because the range of possible frequencies is so wide, the frequencies are normally divided into sub-ranges, or bands. Each band of frequencies has different characteristics, and is thus suitable for different types of electronic applications.

Figure 39: The voice/audio frequency spectrum

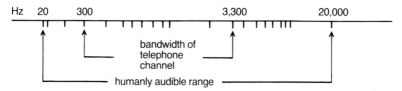

Figure 39 shows the voice/audio frequency spectrum. Sound waves across all of this spectrum are audible to the average human being. However, voice-grade telephone lines cover only a part of this spectrum: normally from 300 Hz to 3,300 Hz, giving a bandwidth of 3,000 Hz. Other types of transmission line may have wider or narrower bandwidths. Broadly speaking, the *wider* the bandwidth, the *greater* the volume of data that can be carried on the line (perhaps by setting up a number of sub-ranges of frequency across the bandwidth) and the *faster* the rate at which data are transmitted.

The speed at which data can be carried on a line and the quantity of data that can be carried are measured in two dimensions: the number of data channels (that is, the number of pieces of data that can be conveyed simultaneously), and the number of bits of data that can be transmitted along a single channel per second. The number of bits per second transmitted need not have any direct correspondence with the frequency in Hz of the carrier signal. It does, however, have a close relationship with another measurement: the baud rate, or the number of shortest pulses that can be used to create a data character, that can be transmitted in a second. However, the rate of data transmission and the baud rate are only identical for certain types of bit-coding methods. They will differ if all bits sent are not of the same length.

The number of bits per second normally transmitted in data communications systems ranges from a few hundred up to several thousand (around 10,000 maximum) serial bits. Parallel transmission enables even higher transmission rates to be achieved.

Serial and Parallel Transmissions

In parallel transmission systems, a number of bits — for instance, all the bits making up a word of the length used in a particular computer (usually one or more bytes) — are transmitted simultaneously. They may be sent down different communication lines, or they may be sent at different frequencies down the same line using multiplexing techniques (we shall discuss these later in this chapter) or other data compression techniques. In serial transmission, by contrast, only one bit is transmitted at a time.

Parallel transmission obviously increases the speed at which large volumes of data can be sent, and because of this advantage it is a technique generally used to increase further the effective speed of high-speed lines, rather than to enhance lower-speed lines that are used for applications where speed is a less vital factor. However, its uses are limited, because:

(1) both the lines themselves and the receivers (but not the transmitters) are comparatively expensive;

(2) it is difficult to synchronize the various parallel signals. For this reason, parallel transmission is not practicable over long distances, over which the synchronization could not be maintained.

Serial transmission is the more common form. The individual bits that are transmitted serially are disassembled from, and reassembled into, computer words by the transmitting and receiving devices (that is, the computer output and input devices). There are two major types of serial transmission, defined by the combined characteristics of the timing of the transmitting and receiving devices, and of the actual signals transmitted.

(1) *Asynchronous transmission* is a form of transmission in which the transmitting and receiving devices are not synchronized to receive data at fixed intervals. Instead, data are transmitted as and when available, and are received in the same manner.

Figure 40: Asynchronous and synchronous methods of data transmission

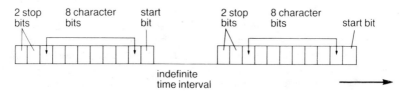

(a) Asynchronous transmission

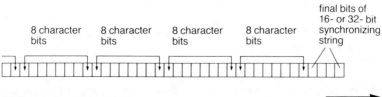

(b) Synchronous transmission

As it is necessary for the receiver to be alerted to the presence of incoming data, each datum to be sent is characterized by a 'start' code, that tell the receiver to begin to sample the data signal at a fixed rate. This will then enable it to be interpreted as a string of binary characters. When the string of bits that comprise the transmission of one number or character is completed, a 'stop' code signals that fact, and resets the receiver, ready to interpret the next piece of data. Figure 40a shows a sequence of asynchronous data transmission, including two bit code strings, each with start and stop signals, and an irregular interval between them, during which no data are transmitted.

Depending upon the transmission code used, both start and stop signals typically consist of either one or two bits of data. The ASCII-type transmission of Figure 40a comprises eight data bits (including a parity bit), one start bit and two stop bits for each character transmitted. In other words, only seven of each eleven bits transmitted actually define the character; the other four are all control bits of various kinds. The large number of control bits that this method of transmission requires markedly reduces its efficiency.

(2) *Synchronous transmission* (see Figure 40b) is handled rather differently. The transmitting and receiving devices are synchronized, by the initial transmission of a set of 'synchronizing' bits (perhaps 16 or 32 bits in all), to receive data in a fixed form, at a fixed rate of transmission. The data are then sent in a continuous string, interrupted by no control bits (except, in some codes, parity bits) at all. The receiving device is able, by its very synchronism, to interpret the signal just as it was sent.

Synchronization needs to be checked and re-established, if necessary, every few thousand bits, to ensure that progressive errors do not creep in. However, the proportion of control bits (including the initial synchronization and the subsequent checks) in this type of transmission is very much lower than with asynchronous transmission, and the efficiency of the method is correspondingly greater.

Synchronous transmission does have two disadvantages, as compared with asynchronous transmission: first, the related equipment is more expensive, as it must incorporate the ability to establish and maintain synchronization; and second, detection of errors is more of a problem. In an asynchronous transmission, an error in transmission (caused by a 'blip' in the line, say) may affect only one or a small number of adjacent bits. Other bits, characterized as they are by their individual start/stop codes, are not affected. In a synchronous transmission, one error may destroy the reliability with which a lengthy batch of code is interpreted.

The timing precision of the associated equipment generally limits asynchronous transmission to a maximum speed of around 19,200 bits per second (b.p.s.). Fully synchronized data communications may be even faster, but at the expense of some flexibility.

Simplex and Duplex

As well as distinguishing between parallel and serial transmission, we must introduce another distinction in methods of transmission. This concerns the availability of *directions* of transmission.

Basically, three methods are available. The terms used to describe them in computer circles differ from those used in the telecommunications industry. We will give the computer terms first, then the telecommunications ones in brackets.

(1) *Simplex* (Single Channel) transmission. In this method, transmission is possible in one direction only: there is a fixed transmitter and a fixed receiver. The method demands the availability of two wires (or other communication links), one to handle the signal itself and one to complete the circuit.

(2) *Half Duplex* (Simplex) transmission. Transmission is again only possible in one direction at a time, but this time it is possible in either direction: that is, the roles of transmitter and receiver can be reversed. A conversation in which two participants take it in turns to speak is an example of this method. Again, this requires only two wires to complete an alternating current circuit.

(3) *Full Duplex* (Duplex) transmission. Information can flow in both directions simultaneously, so both participants can both transmit and receive at the same time. This method requires the availability of four wires: two handle the communication in each direction.

Transmission Codes

In Chapter 1, we encountered one code commonly used to render alpha/numeric information into binary form: the ASCII code. The present U.S. standard ASCII code, accepted in 1968, and its two predecessors dating from 1963 and 1965 are used for the transmission of many binary data today. Their full versions include a number of 'control' codes, listed in Table 10. However, a number of other codes are also in common use. We shall summarize the characteristics of the main ones.

Table 10: Control Codes in ASCII

Code		Abbreviation	Code		Abbreviation
0000000	NUL	Null	0000110	ACK	Acknowledge
0000001	SOH	Start of heading	0000111	BEL	Bell
0000010	STX	Start of text	0001000	BS	Backspace
0000011	ETX	End of text	0001001	HT	Horizontal tab
0000100	EOT	End of transmission	0001010	LF	Line feed
0000101	ENQ	Enquiry	0001011	VT	Vertical tab

Code		Abbreviation	Code		Abbreviation
0001100	FF	Form feed	0010111	ETB	End of transmission
0001101	CR	Carriage return			block
0001110	SO	Shift out	0011000	CAN	Cancel
0001111	SI	Shift in	0011001	EM	End of medium
0010000	DLE	Data link escape	0011010	SUB	Substitute
0010001	DC1	Device control 1	0011011	ESC	Escape
0010010	DC2	Device control 2	0011100	FS	File separator
0010011	DC3	Device control 3	0011101	GS	Group separator
0010100	DC4	Device control 4	0011110	RS	Record separator
0010101	NAK	Negative	0011111	US	Unit separator
		acknowledge	0100000	SP	Space
0010110	SYN	Synchronous idle	1111111	DEL	Delete (rubout)

The Baudot code (named after the eponymous inventor of the baud): is used in some older types of teletype equipment. It is a five-bit code, giving thirty-two possible character combinations. This is not a sufficient number to represent the normal keyboard range of alpha/numeric characters, so the Baudot code adds to this basic code set a device comparable to the 'shift' key on a typewriter. Two special codes, 11111 (letters) and 11011 (figures) designate the manner in which all subsequent codes are to be interpreted, until the opposite code appears in the data string. Allowing for some codes common to both sets, the total Baudot code contains codes for fifty-nine characters.

Binary-Coded Decimal (BCD): derives from the code used in Hollerith punched-card machines. It is a six-bit code, plus a parity bit, with sixty-four character combinations. An Extended Binary-Coded Decimal Interchange Code (EBCDIC) is used on some I.B.M. systems. This version has eight data bits and a parity bit, giving 256 character combinations. (Both these versions differ from the simple use of four binary digits to code one decimal digit.)

Data Interchange Code: is used on newer types of teletype equipment, and particularly on slow-speed narrow bandwidth lines. It has seven data bits, and one parity bit.

The 4 of 8 Code: is an I.B.M. code that has particularly good error detection facilities. Its eight data bits are used only in combinations in which there are exactly four 1's and four 0's: 11001100, for example. This gives only seventy valid characters, in contrast to the 256 possible characters of an eight-bit code, but it is well suited to the characteristics of high-speed, voice grade transmission lines.

Detecting and Correcting Errors

How big a problem are errors in the transmission of data? It varies considerably, both because the percentage of errors itself varies markedly (depending upon the transmission conditions) and because the impact of an error upon the validity of the message varies. In an English sentence, for instance, a number of errors, particularly if they are evenly spaced and not bunched up so as to distort an entire word beyond redemption, need not affect the receiver's ability to read the message. In an arithmetic program, a single error could be disastrous.

In most circumstances concerned with the transmission of data from computer to computer, though, errors must be taken seriously, and attempts to identify and correct them must be made.

First, what causes errors? The error rate is affected by (among other factors):

(1) the amount of traffic on other channels that may cause interference, which varies according to the time of day and the day of the week;

(2) the speed of the line. When a transmission channel is used at close to its maximum data rate, the error rate will normally be higher than at slower rates. (However, fast speed lines need not be particularly prone to high error rates);

(3) the type of line, whether specially leased for data communications, or a dial-up public telephone line. The latter is more error prone, though re-dialling (which will probably engage different lines) may help to solve the problem;

(4) in general, the amount of interference: caused by static, electrical interference, crossed lines and so on.

In general, errors do tend to be 'bunched' rather than evenly spread. A single 'spike' (equivalent to a click or crack heard on a voice transmission line) may destroy a number of adjacent bits. Obviously, a cut in the power supply does the same on a larger scale.

There are three main ways of checking for errors:

(1) The entire message (in suitable small units) is retransmitted from receiver to the original transmitter; and if it differs from the message originally sent, it is retransmitted yet again. This method is not efficient, as about fifty per cent of the errors will occur on the return journey. It is known as loop or echo checking, and is used mainly on short, low-speed lines.

(2) Errors are detected by the receiver, through checking an error code, like the parity bit code, or the error detection aspects of the 4 of 8 code. (The parity code is far from foolproof, of course: it offers no protection against *two* wrong digits in a character, and does not identify which digit was wrongly transmitted. Other codes do better, but at the price of a greater loss in efficiency.) The transmitter is then alerted to the error

(perhaps by the absence of an acknowledgement that the message has been received satisfactorily), and the data are retransmitted.

(3) 'Forward error correction' is the term given to techniques by which the receiver is itself able both to detect and to correct errors. This is possible when the number of errors is relatively low, and the redundancy of the original transmission (the proportion of control and duplicate bits transmitted, compared to the number of bits transmitted in total) is sufficiently high.

Data Compression and Signal Interleaving Techniques

There are three common ways in which the usual serial, binary method of transmitting data can be adapted in order to permit more data to be sent, more rapidly.

(1) Level Coding. Binary digitizing techniques depend upon the use of just two alternative states of the transmitting medium (the wave signal) to represent the alternative binary states of 0 and 1. However, the alternating current voltage that represents the most common form of data transmission signal can be divided into many more than two 'zones' that can represent different coded digits.

Three-level coding, or ternary coding, is one common technique. Another is four-level coding, which often makes use of dibits: the combination of bits into two-bit data units.

The use of four zones allows either four individual digital numbers to be coded (0, 1, 2 and 3, for example) or four *pairs* of binary numbers to be coded. For instance:

00 might be represented by approximately 0 volts
01 might be represented by approximately 1 volt
10 might be represented by approximately 2 volts
11 might be represented by approximately 3 volts.

Figure 41 is a graphical representation of this.

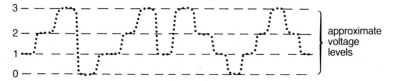

The voltage level sustained at each interval that is measured is interpreted as a pair of binary digits. For example, this transmission sequence begins with voltages 1, 2, 3, 0, 1 . . . which convert into the binary code 01 10 11 00 01.

Figure 41: The dibit transmission technique

When four voltages are used to represent four different binary combinations in this way, in effect a small-scale conversion from serial to parallel is being undertaken; and the signal must, of course, be correctly coded by the transmitter and decoded by the receiver. As a result, more expensive transmitting and receiving equipment (and better-quality lines) are required. However, this technique is commonly used in high-speed (around 9,600 b.p.s.) transmissions over voice-grade lines.

(2) Multiplexing. In the multiplexing technique, each signal still consists of a simple sequence of binary digits; but several signal sequences are transmitted over the same period of time. This is a common requirement in data networks, in which the same communication lines are used to join a number of pieces of electronic equipment. (We shall be going on to look at networks later, see page 200.)

There are a number of reasons why multiplexing techniques are commonly used:

(a) they enable the capacity of a single communications channel to be increased, and thus help to circumvent capacity limitation problems;

(b) they enable channel capacity 'packages' offered by telecommunications companies to be used efficiently; and they may enable the user to take advantage of discounts: proportionately cheaper rates for channels of higher capacity;

(c) they are particularly convenient when the same signal is to be sent out to a number of different devices (for example, to a number of terminals attached to a host computer).

The tasks of multiplexing the signals, and of dividing up the multi-plexed signals back into separate communication channels for forward communication to different devices, are handled by a specific hardware device known as a multiplexer.

There are two ways in which multiplexing can be achieved:

(a) Time Division Multiplexing. In this technique, the multiplexer converts the signals from a number of low-speed data lines into an interleaved sequence of signals on a higher-speed data line. For example, three lines, each with a transmission speed of 2,000 b.p.s., might be multiplexed into a single line with a transmission speed of 6,000 b.p.s. Some time division multiplexers handle as many as thirty-two signals in this way. The signals may be transmitted in a fixed sequence (e.g. signals from or to the terminals A, B, C and D in the fixed character order: ABCD;ABCD;ABCD); or in a variable sequence, with control bits identifying the source and destination of particular signals.

(b) Frequency Division Multiplexing. This alternative technique divides up the bandwidth of a wide band communications channel, much as the level coding compression technique does. It creates a number of parallel channels of lower bandwidths at different frequencies (separated by narrow, unused 'guard bands') in which signals can be sent at the same time, with no cross-interference. Figure 42 presents a graphic summary of the two techniques.

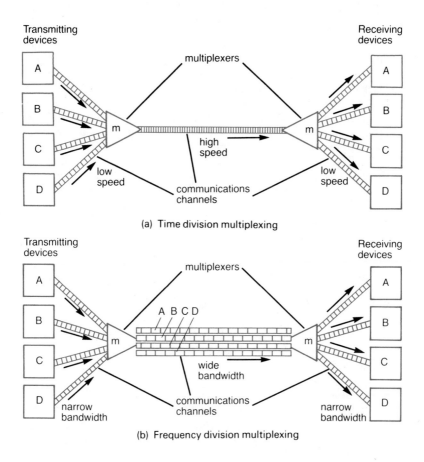

(a) Time division multiplexing

(b) Frequency division multiplexing

Figure 42: Time division multiplexing and frequency division multiplexing

(3) Packet Switching. So far, we have talked about transmitting a message along a line that is circuit switched: that is, the various components of the total communication line connecting transmitter to receiver are switched together, and are dedicated to that particular message-sending task, for the duration of the transmission. An alternative form

of line utilization, packet switching, allows for more adaptable and more intensive usage of available lines.

In packet switching, lines are *not* dedicated to a particular user. Instead, 'packets' of data (consisting typically of 128 characters, or 1,024 bits) are routed along any of the publicly available data routes. The destination of each package is determined by its control codes, just as is the identity of individual characters in dedicated asynchronous transmissions. Successive packets comprising a complete message may be routed along different lines in a public telecommunications system; interleaved with the packets destined for one receiver will be packets destined for other receivers.

A number of public packet-switched networks — including Telenet and Tymnet in the U.S., and Euronet in the E.E.C. — are in use today. They provide a permanently available, low-cost message sending service linking participating computers.

The disadvantage of packet switching lies in the complexity of the interfacing and control that it requires. Today, it is commonly thought that the arrival of a full-scale digital telecommunications system (instead of the currently adopted analog system) will sound the death knell to packet switching. Instead, circuit-switched digital lines will replace this method of transmission.

Communications Hardware

Now that we have examined the ideas and techniques behind data communications, we must go on to consider the hardware: the equipment that handles transmitting and receiving, and the communication lines themselves. We shall look first at the lines, and then at the ancillary equipment.

Transmission media: Copper wires, or wires made of other good conductors of electricity, are still perhaps the most common transmission medium. They are found in the three main forms:
(1) Pairs of open wires, suspended on insulated cross-arms on telegraph poles.
(2) Wire cables, that are rapidly superseding open wires. Many hundreds of wires may be grouped together in one thick cable. Each wire is insulated, and the wires are bound together in a way that minimizes cross-interference. These wire cables form the heart of the telephone system: the underground connections between the subscriber's equipment and the telecommunication authority's exchange. Each pair of wires is normally capable of carrying one voice-grade telephone channel (that is, of full duplex transmission), or conveying signals in both directions at any given time.

(3) Coaxial cables can transmit at much higher frequencies than simple copper wires. One form of these consists of a hollow cylindrical conductor (of copper or some similar material) surrounding a single wire conductor. Insulating rings separate the inner wires from the outer cylinder. A bundle of twenty coaxial cables in a larger cable could handle 18,740 telephone calls or similar communications simultaneously. Coaxial cables are also more efficient carriers of signals than are simple wires. Submarine cables are a special variation of coaxial cable technology.

Optical fibres are increasingly coming to rival copper cables. They carry light signals, generated by lasers or light-emitting diodes. These signals operate at very high frequencies, and thus the fibres have the potential to carry many times as many data as could conventional cables of a similar size. We discuss this technology in greater depth on pages 234 to 235.

Microwave transmission dispenses altogether with the need for a solid transmission medium. The wave signals simply travel through the air, from transmission point to receiving point. As microwave requires line-of-sight contact between transmitter and receiver, it is a technique most commonly used with satellite systems, which reduce the practical difficulties of maintaining such contact.

Satellites can handle many thousands of voice-quality communications simultaneously, and transmit the signals extremely rapidly from one land-based microwave transmitting/receiving point to another. Commercial satellites typically travel at a speed to match the earth's rotation, in very high orbits, so that they appear stationary in relation to the earth.

High-frequency radio waves are also occasionally used for data transmissions, but the high error rates caused by this method of transmission, and the large transmitting and receiving equipment required, limit the practicalities of this method.

Ancillary Equipment: Telecommunications networks themselves, of course, include a great deal of hardware, from satellites to telephone exchanges, but we shall not concern ourselves with this here. We shall discuss the hardware chosen and employed by the user, rather than provided by the communications authority, in data communications systems, or general communications systems adapted to handle data communications.

We have already encountered multiplexers, which handle the interleaving of a number of messages down a single communications channel, and their routeing to the appropriate receiving device. The other main devices that are found in data communications systems are:

'Modems', short for modulator/demodulators. These handle the conversion of binary digital data (in conventional electronic pulse form) into modulated waveforms (modulation), and its reconversion once transmitted (demodulation). They do not initiate any data themselves, though they may

handle ancillary tasks such as automatically dialling up (via the public switched telephone network) a remote computer terminal.

A special type of modem, the acoustic coupler, is often used to convert conventional telephone extensions into temporary data input and output points. The telephone mouthpiece and earpiece are placed on the coupler, which then converts the binary data it receives into and out of a sequence of audible 'blips' that can be sent directly down the telephone line.

'Terminal' is an imprecise term, because simple remote input and output devices, coupled to computers that provide all the necessary processing power and stored data, shade imperceptibly into small computers, complete with their own memory and processing abilities, that merely communicate with another computer. However, the word 'terminal' is often used, and we shall outline briefly the range of equipment to which it is normally applied:

(1) Teletypewriters, low-speed devices that accept typed messages as input, and output printed messages. Some have a limited 'buffer' memory, and very limited control (rather than full arithmetic/logic processing) capabilities.

(2) Visual displays, with either keyboard input or graphical input devices. Most of these have a moderate amount of buffer memory (for example, to hold additional screens full of data), and they normally incorporate a fair range of control facilities.

(3) Remote job entry stations, used mainly for the input of considerable quantities of data. These are generally used in conjunction with higher-speed communications lines. The station may incorporate a variety of input and output media (for instance, card readers, printers, keyboards, a video unit), and they often have a local secondary storage medium (magnetic tape or floppy disc), so that data can be encoded and checked in batches before transmission, perhaps at off-peak periods. Some more sophisticated remote job entry stations incorporate the capability to perform a full range of arithmetic/logic processing operations, as well as microprocessor control functions.

(4) Transaction terminals are normally oriented towards a single task, are lower cost, and work at lower speeds than do remote job entry stations. They handle input and output connected with simple transactions such as supermarket checking-out, basic banking functions, and credit authorization. A local microprocessor-based controller may provide the necessary control functions for a number of terminals; in turn it will be connected to a full-scale computer.

(5) 'Intelligent terminal' is another imprecise phrase. Fundamentally, it is applied to terminals that themselves incorporate a range of computer functions: that is, they are programmable to perform arithmetic/logic operations, as well as being hardwired to perform control operations. Today, most intelligent terminals have visual displays and keyboards; they may also incorporate other input and output devices. More

sophisticated remote job entry stations can be described as intelligent terminals.

From another angle, an independent mini- or micro-computer, when linked by a communications network to a larger computer on whose facilities it can draw, functions as an intelligent terminal.

Front-End Communications Processors are another wide and amorphous class of devices.

Basically, *every* computer has to have some method of switching between, and controlling, its input and output devices. How sophisticated this need be depends upon the quantity and variety of input and output the computer needs to handle. A very simple microcomputer may get by with dedicating a part of its microprocessor chip to these functions. A more complex system will need a separate input and output control chip. And a large and complex mainframe computer, handling a wide variety of input from, and output to, remote devices, determining interrupt priorities and interleaving processing requirements, may need to employ a separate computer to handle these tasks. The front-end communications processor virtually-acts like an intelligent terminal, placed immediately in front of the host computer in the communications network, or like a secretary/receptionist to the main processor.

Some front-end processors are fully programmable and can be adapted to a variety of requirements. Others are non-programmable. These are hardwired to provide a fixed range of communications options to the host computer. These latter devices are also known as 'communications controllers', and as 'transmission control units'.

We shall next summarize the major tasks that may be performed by a programmable communications processor. (Doing so also provides a reminder of the complexity of modern computer input, output and communications systems.) Such a device may:

connect up to several hundred communication lines (with attached data transmission devices) to the computer, and interface the two (that is, handle any compatibility problems).

convert data transmitted in parallel or serial, asynchronous or synchronous form into the form required by the computer, and 'buffer' input in a short-term memory, if necessary, until it can be sent on in suitable units and at suitable time-intervals.

'poll' terminals, to see if they are ready to send or receive a message, and to ensure that their limited control/processing and memory facilities are not overloaded.

cope with a wide variety of codes used for message transmission, and translate into and out of them as required.

log incoming and outgoing messages, providing a permanent record of system usage.

carry out error detection and/or correction procedures, as described earlier.

assign control code, time and date signals to outgoing messages, and remove control codes from, and assign time and date signals to, incoming messages.

handle the message priority system, ensuring that high-priority messages are dealt with rapidly, while keeping overall system efficiency as high as possible.

determine communications routes, monitor them for excessive problems (such as heavy interference leading to a high error rate) and reassign them if necessary.

Local Area Networks

We have already encountered one type of computer-related communications device: the bus that connects the components of a computer system and carries data and control messages between them.

From a wider perspective, the bus can be seen as just one of the phases in a three-phase system of inter- and intra-computer communications. The three are overlapping in some scales of operation, and in function, but they are clearly separable from each other. They are:

(1) The bus, handling communications between parts of a single, co-ordinated computer system.
(2) The local area network, linking a number of autonomous computers and other devices, in a defined area, and permitting the passage of data and of processing requests between them.
(3) The public telecommunications networks, providing data communications on a worldwide scale.

In this section, we shall look at the techniques used in the medium-scale communications systems, known as local area networks.

What is a local area network?: The term 'local area network' (or l.a.n.) is applied to a fairly broad range of networked systems. However, almost all have some basic features in common:

(1) They operate within a defined and limited geographic area: a large office block or a university campus, for instance; and they physically interconnect a range of data processing and communication devices within that area.
(2) The devices are interconnected in such a way that every device can communicate with every other device. This is in contrast with a system that merely links a number of terminals to a host computer, in which the terminals can communicate with the host computer but not with each other.
(3) There are typical data transmission speeds of 1–20 megabytes per second, and typically low error rates. These help to determine the system's operating characteristics.

(4) There is normally a capability to attach at least fifty separate devices (often referred to as work stations, or nodes), to the network.

(5) Most l.a.n.s permit equipment from more than one manufacturer to be connected together. In other words, the communications protocols are reasonably common. However, there are formidable problems in interfacing equipment made to different standards and operated with different software, and the l.a.n.s cannot as yet entirely overcome these. They merely make interconnection possible on defined functional levels (a concept we shall explore in more depth later), and between equipment using defined communications methods.

Typical local area network architectures: The 'architecture' of a local area network is the pattern of interconnections between the various participating devices. There are four common types, which are summarized in Figure 43.

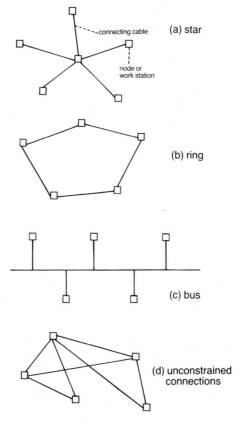

Figure 43: Local area network configurations

(1) The Star. This derives from the mainframe/terminal configuration. All communications pass through a central control point. The advantage is that the failure of any single device, except for the central controller, will not affect the working of the rest of the system.

(2) The Ring. All devices are connected in a one-way (the normal arrangement, though two-way is possible) ring. Special precautions have to be taken to prevent the failure of any device leading to the breakdown of the entire ring structure, but this is an economical layout.

(3) The Bus. This derives directly from in-computer bus architectures. A two-way bus has connection points to which devices can be attached at intervals along its length. The devices do not actually form part of the bus, unlike the devices in a ring structure; they are merely linked to it. As a result, failure of any device need not cause problems to the rest of the network.

(4) Unconstrained Connections. A random net of connections, built up as the need for them emerges, that may open up several alternative data routes between participating devices.

Basic features of local area networks: These are the primary features that identify particular types or 'brands' of local area networks; that determine how they operate, which devices can be attached to them, and how they may develop in future.

(a) *Bandwidth.* We looked at the question of bandwidth — the range of frequency wave signals a channel can carry — at the beginning of this chapter. As you will recall, a wide bandwidth communications channel can be 'sliced up' into a number of parallel channels of narrower bandwidth, each communicating on a different range of frequencies. This technique of frequency division multiplexing (which can be combined with other common multiplexing techniques) enables more data to be sent along a single channel.

Many local area networks use a 'baseband' communications medium: a channel that is not wide enough in frequency range to be divided up in this way. It might be compared to a highway with just two lanes, one for travel in each direction. The alternative, 'broadband', communications could be likened to a motorway with several traffic lanes in each direction. Not only does this permit faster traffic flow; the extra capacity it provides is essential if data-intensive information such as full-colour image data is to be transmitted.

As a result, some commentators believe that with the growth of demands placed on network systems (which might be used, for instance, for videoconferencing as well as for conventional data communications) the generally cheaper baseband systems will be superseded by the more adaptable broadband systems.

(b) *Package handling.* There are difficulties in sending and receiving data efficiently and accurately between just one transmitter and receiver. In an l.a.n., there are many more than two nodes that may either originate or receive data; and the problems of addressing and controlling the data fully and efficiently are comparably greater. Different l.a.n. systems have tackled them in different ways.

Many ring systems, for instance, divide up the message-carrying signal into fixed-length packets that circulate, full or empty, around the ring. When a node is ready to transmit, it can deposit its data into any passing empty packet. All nodes 'listen out' to see if passing packets contain data, and if they are addressed to them. Only if the appropriate address is identified will they actually take in the rest of the message — and indicate in some way to the transmitter that the message has been received.

Alternatively, systems may cater for data packages of varying length. The base signal is not divided up in the same way, and each transmitting node initiates its message when it is ready — after first checking that the line is not in use. This is more efficient in terms of the ratio of control to data bits required, as messages may be much longer than a single fixed packet length. However, it makes greater demands on the receiver.

Instead of all stations in the network listening to messages and identifying their own, the routeing of messages to their intended destinations may be handled by a central controller. This can then alert the individual nodes to receive a message when appropriate.

Yet another difficulty in handling packages of data is that two or more stations may decide that the line is available, and proceed to transmit simultaneously. This leads to inevitable corruption of their data. Elaborate protocols have been devised to avoid such data collisions, or to identify them and to ensure that the data lost are successfully retransmitted.

Of course, the message-handling protocols are far more detailed than this brief summary may suggest. There must be error-handling procedures, for instance, and procedures for dealing with messages that have not been accepted by any station in the network. Each network system has a full set of rules determining how all aspects of message handling are dealt with.

Communications protocols As a first step in establishing a basis from which internationally agreed standards on network design and operation — and the interconnection of independent networks — can be developed, a seven-layer model has been drawn up by the Open Systems Interconnections Subcommittee of the International Standards Organization. This model is *not* an international standard for networks; as yet, no such standard exists, though standards developed for other purposes can be applied to some layers of the model. However, it does give us an indication of how many and various are the problems in interconnecting different types of data handling devices and communications systems. Systems that are compatible on one 'layer' may operate in entirely different ways on another layer.

Figure 44: ISO-OSI reference model for network protocols

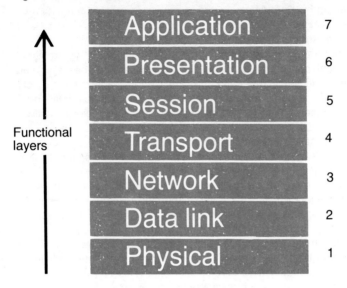

The I.S.O. model is summarized in Figure 44. Its seven layers – working upwards from the pure hardware to the pure software – are:

(1) The physical connections between the components of the system. There are a number of existing standards that can be used in this context; we discussed them in Chapter 14.

(2) The data link layer. This administers the passage of information along the physical channels, and covers some of the package handling issues we have discussed, such as package length and error checking procedures. Again, existing protocols (not part of this model, but compatible with it) cover many of these aspects.

(3) The network layer. This covers the administration of routeing and transmitting messages between communication systems. It covers aspects of control messages such as line connect, line terminate, and confirmation that messages have been received.

(These three 'base' layers can also be applied to data communications using public data networks. For these, the C.C.I.T.T. (Comité Consultatif International Télégraphique et Téléphonique) has developed a standard, known as X25. However, this standard does not form a part of the I.S.O. model. The model is simply a model on which standards can be based, not a standard in itself.)

(4) The 'transport' layer. This is the layer on which end-to-end communications channels for message transfer between a transmitter and receiver are maintained. It handles the 'leapfrogging' of intervening

nodes, and controls message flow. Control of response times, and of some security aspects, may also be handled on this level.

(5) The session layer. This handles the establishment and maintenance of contact between two or more particular transmitters and receivers, on a higher level than that involved in sending a single package of data. It covers the contractual aspects of the exchange of services between participating nodes.

(6) The presentation layer. This handles protocols for the formatting of data, for presentation on output devices such as printers and video screens.

(7) The application layer. This is the layer at which the end user operates, assuming that he or she deals with the system from an applications viewpoint rather than a functional viewpoint. In other words, it forms an interface between the user and the system, interpreting the lower-level demands of the system to the end user.

Typical Local Area Network Systems: We shall next describe three types of system that typify the local area networks currently available. These are not necessarily the best systems; but they are in wide use and indicate how local area network technology is currently developing.

Ethernet was originally devised by Rank Xerox, and its later versions are now being developed primarily by Xerox, D.E.C. and Intel. It is perhaps the best known of all l.a.n. systems.

The Ethernet concept does not involve a central controller and does not lay down any specific form of architecture. Its main features are:

connections between participating devices by baseband (single-channel) coaxial cable. The cables may be up to 1,500 metres long, and data speeds range from 3 megabytes per second (the original specification) to 10 mbs (the updated version).

the technology used to connect devices to the system is comparatively simple, and based on that used in cable television systems.

data are transmitted in packages of variable length.

each device in the system listens to all packages, and identifies its own address when this is transmitted.

The Cambridge Ring concept was originated by M. V. Wilkes and D. J. Wheeler at the University of Cambridge Computing Laboratory, as a means of connecting computing devices in the university area. It has since been developed and extended by a number of other groups.

The system utilizes a ring-type architecture, with a common controller to handle message flow. Its data speed is 10 mbs, utilizing baseband cable. It uses a fixed-length data package, 38 bits long. Of these, 16 bits carry the actual data; the others carry address, error and control information.

P.A.B.X Networks. A private automatic branch exchange (P.A.B.X.) controlling a number of extension lines from the public telecommunications system is itself a form of local area network. As telecommunications technology increasingly switches from analog to digital modes of operation, it is one that will increasingly come to rival the networks offered by the computer industry.

Telecommunications systems use broad bandwidth, voice-quality communications channels. This, together with the fact that most organizations will in any case require a P.A.B.X. system and may find it easier to extend this rather than introduce a parallel local area network system and the easy connections to the international telecommunications network, could make P.A.B.X. the dominant technology in this field.

Mixed local area networks: Combinations of these three types of system are possible. It would be entirely feasible to have a ring or net that has, as one of its nodes, a 'gateway' into the telecommunications system — either into a P.A.B.X. system or through a public branch exchange to the outside world. The constraints that limit this mixing and matching are not technical so much as on the level of protocol or standards, and in the shortage of software that can make the intercommunications between the very widely varying pieces of equipment sensible. For this reason, it is likely that the developments will remain separate for perhaps another ten years. This will be more true where the traffic pattern is not highly foreseeable and fixed, less true where the traffic demands are stable.

Part of the problem lies in the currently different standardization practices of firms in the international telecommunications industry. These tend to move cautiously, because of the international repercussions when any national standard is adopted. The computer industry, by contrast, is more prepared to adopt temporary effective standards, rather than wait for formal ones. Should these temporary standards later be changed, the scale of upheaval would not — at least in the past — have been so great.

16. Printers

Printers are an essential peripheral to all but the simplest computer systems. However, printing technology is a complex field in its own right, and we cannot explore it in depth in this book. We shall simply summarize the range of printers available, and the basic technologies used in them.

The very simplest printers (like those used for printing out sums on a calculator, for instance) cost only a few pounds. The most complex may cost hundreds of pounds. What do you get for your money, as you pay more and more? Some combination of:

(1) a wider character range. Some of the very cheapest printers produce only a basic alpha/numeric (or even just numeric) set of characters. Mid-range printers manage a typewriter-style range. Some technologies incorporate interchangeable character sets, so that different typefaces can be used, or employ more flexible techniques that also allow for the production of a range of graphics symbols. And the top-of-the-range ink-jet and laser printers are 'font free': they can ink the paper in virtually any pattern the computer is able to designate;

(2) better print quality: continuous lines instead of dot-based approximations to characters; clearer definition; better alignment of characters on each line;

(3) faster speed. The simplest teletypes operate at very modest speeds, down to around ten characters per second; the most rapid lineprinters can produce 45,000 *lines* of up to eighty characters each, per minute;

(4) more silent operation. Impact-based lineprinters can be too noisy for operation of them in an open-plan office to be tolerable. Fast mid-range daisy wheel or dot-matrix printers are also noisy. Expensive non-impact printers make virtually no noise at all;

(5) better formatting. All computer printers need to receive software instructions on where to start and end lines; when and how to cross from one sheet to another of a roll of continuous tear-off stationery, or to eject one page and feed in (or wait for) another, and so on. Better-quality systems have superior facilities for the automatic change of fonts, right- and left-hand margin justification of copy, and so on. The intelligence needed to control such layout decisions may be incorporated in the main computer or in the processing facilities of an intelligent printer. (In either case, software compatibility is essential.)

Character-based Impact Printers

The very cheapest printers are teletypes: machines using a typewriter-style mechanism, sometimes with the ability to enter data via a keyboard and sometimes operating simply as an output medium. They normally use a standard cylindrical printing head that is embossed with the available range of characters (often upper case only).

It is not possible to use a standard electric typewriter, just as it is, as a computer output medium. However, if the typewriter is interfaced with a device that converts binary output into electrical impulses that can operate its mechanisms, then it can be used in this way. Some hobbyist systems make use of such an arrangement.

Teletypewriters are basic printers. Their print quality is not high; their speed is low (typically 110–300 bits per second; one-eleventh as many characters per second if an 11-bit character code (including three control bits) is used); they normally use cheap continuous stationery; and they are noisy. However, they do provide a cheap form of hard-copy output.

Typewriter-quality printers, using similar technology but providing better-quality type and lower case, as well as upper-case letters, are also found in some cheap systems. They, too, operate comparatively slowly: their mechanism is adapted from that used by human typists, so operating it much more quickly than a human typist could can cause jams.

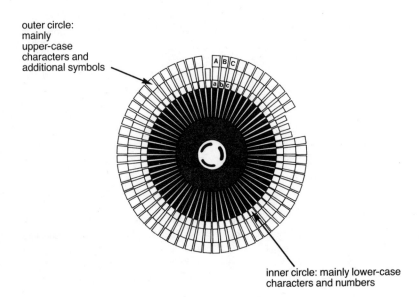

outer circle: mainly upper-case characters and additional symbols

inner circle: mainly lower-case characters and numbers

Figure 45: A daisy wheel print head

The daisy wheel is a similar device to the typewriter-style golfball, but it can be operated much more rapidly. It is a circular plastic disc, with spokes (like the petals of a daisy) on which are embossed its characters. Figure 45 gives an indication of what a daisy wheel looks like. Rotating it selects the correct character to be impacted. Like golfballs, the wheels can be interchanged to provide alternative typefaces.

Daisy wheels provide comparatively high-quality printed output. They are often found in specialized word-processing systems, with elaborate formatting capabilities, where the appearance of the finished work is all-important. They are considerably more expensive than their typewriter-style cousins, but their faster operating speed and superior print quality compensate for this.

Dot-Matrix Printers

Dot-matrix printers are not based around a pre-embossed character set like those found on print cylinders, golfballs and daisy wheels. Instead, they operate by the selective impact of a number of metal or plastic spokes, from an array, made up typically of seven by five, or nine by seven. The impact of each spoke on the paper produces a dot of ink; the array of dots creates a character, as shown in Figure 46.

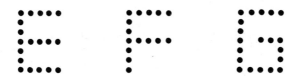

(7 × 5 matrix)

Figure 46: Formation of characters by a dot matrix printer

In some systems, a single vertical row of spokes is moved repeatedly across the paper the required number of times to create each character. Other printers have sufficient rows of spokes to be able to produce an entire character at once; still others have a lengthy array of spokes that can produce an entire line of print in one operation.

Matrix printers produce discontinuous characters that are less visually acceptable to most people than the continuously drawn characters produced by other printing techniques. (Some incorporate an option to produce 'letter quality' print by overprinting each line with a slightly offset array, to produce double the definition.) However, they are reasonably cheap, and they are flexible: some of them can, for instance, be programmed to produce a selection of graphics characters. (As the codes used for graphics characters vary from one computer manufacturer to another, and there is no widely accepted communication standard like the ASCII character code, if you plan to print graphical output it is essential to ensure that the printer is properly interfaced with the computer whose output it produces.)

Line Printers

Instead of producing one character at a time, and then moving horizontally across the page, line printers print an entire line at a time. Their techniques for doing so vary immensely. Some use belt mechanisms that give very poor-quality results; some use matrix techniques; the most expensive use ink jet or other non-impact methods.

Line printers are usually interfaced in parallel fashion to the computers they output from. As a result, they are normally coupled directly to the computer, and not connected by a (serial) data transmission line. This inflexibility of location (which is shared by other parallel printers) can be a disadvantage.

Heat-Sensitive Printers

Special papers, some aluminized and some chemically impregnated, are sensitive to heat: when heated over a small area, they colour as if they have been printed on. These papers form the basis of a sub-set of printing technology, which relies not on the impact of a carbon ribbon on paper, but on the application of heat to produce an impression..Heat-sensitive printers often use a dot-matrix method of creating characters.

Many heat-sensitive papers are produced in narrow (2" (5 cm) or 3" (7·5 cm)) widths, for applications where a very limited amount of output is required (from a calculator, for instance). The need for special paper, and the cost of it, is a disadvantage. However, heat-sensitive printers are generally quiet, and this makes them particularly suitable for some applications.

Ink-Jet Printers

Ink-jet printing is a technology that does not require physical contact between a printing head and the paper. Instead, ink is expelled in a very narrow jet of droplets, from a series of nozzles. The jet is shaped, electrically

Ink-jet printing is expensive, and the various techniques devised to implement this technology have encountered an assortment of arcane difficulties. However, the printing is silent; of high quality; entirely font-free; can be done on a wide variety of surfaces, including some textured and shiny surfaces not easily printed on by other methods; and can be done in a range of colours. This roster of advantages is likely to ensure the further development of the technology.

Ink jets are also extremely fast. The higher-quality systems can operate at up to 45,000 lines per minute.

Laser Printers

Photocopier technology is based on the marriage of printing techniques and optical technology. Today variations on the same techniques are producing a generation of laser printers: high-quality, quiet, non-impact printers. These laser printers use a photosensitive drum, as do photocopiers. An image pattern is written on the drum, using a computer-controlled laser light beam, which scans across the drum by the use of rotating mirrors or photographic plates that can bend the beam, and is turned on and off as required by the computer. Ink particles are then brushed on to the laser-charged parts of the drum surface, and these in turn are transferred to sheets of paper where they are fused on by heat, pressure or a combination of the two.

Different types of laser can be harnessed to produce different qualities of printer. Powerful and expensive gas lasers are used in printers that work at up to 200 pages a minute. Laser diodes are now being developed that can be used in slower printers, producing around 10–20 pages a minute. Both these types of machine, though, will remain top-of-range options, suitable for intensive office use, rather than as personal computer peripherals.

Other Non-Impact Printing Technologies

Yet other forms of non-impact printing technology are also being tried out today. Among them are ion printers, which also use a drum technique, with the stream of ions affecting the electrical charge on areas of the drum; and magnetic printers, which aim to use patterns of magnetism in much the same way. However, these technologies have not yet proved their practicability on a commercial scale.

17. Visual Displays and Graphics

In this chapter we shall be combining two related topics: the technology behind visual displays, and the techniques used to handle graphics (that is, visual data other than alpha/numeric characters) in computer systems. Related, but by no means identical: not all visual displays have a good range of graphics capabilities, and not all graphics are handled on visual displays: for some, hard-copy output methods are used.

Let us start, though, with a very brief look at the technology behind common types of visual display.

The Cathode Ray Tube

The cathode ray tube (C.R.T.) now has a number of rivals, existing or under development; but it is still the dominant technology in visual displays. Figure 47 gives a breakdown of its construction.

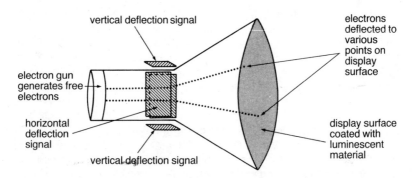

Figure 47: The cathode ray tube (simplified structure)

The cathode ray itself is a thin beam of electrons, generated by an electron gun. The electrons are directed at a display surface, coated with a phosphorescent chemical that glows in small areas where the electrons hit it. The beam of electrons can be moved very rapidly across the display surface, illuminating it in patterns. The movement of the beam is controlled by deflection plates, working both horizontally and vertically (and often in combination) that can themselves be controlled either electrically or electronically.

Movement of the electron beam across the display surface in a repeated pattern generates a picture that is continually refreshed, just as is the information in an array of dynamic read/write memory cells: each element of the picture (that is, each individual piece of data) is renewed before the information on screen fades away. A repeated pattern created in this way is known as a raster.

This is how a conventional television set works. The screen is divided up into a number of horizontal lines (typically 625), and the electron beam scans each of these in turn very rapidly, in a zig-zag pattern. A varying analog signal dictates the degree of illumination (the shade of black/ grey/white on a black and white set) each dot on each line receives: alternatively, a number of different methods have been devised to combine red, blue and green light-signals to create full-colour pictures.

It is not necessary for the electron beam to be moved in a strict zig-zag pattern. Many computer graphics systems instead move the beam in quite different directions across the screen, generating straight or curved lines as required. These are *not* raster systems: they are known as 'vector display generators'.

A cathode ray tube is a bulky device, requiring high voltage current, and these are two of the major shortcomings that have led researchers to look for alternative video technologies. We shall look at light-emitting diodes and liquid crystal displays, two current alternatives used for some types of computer display, in Chapter 19.

Refreshed and Non-Refreshed Displays

A television picture, as we have mentioned, has to be continually refreshed. The illumination generated by the electron beam lasts for only a fraction of a second, and the picture has to be rewritten on the screen (typically between twenty-five and forty times a second) before it fades away. The data that represents the picture (indicating which sections of the screen are to be dark, and which light) must be stored in a memory device, and it is then retransmitted from memory, to the picture-generating circuitry, at these short intervals.

Some visual displays are capable of retaining data on-screen without refreshing it in this way. The data are converted from their stored form (a matter we investigate later) into the pattern of dark and light dots, and then held in this pattern until the instruction comes through to change it. 'Storage tubes' and a number of other technological devices enable these non-refreshed displays to be maintained. We shall not look in detail at their method of operation.

Note that some writers use the word 'video' and 'visual' indiscriminately in talking about displays. Properly, the term 'video' is used in describing the signal in a television set that generates the picture on the screen. There is no comparable signal in a non-refreshed display system, and these latter displays are therefore visual displays, but *not* video displays.

Interfaces to Video Displays

A wide range of visual display units are manufactured specially for use with computers. Most of them contain at least some degree of 'intelligence': that is, they have memory capacity for storing data displayed on the screen, and they may also incorporate some control capabilities. Many, of course, form part of full-scale terminals with keyboard or other input devices, or are integral parts of computer systems. However, conventional television sets are also commonly used as a display medium for use with cheaper microcomputers that do not incorporate visual displays of their own.

When a television set is used as a video monitor ('monitor' is simply the word for a peripheral visual display unit, though it is normally used to describe units with a better display quality than the domestic television), there are two ways in which the binary data can be transmitted to the television's own electronic circuitry. Which will be chosen depends upon the facilities provided by the set, and on the programming of the system.

(1) The data are transmitted exactly as if they were a television signal being transmitted from a distant transmitter, and received by the television aerial, as a high-frequency analog signal, to a pre-tuned channel. The aerial connection is linked to the computer, and the television set then handles the signal exactly as it would an incoming television signal.

(2) 'Direct video': the data are not converted to an analog signal, but are converted directly to the electronic form used inside the set. Transfer of the signal is not via the aerial socket, but via the video socket that is provided on some modern television sets (primarily for use with a video recorder). Direct video circumvents the interference problems that can dog aerial connections; it also avoids the difficulties caused by the different transmission standards used in different countries. However, it *cannot* (nor can the first method) handle the difficulties posed by differing colour television technologies.

Dividing up the Screen

All methods of graphics generation rely upon some method of dividing up the display surface and referring to particular sections of it. There are two basic ways in which this can be done:

(1) The method used in high- and medium-resolution graphics systems. The screen is divided up, like a television screen, into a large number of

dots or tiny squares that are sometimes known as 'pixels'. Each dot or pixel can be designated to be a different shade or colour. The number of dots or pixels, and the sophistication of the shading possible (which might range from a simple black/white option, to various shades of black/grey/white, or to a range of colours on a colour display), varies according to the specification of the system. A typical dot density might be 210 lines of 312 dots each; a typical pixel density, 32 lines of 64 pixels.

(2) The method used in low-resolution graphics systems. The screen is divided up into a smaller number of larger units: perhaps 25 lines, with 40 units on each. Each unit then comprises not a dot, but a character: into it can be written either an alpha/numeric character or a graphics symbol (perhaps a simple black, white or coloured block, or a more complex symbol incorporating areas of several different shades or colours). In the system used for Prestel, for instance, each of the 960 screen locations can be divided up into six blocks that can be handled in a variety of ways. Other systems offer a wider choice of symbols, including the ability to construct convincing curves (the Prestel system produces approximations to curves, made up of visibly block-shaped units).

Memory Mapping and Bit Mapping

Whichever method of dividing up the screen is used, there will need to be a corresponding method for storing the displayed data in memory. The simplest storage methods just designate a memory location to correspond to each screen location. Two methods that use this basic technique, memory mapping and bit mapping, correspond in some ways to the high-resolution and low-resolution screen systems described above.

(1) Bit mapping: if a single dot on the screen can only be either black or white, then its status can be indicated by a single bit in memory. Bit-mapping systems work in this way, matching each pixel to a memory bit, so any one byte of memory will indicate the status of eight specific dots on the screen. This method consumes a considerable quantity of memory space: to store the contents of a 210 × 312 display would take up 8K of memory. If the display were more subtly defined, then more than one bit would be required to describe the shade of each pixel, and far more memory space would be needed.

(2) Memory mapping: in this alternative system, each location on the screen is represented by a byte of memory: so there are 256 alternative ways of describing its contents. These ways might well consist of: (a) the 128 symbols of the ASCII code (minus the parity bit); plus (b) 128 special graphics symbols. The actual repertoire of these varies enormously from system to system. Some systems offer a fairly basic assortment of geometric shapes; others offer specialized symbols for

professional users such as typographers and architects. The binary code that stores the data on the display contents must then be converted into the correct visual pattern, before the memory contents can be displayed on the screen. A software device known as a character generator — normally encapsulated in ROM form (though some can be duplicated in RAM, allowing the user to redefine the character set) — handles this function. Of course, an 'intelligent' visual display terminal will often contain both sufficient memory to store a selection of screen displays and its own ROM character generator.

Clearly it would be more efficient if not every location on the display demanded a location in memory: if, for instance, blocks of a single shade, or lines from one point to another, could be represented by a single coded formula; or if only the changes from one frame to another of an animation could be recorded. Elaborate graphics software could indeed achieve such ends. However, the more usual way to simplify the handling and storage of display data is to use a high-level language, with commands specially designed for manipulating visual data, to describe the required display. The system can then interpret and carry out the commands required to create one screen image at a time. It stores the remainder of the program; but it does not need to hold in a memory map or bit map the displays created by the rest of the program.

As well as special graphics languages, many commonly used multipurpose programming languages contain (or can be extended to allow for) graphics commands. The user need give only one, or a handful, of commands and the system software will translate this into a full screen display. The following are common facilities that enable the user to generate simple graphics simply and quickly:

the ability to 'draw' straight or curved lines from one point on the screen to another;

the ability to 'paint' defined areas of the screen;

Specialist systems, or software, offer the following types of function:

the ability to call up line graphs (plotted to a suitable scale by the computer) to illustrate an algebraic function;

the ability to call up bar charts, pie charts and so on, to illustrate a given set of data;

the ability to draw parallel lines at various angles;

the ability to angle text on the screen;

a 'zoom' facility, to enlarge a designated part of a complex diagram;

the ability to construct repetitive patterns on screen, once an initial section has been composed;

the ability to create and to rotate three-dimensional images.

Systems designed for the creation of animated graphics generally have special facilities to enable content to be carried over from one frame to the next. On these, it is not necessary to redraw unchanging parts of the picture at every successive stage.

Colour

Different colour television standards adopted by different countries generate colour pictures in a variety of mutually incompatible ways. All rely upon creating combinations of the three different primary colours of light (red, blue and green — not yellow, as for pigments), generally by irradiating three sets of phosphorescent particles that glow in these colours. However, their incompatibility means that a computer that uses a colour graphics display will work with only one particular standard. It is therefore essential to check whether a computer with colour video relies upon the U.S./ Japanese, the French, or the Anglo/German colour-generation system, and to use the corresponding type of monitor with it.

Data on the colour of a pixel or a more complex screen location can be simply handled in binary, just as can any other data. The more binary digits dedicated to describing the location, the more precisely can its colour be designated.

Colour graphics was originally seen as an expensive luxury, desirable perhaps, but essential for only a very few applications. However, advances in colour technology, and the pervasiveness of colour television sets, have changed that. Today, even some very cheap personal computers boast good colour graphics capabilities.

Inputting Visual Data

In many cases, the data and instructions determining how a visual display is to be generated are input to computer systems via a keyboard, in conventional alpha/numeric form. Many languages contain graphics commands that enable this to be done. However, some alternative input methods do not rely upon alpha/numeric descriptions: instead, they are exclusive to the input of graphical data.

Light Pens: are widely used for reading bar codes (the striped patterns of black and white that mark an increasing range of consumer goods). However, the pens can be used for inputting any visual data that are presented in a suitable format.

The 'pen' is actually a fattish, ballpen-shaped device that has a light-sensitive transistor at its tip. When the pen encounters a flash of light, the transistor emits a pulse of electricity, that can be handled by a suitably programmed computer as a binary input.

As well as being able to 'read' bar codes, the pen can also be used to 'draw' on a video screen. The screen is scanned in a regular raster pattern by the electron beam, and when the location of the pen is passed by the scanning beam, an impulse is emitted. By comparing the timing of the impulse with the timing pattern of the beam, the computer can calculate the pen's location on – or its movement across – the screen, and then translate that into a dot on, or line across, the screen. Alternatively the pen could be used to point to an item of data displayed on the screen, and thus input the 'choice' of that item.

Touch-sensitive systems: when a light pen is used in this way, it is the pen as well as the screen projection equipment that provides input data to the computer. However, it is also possible to create a touch-sensitive system in which the device that actually does the touching – a pencil, or even a finger – is electrically inert: it inputs data only via its screen touch. The touch completes an electrical circuit, for instance by pressing a grid of wires to a conductive base, or it creates some other form of signal that can be read electronically; and the completion of the circuit generates an electronic pulse that forms the input data.

This technology has been applied to a range of 'graphics pads' and similar devices, in which graphics drawn on a special surface can be stored, then reproduced or manipulated (lines straightened, patterns continued, the scale changed, and so on) on a computer.

Joysticks: are a standard input medium for 'television games' – themselves, of course, programs run on dedicated microcomputers. Moving the stick to and fro controls the movement of a 'bat' or some other moving device on the screen. By an extension of the same technology, joysticks can be used to input drawings directly on to a screen: the stick controls a cursor that 'draws' a line on to the screen. Systems using this input method are particularly useful for those who have difficulty in using a keyboard: small children, for example, or the disabled.

Video cameras: of course, some large computers use video cameras (just like television cameras) for providing direct photographic input. We shall not, however, look at the technology of these cameras here.

Outputting Visual Data

It is one thing to conjure up an elaborate bar chart, in full colour, on a visual display unit; it is quite another to transfer it to paper – as many users have found to their cost.

Printers with daisy wheels, or using other types of character-based impact technology, can be used only to a very limited extent for drawing graphics: they might be able to draw straight lines at fixed angles, for instance, or have a small repertoire of special graphics symbols. Dot-matrix printers are more versatile: their pattern of dots can be programmed to produce crude graphical output. As the demand for colour graphical output grows, cheap dot-matrix printers with the facility to produce this — using interchangeable ribbons — are coming onto the market. More elaborate printers — ink-jet systems, for instance — can produce better-quality graphics in black and white or colour, but at a greater cost.

A variety of devices are available that convert black and white or coloured graphics not into just paper copy, but into full-colour photographs, transparencies, microfilm and other hard-copy media. These are invaluable for the specialist business-user who needs to make regular use of such facilities, but their cost puts them beyond the reach of most personal computer users.

A different route to hard-copy output is via the pen plotter: a device that controls the movement of a pen over a horizontal sheet of paper, rather like a 'graphics pad' in reverse, or a sheet wound round a drum. Electromechanical pen plotters have been used for around twenty years to help produce detailed, accurate diagrams for engineers, designers, architects and other professional drawers of diagrams. Today, a new generation of computer-controlled pen plotters has linked this existing technology to the power offered by computer graphics techniques. Pen plotters can easily incorporate pens of different colours, enabling them to draw a wide range of graphics in several colours.

18. Talking and Writing to the Computer

In this chapter, we shall be looking at two techniques – both in their comparative infancy – that may help to circumvent the massive problems involved in inputting alpha/numeric data (and instructions) to the computer. Keyboard input is slow, tiring and time-consuming: many people have little familiarity with keyboard operation and shrink from using it. Alternative input techniques in common use today – sensors, light pens, touch pads and so on – have only a very tangential application to alpha/numeric data. It would revolutionize our dealings with the computer if we could simply talk to it in natural language, or if it could read our informal, handwritten notes. Is either option feasible? And just how far have computers come today in recognizing speech, and recognizing writing, either typed or handwritten?

As well as trying to answer some of these questions, we shall look at digital techniques for the recording and reproduction of music.

Voice Input and Voice Output

Speaking generates sound waves: and sound waves are an analog form of information that can, without undue difficulty, be sampled and converted into digital data. The sound wave of a person speaking may be described as a 'voiceprint', an analog waveform. By taking sufficiently frequent samples of this waveform – and they must be comparatively frequent, as we shall see shortly, for it is a highly complex waveform – we can produce a digitally coded version of the same data.

And what can we then do with it? We can store it, and reproduce it – with an accuracy that will obviously depend upon the precision and frequency of our sampling – on demand. We can analyse it; and complex techniques have now been devised which enable us to 'clean up' the signal and remove unwanted distortions from it.

But just by digitizing data on sounds, the computer comes no nearer to *understanding* what is being said. How is the computer to set about interpreting these sounds into meaningful commands, and to act upon them?

Each speaker's voiceprint is virtually unique to him- or herself, though identifying voiceprints is a far trickier task (and more prone to error and deliberate deception) than is identifying fingerprints. (Voiceprints are unlikely to replace fingerprints as the staple of identification systems.) But similarly, each word has a 'print' that is identifiable, even though different speakers will produce slightly different versions of it. If the computer knows that the input it receives will be one of a limited vocabulary of words whose typical prints it has in store, it will have a much better chance of deciphering the word. And with the digitized soundwave patterns that make up its vocabulary, it can associate commands that are effectively triggered by those words and patterns.

Pattern recognition — whether the computer has to 'recognize' a letter, a word, or a photographed object as corresponding with the contents of a set previously defined to it — is an extremely difficult operation. By isolating a pattern from any extraneous background, though, it becomes a little easier. Given the print of a single word, uttered in isolation and without too much noise in the background, the computer has a very good chance of matching it to the corresponding print in its memory.

A number of processing techniques are used in this context. These are some of the terms you may encounter:

Feature extraction: distinctive features of the sound wave, such as its amplitude and frequency, are isolated and measured for comparison with the stored examples.

Linear predictive coding: a technique of anticipating the likely shape of the sound wave, and comparing it with the actual shape received.

Dynamic programming: a technique for ascertaining where words or sounds begin and end, so that they can be 'time sliced' for comparison with reference data.

Originally, computers were programmed to recognize words spoken by a single, pre-designated speaker under carefully controlled conditions. Today's systems are more flexible. They can identify the speech of most people, at speeds of anything up to 180 words per minute; they can handle vocabularies of several hundred words. This is sufficient for a system to be able, for instance, to run a stock control operation when it is told the type and number of each good required or sold; for an airline reservation system handling a fairly wide range of destinations, and receiving data on when and how (class? smoking section?) the traveller wishes to fly; for a system that enables a physically handicapped person to control a wheelchair, shouting out the direction and speed in which it is to travel.

Among the speech recognition systems that have been developed for use with personal computers are 'Speechlab' and 'Mike'. Speechlab (made by Heuristics Corporation) consists of an S-100 compatible circuit board, programmed for speech recognition, and a microphone. Its software includes a specially adapted programming language, SpeechBASIC, for programming the computer verbally. It can be taught to recognize between sixteen and sixty-four words, depending upon their length, and to respond differently to each: both to print them out for verification, and to act upon them.

'Mike' has more built-in intelligence and, unlike Speechlab, does not need to be connected to a separate computer. It is manufactured by Centigram Corporation, California, and can recognize up to sixteen words. A typical vocabulary might, for instance, include the digits 0 to 9; enter; cancel; up; down; start; stop, and similar simple control words. It is designed to augment, not completely to replace, keyboard input for busy operators who do not always have a hand free. It 'listens' continually for words it recognizes, and when it finds one it signals its discovery with a code number on screen, and acts by emitting a control signal.

Of course, bigger computers can do more along the same lines. But these simple examples make it clear that such systems *are* useful — and, indeed, many are in use today. They are particularly useful for users who find it difficult — through physical incapacity, distance from the machine, or simply the lack of a free hand — to press keys or knobs to indicate their instructions. What they are *not* useful for — yet — is to take dictation, or to receive and act upon the extremely wide range of instructions delivered in normal speech in uncontrolled circumstances.

Will computers be able to make the jump from understanding these limited, pre-defined vocabularies to understanding natural speech? The problems are formidable. All human languages — and particularly our complex, many-rooted Romance languages — are full of contradictions and ambiguities. We do not always say what we mean; we use confusing idioms; we do not speak clearly and precisely. For a computer to understand us fully, it will need an intelligence that matches or surpasses human intelligence on a very wide front. We do not yet have a computer that can achieve such a thing.

Of course, the lower the accuracy level we can tolerate, the better our chances of success. A system that can provide a very rough 'sketchpad' indication of an executive's speech — full of misspellings, but sufficiently accurate to permit a reconstruction — is not as far in the future as one that will turn out a perfectly laid-out, typed and spelled letter. Today, though, we do not have either.

Recorded Speech and Synthesized Speech

What of a system that speaks to us in words that we did not first say to it? That speaks what we typed, or gives us commands, information or general encouragement? There *are* many such systems already in operation today.

Early 'speaking' machines used recordings of a small number of words, which they then played back to order. The result was rather like a 'Speak your weight' machine: admirably clear, if lacking in inflexion. Today, computers that 'speak' do so by synthesizing their words. This simplifies their operation and gives them (potentially, if not always in practice) greater flexibility. Simple systems are used to provide warnings, commands and confirmations – perhaps as an echo of the limited-vocabulary speech input we have just discussed – in shops, factories, and increasingly in the home. More elaborate ones probably find their major current use in offices, but as the technology improves they may be used increasingly in other contexts.

How does speech synthesis work? There are two different methods in common use:

(1) Waveform digitization. This is an application of the analog-to-digital conversion technique we looked at on pages 94 to 96. A human speaker speaks the required vocabulary of words into a microphone, and the resulting sound waves are then sampled and digitized. The digital information is stored in electronic circuits (typically on a special chip called a 'sound generator') until it is required, when it is converted back into analog form and sent through a loudspeaker to reproduce the original sounds.

(2) Formant synthesis. This technique does not use actual voices. Instead, similar patterns of digital information (perhaps on allophones, or basic speech elements that can be put together to form words, rather than entire words) are artificially generated. They can then be converted into analog form for reproduction in a similar way.

Storing words in digital form takes up a great deal of memory space. Holding a full profile of the sound wave representing the word, with data on its amplitude at each instant, is generally thought to be too inefficient a storage method. Instead, data compression techniques can be used to reduce the quantity of data involved. Data on the make-up of a single word can adequately be stored in 700–2,000 bits of memory, depending upon the quality of reproduction required. Such a demand for memory space seems formidable today, but the increasing cheapness and compactness of memory media may render it entirely acceptable for large-scale uses in future.

The current applications of voice synthesis systems include Texas Instruments' 'Speak'n'Spell' machine, a special-purpose microcomputer that teaches young children spelling, and systems that dictate back to blind typists what they have typed. Some new systems even read in bar-coded information on the sounds they are to reproduce: from codes printed alongside the illustrations in children's picture books, for instance.

Speech synthesis peripherals for microcomputers are also appearing at an increasing rate. Typical of them is the DCP Microdevelopments' 'Speech Pack' for use with the Sinclair ZX81. This is a hardware unit whose main components are a speech synthesis chip, the National Semiconductor 'Digitalker', up to four 8K ROM chips that hold its vocabulary, and a small loudspeaker. Table 11 lists the available vocabulary, to give you some idea how such a system might be used. Some judicious juggling with the available sound elements can enable some additional words to be built up.

Table 11: Typical Vocabulary for a Microcomputer
Speech Synthesis System

(Actual system: DCP Microdevelopments Ltd, 'Speech Pack')

ROM 1 (8K)	ROM 2 (8K)	ROM 3 (8K)	ROM 4 (8K)
THIS IS	CENTI	ABORT	LOAD
DIGITALKER	CHECK	ADD	LOCK
ONE	COMMA	ADJUST	MEG
TWO	CONTROL	ALARM	MEGA
THREE	DANGER	ALERT	MICRO
FOUR	DEGREE	ALL	MORE
FIVE	DOLLAR	ASK	MOVE
SIX	DOWN	ASSISTANCE	NANO
SEVEN	EQUAL	ATTENTION	NEED
EIGHT	ERROR	BRAKE	NEXT
NINE	FEET	BUTTON	NO
TEN	FLOW	BUY	NORMAL
ELEVEN	FUEL	CALL	NORTH
TWELVE	GALLON	CAUTION	NOT
THIRTEEN	GO	CHANGE	NOTICE
FOURTEEN	GRAM	CIRCUIT	OHMS
FIFTEEN	GREAT	CLEAR	ONWARD
SIXTEEN	GREATER	CLOSE	OPEN
SEVENTEEN	HAVE	COMPLETE	OPERATOR
EIGHTEEN	HIGH	CONNECT	OR
NINETEEN	HIGHER	CONTINUE	PASS
TWENTY	HOUR	COPY	PER
THIRTY	IN	CORRECT	PICO
FORTY	INCHES	DATE	PLACE
FIFTY	IS	DAY	PRESS
SIXTY	IT	DECREASE	PRESSURE
SEVENTY	KILO	DEPOSIT	QUARTER
EIGHTY	LEFT	DIAL	RANGE
NINETY	LESS	DIVIDE	REACH
HUNDRED	LESSER	DOOR	RECEIVE
THOUSAND	LIMIT	EAST	RECORD
MILLION	LOW	ED	REPLACE
ZERO	LOWER	EMERGENCY	REVERSE
A	MARK	END	ROOM
B	METRE	ENTER	SAFE
C	MILE	ENTRY	SECURE
D	MILLI	ER	SELECT
E	MINUS	EVACUATE	SEND
F	MINUTE	EXIT	SERVICE
G	NEAR	FAIL	SIDE
H	NUMBER	FAILURE	SLOW
I	OF	FARAD	SLOWER
J	OFF	FAST	SMOKE

ROM 1 (8K)	ROM 2 (8K)	ROM 3 (8K)	ROM 4 (8K)
K	ON	FASTER	SOUTH
L	OUT	FIFTH	STATION
M	OVER	FIRE	SWITCH
N	PARENTHESIS	FIRST	SYSTEM
O	PER CENT	FLOOR	TEST
P	PLEASE	FORWARD	TH
Q	PLUS	FROM	THANK
R	POINT	GAS	THIRD
S	POUND	GET	THIS
T	PULSES	GOING	TOTAL
U	RATE	HALF	TURN
V	RE	HELLO	USE
W	READY	HELP	UTH
X	RIGHT	HERTZ	WAITING
Y	SS	HOLD	WARNING
Z	SECOND	INCORRECT	WATER
AGAIN	SET	INCREASE	WEST
AMPERE	SPACE	INTRUDER	SWITCH
AND	SPEED	JUST	WINDOW
AT	STAR	KEY	YES
CANCEL	START	LEVEL	ZONE
CASE	STOP		
CENT	THAN		
HIGH TONE	THE		
LOW TONE	TIME		
0·2S SILENCE	TRY		
0·4S SILENCE	UP		
0·8S SILENCE	VOLT		
0·16S SILENCE	WEIGHT		
0.32S SILENCE			

Music Synthesis

Many personal computers can be used for playing tunes, or at least for emitting more or less musical sounds — perhaps in conjunction with animated graphics for a really sophisticated video! The more elaborate systems depend upon interfacing with a stereo amplifier and speakers to produce reasonable sound quality; the basic ones have a simple built-in speaker unit.

What characteristics of a sound wave affect the way in which we hear music? There are a number of them and, to produce music really effectively, a computer must be able to allow for most, if not all of them. The basic characteristics are summarized in Figure 48.

In addition, the computer must generate information at a rate that adequately imitates real sounds — or indeed reproduces real sounds, if the

Figure 48: Main characteristics of musical waveforms

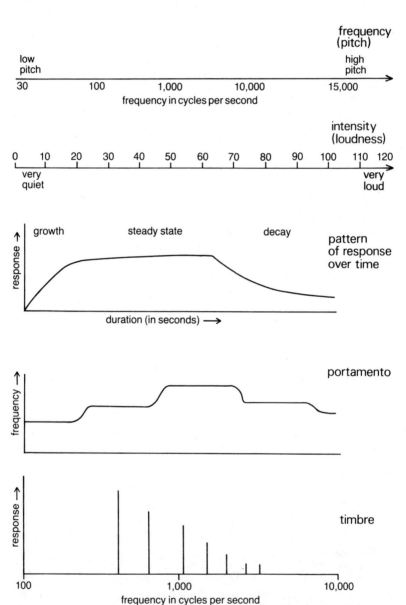

also important: vibrato (= amplitude and frequency modulations) and general pattern of deviations

system is being used to store and then reproduce sounds created by more orthodox musical methods – and it must be able to produce sounds over a frequency spectrum that resembles that which affects our hearing of music. (This is a much wider spectrum than that needed merely to reproduce speech adequately, as you will know from your use of the telephone: fine for speech, but hardly hi-fi for music.) The figures given in Table 12 give some idea of the amount of data that is needed.

Table 12: Parameters Needed for Acceptable Recording or Synthesis of Music

Amplitude resolution (i.e. number of amplitude levels that can be specified): 2^{16}, or 65,536
Decibel range: 96 dB
Sampling rate: 50 kHz (i.e. 50,000 times per second)
Frequency range: 0 to 20 kHz.

Total amount of data generated if these parameters are met:
$16 \times 50,000 = 800,000$ bits per second.

Basic sounds can be produced by generating a square wave pattern of varying frequency. The speed of typical microprocessor operation enables frequencies of up to 2,000 cycles per second to be generated by even very simple systems. The sound quality created, though, is not high: serious music synthesizers must try much harder.

Music synthesis can be handled by a very simple hardware system, with suitable programming: indeed, we write an extremely basic synthesis program for a cheap microcomputer in Chapter 24. The electronic circuits store and generate the signals that can drive speakers; the speakers then vibrate to produce the final sounds. Of course, the output depends upon the quality of the output system. One interesting variation is to use the computer to control, not a speaker, but the playing of notes on a conventional or newly designed musical instrument. An organ or other keyed instrument might be computer-controlled; 'synthesizers' such as the Moog synthesizer are ideally suited to such a form of control.

Typical of the better music synthesizer offerings designed for hobby use with microcomputers is the Music Synthesizer Board from Solid State Music, a circuit board designed to be plugged into an S-100 bus system. The board is programmed from the main computer, and once its initial programming is complete the operator can dictate tunes using a form of ASCII notation: the letters A to G to designate the notes, numbers to distinguish octaves, + and – to indicate sharp and flat, and so on. The board can simulate the sounds of a small selection of instruments – a cello, organ or flute, for instance – and by using several boards in parallel (the software will control up to five) you can orchestrate pieces for a small group of instruments.

Written Input

How can computers 'recognize' writing? There are three basic ways: by decoding magnetically encoded signals, by decoding visual signals, or by decoding touch signals (that is, writing on a special surface).

Magnetic systems depend upon the use of ink that is magnetically sensitive. Such systems are known as M.I.C.R., or magnetic ink character recognition systems. The documents on which the magnetic ink characters are written are passed through a reader that contains a head to magnetize the ink. The magnetized characters then induce electrical signals in a second, 'read' head, that the computer can proceed to decode.

M.I.C.R. systems use strictly defined fonts, and depend upon characters being printed on a fixed position on the document. Cheque-reading systems, for instance, typically use this technology. As a result, the system can be used only when the original writing is done with computer input in mind: it cannot be used to 'read in' paper files of existing documents.

Some typical M.I.C.R. fonts are shown in Figure 49. As you can see, they are very stylized, with a heavy dependence on straight lines of fixed thicknesses.

Figure 49: Typical fonts used by MICR (Magnetic Ink Character Recognition) systems

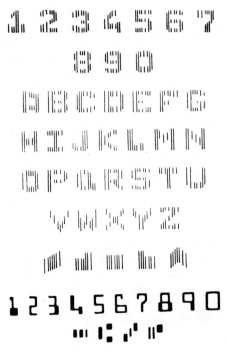

Optical character recognition, or O.C.R., is a more versatile system. The reader contains a video camera which literally 'reads' data on the image presented to it into the computer. Any visual data can be entered; the problem, of course, lies in decoding it!

Figure 50: Typical fonts used by OCR (Optical Character Recognition) systems

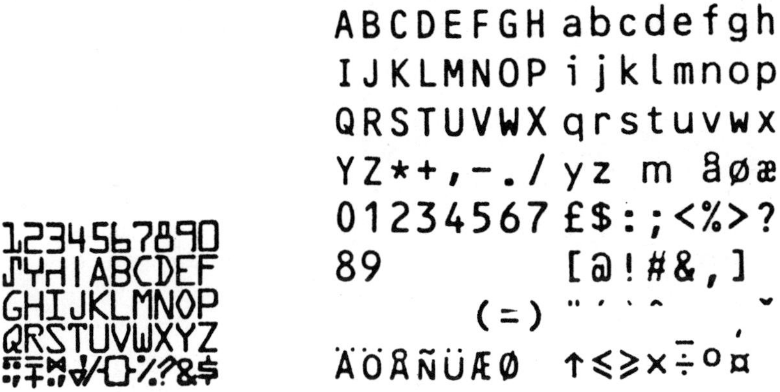

OCR A

OCR B

Originally, O.C.R. systems too depended on fixed, stylized fonts such as those shown in Figure 50. Later, the systems were 'taught' to recognize normal typefaces, and even handwriting: though this latter function was often limited to block capitals carefully printed in a pre-defined segment of a form. Today, the most advanced systems are approaching the ability to decipher normal handwriting.

A major problem is to improve the machine's performance at deciphering input until it can recognize the majority of characters presented to it. A good recognition program can decipher ninety-five per cent of characters correctly on its first attempt. However, it needs to have around 14,000 algorithms representing typical ways of writing letters and other characters with which to compare its input. Systems with around 4,000 algorithms can decipher about eighty per cent of their input: too high an error rate for user acceptability as a regular input medium.

The first O.C.R. systems were used for the large-scale batch input of routine forms. Today, small versatile systems are being developed for use with microcomputers. With them is coming a shift away from a concentration on camera input using ready-completed forms, and towards the use of pads on which the user writes directly: either touch-sensitive systems using ordinary pads and pencils, or electronically sensitive systems using electronic pens. (We discussed touch technology on page 218. One drawback is that many of the pads provided are small, A4 size or even A5 size in some cases.

O.C.R. input is also used with some large word-processing systems. The typists type on ordinary typewriters, and their work is fed into the system via an O.C.R. reader. It can then be filed on disc, recalled on a word processor screen and edited as if it had been initially typed on a word processor.

O.C.R. systems are also acquiring more intelligence. They might, for instance, be programmed to reject obviously invalid entries (a number code where a letter code is required on a form, for example) or to perform simple calculations on the input data.

19. Opto-Electronics

Opto-electronics is the branch of technology concerned with the integration of optical devices (devices concerned with the manipulation of light signals) and electronic devices (devices concerned with the manipulation of electrical signals). The points at which optical signals are converted into electrical signals, or vice versa, vary widely. Indeed, we must also look briefly at 'opto-optics': the information-processing technology that works entirely with light signals.

The field of opto-electronics includes:

light-sensing devices, which pick up light signals and either transmit them or convert them into electronic data signsls;

light -emitting devices, which convert electronic signals into visual output;

light-transmitting devices, which transmit information in the form of light waves;

light-processing devices, which carry out simple logical processing operations on light waves;

and storage devices that are encoded or read by optical means.

We will look at each of these fields in turn.

Light-Sensing Devices

Light is a medium of information: the presence or the lack of illumination in a particular area can make up the basis of a binary information code; or degrees of illumination can be classified in a more complex digital (decimal or binary) or analog manner. A range of devices are used to sense illumination, and to treat it (or its absence) as input to optical or electronic information transmission or processing devices.

We are all familiar with the effect of light rays on the photo-sensitive materials used on camera films. In a similar way, light particles (or photons) have an impact on photo-electric sensitive materials that is analogous to the effect of an electrical input. They can generate an electrical charge in an electrode (forming a simple capacitor, like those we saw storing information on pages 118 to 120), that can then be stored or transmitted when a voltage is applied. Depending on the use to which the device is to be put, data may be transmitted either in analog form (via an electrical current of a voltage directly proportional to the incidence of the photons on the material) or in a binary digital form (in which an arbitrary cut-off point determines the two-state yes/no response).

Arrays of light-sensitive cells can form image-sensing devices, relaying the shape of an object being scanned in electronic form. Still other devices carry out some simple optical processing on visual input, and then transmit or further process the results. These may be used to measure any parameter that can simply be detected visually: speed of rotation, speed of flow, level of a substance, and so on. The light input passes through a mechanical motor, which might, for instance, use a slotted disc rotating at a fixed speed to convert the light signals into pulse form. The pulses can then be counted or directly transmitted through a medium such as fibre-optic cable, which we shall consider later (see page 235).

Light-Emitting Devices

An ordinary light-bulb is a light-emitting device; it turns an electrical current into a light signal. Indeed, light-bulbs were used as an output medium on ENIAC and other early electronic calculators and computers. A more complex light-emitting device is the cathode ray tube. This is used in conventional television sets and in the visual display units of many computers and computer terminals, as a means of converting the information received electrically into visual form. We explored its technology on pages 213 to 214. Today, there is a wide range of other, competing technologies that produce visual output. Some produce output directly for for human consumption; others produce light signals in a form suitable for further transmission or processing.

A variety of technologies generate digital output on small-scale displays (like those used in pocket calculators) and slightly larger displays. Some are tube based, using technologies similar to those used in conventional fluorescent light tubes. The two we shall examine, however, work instead in an array form, dividing the display surface into sections defined by different electronic components.

Light-emitting diodes: The light-emitting diode, or L.E.D., type of display was originally very widely used in calculators, digital clocks and similar appliances. Today it is losing ground to the liquid crystal display, which was formerly (but is no longer) more expensive and less reliable. A major disadvantage of the L.E.D. is that it requires a relatively high-voltage electrical current to activate it, and thus a larger battery. (An attractive feature of optical devices in general is that they consume less power than electronic devices.)

As you will recall, when we looked at the make-up of a simple semiconductor diode, on pages 38 to 39, we observed that it sandwiches together a layer of positively doped semiconductive material (with a preponderance of holes into which electrons might fit) and a layer of negatively doped material (with a preponderance of electrons). Electrical current flowing in the right direction forces electrons from the negatively doped material to the positively doped, where some electrons 'recombine' with the holes, and others continue to flow (in wave form) around the circuit.

When recombination takes place in a manner that takes the electron from the conducting band (in which it is free to move) to the valency band (in which it is attached to a particular atom, or group of atoms), then energy is released in the form of electro-magnetic radiation. The material glows.

Substances that are particularly prone to such 'radiant recombination' (such as gallium arsenide) can be used to make light-emitting diodes, which glow when current passes through them.

Some diodes are 'surface emitting': they glow all over. Others are 'edge emitting'. These glow with greater intensity, but from the edges only, making a light that it is easier to channel into a fixed beamwidth for transmission. These edge-emitting diodes are commonly used in fibre-optic light-signal transmission systems.

Figure 51: Cross-sectional structure of a liquid crystal display

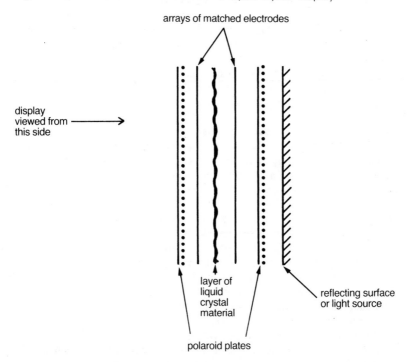

arrays of matched electrodes

display
viewed from ⟶
this side

layer of
liquid
crystal
material

reflecting surface
or light source

polaroid plates

Liquid crystal displays: 'Liquid crystal' is the generic name given to a class of substances that rearrange themselves molecularly when an electrical current is applied to them, in such a way that they switch from being opaque, to being transparent to light. They might be thought of as molecular venetian blinds, switching from closed to open when energy is applied.

A liquid crystal display (L.C.D) is a multi-layered sandwich of materials, made up as in Figure 51. Each segment of the display is defined by a different pair of electrodes, which can be activated separately so that (as with the L.E.D.) the array can form different patterns of illumination.

L.C.D.s require only a low current to activate them, but they do not generate light: they merely allow it to pass through in certain circumstances. As a result, if the display is to be viewed in dim lighting conditions it must be equipped with its own light source.

Gas plasma screens: Gas plasma technology is now capable of making 'flat screen' displays that rival cathode ray tubes. This technology, like that behind neon tubes, depends upon the activation of fluorescent materials, materials that glow when a current is passed through them.

The fluorescent material — zinc sulphite is often used — is sandwiched between two arrays of electrodes: one transparent array and one made of, say, aluminium. Activating a pair of electrodes makes a section of the screen glow.

The great advantage of gas plasma screens over cathode ray tubes is that they take up less depth. As a result, gas plasma technology may be the predominant technology in the production of large and small 'flat screens' for use in the televisions and video units of the near future.

Laser devices: The essential difference between lasers and ordinary light-emitting devices is that the light emitted by a laser has a coherent wave pattern. Ordinary light is incoherent: it consists of a variety of disparate waveforms. Laser light is thus easier to manipulate; it can travel further without being diffused; and by modulation (varying its wavelength), different frequencies of laser light beams (much like different frequencies of radio beams) that can carry different information without mutual interference can be generated.

This property of laser light makes it particularly useful in computing applications. Laser light pens are used to read bar codes on consumer goods, an increasingly common form of computer input. Laser light is used both to write in and to read out stored information. And lasers can be used to generate light beams for transmission.

In optical transmission networks, laser diodes are the main rival of the conventional light-emitting diode we have just discussed. The laser diode must be made of a material with a molecular structure that enables it to generate a coherent light beam. It is difficult to make reliable versions, and the diode is more expensive than its rival. However, laser diodes can be switched on and off much more rapidly; and this quality, together with their superior output in both quantity and quality, ensures a place for them in this field.

Optical Transmission

As we have seen, a jumble of different technologies are competing for the light output market. In contrast, one technology dominates the light transmission market: fibre optics.

Optical fibre is made primarily from silicon, as are microprocessors. However, the fibres utilize not the semiconductive properties of doped silicon, but the transparency of the element. Hair-thin fibres made of glass (which is based on silicon) provide a channel down which light signals can travel for long distances – 7·5 miles (10 km) or more – before it is necessary to introduce a repeater to 'clean up' and boost the signal.

The high frequency of light beams means that they take up less capacity than radio waves, and thus a hair-thin optical fibre can carry as many signals as a conventional copper cable consisting of several thousand wires. The cable is relatively cheap to manufacture, and is becoming cheaper. Since it is so compact, it is also cheap to install, using existing cable ducts. And unlike conventional transmission methods, the optical data are not subject to electro-magnetic interference. The cable is also virtually impossible to 'tap', and thus provides added data security.

Light signals are generated by L.E.D.s or laser diodes, and the wave pattern can convey the same range of coded information as can ultrasonic and other wave-based information media. The development of digital, rather than analog, communication methods makes it practicable for the light-coded data to be converted into electrically coded data as necessary, using the types of device we have already discussed. With the concurrent development of these ancillary technologies, fibre-optic cables are being increasingly used, both for conventional telecommunications and for specialist data transmission applications.

Light Processing

We have already mentioned some simple ways in which light signals can be processed mechanically: for instance, by converting a continuous signal into pulse form. Today, we are seeing an increasing volume of research into ways in which light signals can be made to undergo further processing, without converting them into electronic or other forms of signal.

This field can be divided into two major sections. 'Electronic integrated optics' is the name given to devices comprising integrated circuits in thin films of semiconductive material, which manipulate light signals under the control of electronic signals. These devices depend upon materials, such as lithium niobate, that can change their refractive indices when an electrical current is applied to them. 'Optical integrated optics' are at a more experimental stage. In these devices, the optical signals are manipulated under the control, not of an electronic signal, but of a further optical beam. The processing is not a combination of the optical and the electronic: it is entirely optical in nature.

Optical processors have a number of significant advantages over conventional semiconductor-based processors. They can work much more rapidly – indeed, at the speed of light. There is no need to convert visual input into another form before processing it. Their immunity to interference is especially useful in hazardous or unstable environments, and works in reverse, too: as they do not use high-voltage electrical currents, a failure in the circuit cannot produce a potentially lethal spark.

The devices are especially well suited to parallel processing: that is, to processing in which a number of arithmetic/logic operations are conducted at the same time, rather than in strict time-sequence. This leads to their particular applications in image recognition. Analysing, comparing and 'recognizing' images is a particularly difficult field for conventional computers to handle, and most current methods of tackling these tasks are far from satisfactory. Optical processing, in which all aspects of a complex image can be examined simultaneously, without the necessity to divide it into sections that can then be looked at sequentially, might lead to revolutionary breakthroughs in this area. As a result, the present very limited applications of optical processing systems could evolve into a major presence for this technology in fields such as robotics, medical scanning, and the identification of military targets.

Optical Storage Devices

As optical input and output and optical processing and transmission systems become more sophisticated, it seems clear that there will be a growing role to be played by optical storage media. Today, however, optical storage media (in the sense in which we are using the term) are not primarily media in which information is stored in image form. Rather, they are media in which the reading and/or writing of data is done optically. The data proper may comprise images, or, more likely, alpha/numeric data, or even sound. Whatever they consist of, binary coding of the data is the norm.

We shall next look at two major new optical storage media: the videodisc and the hologram.

Videodiscs: The term 'videodisc' is often used to apply to any disc that contains coded visual (and, usually, aural) information, just as 'video-cassette' applies to cassettes on which are recorded feature films and videos. Some such discs are decoded by reading them optically; others use a more conventional decoding system, similar to that employed by sound discs. Our interest is with those discs that use optical reading and writing methods, whether the stored data be audio-visual or of some other type.

The videodiscs that are used on a small scale today as a form of secondary computer storage are a direct spin-off of the discs developed for the entertainment market. However, the requirements for storage of computer data are rather different from those for the entertainment sector. While mass copies of a single audio-visual work are produced for sale, a couple of copies of commercial data are usually all that is required. Mass-producing recording techniques need to be adapted to meet one-off data writing requirements. Audio-visual discs generate moving pictures; when a computer disc is read, one frame of data may need to be retained on-line for some time. And it is particularly desirable in the computer field that the discs should be capable of being erased and rewritten. This last is a difficult requirement to meet, and it may be that videodiscs will come to be used only for unchanging archive storage. If they are sufficiently cheap, users will be prepared to dispose of them (as they do today of outdated information stored on microfiche) when an updated version of the data is produced.

The optical method of writing data on to, and reading data from, videodiscs involves a laser scanner. The laser 'burns' dark patches on to the recording medium: a layer of tellurium or some similar substance, protected by an inert layer of plastic. The dark and light patches are then 'read' as digital 1s and 0s by a photo-detector, or laser reading device.

Data are generally stored in 'frames' equivalent to the visual frame of a film, or as a screenful of alpha/numeric data, or an A4 page of typescript. The storage density of the discs is high: up to 500,000 frames of data can be stored on a double-sided 12"- (30 cm-) diameter disc. Another great advantage is that the discs are virtually indestructible, and that dirt and scratches on the plastic do not affect the laser's ability to read the underlying data.

The discs are rotated at speeds of around 1,500 to 1,800 r.p.m., so that access to data is fast and pseudo-random. A single frame can be 'frozen' by repeatedly accessing it on successive passes of the disc. As there is no physical contact between the reading device and the recording medium, no wear results from repeated access.

Holograms: Holographic storage media have been greatly discussed, but there have been many technical difficulties in implementing them. Only a few small-scale systems are in current use.

Holograms are generally thought of as three-dimensional photographs. A flat holographic plate rather like a photographic negative, which records three-dimensional data about an object or a scene, is illuminated to reproduce a 3-D image with full parallax. Underlying this technology is the ability to make a record of coherent light-wave data, including both the frequency and the amplitude of the waves, on photo-sensitive paper or in photo-electric form on semiconductive material.

These waves can also be used to record binary data and, by separating out different types of light wave using modulated lasers, many sets of data can be recorded on a single two-dimensional holographic storage device. By making use of different angles within a three-dimensional crystal (a 'thick phase' hologram), even more data can be crammed in.

If a suitable medium is used, the holographic memory should be read/write, rather than read only, and random in access. Together with the very high storage densities envisaged, these advantages should make holographic media a strong contender in the computer storage market of the future. Experiments with recording holographic data on ferro-electric media have been going on since 1968, but not all the problems that have arisen have yet been overcome successfully.

20. The Silicon Chip

In this chapter, we shall be looking at some aspects of silicon chip technology that we have not yet covered: at how chips are made, at the different types of technology used in them, and at some of the frontiers of development, and possibilities for the future, in microelectronics and associated fields of technology.

Let us begin by outlining the differences between the major types of chip components.

Types of Transistor

Two families of transistor types are used in electronic circuits: bipolar transistors and gate transistors. The chips on which they are formed are made in very much the same way, but the circuits themselves have different operating characteristics.

Bipolar transistors: The transistor we looked at on pages 40 to 41 is a bipolar transistor: it is a sandwich containing a central slice of either p- or n-type material, and two poles of the opposite electrical type of material.

The most common type of bipolar transistor technology used in silicon chips is known as TTL: transistor-to-transistor logic. Its advantage is that it operates relatively quickly; as a result, it is used in large computers where fast operating speeds are essential. However, it is not as compact as the rival, gate technology, and it is comparatively power-hungry: it has to be powered by mains electricity (suitably converted), not by a portable battery.

Another type of bipolar transistor logic is ECL, or emitter-coupled logic. This works even faster than TTL: twenty-five times faster, giving it a potential processing speed of 1,000 millions bits per second. However, though individual logic components have been manufactured using ECL, it has not yet proved possible to manufacture entire computers using this technology.

Gate Transistors: Figure 52 shows how a gate transistor works. As you see, the gate transistor is not a continuous sandwich like the bipolar transistor; instead, it makes use of a junction effect to close the gate and allow current to flow through it.

The gate technology commonly used in silicon chips is known as MOS: metal oxide silicon. This acronym is often further extended to designate the particular materials used, or the particular circuit features: nMOS, pMOS, cosMOS and similar terms are frequently encountered. All this family of gates use the general transistor structure of Figure 52.

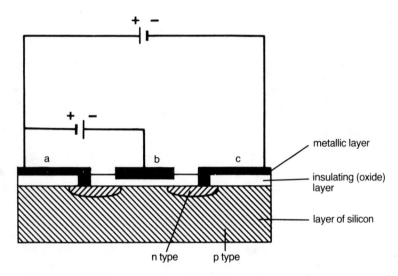

When no electrical charge is applied at (b) (the gate), then current cannot flow from the source (a) to the drain (c) or vice versa. The gate is open. When a charge is applied to (b), the holes in the p-type silicon substrate are negated by the positive charge at (b). This can have an effect even through the thin insulating layer. A narrow n-type region is formed across the gate, and current flows. The gate is closed.

Figure 52: Metal oxide silicon gate transistor

Gates work around ten times more slowly than bipolar transistors: typically at a speed of around 2 million b.p.s. However, they are more compact to manufacture, and a MOS chip will contain perhaps ten times more components than a TTL chip of the same size. MOS technology is also less power-hungry, and can operate from a portable battery power supply. The combination of these advantages means that this is the dominant technology used for the chips found in small computers.

Types of Chip

Of course, these and similar electronic components appear in different formations on chips designed to perform different functions: processor chips, memory chips, and peripheral chips. Let us look briefly at the main types of chips produced for different purposes.

(1) We have already looked at the microprocessor: a chip that contains all
     the components of a computer's central processing unit. A variation on
     the microprocessor chip is the microcomputer chip, that also contains
     some memory capability.
(2) Many logic chips, of course, contain part but not all of the circuitry of a
     c.p.u. Several TTL chips, for instance, may be bit-sliced together (see
     page 108) to make up a complete c.p.u. of a minicomputer or a
     mainframe.
(3) Read only memory (ROM) chips contain arrays of memory cells, into
     which unchanging information has been written. In Chapter 7, we
     looked at the different types of ROM technology: straight ROMS,
     PROMs, EPROMs, and so on.
(4) Random access memory (RAM) chips provide working memory inside
     the computer: information can be written and rewritten into their arrays
     of memory cells.
(5) Chips are also produced specially for many peripheral purposes. We
     have briefly discussed input/output handling chips, and some other
     specialist chips such as speech synthesizers. There are also chips with
     (for instance) special ranges of mathematical and logic functions, for
     use with less specialist microprocessor chips.

The Capacity of Chips

It is difficult to compare microprocessor chips and say that one has greater
capacity than another. The chips all contain a variety of components and a
variety of different circuit patterns, which make direct comparisons all but
impossible. Some new chips *are* clearly superior to older designs; chips that
operate with 16-bit words, for instance, have an obvious edge over 8-bit
chips. (And 32-bit microprocessor chips are now a reality.) But there is no
single measure of chip capacity applicable to microprocessors.

The same is not true, however, of memory chips. Memory chips are made
up of regular arrays of memory cells, and it is easy to identify the difference
in capacity between a 16K RAM and 64K RAM chip.

What is the current state of the art, then? Chip makers currently work on a
quadrupling of memory capacity at each new phase of competition, so chip
sizes have gone from 16K to 64K to 256K. Now (mid-1982), 64K RAM
chips are well established, with a number of competing devices available.
Chips with 256K RAM are already on the drawing board, and many
companies are talking in terms of producing chips with a million or more
components (one-megabit chips) in the very near future.

Of course, not all types of memory chip are equally easy to manufacture at
these densities. Dynamic RAM components can be packed together more
easily than static RAM components, and ROMs are easier still to manufacture at high densities. However, it looks as though 256K chips of all these

three varieties will certainly appear before long, and it is very likely that the megabit chips will follow.

Uncommitted Logic Arrays

One special sub-type of logic chips also has a regular circuit pattern. This is the uncommitted logic array, or ULA.

The microprocessor chips and other logic chips we have discussed so far have 'committed' logic designs: their circuits and components are designed to enable them to perform a fixed range of arithmetic/logic and control operations. The chip models we listed in Chapter 11 were of this type: they all had a fixed instruction set that reflected their circuit design

It is also possible, however, to produce 'half-finished' logic chips, broadly equivalent to programmable ROM chips that have not yet received their data input. The chip is manufactured with all its components in place; the purchaser then decides how they are to be wired together, in order to give the chip a fixed range of capabilities.

If a comparatively small number of chips (say, under 100,000) are required for a particular application — this might be a logic or control application in a certain model of computer, or a control application in an electronically controlled domestic appliance, for instance — then it is cheaper to program a ULA chip than to have a fully customized chip designed and manufactured. ULA chips are not as efficient in operation as fully customized chips, designed from scratch for a fixed application or range of applications. However, they have a firm place in the market for short-run applications.

How Chips are Made

Before it is possible to create the subtle semiconductor effects, dependent on precisely controlled doping, on which chip technology depends, it is necessary to produce a suitable form of silicon base. The silicon must be extremely pure (with not more than one impurity in one thousand million, though most manufacturers work to a hundred times more purity than this), and it must be in crystal form, in which the atoms are arranged in a regular lattice pattern.

The silicon is refined by a method known as zone refining. This takes advantage of the fact that impurities tend to migrate from the border between liquid and solid silicon, towards the liquid substance. If a heating coil is passed down a cylindrical bar of silicon, melting a narrow region as it goes, it will sweep the impurities to one end and they can then be discarded. Repetition of this process can produce silicon of the required purity, and precautions (such as controlling the factory atmosphere and restricting handling) must then be taken to ensure that surface contamination does not build up.

Once the silicon has been refined, it is generally doped with p- or n-type (in practice, normally p-type) impurities, and a crystal is 'grown' in the molten silicon. A single crystal of silicon may be up to 4" (10 cm) in diameter, and 7' (2 m) long. From this crystal are sliced wafers, around 0·2" (0·5 mm) thick, on which a group of chips can be formed. The upper surface of the wafer is highly polished, in preparation for the processes that it will undergo.

The processes that follow are designed to put into (or on to) the basic chip the electronic circuit pattern that will determine how the chip works. There are four basic constituents that make up the chip circuit components:

(1) p-type silicon, doped with boron or indium to create holes into which electrons can flow. As we have just stated, the basic chip is often made of this;

(2) n-type silicon, doped with phosphorus or antimony to give an excess of electrons. The p-type silicon can be converted to n-type if it is sufficiently strongly doped;

(3) traces of metal (aluminium is commonly used) that form the conducting 'wires' of the circuit; and

(4) insulating material to separate the circuit components from each other. Silicon dioxide, oxidized silicon, is a good insulator. Unlike iron oxide (common rust) it is not flaky: it is a glassy layer that can be produced in carefully controlled depths on the surface of the wafer when it is baked in a furnace at around 1,000°C, in an atmosphere of pure oxygen.

The circuit pattern must first be drawn up, before the process of transferring it to the wafer surface is undertaken. Some circuits (for example, the circuits of memory chips with arrays of identical flip-flops, or the 'uncommitted' circuits of ULA chips) are repetitive; in others, the pattern is extremely complex. It can take months or even years to design a complex circuit. Computer-aided design methods help the human engineers to fit together the thousands of circuit elements to form the most efficient layout. The complete circuit is usually broken down into layers (up to eleven of them are commonly used), each containing part of the circuit, which will be printed on to the chip in succession. Great care must be taken to ensure that the successive layers are perfectly aligned. In a final stage, cross-connections between the layers of the circuit are formed.

Producing a circuit layer: Because silicon chips are so small, designers have to work with a circuit image many times the actual size (magnification of 250 times is common) in order to create and check the component layout. Once the layout is finalized, the circuit image is photographically reduced to the actual chip size, producing a dense negative rather like a photographic microdot. This negative is then repeated to create a grid of chip circuit designs, which can be printed in a single operation on one wafer that will later be broken up to form a number of chips.

A photolithographic process is used to 'print' the design on the wafer surface. The wafer is first oxidized to form an insulating layer right across its surface. Then it is covered with a photo-resistant substance that is sensitive to ultra-violet light. When light is shone through the negative on to the surface of the wafer, the exposed portions of the resist material harden and become impervious to acid attack. Dipping the wafer in an acid bath dissolves both the photo-resist that has not been hardened and the oxide beneath it, leaving an etched pattern on the chip.

The exposed portions of the chip can then be doped to convert them from p-type silicon to n-type, or vice versa. This is generally done by a diffusion process. The wafer is exposed to the dopant (in gas form) in a furnace with an oxygen-rich atmosphere, and a few atoms of the dopant diffuse themselves into the silicon substrate. As a final step in this stage, a new layer of oxidation 'closes' the windows of exposed silicon.

This process is repeated until each layer of the circuit has been created on the wafer. Finally, windows are etched through the layers to form contact points to the components, and a thin film of aluminium is evaporated on to the surface, and into these windows. Engraving the aluminium to remove unused portions produces a wiring diagram to which external electrical connections can be made, and this in turn is normally protected by a final insulating layer.

Finally, the wafer is broken up into individual chips, which must be tested carefully to ensure that the circuits have been correctly printed. Acceptable chips are packaged in plastic covers, and connections are hand-soldered between their circuit wires and the external pin-connections of their casings.

Technological Frontiers

How are silicon chips likely to develop in the future? Will they contain even more components than they do today, or are we approaching the limits to their component density? Will new materials seriously rival silicon? Will new properties of semiconductors and electronic components be exploited? We cannot be sure what will happen in the future, but we *can* look at some of the developments and discoveries taking place today.

The scale of electronics: First, how large are the components on silicon chips today? And can we expect them to become smaller?

The size of the components and of the 'wires' connecting them is generally measured in microns. A micron is a millionth of a metre (or a thousandth of a millimetre): that makes it about one-fiftieth the diameter of a human hair.

Using conventional chip-making technology, it is possible to manufacture components and wires about two or three microns wide. Using the newer, more precise forms of chip-making technology such as X-ray lithography, laser processing and electron beam technology, it has proved possible to draw components less than one micron long, and lines less than one-tenth of a micron wide.

At this scale, effects with which we need not normally concern ourselves become of vital importance. It is hardly any wonder that normal photo-lithography methods are inappropriate: the wavelength of ordinary (visible, incoherent) light is itself about half a micron, so it is theoretically impossible to use ordinary light to obtain patterns with greater precision than this. More important, electrons themselves move on a scale that now becomes significant.

On a subatomic level nothing, according to our present theories of quantum mechanics, is certain. We cannot say definitely how particles will behave – we can only make predictions. And as we come to deal with a smaller and smaller number of particles, so the accuracy of those predictions decreases. Like people, electrons *are* predictable *en masse*: their pattern of movement shows up in reproducible electrical and electronic effects. In small numbers, they are *not* predictable. It is not possible to 'push' a single electron in a certain direction and be assured that it will continue to travel in it. We cannot be certain that an insulating barrier will resist *all* electrons, or that a conductive material will induce *all* electrons to flow in a certain direction.

This very unpredictability already has some uses, and we may learn to make even more use of it in future. But it is not well suited to the production of logic circuits that we wish to see behaving in a predictable manner. As a result, it seems likely that before too long we shall approach the minimum scale on which components that will act in a reliable electronic way can be built.

Another source of potential error derives not from the chips themselves but from their packaging. The packaging material radiates a small number of alpha particles (the nuclei of helium atoms) which can corrupt circuits and cause them to behave unpredictably. It is necessary to find ways of circumventing such effects, for instance, by building in a way of recognizing, and bypassing in the circuit, defective components.

Speed: Compared with hand computation, or even with the speed of EDVAC and other early computers, modern computers operate at incredibly fast speeds. But if they are to tackle some highly complex problems – the control of particularly fast-moving operations, the calculation of complex multi-constituent reactions, and so on – they must be made to function even faster.

To some extent, this can be achieved by adjusting the computer's architecture, adapting it from a serial mode of computation (one arithmetic/logic operation at a time) to some more complex simultaneous mode. However, the problem can also be tackled by developing circuits that switch more rapidly, or in which signals can travel more rapidly from component to component.

The switching speed (in other words, the speed at which gates operate) of conventional silicon-based semiconductor technology has already been pushed to its limits: Bell Laboratories have developed silicon chips that can carry out switching operations in 75 trillionths (that is, 75 million-millionths of a second. However, other technologies can do still better. One of these is optics, at which we looked in the last chapter. Optical circuits can operate, of course, at the speed of light. Some other alternatives also deserve our passing attention.

Gallium arsenide: Gallium arsenide is one of a series of materials — including gallium phosphide — known as IIIV compounds. Their main advantage is that electrons can move in them more rapidly than they do in silicon; as a result, circuits on gallium arsenide chips function faster than silicon-based circuits. The electrons move around thirty times faster, but the logistics of circuit design mean that the actual gain in circuit speed is only about two or three times.

Gallium arsenide has another plus: it gives off light in operation. In consequence, it has active and potential applications in opto-electronics.

Needless to say, there are disadvantages. The material is difficult to manufacture to a uniformly high standard, and it is considerably more expensive than silicon. However, some estimates suggest that it may attract up to ten per cent of the chip market by 1990.

Silicon-on-insulator technology: A new technique that involves working with very thin (around one-micron) layers of silicon, formed on top of insulating substances that confine electrical activity to this top layer, may ensure that silicon keeps ahead of rival substances such as gallium arsenide. Because the layer of silicon is so thin, electrons have less far to travel, and the silicon-on-insulator (SOI) chips can work between three and ten times faster than conventional silicon chips. They also open up the possibility of producing three-dimensional chips, sandwiching alternate layers of silicon and the insulating material to compress circuit components even closer together.

SOI technology is still in the experimental stage but, by the time you read this book, you may be encountering the following terms in describing real computer components:

(1) silicon on sapphire (SOS), using synthetic sapphire for the insulating layer;
(2) recrystallized polysilicon, based on a layer of silicon dioxide;
(3) implanted oxide, yet another technique that produces a base layer of silicon dioxide.

Superconductivity and cooling: One very real problem in cramming a large number of components very closely together is that when they operate, they give off heat. This problem is sufficiently serious for today's fastest and most powerful computers, like the Cray 1, to need heavy-duty refrigeration systems to keep their heat generation under control. Another new development not only tackles this heat problem head-on: it makes positive use of cooling effects.

At temperatures close to absolute zero ($-273°C$), some materials (including silicon) acquire a strange property: they lose virtually all resistance to the free flow of electrons and become, not merely conductors of electricity, but superconductors. If a source of current is applied to them, the current will continue to flow even after the original source has been withdrawn. Superconductivity is a fragile phenomenon, though: applying a magnetic field across the path of the current suffices to stop the flow. This effect can be exploited to form the basis of an on/off switch. These magnetic 'junctions' on superconductive material are known as Josephson junctions, after the Cambridge physicist, Brian Josephson.

The Josephson junction effect can be produced by submerging the circuit in liquid helium, which has a temperature of $-269°C$. In these circuits, circuit switching speeds of 13 trillionths of a second — substantially faster than even the fastest of today's computers — can be achieved.

There have been many problems in creating a working computer based on Josephson junctions: for instance, it is difficult to cope with the differential contraction of circuit parts made at room temperature, when they are cooled to these incredibly low temperatures. However, I.B.M. are actively pursuing research in this area, and it seems possible that Josephson junction technology will form the basis of the supercomputers of the future.

We end this chapter with a brief look at a very different futuristic technology. The development of biotechnology has opened up the prospect of our making chips out of living material.

The living chip: Can a computer be alive? This curious question is in some ways a counterpart to a question we shall be asking later in the book: can a computer think? Neither is a rhetorical question by any means. For as more and more of the characteristics by which we have defined living, thinking beings come to be reproducible in man-made constructs, so we are having to think harder and harder about what we mean by life and thought.

What *is* a living being? Many biologists place at the core of their definition the idea of an independently recognizable, self-organizing system. The components of the system — the atoms, the molecules, the cells — build up to form a whole that is somehow greater than the parts. They cooperate, they specialize: and though the actual components may change (for instance, as the being takes in food, and excretes waste matter), the identity of the system, and its structure, persists over the course of time.

There is nothing inherent in the idea of a self-organizing system to rule out things and groups of things that we would not normally describe as living (except perhaps in a metaphorical sense). Social groups, for instance, self-organize: political parties, religious movements and so on persist, even though their individual members come and go. In some circumstances, groups of machines, or components or capabilities within a single machine, *can* self-organize. Much work at the Biological Computer Laboratory at the University of Illinois, headed by Heinz von Foerster, was concerned with research into self-organizing systems.

What distinguishes any self-organizing system from a living being, then? An insistence upon an individual identity – in other words, a boundary that circumscribes the system's components and excludes non-components of the system – cuts out larger-scale social phenomena, but not self-organizing machines. Some biologists lean heavily on the idea of self-reproduction; others find it difficult to make this the *central* feature that defines life. And in any case, we are now at a point in technology where machines can build other machines, identical to themselves or even incorporating improvements upon their own designs. Once again, it becomes all but impossible to produce a definition of life that does *not* include computers.

The problem becomes even greater, however, when we consider computers that not only imitate the organization of living beings, but also use the same components. This is the field of biotechnology: the 'engineering' of biological substances to meet technological requirements.

How does biotechnology – which is often thought of in terms of improving crop yields, or manufacturing new drugs from natural ingredients – fit in with computer technology? It makes use of the fact that living cells, like computers, have input, process information, and produce output. They can organize their own resources and build on data provided: DNA quite literally 'bootstraps' an embryo into a fully grown creature, much as a conventional computer has starter programs that bootstrap its more complex programs into operation. And the bio-based computer technology also makes use of the redundancy of some parts of the living organism – a feature of our brains, for instance – to help it cope with breakdowns through the automatic replacement of malfunctioning parts by previously unused ones.

Research into biologically based computer systems is still in its infancy, though much interesting work has been done. But it is a fascinating prospect for the computers of the foreseeable future.

21. Assessing Computers

Which are the best currently available computers?

That question is all but meaningless. It depends on what you want a computer to do; how much money you have to spend; what your priorities and preferences are. A computer that seems ideal to one person will madden another one, and vice versa; one computer from a particular manufacturer may mysteriously prove much more satisfactory than an apparently identical one. But, of course, there *are* a number of factors according to which you can 'score' machines and ascertain just what they offer. It is entirely up to you to decide what weight you will give to each factor.

The range of available computers is immense, and it changes constantly. Entire books have been written comparing machines and recommending or rejecting them; entire books have even been written about assessment criteria. We shall not be providing any recommendations in this book. We *do* describe two particular computer systems: they are the systems we use ourselves, but we are not necessarily recommending them to our readers: their requirements may be entirely different from ours. What we shall do, in this chapter, is provide a brief rundown of some of the factors you should be considering when choosing a computer.

Who Makes It?

Does the company have a good reputation? Do they appear stable? (Bankrupt companies may mean difficulties with having the machine serviced, and a disappearance of all after-sales support.)

When can it be delivered?

In what state is it delivered? Ready to use, needing some checking over, or in parts awaiting assembly?

What after-sales support is available?

Does the company or the retailer provide good sources of advice? Particularly if you are a novice, do they provide training programmes?

What maintenance arrangements are available? What are the average and maximum call-out times? Are there different levels of maintenance packages to suit different users?

What other users are there in your area?

Will the company or retailer name any of them? What do they think of the system?

Many popular computers have 'users' clubs' that meet or circulate newsletters and provide practical and moral support. Are there any in your area, and for which machines?

What is the machine itself like?

Does it appear robust? Is it portable? Do you like the look of it? Does it have a modular design (separate visual display unit, keyboard, disc units), or is it one-piece?

What about its basic operating features:

(1) What is the c.p.u. architecture? Operating speed? (See pages 173 to 174.)

(2) How much RAM does it have, and how much of that is available for the user when the operating system is loaded?

(3) What is the keyboard like? Key configuration? (Full alpha/numeric, upper and lower case, with special characters you will need? Or more restricted? Separate numeric keypad?) Are the control keys clearly labelled and sensibly designed for use? Is there a 'repeat' function on every key?

(4) What is the visual display unit like? Is it attached to the keyboard, or can you angle them separately? Does it tilt? How large is the display area, and what is its display capacity? What colour is it? (normally green/black, bronze/black, or black/white). If black/white, does it offer 'reverse video' (white/black)? Are there brightness and contrast controls? Check out its operating characteristics, too: its cursor arrangement, its scrolling abilities, its graphics capabilities. Is the video unit in colour, or is a colour monitor available? (This is good for games, graphics, viewdata reception.)

(5) What are the secondary memory options? Cassette, floppy disc, hard disc? Densities of storage? Operating characteristics (access time, etc.)?

What Hardware Options are Available?

These might include:
(1) Different amounts of RAM. If you choose a small system, how easy is it to expand?
(2) Different secondary storage media. Again, how easy is it to upgrade the system?
(3) Peripherals, such as printers or pen plotters, light pens, joysticks, provided by the manufacturer or available (and compatible) from other sources.
(4) Is the machine designed in a way that makes it possible to add other firmware to it?

How About Interfaces and Communications?

What connection ports are provided, and do they match up to widely recognized standards? At what transmission speeds can communication ports work? Are the interfaces adequate for connecting any peripherals you are buying or may wish to buy in future?

If you wish to use the machine in a local area network, will it function and communicate correctly? Do you have to buy any extras (e.g. a communications software package) in order to use it in this way?

What About Software?

What operating system does the machine use? This could be a vital factor if you wish to use programs written with other machines in mind, or to communicate with other machines.

What languages does it support? Is the range adequate for your purposes?

What applications packages are available direct from the manufacturer?

What applications packages or simple programs are available from other sources (software houses, your local computer store, users' groups, listed in magazines)?

How easy is the machine to program? Are there software aids (e.g. editors) available for use by programmers?

How well is the software documented?

What About Documentation?

What written information is included? Training manuals? Do they teach you any languages you will be programming in, or assume you are an experienced programmer? Operating manuals? Is their information clear to you? Detailed engineering data? Do you plan to tinker with the machine yourself, or might your friends? Can you obtain any data that is not automatically provided, or does the manufacturer jealously guard all technical details?

And — last but not least —

Do You Like It?

No checklist is complete: and no checklist is a substitute for sitting down and trying out the machines you have shortlisted. Do you feel happy with your choice? If not, think again.

22. A Simple Microcomputer: The 'EMMA'

'EMMA' is a board computer assembled and programmed by LJ Electronics Limited of Norwich, England. It is designed primarily for training would-be technicians in the basics of computing and microelectronics, and it is particularly clearly and spaciously laid out for this purpose. However, the circuits in EMMA, and their general layout, are similar to those found in other microcomputers: both 'breadboard' self-assembled systems like the Altair we discussed in Chapter 6, and more commercial microcomputer systems.

In this chapter, we shall be looking at EMMA's layout: at its components, how they are fitted together, and what they do. In the process, it should become clearer to you how many of the aspects of computer technology we have described earlier in this book fit together. In Chapter 24, we shall go on to use EMMA as an example when we discuss programming a microcomputer in machine code.

Why EMMA?

First, why are we choosing EMMA as an example? For two basic reasons:
(1) its clear and spacious layout makes it particularly easy to explain how it is put together, and what components it contains;
(2) it has a particularly good range of peripherals, which we will be using in Chapter 24 to illustrate the versatility of simple control programs written in machine code.

EMMA's Layout

Figure 53 shows EMMA's main components: its integrated circuit (i.c.) chips, other electronic components, and some of the wires connecting them. They are divided into nine main functional areas, which we will be discussing one by one. Finally, we shall take a look at the features of EMMA that do not fit neatly into this functional division.

In fact, the diagram is also a very good indication of what EMMA (as it is sold) actually looks like. EMMA doesn't have a casing: all its components are exposed to view, just as you see them in the diagram. They are all mounted on a rigid green fibreglass board, that is actually about 12" × 9" (30 cm × 22 cm), and that is in turn suspended (by six metal pins) about $\frac{1}{2}$"

(12 mm) above an even thicker baseboard. (Some of the thicker components, and particularly the ports along the left-hand side of the diagram,
protrude into the space between the two.) As a result, it is easy to add and
remove components, or to plug directly into the buses to monitor the
machine's activities. All the legends on the diagram are also marked on the
EMMA board itself.

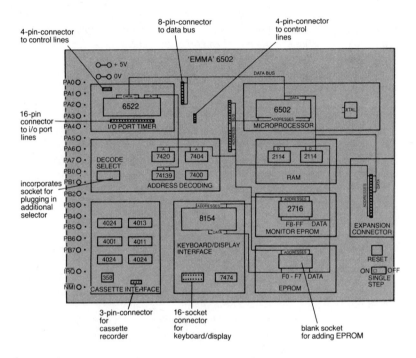

Figure 53: Outline of the 'EMMA' microcomputer

EMMA's Components

(1) **The microprocessor:** EMMA uses a 6502 microprocessor: the same
microprocessor that we looked at in Chapter 11. It is a 40-pin
integrated circuit: that is, it has forty connection points with the rest of
the computer circuitry. The functions of these are summarized in Figure
54. As you can see, they may be divided into three types, which
correspond with the three internal bus systems:
(a) address signals: there is a 16-bit address bus that, as you will recall
from page 133, is one-directional (signals go out from the microprocessor to the other components).

(b) data signals: there is a bi-directional 8-bit data bus.

(c) control signals: we shall be looking in detail at some (but not all) of these later.

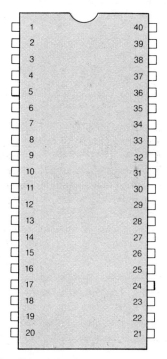

1 – 8	Control signals:
	power supply
	ready
	clock signal out
	IRQ interrupt
	(5 not used)
	NMI interrupt
	sync (fetch signal)
	power supply
9 – 20	address bus lines 0 – 11
21	power supply
22 – 25	address bus lines 12 – 15
26 – 33	data bus lines 7 – 0
34 – 40	Control signals:
	read/write (controls data transfers)
	(35 and 36 not used)
	clock signal in
	set overflow (not used in practice)
	clock out (second phase)
	reset

Figure 54: Pin connections on the 6502 microprocessor in EMMA

You may also recall from Chapter 11 that the 6502 needs an external periodic device to control the speed of its internal clock circuits. The device to the right of the microprocessor on the board is a crystal that is oscillated at 1 MHz. This means that this particular computer has a cycle time of one-millionth of a second.

(2) **Random access memory:** In the RAM section of the board are two identical integrated circuit chips. Each provides 1,024 × 4 bits of random access memory, and they work in tandem to provide a total RAM capacity of 1,024 bytes (remember, one byte equals eight bits). The actual chips used are model 2114s, which are MOS (metal oxide silicon) technology devices, using n-channel silicon gate technology. They are static technology chips, so they need no refresh circuitry.

Each 2114 is an 18-pin i.c. The 16 connections are used as follows: 10 to provide addressing signals; 4 data lines (remember, these are four-bit chips); 4 control lines, handling 'read enable', 'write enable' and other control operations.

Integrated circuit RAM is, as you will recall, a fast-access memory medium. The maximum access time for read or write operations is 450 nanoseconds (one nanosecond is one thousand-millionth of a second).

(3) **Read only memory:** The only read only memory on this model of EMMA is in EPROM form. As we stated in Chapter 7, this means that it can be erased and reprogrammed: in the case of this particular chip, it is erased under ultra-violet light, and reprogrammed electrically. For the non-technical user who does not intend to change the ROM programming, it is no different in use from ordinary ROM chips.

The EPROM chip is a 2716 model, which provides 2K bytes of memory capacity, or 2,048 eight-bit words. This means that the chip needs eight data lines. In fact, there are 24 connecting pins, used as follows: 8 data lines; 11 address lines; 5 control signal lines. Just like the RAM on this machine, the EPROM has a maximum read/write access time of 450 nanoseconds.

Finally, note the legend 'F8-FF' written under the chip. This refers to the addresses given to the memory in the EMMA system. They are written in hexadecimal form: this, as you will remember from Chapter 1, means a sixteen-base numerical system. As a result, four hexadecimal digits can hold the data from sixteen address lines. The addresses that access the information held on this particular chip are those starting with the digits F8, F9, FA, FB, FC, FD, FE and FF.

The monitor — the microprocessor operating system programs — actually takes up 512 bytes of memory space: only a quarter of the 2716's total capacity. These programs are held in the addresses FE00 to

FFFF in the system. In the other addresses on this EPROM, F800 to FDFF, are an assortment of demonstration programs.

(4) **EPROM expansion:** Directly below the Monitor EPROM is a socket for adding a second EPROM chip, which is simply labelled EPROM. As you can see, it would be located at addresses F000 to F7FF in the system. However, the second EPROM socket is not used in our particular system.

(5) **Expansion connector:** An expansion unit that gives EMMA additional capacity is available from the manufacturers, and this is connected to the original EMMA board at this point when required. You will see that the expansion connector consists of a 34-pin connection point, which is linked to the power supply, timing and bus circuits of EMMA. We shall discuss EMMA's expansion capabilities later, but shall not be using the expanded system for our programming examples, and shall not look in detail at the mechanics of expanding the system.

(6) **Keyboard/display interface:** The main component in this functional area is another i.c. chip: model 8154, which provides two different facilities:
(a) an additional 128 bytes of random access memory;
(b) two eight-bit ports, programmable to handle either input or output. These are used for two different functions: fourteen of the sixteen lines are used to interface to EMMA's keypad and display (which we shall look at on page 259); the remaining two are used to interface to a cassette recorder, if one is used for secondary memory.

The 8154 has 40 connection pins, which are allocated as follows: 8 data lines; 8 lines to connect to 'port A'; 8 lines to connect to 'port B'; 16 address and control signal lines, which we shall not discuss in detail.

The smaller i.c. at the bottom right of this area is a 7474. This is a 'bistable' unit: it provides the signals required to interrupt the microprocessor so that it can stop after each step of program operation.

Finally, at the bottom left is the connection point for the cable to the keyboard/display unit: a 16-pin connector, for the fourteen control lines from the 8154 and two power lines.

(7) **The cassette interface:** As you can see in Figure 53, the 'cassette interface' section of the board contains a number of small i.c.s and other components. We shall not look in detail at their functions: basically they convert binary 1 and 0 signals into and out of audible frequency signals that can be stored on audio tape, on a standard domestic cassette tape recorder. The monitor handles the timing and

control of read/write operations. Tape is the only secondary memory medium for which the basic EMMA system makes provision.

The interfacing system meets a standard known as CUTS: the Computer Users' Tape Standard.

(8) **Address decoding:** The four i.c.s to the right of this area provide manipulative circuits that act to 'decode' part of the memory addresses and ensure that signals are sent to the right chip on the EMMA board. We shall not look in detail at their operation.

To the left is a connection point labelled 'decode select'. If an expanded EMMA system is to be used, the address decode circuits will need to be modified to allow for the different memory configuration. This can be done by plugging an additional component into the 'decode select' slot.

(9) **The input/output port control/timer:** In this section of the board is a 6522 chip that performs the following functions:

(a) it handles control functions (including programming as input or output) for the two 8-bit ports, port A and port B, that are marked down the left-hand side of the EMMA board;

(b) it provides two 16-bit timer/counters, that can be used to simplify the programming of control programs that need to repeat their operations at specific time intervals;

(c) it provides an 8-bit serial data transfer register.

We can put this differently by saying that the 6522 is a programmable interface adapter chip: a type of special input/output control chip. It controls the sixteen input/output points in such a way that they can be addressed by the microprocessor as if they were ordinary memory locations, and acts as a 'buffer' between their input and the system operation.

(10) **Other system components:** The nine functional areas we have looked at cover the main integrated circuits and electronic components of EMMA. However, we need to mention briefly some of the other hardware features of the machine:

(a) The power supply. The EMMA board does not incorporate a power supply: this has to be produced externally at the 5 volts d.c. EMMA demands. The EMMA system is often sold together with a power unit that can provide power for the EMMA, its expansion board, and a number of the teaching peripheral devices that can be used with it. The power is then supplied to the board itself via two of the plug sockets at the top left-hand corner. The other two sockets can be used to run a peripheral device directly from the EMMA board.

(b) Connection points. The ports down the left-hand side of EMMA are actually provided in two different forms: 0·16" (4 mm) standard plug sockets, and 0·01″ (0·25 mm) spacing connector pin points. The latter are the small points you can see just to the right of the large sockets. There are many more connector pin points available around the board, in both pin form and socket form. These are designed for monitoring and testing system operation, and the large number of them reflects EMMA's prime purpose as a technician-oriented system.

(c) The ports. As you can see from the circuit diagram, there are eighteen 0·16″ (4 mm) sockets down the left-hand side of the board. The top sixteen are the input/output points of the ports A and B controlled by the 6522 chip. They can be connected to peripheral devices, as we shall see in Chapter 24. The lower two, labelled '$\overline{IRQ}$' and '$\overline{NMI}$', are concerned with the computer's interrupt facilities. (They stand for 'Interrupt Request' and 'Non-Maskable Interrupt': two forms of interrupt that the system handles differently.) We shall not look in detail at these interrupt procedures.

(d) The reset button. This is the button near the lower right-hand corner of the board; it is a red plastic button. It is used to reset the system: that is, to switch from the running of an application program back to the monitor programs.

(e) The 'single step' button, just below the reset button. EMMA has the facility to work step by step through application programs. After executing each program statement, the system switches to a subroutine that displays the contents of the microprocessor registers. Provision of this facility again reflects EMMA's intended uses as a training system. It is also a useful aid in debugging programs (see Chapter 28).

(11) **The keyboard/display:** EMMA'S keyboard and display is provided on a small separate board, about 6″ (15 cm) square, which is sketched out in Figure 55.

As you can see, this version of EMMA does not have a full alpha/numeric keyboard. Instead, the keys available are: (a) a hexadecimal key set, covering the digits 0 to F in hex; and (b) eight 'control' keys which we shall discuss when we come to write programs for the machine in Chapter 24.

The keys are 'read' by the monitor program held in EMMA's EPROM; the circuitry on the keyboard itself does not carry out all the necessary control functions.

EMMA's display consists of eight seven-segment light-emitting diodes. By programming EMMA appropriately, the user can illuminate any selection of the seven segments of each digit, to produce alpha/numerics or other symbols.

The integrated circuit between the keys and the display is a 7445 'binary decoder'. This carries out two functions: (a) 'decoding' the control signals the monitor sends (via the 8154 chip on the main board) to check for key operation; and (b) 'decoding' the monitor's signals to the display.

The 7445 has a three-bit architecture. The monitor works on a three-port basis to handle both keyboard and display functions, and the 7445 interfaces the three-bit signals it sends with the various display units.

The keyboard/display unit is connected to the main computer board via a 16-channel ribbon cable, as discussed above.

Figure 55: EMMA's keyboard display

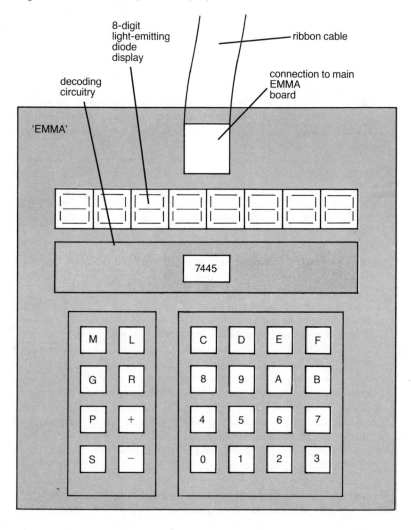

EMMA's Software

EMMA is a system designed for teaching programming and microcomputer design, rather than a 'personal computer' system in the commercial sense. As a result, it does not come with a large selection of software. The primary idea is to program it for yourself, though a selection of control programs (for controlling the peripheral devices that LJ also sell) are available in EPROM form.

What EMMA *does* have in the way of software are:
(1) the monitor program mentioned above that performs basic control operations. We shall encounter some of its features when we look at programming EMMA in Chapter 24;
(2) a number of short demonstration programs, for checking out the system and demonstrating its capabilities: programs that display predefined moving messages, for instance, or that operate some of EMMA's peripheral units.

EMMA's basic system does not include any high-level language capability, or even an assembler program for programming in mnemonics. It has to be programmed in machine code. The expanded system has more software capability, as we shall see later.

EMMA's Peripherals

As we have seen, the basic EMMA system consists of three components:
(1) the microcomputer board we described;
(2) a separate keyboard/display board;
(3) a power supply, which may be provided by the separately available power pack.

These components are sufficient to produce a working computer system; it can be used 'as is' to run programs that fit into its fairly restricted memory capacity. EMMA is designed primarily as a control system, though; to be seen at its best it needs to have some equipment to control. As a result, the basic EMMA is frequently sold as a package with some peripheral devices that can be used to demonstrate its controlling abilities. (The package is known as a 'basic microprocessor application system'.) Included in the package are:

a 'switch pad' with eight switches that can be used to provide 0 or 1 input signals to one of the input/output ports (e.g. to the eight lines of port A on the left of the microcomputer board);

a 'buffered loudspeaker' that can be used together with the switchpad to make a simple eight-note 'electronic organ'. We shall see this at work in Chapter 24;

an input/output port monitor, with eight ports in series with eight light-emitting diodes. Its ports can be connected to EMMA's input/output ports to give a visual indication of the signals they emit;

an analog/digital converter, so that analog equipment can be used with the system;

a strain gauge, that can be used with the analog/digital converter to act as a simple weighing device;

an oscilloscope, for monitoring system activity.

As we saw, EMMA has provision for a cassette recorder to be connected to it, and this forms yet another peripheral device.

We shall see many of these devices being used when we come to look at EMMA in action later in this book.

Of course, EMMA's abilities are not limited to controlling the devices provided with it. It can control a wide variety of real-life devices, as well as the experimental modules sold as part of the teaching package it belongs to. And there are more advanced EMMA kits that contain yet other peripherals. Before we look at those, however, let us look at how EMMA's actual computing abilities can be expanded.

Expanding EMMA

When we looked at the basic EMMA board, we mentioned the expansion connector as one of its functional parts. Among the devices that can be plugged into this connector is a computer 'expansion board', known as VISA. VISA gives EMMA the following additional hardware and software facilities:

(1) The ability to control a full alpha/numeric keyboard, typewriter-style with fifty-four keys. (The keyboard is available as an additional peripheral with the system.)

(2) A video display capability. A visual display unit is also available as a separate peripheral. It has a 12" (30 cm) green phosphor display screen. VISA has the ability to hold data on two screens full of information, using a 32 × 32 character memory-mapped display (see Chapter 17 for explanations of these terms).

(3) The ability to run a printer. The printer that comes with the EMMA/VISA system is run by a separate EPROM device, which can be plugged into the vacant slot in the basic EMMA board, or into the VISA board. It is a simple dot-matrix device, printing characters with a resolution of seven dots by five.

(4) A more sophisticated monitor program, taking up an additional 2K of EPROM.

(5) An assembler/disassembler program, for writing and inputting programs in assembly language (that is, mnemonic codes) rather than machine code. This takes up 4K of memory space (in EPROM form).

(6) A BASIC interpreter, for writing and inputting programs in the high-

level BASIC language. This takes up 8K of memory space. (Again, it is in EPROM.)

(7) An additional 8K of random access memory for use by the programmer/operator.

(8) A socket for a floppy disc controller. VISA does not actually include the disc control circuitry, but it can have the control circuitry added to it, permitting floppy discs rather than cassette tapes to be used as a secondary storage medium.

(9) A socket for a light pen module. Again, the light pen comes with control circuitry that also provides some additional software options on VISA's video screen. The pen can be used, for instance, to indicate a choice of options from a menu, or to select an alpha/numeric or graphics character from a set shown on screen, for use in building up a diagram on a second screen.

The VISA system also increases EMMA's power to control other peripheral devices, though many devices not included in the basic EMMA application set can be run without the aid of the VISA board. A number of the devices sold with EMMA and VISA are specialized aids for learning about microelectronic technology and control techniques, about techniques for programming EPROMs, and so on. The following is a random selection of the more 'general-interest' peripherals that L.J. sell for use with the system:

a stepper motor, a form of motor which can accept digital input and which provides an indication on a small scale of the action of motors controlled by microcomputer (or larger computer) systems;

a temperature sensor, an analog device used with the a/d converter;

a traffic-light simulator, which provides a model of a complex road junction with four sets of traffic lights to be programmed, including the facility to simulate the effect of traffic movement;

a robot arm, a simple robot that can make five different types of movement, rotate through 360°, and lift loads of up to 750 grammes. It is run by stepper motors and provides a more advanced indication of how the computer's control abilities can be put to use.

EMMA's Documentation

Of course, EMMA would not be complete without its instruction manuals: even the most expert user would be hard pressed to make much of the system without them. A series of manuals, some intended for teachers and some for students, explain EMMA's hardware and software, and take the student through a series of programming exercises.

23. A Small Business Computer System

Tandy ('Radio Shack' in the U.S.) market a series of computers in the TRS-80 range, from a basic home computer to small business systems. We use the Model II, which is designed primarily for small business use, in our own business, and we shall use it in this book to contrast with the EMMA, as an example of how a rather more ambitious microcomputer system is put together.

We shall describe the system we use, then look at some of the options that enable it, and the other computers in the range, to be tailored to users' specific requirements.

Like all the TRS-80s, the Model II is a microcomputer: at its heart is a single microprocessor chip. The chip it uses is a Z80A, an eight-bit chip working at its maximum design speed of 4 million cycles per second.

Inside the computer casing there is room for eight circuit boards, linked together by a bus system. Four of the slots are taken up in the basic system: one for the processor and associated circuitry, one for circuitry controlling the video display, one for the floppy disc controller, and one for the random access memory (RAM). Our system has 64K bytes (remember, 1K = 1,024 bytes) of RAM; systems with only 32K are also available. (To expand these to 64K demands the addition of a second 32K RAM board, taking up another slot.) The spare slots can be used to enhance the system with additional capabilities.

As well as the processor chip, there are separate chips to control the video display (handling display refresh and similar control functions) and the keyboard.

The computer contains only a very small amount of read only memory (ROM). This holds a bootstrapping sequence. It is accessed by the processor during the 'power up' operation, and is then switched out, so that it does not demand any address space while the computer is in operation. All other system software is loaded into the system on power-up, from the floppy discs on which it is stored.

Model II, like most Tandy machines using floppy discs, uses single-sided, high-density 8" (20 cm) floppies. These each have a capacity of 509,184 bytes: this is high by floppy-disc standards. The computer console has one built-in disc drive into which a single disc can be inserted at any time. (The discs can be interchanged during system operation.) Another three floppy disc drives can be 'added on' if required. Our system has a single additional drive, contained in a separate cabinet. In other words, we work with 'Drive 0' (the built-in drive) and 'Drive 1' (the expansion unit).

Data can be transferred between the disc and RAM at a rate of up to 500,000 b.p.s. When a systems software program is actually being used, it is 'loaded' from the disc into RAM for faster access. The systems software takes up a varying amount of space on the disc. Tandy's Disc Operating System, TRSDOS, in its usual version (it can be 'slimmed down' by omitting some utilities if space is at a premium for a particular application) occupies 39,040 bytes on the 'system' disc (that is, the disc that contains it). Of course, additional discs used in the expansion unit need not contain the systems software.

Address
(in decimal)

Address	Description
0 10240	Used exclusively by Operating System
10241 12288	Mainly user area, but used by some Operating System commands
12289 'TOP'	User area not touched by Operating System
'TOP' 32767 (or 65535)	Area which may be reserved by Operating System for special programming requirements

'TOP' is a 'memory protect address', between 12289 and the last address (32767 on 32K byte systems, 65535 on 64K byte systems), which is set by the Operating System itself. It then 'protects' higher addresses by reserving them (if required) for special applications.

Figure 56: Memory map for the TRS-80 Model II

Figure 56 shows how the operating system programs are allocated to RAM addresses. Some of them are permanently in memory during system operation; some are loaded only when necessary. (We look at the functions in the operating system on pages 270 to 271.) The space in RAM and on the disc that is not used by the operating system can, of course, be allocated by the user to:

additional systems software (for instance, a high-level language interpreter);

program or data files;

working space that is needed while a program is running.

The basic computer unit consists of: a cabinet containing the main circuitry, the video display unit, and the integral disc drive; and a keyboard, housed in a separate unit that is connected to the main unit by a short cable. Our own system also comprises: the disc expansion unit we mentioned above, and a printer, which we shall discuss later.

Figure 57: A small business system based around the TRS-80 Model II

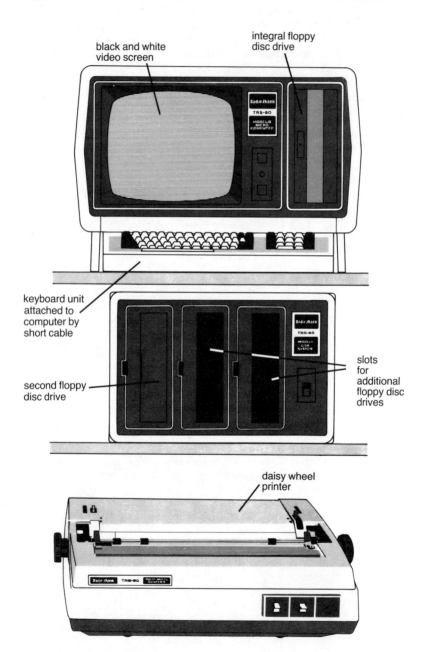

Figure 57 gives an impression of what our set-up looks like. The main console measures approximately 21″ (53 cm) wide by 14″ (36 cm) high by 15½″ (40 cm) deep: the disc expansion unit is a fairly hefty 20″ (51 cm) wide by 11″ (28 cm) high by 18½″ (47 cm) deep; and the printer is approximately 22″ (56 cm) wide by 9″ (24 cm) high by 15″ (37 cm) deep. Total keyboard unit size is 18″ (45 cm) wide by 2″ (5 cm) high by 7½″ (19 cm) deep. In other words, the entire system fits comfortably into our small home office. Of course, it operates at a fair range of normal room temperatures, from a conventional domestic power supply.

The Video Display Unit

As this is a fairly cheap business system, it has a black-and-white display, not the colour display that some less business-oriented home computers boast. There are brightness and contrast controls, and the display can be reversed to show either black characters on white or white characters on black.

Figure 58: Graphics characters available on the TRS-80 Model II

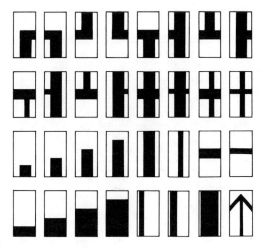

The screen is approximately 12″ (30 cm) across, and it can be used with two character sizes: to display 80 characters × 24 lines, or 40 characters × 24 lines. (The former is perfectly adequate for word processing and other routine business uses.) It displays a full set of ASCII characters, upper and lower case, and a set of thirty-two special graphics characters (see Figure 58). Its display can be addressed in two different modes: in 'graphics' mode, it can be thought of as a matrix with 40 or 80 column positions by 24 line positions; in 'scroll' mode, it functions as a continuous string of character positions, scrolling across the screen and back. Figure 59 summarizes the difference between the two modes.

Figure 59: Scroll and graphics modes on the TRS-80 Model II's display

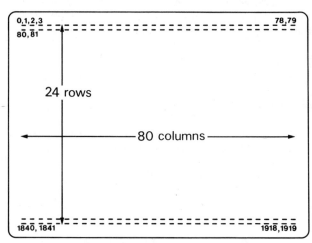

SCROLL MODE
When cursor is moved appropriately, screen display can be 'scrolled' up or down to fit in additional data at the top or bottom.

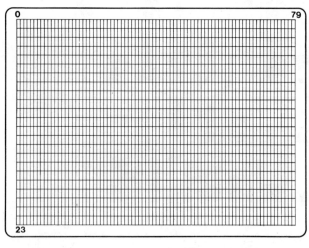

GRAPHICS MODE
Screen can be thought of as an 80 x 24 matrix. Moving cursor to edges 'wraps' display: e.g. figure in column 79 moves to column 0, same row; or in row 23 moves to row 0.

The Keyboard

Our Model II has an alpha/numeric keyboard that is much like a conventional electric typewriter keyboard, with the addition of a few extra control keys. To the right of this is a separate numeric keypad, again with some control keys, including the 'arrow' keys that control the movement of the cursor (the marker that determines where the next input will appear on the video screen). Figure 60 shows the total layout. We shall discover the function of some of the special keys when we look at programming the system in Chapter 26.

Figure 60: The TRS-80 Model II's keyboard layout

The Printer

Tandy markets a range of printers; printers from other firms can also be used with the computer. Our own printer is a TRS-80 Daisy Wheel Printer II which produces good letter-quality type, justified if required, at a speed of around forty-three characters per second. The daisy wheels can be interchanged, to allow it to print at ten or twelve characters per inch, in a number of different fonts, or to produce proportionally spaced output.

The printer operates in parallel mode, and there is a parallel 'ribbon' cable to link it to the computer console. (A similar cable connects the disc expansion unit.)

Interfaces

The interfaces with which the computer is supplied largely determine to what additional equipment it can be connected. Our model has the following ports, on the back panel illustrated in Figure 61:

Figure 61: Interfaces on the TRS-80 Model II

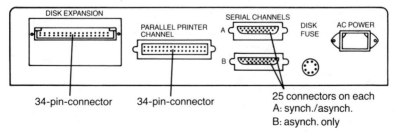

two serial input/output channels, conforming to the RS-232C standard. One of these can be used for either asynchronous or synchronous transmission; the other for asynchronous transmission only. They could be used, for instance, for connecting a serial interface printer; a modem for long-distance communication with a terminal or another computer; or a plotter or similar device;

a parallel input/output channel for connecting a parallel interface printer. This can output eight bits in parallel, and input four bits in parallel. In total, there are 34 connector pins, and all but four of the additional channels are used for various control purposes;

a parallel input/output channel for connecting a disc expansion unit.

The Systems Software

As already stated, the basic piece of systems software, which is supplied with the computer, is the TRSDOS (Disc Operating System). What exactly does this do?

TRSDOS has three types of utility: library commands (subroutines called up by a single-word command); utility programs (rather larger in scope); and system operating routines. The library commands are an integral part of the basic TRSDOS program; they are always available when TRSDOS is on-line to the computer. The utility programs are separate programs provided with the operating system on the system disc; they can be erased from the disc if they are not required for particular applications. We shall next look at some of each, to give an indication of what the operating system does:

Library commands: Among those available are commands that:
clear user memory;
clear the screen;
copy a file to create a duplicate for backup;
create a new file on disc;
control a Debug program that enables machine language programs to be entered, tested and debugged;
delete unwanted files from disc;
display a real-time clock (a clock that tells the time, as opposed to an internal timer) on the screen;
enable the system to act as host to a remote terminal via a modem;
help with information on available commands;
list the contents of a file on disc;
list the directory of file names on disc;
print a specified file.

Utility programs: There are a smaller number of these. The basic ones serve to:

BACKUP: this duplicates the data on a disc to a second disc (either held in an additional drive, or swapped with the original at intervals during the backup process);

FORMAT: the computer uses soft-sectored discs: discs on which the space is not pre-allocated in any fixed pattern. Formatting a disc allocates space in a pattern that the system uses when TRSDOS is running. It divides the total available space on the disc into 77 tracks (numbered 0 to 76) with 26 sectors on each (numbered 0 to 25). Each sector has room for either 128 or 256 bytes of data. It also divides the sectors into 'granules' containing 1,280 bytes each, divisions that are used when file space is allocated to individual named files. The FORMAT program also writes on to the disc essential system files, and provides a directory structure;

MEMTEST: this checks out the operation of the RAM;

PATCH: special utilities for changing the contents of existing disc files;

TERMINAL: a communications handling program that sets up the system to communicate with another computer. For instance, it defines part of the RAM space as a 'buffer' for handling incoming and outgoing messages, and can detect some errors (e.g. parity errors) in incoming messages.

TRSDOS does not itself contain a high-level language interpreter or compiler. The basic TRSDOS-operated system can be used for programming in machine code. However, among the software also supplied with the computer is a BASIC interpreter, which comes on the same floppy disc as TRSDOS. (Of course, when it is not required, it need not be loaded into the system.)

Tandy have a number of different versions of BASIC, used on systems with different amounts of memory to play with. The Model II BASIC is a powerful dialect: we shall be looking at some of its features in Chapter 26. It takes up 17,920 bytes on the system disc. When the system is being used to program in BASIC, the interpreter must be loaded into RAM, where of course it occupies the same amount of space.

Hardware Options on the TRS-80

Of course, the exact system set-up we have described is only one of a number of options. Cheaper models in the TRS-80 range will not have all the facilities of our system. Alternatively, our system can itself be upgraded to provide more powerful facilities. Let us look at some of the hardware options, to give an indication of the range of power that microcomputers like this can offer.

Internal memory: Our system has 64K bytes of RAM, a respectable, if not overwhelming, amount. By contrast, the smallest Model III comes with as little as 4K RAM. The greatest amount of internal memory that can currently be provided to the TRS-80 series is 256K but, to handle the addressing of all this, a second processor chip is necessary.

The processor option:: Tandy's newest (at the time of writing) and biggest microcomputer, the Model 16, has two processor chips: the Z80A that is found in the Model II, and the 16-bit MC68000. The Model II, too, can be upgraded to add the MC68000 chip. This gives it greater speed and power, and (as mentioned above) the ability to address a greater amount of RAM. The two chips are used for different functions: the 68000 handles the processing tasks, while the Z80A deals with input/output and other 'housekeeping' operations.

External memory: Floppy disc drives such as those our system boasts are not standard on all TRS-80 machines. The cheapest Model III does not come with any secondary memory capacity. To provide some at minimal cost, it is possible to interface a cassette player to it, giving it access to a slow but useful sequential memory medium.

Model II, and some other models in the range, can be interfaced with a hard disc unit, as an alternative to floppy discs. As we saw in Chapter 7, hard discs have many advantages over floppies. They do not suffer from wear as floppies do and thus are more suitable for continuous intensive use. Their storage capacity is also much greater. The hard disc drive that Tandy sell for interfacing with their microcomputers offers 8·4 million bytes of storage space. The drive contains two double-sided 8" (20 cm) discs (not removable, as are the floppies), with one movable read/write head to each side. Data can be transferred at a rate of 4·34 megabits per second: much faster than with the floppy disc drive. Up to three of these drives can be added to the Model II or Model 16 systems.

Printers: The daisy wheel printer that we use with our system is a top-of-the-range option: not necessary for data processing or entertainment uses, but highly desirable if, like us, you use the system for word processing. However, the system can be equipped with a cheaper printer, of course, or even with no printer at all. Tandy offer a range of dot-matrix serial printers for basic-quality printed output, and dot-matrix line printers for faster output, also of modest quality.

Ready-written Software

The computer system we have just described is, of course, all ready to be programmed in machine code or BASIC, prior to performing actual applications on it. But there are in addition a wide variety of ready-written system and application programs available for the various computers in the range.

We shall look, first, at the software we use ourselves, then at some of the other software Tandy sell. Of course, a number of software houses also sell programs that will run on this range of machines.

Word processing: We use SCRIPSIT, Tandy's own word-processing package, as we do a great deal of word processing on the system. SCRIPSIT requires a fairly large RAM working memory, so it can be used only on systems with 64K or more of RAM. (Some less powerful word-processing systems can be run on less.)

SCRIPSIT works quite differently from TRSDOS: it formats files differently, and contains its own operating system. So, to run word-processing applications, you remove the TRSDOS disc from the system and insert a SCRIPSIT disc instead. It, too, has utilities that perform system functions like duplicating discs, formatting new discs for use with it, maintaining indexes of disc contents, and so on.

To work with SCRIPSIT, it is not necessary to use a specific high-level language like BASIC. SCRIPSIT has a menu structure, and its own collection of commands: most of them single-key inputs like 'F1' (the key on the right of the keyboard) for 'enter text', 'F2' for 'delete a defined amount of text', or 'M' for 'move a section of text on to another page'. In other words, the SCRIPSIT software is entirely self-contained. It can, however, be interfaced (on a software level) with files created by different programs, like the PROFILE filing package we shall be looking at next.

SCRIPSIT comes as a package. There is a floppy disc containing the SCRIPSIT program and utilities (together with some empty space for user files); an audio-cassette and handbook training course, for teaching operators (who need not be familiar with the workings of TRSDOS or with computer programming) to use the package; and a reference manual.

File handling: We also possess Tandy's file-handling package, PROFILE.

Unlike SCRIPSIT, PROFILE does work within the normal parameters laid down by TRSDOS: it has the same formatting system, and so on. However, it, too, comes as a self-contained master disc: to run PROFILE, you remove the TRSDOS disc from the system and replace it with the PROFILE disc. This contains some of the TRSDOS operating system features, plus the file-handling program.

PROFILE effectively creates a database system. It allows the user to set up files, defining their structure (what headings are to be used, how much data can be stored under each heading, how the file is to be sorted, and so on), defining how they are to be interrelated, and defining how they will be updated and recalled (by planning screen layouts that act as prompts for inputting new data). The PROFILE system also allows some arithmetical operations to be carried out on stored data. However, its prime function is to act as a database; arithmetic operations are secondary and limited.

Files created and formatted according to PROFILE can, in turn, be used as data in other application programs.

PROFILE, too, comes in a package: a floppy disc containing the program itself and a manual that tells you how to use it. It does demand more computing know-how than does SCRIPSIT, though: and there is no cassette-based training course.

FORTRAN compiler: As well as BASIC, the TRS-80s currently support two other high-level languages, FORTRAN and COBOL. We use the FORTRAN package for writing application programs in FORTRAN.

Just like the other software packages we have mentioned, the FORTRAN compiler comes on a floppy disc, complete with a reference manual. This contains technical detail, but it is not a course in FORTRAN programming: it is aimed at the practised programmer. Anyone inexperienced in FORTRAN programming would need to buy an additional training course, or learn elsewhere before using the package.

The FORTRAN compiler works in conjunction with TRSDOS files, but not, of course, the BASIC interpreter. The additional FORTRAN files are five in number:

the FORTRAN compiler itself;

a text editing program;

a linking loader (remember, this is a compiler, not an interpreter; the compiler program converts the FORTRAN program entered by the programmer into an intermediate code, and stores it on disc. The load program then obtains this code from the disc, converts it into machine code, loads it into memory, and executes it):

a subroutine library, containing a number of additional subroutines that can be called up from FORTRAN programs;

and a utility program that handles tasks like printing out program listings.

Both the FORTRAN compiler and PROFILE demand 64K of user memory. To merge their files with files created by other utilities, it is virtually essential to use a second disc drive.

Additional software: Among the additional software that Tandy sell for this range of computers are the following programs and packages:

Visicalc: A widely known management planning package that calculates project plans using a 'worksheet' on screen. Designed for use by non-expert programmers.

General Business Accounting Programs: including Payroll; Accounts Payable and Receivable; Mailing List file-creation packages; General Ledger programs; Sales Analysis. Most of these are 'parameterized' in a number of different ways, to fit on to different sizes of computer system and to meet different user needs.

Packages aimed at special types of business: there are packages for lawyers, including 'Time Accounting' for billing the time spent by individual lawyers to individual clients; and a legal filing system. In the U.S., Tandy also provide an interface package that enables a user with a suitable modem to remotely access the 'Westlaw' electronic legal library.

There is a package for medical practices, a job-costing package for small contractors, and many more.

Programming aids: an assortment of editing and assembler utility programs, for use when programming either in assembly language or in a high-level language.

Communications packages: these and special program and data 'reformatting' utilities enable the TRS-80s to communicate with a variety of other manufacturers' computers, including I.B.M. and D.E.C. machines, that use different protocols.

Educational software: ready-to-use teaching programs, including courses on reading, mathematics and computer programming; and some special packages to enable teachers to write their own instruction material, using the PILOT and AUTHOR programming languages specially designed for this purpose.

Graphics: as we saw earlier, Tandy's BASIC contains a set of graphics characters, which can be used for drawing up low-resolution graphic designs. As an alternative, though, a special Graphics package can convert the screen into a high-resolution graphics mode, using 153,600 pixels (640 × 240). The Graphics package uses additional BASIC commands, and enables users to 'paint' in screen areas (filling them with a variety of dense patterns), or 'line' draw point-to-point on the screen, to produce tables, charts, maps or even animated videos.

Unlike the other software packages we have mentioned, the Graphics package contains some hardware. It consists of an additional circuit board (plugged into one of the vacant slots in the console), with an additional 32K of RAM dedicated to graphics use. There is also a disc with the software programs (extended Graphics BASIC, and a library of graphics-oriented subroutines), and a user manual.

Games: Model II is marketed primarily as a business system, but the more 'home'-oriented models in Tandy's range, and particularly the 'Colour Computer' (a low-cost computer that can use a colour television as a video monitor), have a wide selection of games programs available. Among them are: Chess; Backgammon; 'Space Assault' and other 'space' games; a simple music-writing package; a 'Rubik cube' package, which lets you go backwards to scrap mistaken moves; 'ELIZA', the amateur psychologist (an artificial-intelligence program, which appears to discuss your personal problems with you); and astrology programs.

Part Four: Programming and Languages

In Part Three we concentrated on the hardware of computers, concluding with a look at two specific machines. In this section, we shall be using those two machines as our examples as we come to look at aspects of programming a computer.

This book is not a programming manual and we shall not attempt to teach you how to program a computer. What we *do* hope to do is to show how programs are put together, and to explain some of the basic principles behind programming and the development of software.

The first chapter of Part Four will look at programming in machine code, the most basic type of programming, and one that is particularly helpful in making clear how the programmer uses the computer system's resources. Then we shall look at some aspects of how data are structured, as a basis for our brief examination of programming in a high-level language, BASIC.

We shall then examine briefly some other high-level languages, ending with a chapter (Chapter 28) that explores some of the aspects of programming in practice that we shall not be able to cover in our actual program examples.

24. Programming in Machine Code

In this chapter we shall be looking at some of the basic principles of programming in machine code, working up to the writing of very simple arithmetic and control programs.

As we stated in Chapter 9, machine code is machine-specific: its instructions depend upon the instruction set of the microprocessor used in the computer system. As a result, we cannot look at machine code programming in isolation: we must use a specific instruction set belonging to a specific microprocessor. We shall be using the 6502 instruction set, the set of instructions found on the EMMA microcomputer that we looked at in Chapter 22. Computers using different microprocessors will, of course, have slightly different instruction sets, and the machine-code instructions will in turn be different from those we use. However, the general principles we shall be introducing are applicable to all programmable microprocessors.

The 6502 Instruction Set

First, then, let us introduce the instruction set we will be using. Table 13 gives an alphabetical list of the mnemonic codes for the 6502's instructions, with a brief explanation as to what they mean. To use them correctly, we would need a fuller explanation of what exactly they do; however, space prevents us from including this for every instruction here. We shall be using only some of the instructions in this chapter, and we shall discuss their use and impact when we do.

Table 13: Instructions on the 6502 Microprocessor (listed alphabetically)

ADC	Add Memory to Accumulator with Carry
AND	'AND' Memory with Accumulator
ASL	Shift Left One Bit (Memory or Accumulator)
BCC	Branch on Carry Clear
BCS	Branch on Carry Set
BEQ	Branch on Result Zero
BIT	Test Bits in Memory with Accumulator
BMI	Branch on Result Minus
BNE	Branch on Result not Zero
BPL	Branch on Result Plus

BRK   Force Break
BVC   Branch on Overflow Clear
BVS   Branch on Overflow Set

CLC   Clear Carry Flag
CLD   Clear Decimal Mode
CLI   Clear Interrupt Disable Bit
CLV   Clear Overflow Flag
CMP   Compare Memory and Accumulator
CPX   Compare Memory and Index X
CPY   Compare Memory and Index Y

DEC   Decrement Memory by One
DEX   Decrement Index X by One
DEY   Decrement Index Y by One

EOR   'Exclusive-OR' Memory with Accumulator

INC   Increment Memory by One
INX   Increment Index X by One
INY   Increment Index Y by One

JMP   Jump to New Location
JSR   Jump to New Location Saving Return Address

LDA   Load Accumulator with Memory
LDX   Load Index X with Memory
LDY   Load Index Y with Memory
LSR   Shift Right One Bit (Memory or Accumulator)

NOP   No Operation

ORA   'OR' Memory with Accumulator

PHA   Push Accumulator on Stack
PHP   Push Processor Status on Stack
PLA   Pull Accumulator from Stack
PLP   Pull Process Status from Stack

ROL   Rotate One Bit Left (Memory or Accumulator)
ROR   Rotate One Bit Right (Memory or Accumulator)
RTI   Return from Interrupt
RTS   Return from Subroutine

SBC   Subtract Memory from Accumulator with Borrow
SEC   Set Carry Flag
SED   Set Decimal Mode
SEI   Set Interrupt Disable Status
STA   Store Accumulator in Memory
STX   Store Index X in Memory
STY   Store Index Y in Memory

TAX   Transfer Accumulator to Index X
TAY   Transfer Accumulator to Index Y
TSX   Transfer Stack Pointer to Index X

TXA   Transfer Index X to Accumulator
TXS   Transfer Index X to Stack Pointer
TYA   Transfer Index Y to Accumulator

We have used all the terms mentioned in Table 13 earlier in this book; if you are not clear what some of them mean, they are also explained in the Glossary (see page 428). However, the function of the instructions will become clearer as we go on to actual programming.

The 6502 uses basic one-byte instructions codes, so there is a set of 256 codes in all: the number of different codes that can be expressed in eight binary digits. However, you will see that there are only fifty-six instructions in the list comprising Table 13. This discrepancy is due to the fact that we have not yet allowed for addressing modes. Each addressing mode used by an instruction demands a different numeric code, and the various instructions in the list may be usable with anything from one to eight different addressing modes. In total, there are 150 different instruction/addressing combinations. These are summarized in Table 14. One other code is used: 00 for 'Break'. The remaining codes are reserved for future expansion and are not used on the system we will be looking at.

Table 14: Summary of Instruction Codes/Addressing Modes on the 6502 Microprocessor

	Accumulator	Immediate	Zero page	Zero page, X	Zero page, Y	Absolute	Absolute, X	Absolute, Y	Implied	Relative	(Indirect, X)	(Indirect, Y)	Absolute Indirect
ADC	.	69	65	75	.	6D	7D	79	.	.	61	71	.
AND	.	29	25	35	.	2D	3D	39	.	.	21	31	.
ASL	0A	.	06	16	.	0E	1E	.	.	.	.	.	.
BCC	.	.	.	.	.	.	.	.	.	90	.	.	.
BCS	.	.	.	.	.	.	.	.	.	B0	.	.	.
BEQ	.	.	.	.	.	.	.	.	.	F0	.	.	.
BIT	.	.	2C	.	.	.	.	.	.	.	.	.	.
BMI	.	.	.	.	.	.	.	.	.	30	.	.	.
BNE	.	.	.	.	.	.	.	.	.	D0	.	.	.
BPL	.	.	.	.	.	.	.	.	.	10	.	.	.
BRK	.	.	.	.	.	.	.	.	00	.	.	.	.
BVC	.	.	.	.	.	.	.	.	.	50	.	.	.
BVS	.	.	.	.	.	.	.	.	.	70	.	.	.
CLC	.	.	.	.	.	.	.	.	18	.	.	.	.
CLD	.	.	.	.	.	.	.	.	D8	.	.	.	.
CLI	.	.	.	.	.	.	.	.	58	.	.	.	.

	Accumulator	Immediate	Zero page	Zero page, X	Zero page, Y	Absolute	Absolute, X	Absolute, Y	Implied	Relative	(Indirect, X)	(Indirect, Y)	Absolute Indirect
CLV									B8				
CMP		C9	C5	D5		CD	DD	D9			C1	D1	
CPX		E0	E4			EC							
CPY		C0	C4			CC							
DEC			C6	D6		CE	DE						
DEX									CA				
DEY									88				
EOR		49	45	55		4D	5D	59			41	51	
INC			E6	F6		EE	FE						
INX									E8				
INY									C8				
JMP						4C							6C
JSR						20							
LDA		A9	A5	B5		AD	BD	B9			A1	B1	
LDX		A2	A6		B6	AE		BE					
LDY		A0	A4	B4		AC	BC						
LSR	4A		46	56		4E	5E						
NOP									EA				
ORA		09	05	15		0D	1D	19			01	11	
PHA									48				
PHP									08				
PLA									68				
PLP									28				
ROL	2A		26	36		2E	3E						
ROR	6A		66	76		6E	7E						
RTI									40				
RTS									60				
SBC		E9	E5	F5		ED	FD	F9			E1	F1	
SEC									38				
SED									F8				
SEI									78				
STA			85	95		8D	9D	99			81	91	
STX			86		96	8E							
STY			84	94		8C							
TAX									AA				
TAY									A8				
TSX									BA				
TXA									8A				
TXS									9A				
TYA									98				

Note that the codes in Table 14 are given in hexadecimal form: using the sixteen digits 0 to 9 and letters A to F as the basis of a base-sixteen numbering system. This means that two hex digits can indicate the data held in one byte of memory. (We glanced at the hex system in Chapter 1.) The EMMA keyboard has a hex keypad, you will recall, so we shall be writing our machine code programs in hex, and entering them in this way.

As you can see, there are thirteen different variations on the addressing mode, and most of these should be familiar to you from our discussion in Chapter 10. We shall be using some of these, and discovering how the choice of addressing mode affects the way we write our program, soon. There is one we have not yet met: the 'Zero Page' mode. This is a special immediate addressing mode, that applies only to the first 'page' of memory: that is, to memory locations whose first two address digits are 00. As the '00' is assumed, the address can be given in one byte, rather than the two needed for other addresses on EMMA.

You may also like to examine the data given in Table 15, where the execution times for the different instruction addressing modes are listed. As you see, the fastest instructions take only two machine cycles (remember, one machine cycle on the EMMA takes one millionth of a second) to carry out. More complex instructions can take up to seven instruction cycles.

Table 15: 6502 Microprocessor Instruction Execution Times (in clock cycles)

	Accumulator	Immediate	Zero page	Zero page, X	Zero page, Y	Absolute	Absolute, X	Absolute, Y	Implied	Relative	(Indirect, X)	(Indirect, Y)	Absolute Indirect
ADC	.	2	3	4	.	4	4*	4*	.	.	6	5*	.
AND	.	2	3	4	.	4	4*	4*	.	.	6	5*	.
ASL	2	.	5	6	.	6	7	.	.	.	.	.	.
BCC	.	.	.	.	.	.	.	.	.	2**	.	.	.
BCS	.	.	.	.	.	.	.	.	.	2**	.	.	.
BEQ	.	.	.	.	.	.	.	.	.	2**	.	.	.
BIT	.	.	3	.	.	4	.	.	.	.	.	.	.
BMI	.	.	.	.	.	.	.	.	.	2**	.	.	.
BNE	.	.	.	.	.	.	.	.	.	2**	.	.	.
BPL	.	.	.	.	.	.	.	.	.	2**	.	.	.
BRK	.	.	.	.	.	.	.	.	.	.	.	.	.
BVC	.	.	.	.	.	.	.	.	.	2**	.	.	.
BVS	.	.	.	.	.	.	.	.	.	2**	.	.	.

	Accumulator	Immediate	Zero page	Zero page, X	Zero page, Y	Absolute	Absolute, X	Absolute, Y	Implied	Relative	(Indirect, X)	(Indirect, Y)	Absolute Indirect
CLC									2				
CLD									2				
CLI									2				
CLV									2				
CMP		2	3	4		4	4*	4*			6	5*	
CPX		2	3			4							
CPY		2	3			4							
DEC			5	6		6	7						
DEX									2				
DEY									2				
EOR		2	3	4		4	4*	4*			6	5*	
INC			5	6		6	7						
INX									2				
INY									2				
JMP						3							5
JSR						6							
LDA		2	3	4		4	4*	4*			6	5*	
LDX		2	3		4	4		4*					
LDY		2	3	4		4	4*						
LSR	2		5	6		6	7						
NOP									2				
ORA		2	3	4		4	4*	4*			6	5*	
PHA									3				
PHP									3				
PLA									4				
PLP									4				
ROL	2		5	6		6	7						
ROR	2		5	6		6	7						
RTI									6				
RTS									6				
SBC		2	3	4		4	4*	4*			6	5*	
SEC									2				
SED									2				
SEI									2				
STA			3	4		4	5	5			6	6	
STX			3		4	4							
STY			3	4		4							
TAX									2				
TAY									2				
TSX									2				
TXA									2				

	Accumulator	Immediate	Zero page	Zero page, X	Zero page, Y	Absolute	Absolute, X	Absolute, Y	Implied	Relative	(Indirect, X)	(Indirect, Y)	Absolute Indirect
TXS	.	.	.	.	.	.	.	.	2	.	.	.	.
TYA	.	.	.	.	.	.	.	.	2	.	.	.	.

* add one cycle if indexing across page boundary
** add one cycle if branch is taken, add one additional if branching operation crosses page boundary.

Monitor Subroutines

As you will remember, instruction codes are only the most basic layer of software a computer can offer. Even a simple system like EMMA has a few subroutines stored away in its EPROM monitor. To give you an idea of how these extend the instruction-code capabilities, we list them in Table 16. You will see that many of them are concerned with interfacing the microprocessor with the EMMA keyboard and display.

Table 16: Some EMMA Monitor Subroutines

Write 4
FE00*   Displays the contents of the locations specified by the address given in the X register, and the three previous addresses, in ascending order.

Display
FE0C   Displays seven-segment codes stored at (0010–0017). If (000E) < #80, display is scanned only once per subroutine call. If (000E) > #80, display and keyboard are scanned until a key is pressed, when accumulator is loaded with the value of the key. If a Hex key, carry flag is cleared; if a Command key, it is set. (000E set to FF on RESET.)

DISPM
FE5E   Converts the contents of the locations specified by the address given in the X register, and the subsequent address, into seven segment codes, and stores them in locations 0016 and 0017.

DISPA
FE60   Converts the contents of the accumulator into seven-segment codes and stores them at locations 0016 and 0017.

* Hexadecimal addresses in left-hand column indicate position of subroutine in EMMA's memory.

DIS4

FE64   Converts the contents of the locations specified by the address given in the X register and the subsequent address, into seven-segment codes and stores them at locations 0011, 0012, 0013 and 0014 respectively.

GETKEY

FE88   Shifts in new data entered from keyboard into the locations specified by the address given in the X register and the subsequent address and displays the information on the left-hand side of the display (using subroutines at FE64 and FE0C).

TOTAPE

FEB1   Sends a byte to tape. The byte is sent from the accumulator.

FROMTAPE

FEDD   Fetches a byte from tape. The byte is read into the accumulator.

FONT

FFEA   Font for Hex to 7-segment code conversion. Occupies locations FFEA to FFF9.

Control Keys

What else do we need to know before we can start to program EMMA? Well, we need to know what the keys on its keyboard actually do. As a reminder, the EMMA keypad is reproduced in Figure 62.

Figure 62: EMMA's keyboard layout

On the right are a set of hex keys (digits 0–9 and A–F) that can be used to enter in hex form any type of information: instructions, addresses or data. On the right are a set of control keys, which tell EMMA how to interpret the data entered via the hex keys. These have the following functions:

M   the 'memory' key. When this is pressed, the digit 'A' (for 'address') appears in the left-hand position of EMMA'S display. EMMA interprets data entered on the rest of the display as follows: data in the next four locations (these are accessed when 'M' is first pressed) : the address of a memory location, in hex form. Keying in new characters changes the address being accessed.

data in the two right-hand locations (these are accessed when 'M' is pressed a second time): data to be stored in the memory location whose address is displayed. Again, keying in new characters can change these pieces of data (unless the address is of a location in ROM, in which case the keys will not be able to alter their contents).

Figure 63 should help to make this clear. It shows location address 0020, which is to be loaded with data FF. Pressing the 'M' key yet again will load the data, then a new operation can be carried out.

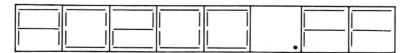

Figure 63: EMMA's display in 'M' mode

G   the 'go' key. Pressing this once lights up a rather odd-looking 'G' symbol in the left-hand position and enables the user to specify (in the second to fifth locations of the display) the address at which a program begins. Pressing 'G' again then runs the program. (This may cause the display to go blank, or a message may be displayed if the program instructs the system accordingly.)

P   controls the 'break' point in a program — a point at which program execution stops so that the programmer can check out in detail how it is being executed. This is an essential facility for debugging programs.

S   the 'store' key. This key is used to define data to be stored on cassette, if one is being used with the system, and to carry out the 'store' operation.

L   the 'load' key: for loading data stored on cassette.

R   restores program running after a break, or 'pages' through program steps when the 'single step' switch is on.

+   'memory increment'. Pressing this increments by one the memory address displayed (whose contents can be changed via the keyboard).

—   'memory decrement'. Works like the ' +' key, but in reverse.

EMMA'S User Memory

Not all of the RAM in EMMA in available for use by the programmer. Some of it is reserved for special uses by the monitor programs. What memory *is* available, then, and what are its addresses?

Figure 64: EMMA's memory map

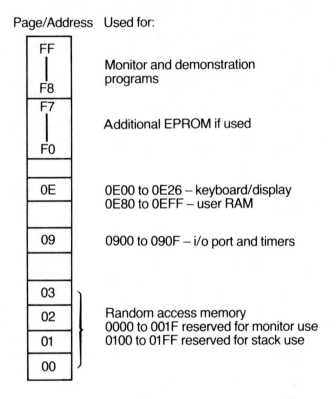

Figure 64 shows a 'memory map' of EMMA: the addresses of its memory locations, and an indication of what they are used for. This includes both read only and read/write locations.

EMMA's RAM can be divided into four and a half 'pages', with 256 bytes of memory to a page (that is, 256 addresses). These are as follows:

Page 0   This includes locations with the 16-bit (four hex digit) addresses from 0000 to 00FF. It is the page used for the 'zero page' addressing mode mentioned above.

   Locations 0000 to 001F on this page are used by monitor routines, so they are not available for use in user programs. Locations 0020 to 00FF *are* available.

Page 1   This page comprises addresses 0100 to 01FF. It is used for the 'system stack': its locations are accessed via the stack pointer. It should not be used by user programs.

Page 2   This page comprises addresses 0200 to 02FF. All these memory locations are available for user programs.

Page 3   Similarly, all the locations 0300 to 03FF can be used for programs.

Page E   While the previous RAM we have mentioned is located on the two RAM chips, page E is located on an interface adapter chip, the 8154 (see page 257). It is a half-page of memory, with the addresses 0E80 to 0EFF.

As well as bearing in mind which memory locations we can use for data or instructions in the course of our programs, we must also remember some special addresses that we will be using.

Thanks to the way in which the 6502 handles input and output, EMMA can treat its input and output ports in many ways as if they were memory locations: so data can be sent to them, or read from them, by specifying the memory addresses that apply to them. In dealing with the main input/output ports, A and B, we use the following addresses:

0900   Port B data register
0901   Port A data register
0902   Port B data direction register
0903   Port A data direction register.

The 'data direction registers' are (as you may recall) the registers in the 6522 microprocessor that keep track of whether the lines in the port are being used for input or output (1 signifying output, 0 input). We can program the eight data lines of each port in different combinations of input or output, by storing different data in these registers.

When the data lines are programmed for output, we can then send data to them (that is, to their 'data registers', which effectively comprise the ports themselves and their buffers). When the data lines are programmed for input, we cannot send any data to them: the computer receives data *from* them.

Various locations on the E memory page (not in the available range) are similarly used to interface with the keyboard and display (which, you will recall, is handled by the 8154 chip which contains this block of RAM) and to handle the cassette interface. Two ports are handled by the 8154, known (like the 6522 ports) as A and B. However, it is not the case that one controls the cassette and one the keyboard/display. Instead, their lines are used as follows:

Port A, lines 0 to 2: to determine which locations of the display (of the eight available) are used for any particular function;

Port A, lines 3 to 5: handle input to the keyboard;

Port A, line 6: output to the cassette;

Port A, line 7: input from the cassette;

Port B, all lines: define the segments of the seven-segment (plus stop) L.E.D.'s in the display that light up.

The addresses of the 8154 ports are as follows:

0E20   Port A data register

OE21   Port B data register
OE22   Port A data direction register
OE23   Port B data direction register

However, it is not necessary with the 8154 ports to program them for input or output before using them. The monitor program handles this, in the pattern demanded by the uses specified above.

In addition, other specific memory locations are used to describe the interrupts and various other functions of the machine. We shall not be using these in the very simple programming we shall do in this chapter.

Planning and Writing a Program

With all this basic information behind us (and it is only the tip of the iceberg of the information we would need if we used EMMA to the fullest), we can now go on to write our very first simple program. We shall look first at a couple of very short arithmetic programs, and then go on to use EMMA for some control programs.

What must we do before we write a program? The usual procedure goes like this:

(1) **Analyse the problem:** First, we must decide just what the program is to do. The level of detail at which we will do this depends upon the complexity of the program: for a very complex program, we might sketch it out first in broad outline, then work on it in detail, section by section. For our very simple program, we shall try to be exhaustive this first time around.

It is very common to use a flowchart as an aid in analysing what we want the program (and, by extension, the computer) to do. The flowchart is purely an aid to the programmer in visualizing the program steps: it traces out the algorithm, or the general shape of the solution to our problem. As such, it is part of the program documentation (a subject we shall discuss in Chapter 28), but not of the program itself.

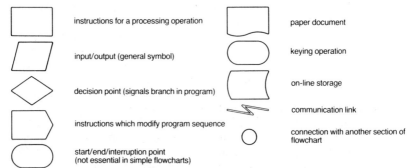

instructions for a processing operation	paper document
input/output (general symbol)	keying operation
decision point (signals branch in program)	on-line storage
instructions which modify program sequence	communication link
start/end/interruption point (not essential in simple flowcharts)	connection with another section of flowchart

Figure 65: Conventional symbols used in flowcharts

There are a number of conventions about the shape of the boxes and the types of lines used to connect them in drawing flowcharts. The few we shall need are summarized in Figure 65. We shall use them in drawing up a simple list of what we must tell the computer to do to, say, add 35 and 40.

Admittedly, it would be no trouble to do the arithmetic mentally without the aid of the computer, but at this stage that is a bonus: we can see when we get the result whether we did the right things!

A flowchart for adding 35 to 40 is shown in Figure 66.

Figure 66: Flowchart for adding two numbers (35 and 40)

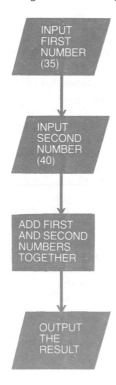

(2) **Decide how the computer will carry out the program:** For many problems, including this very simple one, there are a number of ways we can use the computer's resources. What resources? Well, we have to decide: where in the computer we shall enter our data and instructions; which instructions (from the basic instruction set, or monitor subroutines, or more elaborate instructions if they are available) will fit the bill; how the output is to be communicated to us.

(3) **Write down in detail the instruction steps, and the addresses and data that we plan to use:** It is usual to do this in mnemonic form, using (for instance) the instruction mnemonics that were listed in Table 12. Choosing addresses (in memory, or microprocessor registers) for our data will enable us to select a particular addressing mode — or vice versa. Our data we already have, but at this stage we shall need to convert it into hex form.

(4) **Write down the machine-code listing that we want to enter into the computer:** We shall compile this with the help of the codes given in Table 13.

(5) **Enter the machine-code listing into the computer:** To do this, we shall need to use the control keys discussed above.

(6) **And, last but not least, Run the program.**

With all that in mind, let us go through steps 2–6 for the EMMA.

Step 2. How shall we use the computer's resources to carry out our very simple algorithm? In theory we could input our two pieces of data into any available memory or microprocessor location, but it seems clear that we shall find it easiest to input one of them into the accumulator. We can then use instruction code ADC (Add Memory to Accumulator with Carry). Then we shall designate memory locations to contain our instructions and find a suitable location for the second piece of data. By using a zero page location for the data, we shall be able to use the shortest and simplest form of instruction available to us. Of course, we could choose some other memory location, and then we would need to choose a different addressing mode to access it.

We have only one output medium available to us: the L.E.D display on the keyboard unit. However, there are two alternative ways in which we might obtain our output:

(1) As novice programmers, we might simply take a look at the result as it is stored in memory, when our program has finished running. Of course, to be sure of a correct answer we would also have to check the status of the 'overflow' bit, or the 'carry' bit (which one depends on which arithmetic mode we select — binary, signed or binary-coded decimal) to make sure that the answer had not overflowed beyond the accumulator's eight-bit capacity.

(2) We might program the system to send the result to the output ports that control the display, and to convert it into the form we require.

Resolving these points brings up yet another point: EMMA (as we discovered in Chapter 22) can handle arithmetic in three different modes, binary, binary using a sign bit, or binary-coded decimal. Which shall we use? Well, let us write two alternative programs. First, we shall do a simple version, in binary, in which we simply look at the accumulator contents to obtain our answer (Program A). Second, we shall do a version that enables us to input our data, and receive our answer on the display, in binary-coded decimal (Program B).

Step 3 – Program A. For the easy version, then, this is what we shall need to do:

Clear Decimal Mode: CLD

Clear the Carry Flag: CLC

Load Accumulator with Memory (immediate mode: data follows): LDA # 23

Add Memory to Accumulator with Carry (immediate mode: data follows): ADC # 28

Store Accumulator Contents in Memory (zero page mode: two address digits follow) STA 30

Note the 'hash' symbol (#) that we use in front of data, to distinguish between data and addresses in which data are to be stored.

How many memory locations shall we need to store these instructions? Not many, but our normal best practice is to start at the beginning of a page in RAM, and then work down consecutive locations, using the 'memory increment' key to enter the data and instructions. So we shall start at address 0020, on the first page of RAM, and work down until we reach the end.

Finally, we need to stop our program. Some microprocessors have stop instructions; ours does not, so we need to tell the machine to 'do something sensible' when the program is complete. The usual default option is to Jump to a memory location in the monitor program. The 'Jump' instruction (JMP) can be used only with the absolute or indirect addressing modes: we shall use the absolute, the more straightforward, followed by the monitor address FEF3. (EMMA always accepts the 'low' half of an address first, followed by the 'high' half (if not zero).)

Step 4 – Program A. And now we can write our machine code program.

Address	Mnemonics	Data
0020	CLD	D8
0021	CLC	18
0022	LDA # 23	A9, 23
0024	ADC # 28	69, 28
0026	STA 30	85, 30
0028	JMP F3, FE	4C, F3, FE

Note that we only list the addresses with which each new program statement (the instruction and its associated addresses and data) begins. The intermediate addresses are implied: so, in fact, A9 will go in address 0022, 23 in address 0023, and so on. This is the usual convention in listing machine code.

Note too the form of our arithmetical data: not decimal 35 and 40, but hex 35 and 40: 23 and 28 respectively.

Step 5 – Program A. How do we enter this listing into the computer? Quite easy, really. We 'reset' the computer to undertake a new task (using the button on the bottom right-hand corner of the main EMMA board), then input all these instructions using the 'M' and ' +' (memory and memory increment) control keys. Then we tell the computer to 'G 0020' (go to the start of the program) and to 'G' again (run the program).

Finally, how do we obtain our result? We told the computer to place the accumulator contents in address 0030 (the first two zeros being assumed in zero page mode), so all we need to do is to look at the contents of this location. (We do this using the 'M' key, entering 0030 as the location we want to inspect or change.) A brief check ensures that this location holds the number 4C (in hex, 75 in decimal).

Program B. How could we modify this program to carry out the additional functions we specified above: that is, to accept decimal input, give decimal output, and to display the output for us without further prompting? The following changes would be necessary:

(1) We would not clear, but set the decimal mode at the start of the program.

(2) We would obviously change our data input to decimal form.

(3) We would need to build into the program a check to ensure that the carry flag was not set by the operation. (The carry flag – not the overflow flag, as you might think – is the important one here: the overflow flag is not a reliable indicator in binary-coded decimal operations.)

(4) And we would need to find a way of programming the display function. The last of these is obviously the most demanding. The 6502 instruction set does not give us much help with displays: we have to handle the display orders step by step in machine code, telling the machine where to send its output and exactly what to do with it (which digits in the display to light up, which segments of them to light up, and so on). However, the brief list of monitor subroutines we gave in Table 15 *does* mention displays. To save us from programming the display in depth, we can write our program so as to use one of these subroutines.

Let us take, for instance, the subroutine stored at FE88. This effectively takes the data stored in the address held in the X register, and the subsequent address, converts them into display form, and displays them on the left-hand side of the display. How could we incorporate this subroutine into our program?

(1) by sending our result to a memory location as before;

(2) by sending the address of this memory location to register X;

(3) by ensuring that the subsequent location in memory contains the data 00 (in hex), so that the full display will be clear. To do this, we would need to load 00 into a suitable location (say, register Y, which we are not using yet) and store it in the memory location;

(4) and by 'jumping' to the subroutine (with a 'JMP' instruction and the subroutine address).

How could we check the carry flag? In the instruction set, you will recall, there is an instruction to branch if the carry flag is set, or alternatively to branch if it is clear. Both of them demand relative addressing: that is, we follow the instruction byte with a second byte that contains an offset value to be added to the program counter. In the given circumstances, the program will then branch to this new address for its next instruction. We shall use the 'branch if set' instruction, amending subsequent steps to allow for a carry bit if one is required.

Table 17: Program for Adding 35 to 40 in Machine Code

Address	Mnemonics	Data
0020	SED	F8
0021	CLC	18
0022	LDA #35	A9, 35
0024	ADC #40	69, 40
0026	STA 40	85, 40
0028	LDX #40	A2, 40
002A	BCS 6	B0, 06
002C	LDY #00	A0, 00
002E	STY 41	84, 41
0030	BCC 4	90, 04
0032	LDY #01	A0, 01
0034	STY 41	84, 41
0036	JSR FE88	4C, 88, FE
0039	JSR FEF3	FC, F3, FE

Table 17 gives the mnemonics and machine-code listing for a program that could accomplish all these things. You should be able to follow its structure with the help of the instruction set and other listings in Tables 13, 14 and 16. Note the following points:

(1) Address 002A: This is our 'branch if carry set' instruction. Note the number that follows: 06 is the number of program steps (i.e. memory addresses) we want to omit if the branch is taken. The 'branch if carry clear' instruction at 0030 works the same way.

(2) Address 0028. We must be careful here: we do not want to load register X with the data *in* location 40 (which is where we put our result, in addresses 0026/7) but with the *data* 0040 — that is, the address of the location whose contents we want to be displayed. So we want immediate mode, and not zero page mode, for our instruction.

(3) We have included a routine for coping if our arithmetic operation overflows. We branch if 'carry' is set to enter 01 into memory location

0041, the second location we display. If we then added, say, 35 and 99, the display would still come up with the right answer.

From Arithmetic to Control Programming

Doubtless you are not particularly impressed by EMMA's performance so far. It has taken fourteen different instructions to make the computer carry out a simple arithmetical operation that you could have done in your head in a fraction of the time. If this is typical, why do we bother? Well, some of the reasons are:

(1) If the problem were much more complex, EMMA could still be programmed to carry it out rapidly and without error: though not easily programmed, admittedly, allowing for the limitations of its instruction set.

(2) If you wanted to repeat a complex series of mathematical manipulations on a series of different data, then you would not have to go through the chore of writing the program from scratch each time. You could save it on cassette, and simply change the data each time.

However, EMMA's real forte is not arithmetic at all. Though (as we have shown) the machine *can* be used for arithmetical operations, its qualities show to much greater advantage when it is used for control operations. While machine code is poorly adapted to complex arithmetic, it *is* well adapted to the repetitive, specific operations of controlling equipment via the peripheral ports. And we shall now go on to look at how EMMA sets about controlling two simple pieces of equipment from its companion set of peripherals.

A Simple Electronic Organ

Among EMMA's peripherals are two gadgets that can be used together to make a very simple electronic 'organ': a switch pad, with eight keys, and a buffered loudspeaker. The switch pad can be used to send input to the computer: pressing each switch will send a 0 or a 1 impulse to the data line to which it is connected, depending upon which way round the switch pad is wired. And the organ can be used to receive output from the computer. Generating a simple square wave at a fixed frequency (the usual form of digital output) will cause it to emit a note of that frequency. It is quite an easy job to cause each of the eight input channels to which the switch pad is connected to trigger the generation of a different frequency of wave, then as the switch pad keys are pressed they will play a very simple one-octave tune.

The hardware: First, let us look at Figure 67, which shows the hardware configuration we shall be working with. We shall connect the switch pad to port B of the two ports controlled by the 6522 microprocessor. This is simply done by plugging in leads that connect each of the eight switch pad channels with each of the eight port lines.

Figure 67: Hardware configuration for an electronic organ

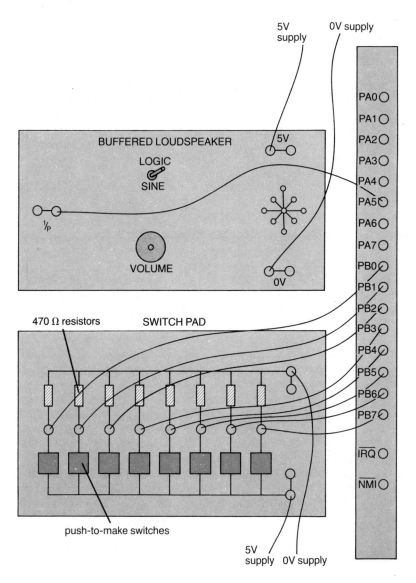

The switch pad also needs a 5V power supply: it can be run either off the two spare sockets on the EMMA board or directly from the power pack. As you can see, it can be connected either way round: with the 5V input at the top or the bottom right-hand corner, and the 0V at the other input point. The series of eight 470 ohm resistors, one in series with each switch, determines the direction of current flow. Arranging the 5V supply at the bottom and the 0V at the top means that the switches must be depressed (completing the simple circuits) before power will flow back to the input ports. In other words, pressing a switch sends a series of 1 impulses, for as long as the circuit is connected. If a switch is not pressed, then input is at the 0 level.

The loudspeaker unit also needs a 5V power supply, but this time the direction is fixed. It has only one effective input point, so it can be connected to only one data channel of Port A. How do we choose which? It depends how we program the system: for instance, we could arrange for different wave frequencies to be associated with each. For now, we will plug it into PA5.

As you can see, the loudspeaker also has a volume control, and a logic/sine switch. For our purposes, we want this to be switched to 'logic'. Switching it to 'sine' enables the loudspeaker to be used to amplify low-level analog signals.

Outputting a variable waveform: As you already know, the output from the microcomputer is in the form of a variable electrical impulse. In our particular system, a level of approximately 5V indicates a logical 1, and a level of approximately 0V a logical 0. When a stream of 1s and/or 0s are output (one at the end of each instruction cycle, or every millionth of a second, the microprocessor cycle time), the result is a 'square wave', which switches from one voltage level to the other, and back again, as shown in Figure 68a.

By altering the intervals at which we switch from one logic level to the other, and back again, we can produce waves of varying frequencies. Figure 68b shows how this is done. The eight channels here represent eight output lines, just like the eight lines of port A. In each successive horizontal line, we are 'incrementing' the signal: adding a binary 1 to our output. And you will see that the result is a wave of a regular frequency that is doubled at each successive output channel, going from left to right.

The result of this simple operation (which requires no independent input) would be the production of continuous notes of a fixed frequency, with a different frequency of note being produced at each output channel. To alter the frequency of the note being output at a single channel, like the PA5 to which we have connected our loudspeaker, we need to change the rate at which its signal changes from 0 to 1 and back again. The principle involved is just the same. We could make such a change by drawing up a 'look-up' table of successive values, just like the table in Figure 68c, but with a more complicated content, and sending each successive piece of data to the

Figure 68: Outputting waveforms

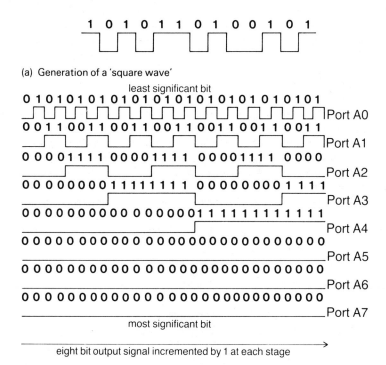

(a) Generation of a 'square wave'

(b) Waves of varying frequency generated at the eight lines of port A by incrementing the output signal

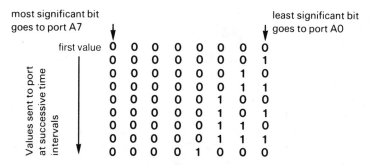

(c) The initial data to produce the waves shown in (b), in the form of a look-up table. (only the first nine values are shown)

output port as required. Alternatively, we could do so by tying the output to a variable·input, like the input we shall be receiving from our switchpad.

Of course, we do not want the frequency of the note to change at every instruction cycle! We want a note of a recognizable frequency to be sustained for a minimum time that is at least sufficiently long for us to hear it. In order to do this, since the microprocessor works so fast compared to the responses of the human ear, we need to build time delays into our system.

How can we program a time delay? There are two simple ways of doing so:

(1) We can build a 'delay loop' into the program. For instance, we might put a suitable value into one of the microprocessor registers (say, X) and then decrement the register. After each decrement, we would check the contents, branching back to decrement again if they had not reached 0, and going on to carry out the rest of the program if 0 had been reached. Figure 69 shows the flowchart for this simple operation.

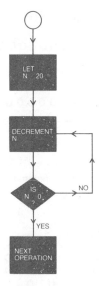

Figure 69: Flowchart for a simple delay loop

(2) We could program a timer, like the timers contained in the 6522 chip, to time our delay for us. This method has the advantage that the microprocessor is not fully occupied while the delay is being counted. It can be used to perform other tasks then, when the delay is complete, the timer will interrupt it with an interrupt signal.

For our simple program, requiring a relatively short delay period, we will use the first of these methods.

How do we set about writing the program? Let us follow the steps outlined above, and start by analysing our problem and writing a flowchart to indicate our algorithm.

What do we need to do? We certainly need to tell the computer that port B will provide input, and a channel of port A will need to act as output. We can do this by programming the data direction registers, as discussed above. Then we need to find a way of telling the computer what to do with the input from port B, and how to turn it into output for port A. As we have just seen, a simple way to produce a sound we might optimistically describe as an 'electronic organ' is to increment port A (that is, the port A data register), with a time delay between increments that is proportional to the code we read in from port B. This will generate square waves that halve in frequency at each bit from PA0 to PA7. Depending which data channel we plug the loudspeaker into, we shall hear a different series of notes when the switches are pressed.

Figure 70 shows the flowchart for this simple operation.

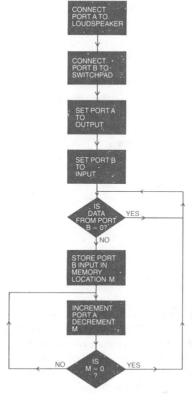

Figure 70: Flowchart for a simple electronic organ program

What about the computer's resources? We have already decided to use port B as input and port A as output, and the data registers and data direction registers are fixed for us. Which instructions and registers should we use? We will try the following ones:

(1) We shall load the data direction registers from the accumulator.
(2) We shall load the input from port B into index register X. Then we can use other instructions to tell the system to act according to the contents of X.
(3) The BEQ instruction (branch if result zero) will enable us to keep inspecting the input (as stored in X), and to loop around doing no more until some positive input (a key being pressed) is received.
(4) The INC instruction will enable us to increment port A, if a key is being pressed. At the same time, we shall use DEX to decrement the X register (that is, the input). By doing so, we are effectively building in a variable time delay.
(5) The BNE instruction will enable us to check for when we have decremented the input to zero. When it is not zero, we can loop around and decrement again; when it *is* zero, we shall need to go back to load X again with the input, checking if there is still some positive input we should be acting on.

Our program, in mnemonic and machine code form using these instructions, is given in Table 18.

Table 18: Program to Produce a Simple Electronic Organ (in Machine Code)

Address	Mnemonics	Data	Comments
0200	LDA #FF	A9, FF	
0202	STA 0903	8D, 03, 09	initialize i/o
0205	LDA #00	A9, 00	ports
0207	STA 0902	89, 02, 09	
020A	*LDX 0900	AE, 00, 09	Input to X
020D	BEQ*	F0, FB	wait for positive i/p
020F	INC 0901	EE, 01, 09	increment o/p port
0212	**DEX	CA	variable delay dependent on
0213	BNE**	D0, FD	input value
0215	JMP*	4C, 0A, 02	check key still pressed?

NOTE: Line 020E/0214: Note form of backwards relative address: count back *from* hex FF.

When the program is run, the display will go blank, and the program will continue to loop around until it is stopped by the Reset button. (Hence we have no need for a final 'Jump' instruction, as in our earlier programs.) Pressing the keys on the switchpad does indeed play a very simple tune over the loudspeaker.

How might we enhance the program? We could improve the frequencies of the notes, from the very basic half scale we just used, to something more harmonic. We could program the computer to play a specific tune we had composed. And in EMMA's set of monitor demonstration programs, there is a listing that enables the computer to 'learn' a tune we play, and play it back to us. All these operations can be done in relatively short machine-code programs that fit into EMMA's modest memory capacity.

A Simple Weighing Machine

We will close this section on control programs with a program to control a piece of equipment that works in analog fashion: a strain gauge that can operate as a simple weighing device.

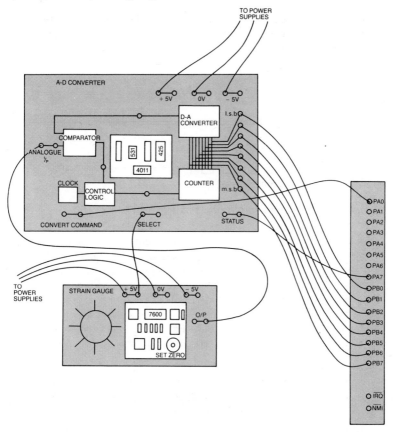

Figure 71: Hardware configuration for a simple weighing machine

Figure 71 shows the hardware configuration we shall be programming. Before we discuss the program, we shall introduce the two new peripherals: the analog-to-digital converter and the strain gauge itself.

The analog-to-digital converter: How does the a/d converter work? Figure 72 summarizes its mode of operation.

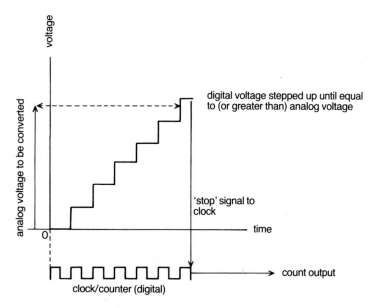

Figure 72: How the analog to digital converter works

As you can see, there is a clock that counts up a number of digital pulses at regular intervals. While the clock is running, a voltage is generated, and stepped up at intervals, to make the 'ladder' effect shown in the figure. At each step, this digitally produced voltage is compared with the analog input voltage. When the two are identical (or the former is greater than the latter, since there may be no point at which they are precisely identical), an inhibit signal stops the clock-counter. The clock-counter then holds a number that is proportional to the size of the original analog input, and this forms the digital output.

In the centre of the a/d converter are two integrated circuit chips, the Ferranti ZN 425, that produces the digital voltage, and the 4011, that carries out the clocking and control logic operations. Also in the central module are a 531 operational amplifier, that allows comparison to be made between the ZN 425 output and the analog input, and two variable resistors, one of which is a 'set zero' control and the other a sensitivity control to ensure an appropriate range of output responses.

For our purposes, the most important components are the connection points. You can see that the unit needs three electrical inputs, rated at +5V, 0V and −5V. It has the following additional connection points:

(1) an analog input point on the left-hand side, into which the analog input (in our case, the output from the strain gauge module) is plugged;

(2) an eight-channel output port. We shall connect this to the eight channels of the computer's port B;

(3) and three control signal input/output points:

(a) Convert command. This is an input point. It must receive a logical '0' signal, followed by a logical '1' signal. This causes it to initiate an a/d conversion,

(b) Select. The unit can also be used as a digital/analog converter, and this input selects its mode of operation. For a/d operation, it must receive a 1 input;

(c) Status. This is an output point that acts to indicate when the output is ready to be read. When the 'convert command' input receives its 0 signal, it sets the unit counter to 0, and the status output to 1. The counter then proceeds to increment, once the 1 signal has been received by the convert command, until the a/d converter output is equal to the analog input. At this point, the control logic inhibits the system, and the status output goes from 1 to 0. The data output can then be read.

We shall connect these points as follows:

(a) 'Convert command' to Port A0. We must then send this the correct initiating sequence of 0, then 1.

(b) 'Select' to a 5V point, that will keep it at logic state 1.

(c) 'Status' to Port A7. How can we check to see that it is zero? We are using a 'most significant bit' of a data register, the bit that is used as a sign bit in signed arithmetic. If we check to see if the 'number' contained in the register is negative, we shall in fact be checking the status of this bit: and we can build a branch into our program accordingly.

The strain gauge: On the left of the strain gauge unit is an aluminium disc, 1" (2·5 cm) in diameter, which acts as a simple weighing platform. Beneath it are a cantilever beam and four thin-film strain gauges. This arrangement and the associated amplification circuitry in the middle of the unit combine to cause a voltage to be output that is proportional to the weight placed on the disc.

The strain gauge is simple to connect: power supplies, as you can see, and an output point that becomes the input to the a/d converter.

Figure 73: Flowchart for displaying strain gauge readings

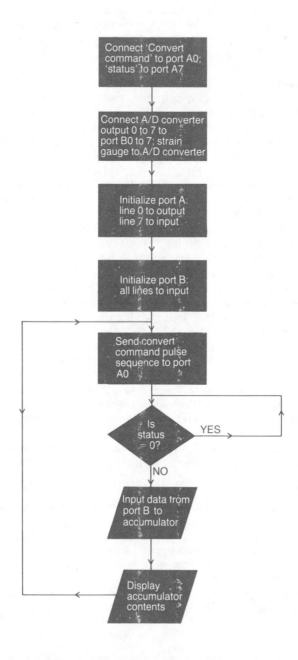

Programming the strain gauge system: What points do we want to allow for in our program, then?

We want to ensure:

(1) that the appropriate ports or port lines are set to input and output;

(2) that all the control signals required by the a/d converter have been programmed in;

(3) that the necessary checks are included in the program to ensure that the peripheral circuitry has time to do its work, and to ensure that the output is correct;

(4) that the system has been programmed to provide the required output. We must consider two factors here:

(a) What form we we want our output in − hex, or binary-coded decimal? And do we want it to be expressed in grammes, or some other weight scale? If so, we would need to perform the necessary conversions to change the simple proportional output to the right measure. In our case, we shall simplify our program by producing a simple output in hex form. It will then vary proportionally as different weights are placed on the strain gauge, but will have no direct reference to any conventional weighing scale.

(b) How are we going to handle the programming of the display unit? To simplify the program, again we shall use monitor subroutines. However, we cannot use the subroutine we used in our arithmetic program: the way it is programmed means that it will only display one output, and will not vary its display as the input varies. Instead, we shall use the two subroutines that form part of the FE88 subroutine: FE64 and FE0C. We will then need to send the contents of the input port B (once the status digit has been checked) to a memory location whose contents will be displayed by these subroutines. And we will need to remember to enter 00s into the other memory locations that will be displayed.

Figure 73 shows the flowchart for our program, and Table 19 lists the program itself, in mnemonic and machine-code form. Take a look through the listing to make sure you understand the significance of each step.

Table 19: Program for Producing a Simple Weighing Machine (in Machine Code)

Address	Mnemonics	Data	Comments
0200	LDA 01	A9 01	initialize port A
0202	STA 0903	8D 03 09	(0 to o/p; 7 to i/p)
0205	LDA 00	A9 00	initialize port B (to input)
0207	STA 0902	8D 02 09	
020A	LDA 01	A9 01	send 1 signal to convert
020C	STA 0901	8D 01 09	command
020F	LDX 08	A2 08	time delay set

Address	Mnemonics	Data	Comments
0211	DEC 0901	CE, 01, 09	0 signal to convert command
0214	*DEX	CA	time delay (8 loops)
0215	BNE*	D0 FD	
0217	INC 0901	EE 01 09	1 signal to convert command
021A	**LDA 0901	AD 01 09	check status signal
021D	BMI**	30 FB	
021F	LDX #00	A2, 00	
0221	TXA	8A	
0222	**STA 10, X	95, 10	send data 00 to memory
0224	INX	E8	locations 0010 to 0017
0225	CPX #08	E0, 08	
0227	BNE**	D0, F9	
0229	LDX #20	A2, 20	indicate memory location
022B	LDA #30	A9, 30	which holds indirect
022D	STA 0020	85, 20	address
022F	LDA #00	A9, 00	and 2nd digit of i.a.
0231	STA 0021	85, 21	
0233	LDY 0900	AC, 00, 09	input from a/d to Y reg. and
0236	STY 0030	84, 30	then to address given above
0238	JSR FE5E	20, 5E, FE	display contents of i.a.
023B	JSR FE0C	20, 0C, FE	
023E	JMP 020F	4C, 0F, 02	repeat procedure

Conclusions

Writing machine-code programs is a pretty arid operation if you do not have a computer handy on which to enter them and see how they work. But we hope the few short programs we have written will have given you some 'feel' for what factors you need to consider in writing programs on this level, and for how the computer gets to work. It is comforting to know that, even in one short chapter, we can reach a stage where we can actually write programs that work. Of course, we have omitted to describe all the mistakes we made in writing them — listing the working version is only the tip of the iceberg! In Chapter 28 we shall be looking at some of the practicalities of testing and debugging programs, which will be very real to you if you use and program your own computer.

Of course, the programs we have listed are unsophisticated and do not allow for all the factors we would need to consider if we were running equipment in real life. But they *are* an indication of how such a very simple computer system can be put to use. EMMA has only a tiny RAM, by comparison with many commercial computers. But in machine code, we can cram a lot into it. Our programs take up only a fraction of EMMA's capacity. High-level languages, which we shall be looking at later, are much more profligate with memory space.

If you yourself tried to write programs for any of the simple examples we have used, or if you have done any other machine-code programming, you will realize just how difficult and time-consuming it is to program a computer in this fashion, though. It is no wonder that easier methods were soon developed. Most control engineers still *do* program in machine code, but they use assembler programs to enable them to enter the mnemonics without having to look up the codes themselves. The majority of other computer users program primarily in high-level languages. In Chapters 26 and 27 we shall go on to look at some of them.

25. Structuring Data

Before we go on to look at some aspects of programming in a high-level language, we need to look at a rather different aspect of programming: the ways in which data can be structured. This was something that did not unduly concern us in machine-code programming, but which *is* of great significance in writing programs in high-level languages, also in using many program packages.

Whatever our data relate to, they almost invariably have two basic characteristics:

(1) The total amount of data employed by a program or system divides itself up naturally into units that might be of almost any size. For instance, single letters, pages of a book, or even whole books might form data units in different contexts: text-editing programs, book-indexing programs, or library-cataloguing programs.

(2) The units that comprise the data are related to each other: either by formal logical relations such as those of Boolean algebra, or in other, less easily defined ways.

As a result, the ways in which a computer can store and manipulate data need to reflect these two features. They need to allow for the differing sizes of the natural units of data applicable in different circumstances, and they need to allow for the different, and often complex, ways in which pieces of data are related to each other.

We shall look very briefly at some of the basic ideas and terms that have emerged from the technology of data handling.

Variables

A variable is simply a location in read/write memory: one computer word, or more than one word, or even part of a word, as necessary, that is to be treated as an unit for a particular purpose. The data held in the memory location may change, but two aspects remain the same:

(1) the actual computer location in which the data are held;

(2) the function of the data in the program. This is often reflected in the names we give to variables in high-level languages: names that are effectively mnemonics for their function.

In a very simple way, we encountered variables in some of our machine-code programs. When we designate a memory location by its address — say, 0030 — and use it as the repository for data that will be defined (and perhaps changed) in the course of a program, then we are setting up a variable location. In such a location we might opt to store, for instance:

the number of pieces of data tested by a program that meet a particular condition — e.g. holidays costing less than $200, or numbers exactly divisible by 3 and 17;

the 'best' fitted piece of data the program has found, according to a particular condition — e.g. the shortest route from London to Birmingham, or the best-matched date for a person on a dating agency computer;

the varying attribute of an item being monitored — e.g. the weight reading given out by the strain gauge; the price of a particular share on a stock exchange system; the temperature registered on a heating system.

In order to keep track of the variable information when writing a machine-code program, we have to recall in which location in memory we stored it. In high-level languages, it is not necessary to do so. Instead, we give the variable (location) a *name* — which might be a simple name like A or B, or a more descriptive name like WEIGHT or BESTROUTE, according to the rules of the language we are using — and refer to the name whenever we want to access or manipulate the variable information. The software then handles the function of relating the variable name to the actual memory location it refers to.

In many languages — BASIC is one of them — it is not even necessary to 'set up' variables before a program is entered. The software will auto-matically handle the task of allocating a suitable amount of space for each variable, as and when it is required.

The contents of a variable, of course, will be a piece of binary code. But there are a number of ways in which a computer might interpret this code: as numbers, as letters, as a description of a graphics character, or whatever. In BASIC, as we shall see, we can tell the computer by our choice of variable name what kind of data it should interpret the variable information as being.

Strings

What is a string? Essentially, it is a kind of data that can be stored in a variable location. A string is a simple, one-dimensional sequence of data that forms one data unit: so it needs only one variable location (which may consist of more than one memory address) to hold it.

Strings are essentially strings of characters: sequences of data that are input from the keyboard, and held in ASCII (or some other character code) form. As you will recall from Chapter 1, this means that they *can* include numbers, but that the computer will not be able to carry out any arithmetical manipulation on those numbers.

Figure 74 gives some examples of typical strings, data groups that the computer will treat as a whole.

Figure 74: Examples of character strings

"THIS IS A CHARACTER STRING"

"and so is this"

"This one has numbers in too: 12345"

"and this one graphics characters: ▄ █ ▀ ▐ ▄ ▌"

"234.567"

"   note the spaces at the start of this string"

"   "

How do languages vary in their handling of strings? They may:

have particular protocols for designating a string as apart from other types of data. In BASIC, for example, a string in a program is enclosed in inverted commas, and the variable name for a location to hold a string always ends in a '$' sign;

limit the length of strings that can be handled, in general, or in a particular application program;

have limitations upon their ability to sort or manipulate strings.

The string concept should not be confused with the computer's word length (whether it works in units of 4, 8, 16 or 32 bits). The word length is the size of the computer's memory locations, each with an individual numeric address; the string is the piece of data which has to be fitted into them. Data do not usually come in fixed-length chunks, and the strings have to be manipulated to make them fit into the fixed units with which the computer works. One string may spread over several words, that will be given a single variable name to designate them.

Before we leave the subject of strings, let us look briefly at some of the other ways in which variable contents can be designated.

In the particular dialect of BASIC that we shall be using in this book (TRS-80 Model II), the fundamental distinction is between strings and numeric data. (Strings of up to 255 characters can be handled.) Three types of numeric data are distinguished:

(1) Integers. Our system allocates two bytes of memory to an integer, so the integer data must be a whole number in the range from -32768 to 32767. Typical integers are:

    1
    -3000

(2) Single-precision numbers. To these are allocated four bytes of memory, which allows them to have up to seven significant digits (in decimal form). These numbers are stored and represented by the system in 'normalized' form, a type of floating-point representation in which only one digit appears to the left of the decimal point. The exponent of the number is then given at the end of it. Single-precision numbers can be stored with exponents of up to $+$ or -38, so the range available is:

from -1×10^{38} to -1×10^{-38}, and

from 1×10^{-38} to 1×10^{38}

The computer uses a special code, E, to represent the exponent. So in the format in which they could be used in a BASIC program (which is not always normalized form), typical single precision numbers would be:

10.001

1.774E6

-200034

6.024E–23

(3) Double-precision numbers. The range of double-precision values is just the same as the range of single-precison values, but the number of significant digits permitted (that is, the accuracy with which numbers are represented) is greater: seventeen as opposed to seven. Eight bytes are allocated to each double-precision number.

There are complex rules for designating which variable names will hold which type of string or numeric data.

Arrays

A string is a single data unit that can be linked with other data units; an array is fundamentally a way of associating data units, that may themselves be single bits, or fixed-length words, or strings. Strings and numeric variables of the kind we looked at just now are data; arrays are structures into which data can be fitted.

Figure 75 indicates graphically what arrays are like. They might be thought of as table structures in a single dimension, or in the two dimensions of a statistical table, or the three dimensions of a cube, or more dimensions if necessary, which provide a formal arrangement of 'slots' (single-storage locations, or sequences of linked storage locations with a single variable designation) into which data can be posted. The data in the array are related to each other, simply by sharing the array structure; more concretely, the dimensions of the array may form axes measuring or ordering particular attributes, along which the location of the data has a special significance. If this is not clear to you now, it may well become clearer when we write a simple program, using the array concept, in Chapter 26.

Figure 75: Array structures

Address	Address	Address	Address	Address	Address	Address
Name	Name	Name	Name	Name	Name	Name
Data	Data →	Data	Data	Data	Data	Data

(a) One-dimensional array.
Contents might comprise: Addresses: locations 10000 to 10006
Names: A1 to A6
Data: Six temperature readings: 1.0
1.1
1.2
1.1
1.2
1.1

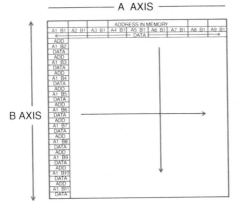

(b) Two-dimensional array:
9 locations (A axis) × 11 locations (B axis)

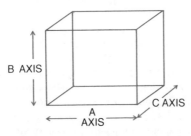

(c) Three-dimensional array

In our version of BASIC, arrays can be handled by giving them a single variable name, and listing their dimensions. The BASIC statement that is used to do this looks like this:

DIM A(12,10)

This particular statement sets up an array with the name A, that has 13 rows of elements, numbered 0 to 12 (in our dialect, 0 is always assumed to be the starting point; in other dialects, 1 can be designated instead); and 11 columns. A single element (that can contain a single piece of variable information) can then be referred to as, for instance,

A(6,6).

Our BASIC will even include a default second dimension (11 columns deep) to an array in which the user defines only one dimension.

Obviously the computer has a harder task when the array contains not numbers to which a fixed amount of storage space can be assigned (as we saw above), but strings that can be of any length up to 255 characters. It would not be practicable for the computer to set aside room for 255 characters in every element of a large array. Instead, the system organizes in the array a set of pointers, that will hold the starting addresses of the memory locations in which the actual data are held.

Files

Paper files are familiar to anyone who has worked in an office. Filing systems are simply conglomerations of data, kept together under a single heading or file name. They might contain, for instance:

data on customers' orders (file name: 'customer files');

data on employees' work record and personal details (file name: 'employee files');

data on events that took place within fixed periods (file name: 'date files'):

Some files are structured: they contain fixed types of data, arranged in a definite way. Some are unstructured: the name of the file is a 'catch-all' under which every relevant piece of data is stored.

Computer 'files' are exactly the same as paper files in concept: they are given names that act as reference points for locating a fixed assortment of data. Sometimes the data are unstructured, like the data in an office letter file; sometimes they are highly structured. We shall concentrate here (briefly) on the handling of structured files.

A structured filing system will contain a number of 'records': individual folders, perhaps, in a paper-based system, each of which holds data on one particular customer, employee, month or whatever. Each record will then contain a number of pieces of data that can themselves be given titles; for instance:

the address

phone number

credit/debit balance

of the customer or employee concerned.

These file sub-units are usually known as fields, or elements. Computer programs that set up file structures may — depending on how they allocate memory space — either:

(1) provide fixed-length fields (that is, slots in memory that can only hold a fixed amount of data, each associated with a field title in a particular file); or

(2) allow for fields of variable length, depending upon the quantity of data to be stored in them.

Similarly, they will allow for a fixed number of records — perhaps a default number — that in some systems can be changed if the requirements of the system change.

A very simple file system will reference files only by their names; in other words, to obtain a piece of data the user might first give the name of the file, then give the name of the record, then give the title of the field that holds the data. Bear in mind that these are quite different types of information. The name of the file or record is a specific piece of data (for example, Jones, Mary; or January 1982); the title of the field is a generic name given to it (for example, name of employee; or credit balance). Giving the title of the field is not the same as giving the data in the field: that is what the computer will provide.

This simple schematic may seem tidy, but it is extremely limited, as any user of paper files knows. The user may want to start with the contents of a field, for instance, and track down the records that have a fixed piece of data in that field. Say the records consist of data on individual employees, and one field within the file is length of years' service. That is fine if you want to know how many years' service Mary Jones has given; but not if you want to know which employees have worked for the firm for ten or more years. To obtain such information using paper files is a laborious job. Most well-programmed structured computer files, however, can sort and select according to field data, as well as file or record data.

As an example, let us look quickly at PROFILE PLUS, the file-handling package we use on our TRS-80. PROFILE PLUS allows us to name (with names of up to eight characters) files, and then to define their structure in a variety of ways. Each file can contain up to four 'segments', areas of storage in which data can be placed. In each segment, the space available (up to 85 characters in segment 1; up to 256 characters in the other segments) can be divided up into fields, with anything from one to almost the maximum number of characters. Depending upon the length of the fields, there can be up to 99 of them: obviously, if a field is to contain a lot of data, there will be less room for other fields. The user names each field, too.

The user also specifies how many records (up to several thousand, depending on the way in which the files are set up) are to be held on the file. Records as such do not have names: they are referenced numerically. And the records can then be updated, accessed individually, or sorted and output in a report format, as the user defines. Sorting can be carried out alpha/numerically by any of the fields that are included in 'segment 1'.

For instance, we hold a file of our freezer contents on PROFILE PLUS (or, strictly speaking, on a floppy disc that contains both the PROFILE PLUS program and some storage space that the program manipulates). We have called our file FREEZLOG, and allocated room for sixty records — the maximum different number of items we expect to hold in the freezer. And we have defined fields to hold:

(1) the general type of dish: meat, fish, vegetable, and so on (according to a simple one-letter code);

(2) the exact dish: minced beef, goulash, fish steaks or whatever (we allow 20 characters for this);

(3) the quantity of the dish in store (8 characters);

(4) the date the food was stored;

(5) and the date by which the food should be eaten.

As there are only a few fields, we have included them all in segment 1: the 'sort' segment.

We update the file once a fortnight, and run off two reports on our printer: one listing the dishes by general type (so we can choose something for supper), and one listing them by expiry date, so we can check that we are not storing anything for too long.

Unstructured files: A perfect example of unstructured files is the file of BASIC programs we keep on our system. When we write a program that we wish to keep for future use, we give it a name and ask the system to SAVE (another BASIC command word) it on disc. On the floppy disc is a file of different programs, that can be accessed by asking the system to LOAD (followed by the program name).

Our particular system also enables us to store files of data on disc, for access while we are writing or running BASIC programs. There are two ways of storing these files: sequentially or by direct access (sometimes referred to as 'random access', though this is a slight misnomer).

When the records in a file are stored sequentially, the system simply loads them (with codes to indicate where they start and end) into the next available space on the disc. To find a file, it then has to hunt sequentially through all the file contents until it comes across the start of the required record.

Direct access means that the user sets up a specific file structure, in which records will be held: not dissimilar, in fact, to the type of file structures that PROFILE PLUS uses. The user has to define the number and length of fields in advance, just as with the PROFILE PLUS package. Once this has been done, though, it is possible to access a specific record directly (the 'random' part), without hunting right through the file for it. There are also some other advantages to the direct access method, concerning the procedures used for reading data from, and writing data to, a file — but we shall not look at these here.

Databases

When a group of files are held in a structure that enables their contents to be retrieved, altered and sorted on a variety of levels, the result is often called a database. The term 'database' is often applied indiscriminately to the data structure, and to the data held in it, just as the term 'file' is used for both purposes.

Note the essential difference between file structures and database structures. A file is a structure that links fields and records; a database is a structure that links files (which in turn link fields and records).

The essence of a database is that it is independent of the application programs that will use the data stored in it. It is a computer system resource, which can be used by a wide variety of different application programs, and the system will normally run so that programs that merely need to access the data cannot accidentally erase or alter it. The database might contain, for instance:

all data relating to a firm's customers, sales, purchases, stock levels, employees and other measurable activities, arranged in a complex file-based manner;

or all data relevant to the members of a particular club, organization or interest group;

or data provided by an organization for use by its agents (e.g. data on flights and seat availabilities, provided by airlines for use by travel agents; data on motor insurance rates, provided by insurers for use by insurance brokers).

Many databases are highly structured, so that clearly defined data can be simply and reliably accessed. For other purposes, however, it is not possible to structure the data so tightly, just as it is impossibly difficult to cross-reference the information held in a correspondence file in every possible way. Loosely structured databases, or databases structured only on a relatively abstract level, resemble libraries with catalogues, rather than structured file systems. They are sometimes described instead as databanks.

The data held in a widely used database must be carefully 'managed' to ensure that it is accurate and up-to-date, and that it is stored efficiently in the computer's memory. Often, as we have indicated, the system is structured so that application programs cannot alter the stored data. Alteration, updating, deletion of dead records and other 'housekeeping' tasks are instead the province of a systems software program, or suite of programs, known as a 'database management system' (D.B.M.S.). Proprietary D.B.M.S.s offer various structures into which data can be fitted, routines for updating the data, and perhaps other facilities such as security routines for screening out unauthorized users.

26. Programming in BASIC

In this chapter, we shall be looking at some aspects of programming a computer in a high-level language. The language we shall be using is BASIC, both a widely used language and one that is comparatively easy to learn. In Chapter 27 we will be taking a brief look at how programs in other high-level languages differ from BASIC programs.

One of our prime aims is to contrast high-level language programming with the machine-code programming we looked at in Chapter 24. As you will discover, many things that the machine-code programmer has to take into account are handled by the system for the BASIC programmer. As a result, it is very much easier to write many types of programs in BASIC than in machine code.

Not all, however. Machine code, and assemblers that enable machine-code programming to be performed more rapidly and efficiently, still have a part to play, particularly in control programming. BASIC, as we shall see, is not good at controlling a wide range of peripherals for the sort of applications we looked at in Chapter 24. We shall *not* be duplicating in this chapter the control programs we wrote earlier: to handle those in BASIC would be a relatively complex job. What we *will* do is to concentrate on some applications that BASIC is well suited for: text handling, interactive programming (in which the user inputs data from the keyboard while the program is running), and graphics manipulations. These are all types of applications that we can illustrate with short, simple BASIC programs, but that would be extremely difficult to handle on, say, EMMA.

The Tools of BASIC

You will recall that, in introducing machine-code programming, we started by listing the instruction codes that our microprocessor enabled us to use. The equivalent in BASIC is our list of functions and commands, or key-words. (Different people and different systems use different words to describe these.) The keywords that we can use in TRS-80 Model II BASIC are given in Table 20. The code on the left is what we enter into the system; on the right is a brief explanation of what it tells the system to do.

Not all of these keywords will be clear to you at this stage. Do not worry: we shall not be using many of them, and we shall not try to explain in detail what all of them do. Let us stop at this stage, though, to draw out some points about the *type* of operation we can do in BASIC, that you should be able to relate to the data in the table.

Table 20: BASIC Keywords on the TRS-80 Model II

COMMAND STATEMENTS intended primarily for use in command mode, outside a program.

Keyword	Action
AUTO	Number lines automatically
DELETE	Erase program lines from memory
EDIT	Edit program line
KILL	Delete a disc file
LIST	List program to display
LLIST	List program to printer
LOAD	Load program from disc
MERGE	Merge disc program with resident program
NAME	Rename a disc file
NEW	Erase program from RAM
RENUM	Renumber program
RUN	Execute program
SAVE	Save program on disc
SYSTEM	Return to TRSDOS (Operating System)

PROGRAM STATEMENTS intended primarily for use inside programs.

Definition and Initialization Statements primarily for use at the start of a program.

CLEAR	Clear variables and allocate string space
DATA	Store program data
DEFDBL	Define variables as double-precision
DEFFN	Define function
DEFINT	Define variables as integers
DEFSNG	Define variables as single-precision
DEFSTR	Define variables as strings
DEFUSR	Define entry point for USR routine
DIM	Dimension an array
ERASE	Erase an array
RANDOM	Reseed random number generator
REM	Comment line (remarks)
RESTORE	Reset DATA pointer

Assignment Statements primarily concerned with the values of variables

LET	Assign value to variable
LSET	Left-set data in direct access disc buffer
MID$	Replace mid-string
READ	Get value from DATA statement
RSET	Right-set data in direct access disc buffer
SWAP	Exchange values of variables

Program Sequence Statements for changing the sequence in which program statements are executed.

END	End program

FOR/NEXT	Set up loop
GOSUB	Call subroutine
GOTO	Branch to line number (given)
IF . . . THEN . . . ELSE	Test conditional expression
ON . . . GOSUB	Multi-way subroutine call
ON . . . GOTO	Multi-way branch to line numbers
RETURN	Return from subroutine

Input/Output Statements

INPUT	Input value from keyboard
LINE INPUT	Input line from keyboard
CLS	Clear video display
PRINT	Print to video display
LPRINT	Print to printer
CLOSE	Close access to a disc file
FIELD	Organize a disc buffer (direct access)
GET	Get a record from a disc file (direct access)
INPUT#	Read from a disc file (sequential access)
LINE INPUT#	Read a line from a disc file (sequential access)
OPEN	Open a disc file (direct or sequential access)
PRINT#	Write to a disc file (sequential access)
PUT	Put a record into a disc file (direct access)

Debugging Statements for use in checking program accuracy.

CONT	Continue execution of program
ERL	Get line number after error
ERR	Get error code after error
ERROR	Simulate error
ON ERROR GOTO	Set up error-trap
RESUME	End error-trap
STOP	Stop execution
TROFF	Turn trace off
TRON	Turn trace on

Numeric Functions that result in the system producing a number

ABS	Compute absolute value
ASC	Get ASCII code
ATN	Compute arctangent
CDBL	Convert to double-precision
CINT	Return largest integer not greater than argument
COS	Compute cosine
CSNG	Convert to single-precision
EXP	Compute natural exponential
FIX	Truncate to whole number
INSTR	Search for specified string
INT	Return largest whole number not greater than argument
LEN	Get length of string
LOG	Compute natural logarithm

RND	Return pseudorandom number
SGN	Get sign
SIN	Compute sine
SQR	Compute square root
TAN	Compute tangent
VAL	Evaluate string

Numeric Operators

+	addition
−	subtraction
*	multiplication
/	division
\	integer division
↑	exponentiation
MOD	modulo arithmetic

Logical Operators

<	less than
>	greater than
=	equal to
> < or < >	not equal to
= < or < =	less than or equal to
=> or > =	greater than or equal to
AND	AND logic
OR	OR logic
XOR	Exclusive OR logic
EQV	Equivalent logic
IMP	bit manipulation function
NOT	NOT logic

String Functions involving the manipulation of character strings.

CHR$	Get specified character
DATE$	Get today's date
ERRS$	Get latest TRSDOS error number and message
HEX$	Convert decimal value to hexadecimal string
LEFT$	Get left portion of string
MID$	Get mid-portion of string
OCT$	Convert decimal value to octal string
RIGHT$	Get right portion of string
SPACE$	Return string of spaces
STR$	Convert to string type
STRING$	Return string of characters
TIME$	Get the time

String Operators

<	precedes
>	follows
=	has the same precedence
< >	does not have the same precedence
< =	precedes or has the same precedence
> =	follows or has the same precedence

INPUT/OUTPUT FUNCTIONS that perform input and/or output to the keyboard, video display, printer and disc files.

INKEY$	Get keyboard character if available
INPUT$	Get a string of characters from keyboard
POS	Get cursor column position on video display
ROW	Get cursor row position on video display
SPC	Output spaces to video display
CVD	Restore data from disc file to double-precision (direct access)
CVI	Restore data from disc file to integer (direct access)
CVS	Restore data from disc file to single-precision (direct access)
EOF	Check for end of file
INPUT$	Input a string of characters from disc file (sequential access)
LOC	Get current disc file record number (direct or sequential access)
LOF	Get disc file's end of record number
MKD$	Make double-precision number to string for disc write (direct access)
MKI$	Make integer to string for disc write (direct access)
MKS$	Make single-precision number to string for disc write (direct access)

SPECIAL FUNCTIONS

FRE	Get amount of free memory or string space
MEM	Get amount of free memory
USRn	Call machine-language subroutine
VARPTR	Get absolute memory address

Modes of BASIC operation: You will see that the keywords are broken up into a number of functional areas. One basic distinction is between 'command' keywords and 'program' keywords.

Let us go back briefly to EMMA. You will recall that we could operate EMMA in a number of modes that we selected by pressing the control keys on its keypad. In 'M' mode, for instance, we could alter the data held in specific memory addresses; in 'G' mode, we could run a program. The modes in which BASIC can be used are comparable to these operating modes that we have already encountered.

Some sequences of input involving keywords, when we enter them via our keyboard, make the computer *do* something straight away. Using the system in this way is known as 'command mode'. At other times, we want to enter an entire program – as we did for EMMA – and then afterwards run it. We make it clear to the system – primarily by entering program 'line numbers', which the system interprets as signifying this – that we are entering, not commands, but program data, using the 'program' keywords (and other necessary input). Then we move into 'execute mode', and the system proceeds to execute the program. While the program is running, the system's keyboard and display are not controlled directly from the keyboard, but by the program itself.

Finally, our version of BASIC has an 'edit mode', used for editing program statements that have already been (wrongly) entered into the system.

Data handling functions: In the last chapter we talked about variables, the way in which we tell the computer, when programming in a high-level language, to allocate storage space to a piece of data; about strings, or non-numeric data; and about arrays. You will see all these concepts reflected in the BASIC keywords, which give us a number of ways of defining ways of handling data, and of manipulating data.

Note, too, that the range of arithmetical and logical functions that we can specify with just one instruction is much greater than was the case using the 6502 instruction set as our only tool.

Of course, using BASIC we do not have to input our data in hexadecimal form. We input in decimal numeric form (for use in any of the three numerical formats we described on pages 312 to 313) or direct from the keyboard in alpha/character form. And the system handles the task of translating its output into the corresponding formats.

Input and output functions: With EMMA, we had a small number of input and output ports; and we had to tell the system (with the help of the monitor programs) exactly how to use them. As you can see, there is no reference to ports in the list of BASIC keywords. There are a number of references to the keyboard, the display and the printer, though.

The input and output commands make life very easy if we simply want to input data from the keyboard and output it via the display unit or the printer. What if we want to use other forms of input and/or output, though?.

BASIC does not handle many more complex aspects of input/output and communication directly. We *can* perform many input/output and communication tasks on the Model II, though: as you will remember from Chapter 23, it has a number of ports designed for use in different ways. However, to use them, we go outside BASIC and use other types of systems software. And it is at those that we must look now.

Interfacing BASIC with Other Systems Software

As you know, the BASIC interpreter is just one piece of software to be found on the computer we are using, the TRS-80 Model II. As well as the interpreter, we have an operating system, TRSDOS, that handles many aspects of system management.

When we start to use BASIC on this particular system, we take the following steps:

(1) We put into the disc drive a floppy disc that contains both the TRSDOS programs and the BASIC interpreter. TRSDOS boots the system into full operation, and the screen comes up with the initial 'TRSDOS Ready' message that characterizes the system.

(2) We then tell the system that we wish to communicate with it in BASIC. We type in 'BASIC', perhaps together with some system commands telling the system to set up some files for use with BASIC. And the system will then load the BASIC interpreter from the disc into RAM, and come up with a further message that tells us that BASIC is ready for us.

To use a different high-level language with our system (FORTRAN, for instance), we shall take a similar sequence of steps, but load the appropriate alternative compiler or interpreter instead.

Of course, other computer systems that have both operating systems and high-level language utilities work in a very similar fashion.

When the BASIC interpreter is loaded, though, TRSDOS remains in the system: we do not switch it out. And this means that we can:

(1) move from BASIC into TRSDOS, so that we can use some TRSDOS commands and subroutines in conjunction with our BASIC programs; or

(2) switch from BASIC into machine code, if we want to perform an operation that can be performed more easily in machine code, or to check on aspects of system operation (what data are held in a fixed memory location, for instance).

Of course, there are fixed protocols that determine how we switch from one software utility to another. You will recognize some of them in the list of BASIC keywords: SYSTEM, ERRS$ and USRn, for instance.

The fact that BASIC runs in close collaboration with TRSDOS, and not in isolation, is one reason why our dialect, and the programs we write in it, are to some extent machine-specific. BASIC dialects used on other computers have many of the same keywords; but, of course, they will not have keywords that interface with quite different system utilities in exactly the same way as our system does. Instead, their system interfacing will reflect their system's set-up and capabilities.

To clarify the way in which BASIC and TRSDOS interrelate, we shall list some simple TRSDOS commands and utility sequences in Table 21. You will see that these reflect TRSDOS's function as a disc operating system, but they also cover other aspects of system management, communication, and machine-code programming.

Table 21: TRSDOS Commands and Utilities

Keyword	Function
AGAIN	Re-executes last command
APPEND	Appends one file on to another
ATTRIB	Changes file protection
AUTO	Automatically executes specified command
BACKUP	Copies disc data on to second disc
BUILD	Creates file of commands for automatic execution
CLEAR	Clears: user memory; screen; stack
CLOCK	Switches on real-time clock display
CLS	Clears video display
COPY . . . TO	Copies a file
CREATE	Creates a file (allocation to be defined)
DATA	Displays or resets date/time
DEBUG	Starts debugging utility
DIR	Lists disc directory
DO	Executes BUILD file
DUMP	Dumps machine-code program in RAM into a disc file
ERROR	Displays error message associated with specific error code
FORMAT	Formats a disc
FORMS	Sets printer driver parameters
FREE	Displays granule allocation map
I	Used after swapping discs in drives
KILL	Deletes file
LIB	Lists all library commands
LIST	Lists file contents
LOAD	Loads machine-code file into memory
PAUSE	Pause until operator presses ENTER key (used inside DO file)
PURGE	Rapid deletion of files
PROT	Changes file/disc passwords
RENAME	Renames file
SETCOM	Initializes RS-232C communications port
TIME	Displays time and date/resets time
VERIFY	Checks disc sector integrity after write operation

Building up a BASIC Program

The keywords we have listed are the primary building blocks of BASIC programs: they are the words that instruct the system to carry out specific manipulative operations. But a BASIC program is not made up of keywords alone. What else is in it, and how is it structured?

An important unit in compiling our program is the line. BASIC programs, like programs in other languages (and even machine-code programs) consist of lines that contain one or more program statements. A statement, you will recall, is a program unit that tells the computer all it needs to know in order to perform a specific operation: including both commands or keywords, and data, or details on where data are to be found: and sometimes other elements as well, as we shall see.

In BASIC (but not in all high-level languages) we number the lines of our program. The line numbering tells the computer in what order it should execute the statements, unless it is given overriding instructions in the program itself. Entering line numbers also tells our system that we are entering data for a program, and are not entering commands for immediate execution.

It is normal to number program lines using intervals of ten: 10, 20, 30, and so on. This gives you room to fit in new lines if you find you need them, without renumbering the whole program. It makes no difference to the way in which the program is stored and executed by the computer.

What about data? We need to make a number of points about how data is handled by BASIC:

(1) It is common to discriminate between data and keywords by writing the keywords in capital letters, and the data (including variable names) in upper/lower case, if the computer can handle both. The system *must* receive the keywords in capitals, or it will not interpret them correctly. However, it is quite indifferent as to how it receives string data. If you particularly want the data to be output in upper or lower case, then you enter it in that way.

(2) It is possible to give the system data within a program. You tell the system (via the program statements) how the data are to be arranged, for instance by specifying an array structure; and at a suitable point, you include a few lines starting with the keyword DATA. We do this in the program we write on page 333.

(3) It is possible to enter data from the keyboard, for use in a program, while the system is in execute mode. We will see how this is done on page 329.

(4) It is possible in BASIC to include in a program data that the system will not need at all, but that the *programmer* needs, in order to remind him/her simply how the program works, and what it does. This is a form of documentation: an issue we examine in Chapter 28. In BASIC, we use the REM keyword to designate lines on which details are entered purely for the programmer's (and subsequent users') information.

Let us look briefly, too, at the sequence of program instructions. Normally, as we have seen, the computer will execute the lines of program one by one, in the order defined by their numbers, or designated by the program itself. But how does it order the execution of several instructions within a single statement?

For most types of instruction, the system simply works from the beginning to the end of the statement, dealing with instructions and data as it comes to them. When the programmer is specifying arithmetical operations, however, this is not a suitable mode of execution. Instead, the system has an order of priority in which it will execute arithmetical operations contained in a single statement. This order is summarized in Table 22. The inclusion of this ordering facility means that it is possible to write algebraic expressions in BASIC in a reasonably 'natural' order, and not in a convoluted order to meet the demands of the system.

Table 22: Order of Priority for Executing Functions in TRS-80 Model II BASIC

Operators are listed in decreasing order of precedence. Operators listed on the same line have the same precedence: they are executed from left to right in the program statement.

↑ (exponentiation)
+ − (only when used as signs, not for addition/subtraction)
* /
(integer division)
MOD
+ − (when used for addition/subtraction)
<, >, =, < =, > =, < >
NOT
AND
OR
XOR
EQV
IMP

A Simple Arithmetic Program

Enough of the introduction: let us get on to a program. We will start with a very simple program that does the same as our first program in Chapter 24: it adds 35 to 40.

In fact, as there is only one statement involved, we do not need to go into 'program' mode at all to perform this operation. We can simply type into our system, once we are in BASIC,

PRINT 35 + 40

press the ENTER key (many systems have a RETURN key instead) to tell the system to act on this data, and the screen will come up with

75

That alone is as well as we did on EMMA: but in BASIC, we can easily elaborate our program. If we tell the system, for instance,

PRINT "35 + 40 =" 35 + 40

then it will come up with the message:

35 + 40 = 75

Why? As the first '35 + 40 =' was enclosed in inverted commas, the system interpreted that as a string. No arithmetical operation was performed on it; it was simply printed, as the PRINT keyword instructed. The second '35 + 40' was *not* enclosed in inverted commas, so the system acted upon the arithmetical operator ' +', and printed the result.

Let us go one step further, and write a proper program (which we could name and store, if we wished) to carry out this sequence of operations.

    10 REM Program to add 35 and 40
    20 PRINT "35 + 40 = " 35 + 40
    30 END

Enter all this, type RUN, and the program will run.

Interactive Programming

Let us build on this very simple program, to do two new things. First, we shall turn the data into a 'variable' format, so that we can run the same program using different pairs of numbers. Second, we shall make it interactive, so that the new input can be entered while the computer is in 'execute' mode.

BASIC dialects vary in their rules for assigning variable names. In our dialect, we can give the system names as long as we like, but it will ignore all but the first two digits: so that MA, MARY and MARGARINE are all the same to it. The first digit must be a letter (A–Z, upper case); the second can be a letter or a numerical digit, 0–9. There are additional rules for determining whether the variable will contain single-precision, double-precision or integer numbers, or a string. We need not go into these here: we shall just add (as we mentioned earlier) that string variable names must end with a '$' sign.

We want two variable locations, into which the computer can put our two numbers, so we shall call them 'A' and 'B'. And they will be numeric, not string variables, so no $ is needed. However, we *will* use a string variable to allow us to answer yes or no to the question whether we wish to repeat the program operation.

The INPUT keyword enables the computer to receive input from the keyboard during program operation. The system stops and outputs a '?', until the input is received. To make it clear what the input should be, we can also use INPUT to print out a string of characters that ask us more politely for the two numbers. There is no need for an additional PRINT keyword, though we could have used one if we wished.

Our program will look like this:

    10 REM Program to add two numbers input from keyboard
    20 INPUT "What is first number"; A
    30 INPUT "What is second number"; B
    40 PRINT A " +" B "=" A + B
    50 INPUT "Do you want to repeat? Y/N"; C$
    60 IF C$ = "Y" THEN GOTO 20
    70 END

When we 'RUN' the program, a dialogue such as the following will be built up on screen. The computer's output is in normal typeface, our input in italics:

What is first number? *75*
What is second number? *40*
75 + 40 = 115
Do you want to repeat? Y/N? *N*
Ready

Note that the question marks were added automatically to the computer's message as part of the INPUT function. Note, too, that any input other than 'Y' (including 'y', 'yes', and so on) in response to the question 'Do you want to repeat?' would terminate the program. Of course, we *could* have written the program to allow for a greater variety of positive responses. And finally, note that on line 60, we did not need to specify what would happen if the C$ input was *not* 'Y'. In that case, the computer automatically proceeds to execute the rest of the program in sequence, unless given contrary instructions (for example, by an ELSE command).

Handling Text Data

Enough of arithmetical programs: let us go on to look at some short programs that manipulate text instead. Text, of course, is merely a subset of possible character strings to the computer. In this type of simple program, the system does not concern itself with what the words *mean*, only with what we want it to do with them.

We can hold a 'conversation' with the computer by using character strings in an interactive program format. The following simple program does just that:

```
10 INPUT "What is your name"; N$
20 PRINT "Hello " N$ ". How old are you"
30 INPUT AGE
40 PRINT "Fancy that. You were born" AGE – 3 "years before I was
   made"
50 END
```

Alternatively, we can simply manipulate textual data within the program itself: perhaps using the data handling facilities we have already outlined. Let us do that next, to show how we could program the computer to play a short game.

Our game is called 'Consequences'. It is based on a party game, in which each participant writes a short 'story' to a fixed format: man meets woman, in a specified place, they have a brief conversation, and something ensues. The story elements provided by the different participants are then jumbled together, and drawn out at random to produce amusing 'nonsense' variations on the theme. The data in this case will be the variable story elements: the names of the man and woman, the place where they meet, their conversational exchanges, and the 'consequence'. The program will provide the framework of the story and randomize the data elements to produce the individual stories. A flowchart algorithm for 'Consequences' is given in Figure 76.

Figure 76: Flowchart for the 'Consequences' program

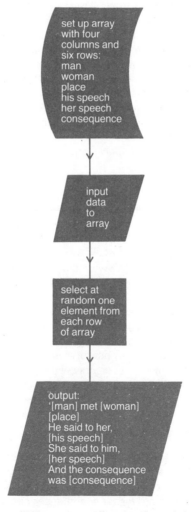

This short program will illustrate array structures and the use of the DATA keyword to include the data in the program itself. We shall use the READ statement to feed our data from the program into the memory array we specify; and then we shall use the RND keyword to select story elements to fit together.

First, we explain some aspects of the use of the program elements we shall be employing.

(1) Nested loops: We have already encountered the idea of a loop: as you will remember, we used loops in our programs for EMMA; and we pointed out then what a powerful tool they are. There are a number of ways of writing loops in BASIC programs, but perhaps the simplest is the FOR . . . NEXT sequence of keywords that we shall use. Our construct is a very useful one when we know how many times a program loop is to be repeated. The FOR statement specifies how often the successive statements are to be executed, and the NEXT statement sends the program execution back to the FOR point which precedes it.

It is perfectly possible to use a number of FOR . . . NEXT pairs nested inside one another, identifying each by a different variable name. However, it *is* important to ensure that the loops are neatly enclosed inside one another and not jumbled together; otherwise, the program would run incorrectly or not at all.

We shall use a double loop to READ data from our DATA statements into the elements of a two-dimensional array: using one loop to work along the rows of the array and the other to work along the columns. Each row will then contain the variables for a single story element (all the possible men's names, for instance), and each column a different set of story elements.

(2) Handling arrays: The DIM keyword allows us to specify how large an array is to be set up, and how many dimensions the array is to have. It *is* possible in our version of BASIC to set up an array by default, without using DIM; however, in this case the use of DIM will be clearer.

We indicated briefly on page 315 how the DIM statement is structured. For our purposes, it is important to remember that the array always begins with row 0 and column 0; so to produce an array with four rows and six columns, we need to dimension our array with the statement DIM A$ (3,5). ('A$' acts as our variable name for an array to contain character strings.)

Once the array is set up, we can enter data either from the program itself, using the READ keyword (as we shall in fact do), or from the keyboard, using an INPUT sequence.

(3) Random numbers: Our BASIC will automatically produce a random number from within set parameters that we specify in the program. To ensure that each run does not produce the same set of numbers, we begin the sequence by 'reseeding' the random number generator: making it start work at a different point. The RANDOM keyword accomplishes this.

Many BASICs produce random numbers in the range from 0 to 1, and a special program sequence is then needed to convert these into integers of the desired range. Our version can also produce integers, in a range starting at 1. This is a little inconvenient for our purposes, since our array numbering starts with 0; so we will need to produce a random choice in the range 1–4, and then subtract 1 from the result to produce a random number in the range 0–3 (for our rows, and similarly for our columns).

Our program is reproduced in Table 23. A sample run might produce the following output:

George Washington   met Marilyn Monroe
in the bath
He said to her, Rather wet today
She said to him, Never again
And the consequence was explosive

Table 23: 'Consequences' Program (in BASIC)

```
10    CLS
20    REM Consequences
30    REM Dimension array
40    DIM A$(3,5)
50    REM Read data into array
60    FOR N = 0 TO 5
70    FOR I = 0 TO 3
80    READ A$(I,N)
90    NEXT I
100   NEXT N
110   REM Select data at random
120   RANDOM
130   REM Print story
140   PRINT A$((RND(4)−1),0), "met " A$((RND(4)−1),1)
150   PRINT A$((RND(4)−1),2)
160   PRINT "He said to her, " A$((RND(4)−1),3)
170   PRINT "She said to him, " A$((RND(4)−1),4)
180   PRINT "And the consequence was " A$((RND(4)−1,5)
190   REM Data follows
200   DATA "George Washington", "Idi Amin", "Julius Caesar", "Albert Einstein"
210   DATA "Jane Austen", "Marilyn Monroe", "Golda Meir", "Queen Elizabeth I"
220   DATA "in the bath", "at a party", "in hell", "In Paris by moonlight"
230   DATA "Rather wet today", "Shall we dance?", "Do you come here often?",
          "How romantic this is"
240   DATA "Never again", "If you say so", "Not tonight, thank you", "Maybe next
          time"
250   DATA "unspeakable", "he cried", "explosive", "she cut off his head"
260   END
```

Handling the Screen: From Printing to Graphics

Let us build on this rather ridiculous program, to look at how we might improve the quality of our output. Learning to manipulate PRINT statements so as to produce attractive output on screen (or, indeed, on a printer) is a first step towards the use of low-level graphics. We shall go on to look very briefly at graphics handling later. However, this is a very machine-specific issue, and different dialects of BASIC use very different methods for producing graphical output. In consequence, we shall not look at graphics handling in depth in this chapter.

When we simply tell the system to PRINT something (a string or the result of an operation), it will, in default of other instructions, print it either in the next available space on the screen, or (if the screen is cleared by a CLS command) at the top left-hand corner. If we are printing a number of items, we can space them very simply by varying our program punctuation. In our system (as in many), for instance, a comma that is used to separate items to be printed moves the print position on to the next tab position, from five preset on each screen line (or on to the next line if necessary); a semicolon, on the other hand, does not space items . . . and the system ignores blanks. To print a blank, it is necessary to include it within quotation marks, making a short string out of it. So, for instance,

        PRINT "Matthew", "Mark", "Luke", "and John",
and   PRINT "Matthew"; "Mark"; "Luke"; "and John";
and   PRINT "Matthew "; "Mark "; "Luke "; "and John";
will emerge respectively as

        Matthew   Mark   Luke   and John
        MatthewMarkLukeand John
        Matthew Mark Luke and John

We can be more selective still about how our output appears by telling the system exactly where to place the output. We do this by following the PRINT keyword with an '@' command which specifies a particular space on the screen. As you may recall from Chapter 23, in the normal mode our screen consists of 24 rows (numbered 0–23) and 80 columns, numbered 0–79. (There are some alternative ways of using the screen, which we will not go into.) We can give the system a row number and a column number, and our screen output will appear at that point. So, for instance,

        PRINT @ (10,40)
will tell the system to start printing at column position 40 on row 10: just above the middle of the screen.

If we want to produce a design of graphics characters, or set of alpha/numeric output that builds up on screen as the program continues to run, then we can achieve this by manipulating our 'PRINT @' commands. The best way to do this is by using variable names to describe our print positions. So we would include a program line that says, for instance,

        PRINT @ (A,B)

and tell the program in advance how to calculate A and B at any point in the program run. We might, for instance, loop round, incrementing or decrementing A and B; or we might randomize our choice of A and B from among the range of permissible print positions.

Let us expand our 'Consequences' program, to do two things along these lines. First, we shall space the lines of output evenly down the screen, rather than jumbling them up in one corner. And second, we shall use a very simple graphics technique to 'rub out' the 'Consequences' story before the program run is completed.

Using Reverse Video

Our system, like many, has a 'reverse video' capability: it will print in white on a black background (the usual option) or in black on a white background (the 'reverse' option). We designate which option we want to use by a simple video command:

PRINT CHR$ (26)

for reverse video, and

PRINT CHR$ (25)

for normal video. These two commands come from a set of screen manipulation and graphics character commands that are available on our version of BASIC. The CHR$ keyword is followed by a code, from a set based on the ASCII codes.

In reverse video, blanks show up as white spaces. So by printing sequences of blanks after a 'reverse video' command, we actually produce a sequence of white rectangles on the screen. We can build up patterns in this way, by jumping from one video mode to the other and back again.

We shall include a very simple sequence in our program that starts at the top left-hand corner and proceeds to 'white out' the screen and the message on it, row by row.

The expanded 'Consequences' program listing is given in Table 24. Take a look at it, and see if you can work out exactly how it is built up, and what it will do. (If you have a computer that runs a similar version of BASIC, you may like to try it out.)

Table 24: 'Consequences' Program (expanded version)

```
10    CLS
20    REM Consequences
30    REM Dimension array
40    DIM A$(3,5)
50    REM Read data into array
60    FOR N = 0 TO 5
70    FOR I = 0 TO 3
```

```
80    READ A$(I,N)
90    NEXT I
100   NEXT N
110   REM Select data at random
120   RANDOM
130   REM Print story
140   PRINT @ (4,20),A$((RND(4)-1),0), "met " A$((RND(4)-1),1)
150   PRINT @ (8,20), A$((RND(4)-1),2)
160   PRINT @ (12,20), "He said to her, " A$((RND(4)-1),3)
170   PRINT @ (16,20), "She said to him, " A$((RND(4)-1),4)
180   PRINT @ (20,20), "And the consequence was " A$((RND(4)-1),5)
190   REM Data follows
200   DATA "George Washington", "Idi Amin", "Julius Caesar", "Albert Einstein"
210   DATA "Jane Austen", "Marilyn Monroe", "Golda Meir", "Queen Elizabeth I"
220   DATA "in the bath", "at a party", "in hell", "in Paris by moonlight"
230   DATA "Rather wet today", "Shall we dance?", "Do you come here often?",
      "How romantic this is"
240   DATA "Never again", "If you say so", "Not tonight, thank you", "Maybe next
      time"
250   DATA "unspeakable", "he cried", "explosive", "she cut off his head"
260   REM Reverse video
270   PRINT CHR$(26)
280   REM White out screen
290   FOR S = 0 TO 24 * 80-1
300   PRINT " ";
310   NEXT S
320   END
```

Moving Graphics

This very crude sequence is in fact our first step towards moving graphics:
building up pictures on the screen, and then moving them around in
successive loops of our program. Let us end the chapter by building on this
theme and producing a moving shape that might have an application, for
instance in a game of 'Battleships'.

The shape shown in Figure 77 is made up, as you can see, of simple
rectangles. It is intended to bear a very rough resemblance to a ship, seen
head-on. We can produce it on screen just as we produced the 'white-out'
above: by moving into reverse video, and telling the system to print blanks
at specified spaces on the display.

Let us write a program that 'draws' this shape on the screen and then
proceeds to move it around at random, to produce a 'moving target'. To
simplify matters, we shall keep the shape on the same rows of the display,
and simply change its column positions. And we will give it a random

Figure 77: A very simple 'ship' shape in reverse video

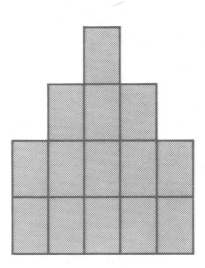

(drawn as black on white: on screen,
would appear as white on black).

choice of three moves at each program pass: stay still, move one column to the left, or move one column to the right.

We can produce a random number between −1 and +1 just as we produced one between 0 and 3 in 'Consequences': by specifying the appropriate size of number range, and then subtracting a constant to produce the scale of number range we want. We shall designate our reference column position by the variable name 'A', and place it initially at 40. We shall then describe all the successive rows of our shape in terms of the A column plus or minus a number, and when we want to move the entire shape at once we shall simply have to change the value of A, using a randomizing sequence.

Some further refinements are necessary. In order to make our shape move, we have to 'black out' its previous position each time we shift it to a new position. We can do this by surrounding our reverse video rectangles with a border of normal video blanks, which also move with reference to the value of A. As the shape will only move by one column in any direction on a program pass, our border also will need to be only one blank wide.

Next, we have to ensure that the value of A does not fall below 0, or exceed 79; and to allow extra room on top of A (which we will place at the left of the shape, as you can see in Figure 78), for the rest of the shape to fit on the screen. (We print at positions up to A +5.) We shall do this very simply by checking the value of A and repeating the randomizing operation, if it is out of our range. This is not a particularly satisfactory method, for our shape will tend to 'linger' at the screen borders; for a proper games program, we would include a more sophisticated routine.

Figure 78: The 'ship' shape with border and reference grid

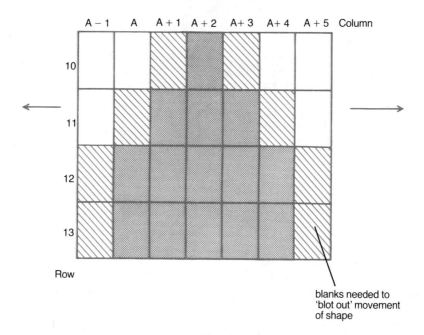

blanks needed to
'blot out' movement
of shape

Finally, we want to decide how quickly the shape is to move. Think back to our machine-code program for generating sound waves: as we saw, the very length of the program sequences we used, and the time taken for the machine to execute them, created a certain output frequency. To vary this frequency, we either vary the sequence length, by building in a 'delay' loop, or resort to the use of a timer. For our present example, we shall use a simple delay loop: repeating a non-existent operation a fixed number of times, that we designate by a FOR ... NEXT sequence. We have chosen to repeat 50 times, but if you run this program, or a variation upon it to suit your own machine, you may like to try out the effect of including smaller or larger delays, or of omitting the delay altogether.

Figure 79: Flowchart for the 'Ship' program

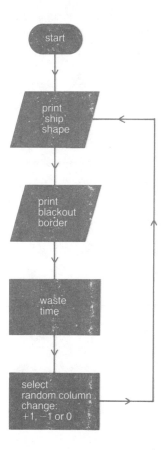

Our flowchart algorithm is given in Figure 79, and the program listing itself in Table 25. Note that we loop around repeatedly, without ever reading the END statement. When you get fed up with the ship moving, you have to BREAK (a command key on our keyboard) the program execution in order to exit from it.

This is a very crude program, and there are many more elegant ways of achieving the same effect in our version, and other versions, of BASIC.

If you have a computer on which you can run these programs or suitable adaptations of them, you will certainly want to go further with programming, using a proper programming manual. We are not trying to provide that here, though: merely to give you a taste of how programs are constructed. And if you do not have a computer to practise on, you will probably find our small sample of programs more than enough to look at. Programs in the abstract are pretty boring, except to the programmer.

In the next section we go on to look at how some other common high-level languages differ from BASIC in their tools for program writing.

Table 25: 'Ship' Program (in BASIC)

```
10   REM Ship (program to illustrate moving graphics)
20   REM Reseed random number generator
30   RANDOM
40   CLS
50   REM Locate initial print position
60   LET A = 40
70   REM Reverse video
80   PRINT CHR$(26)
90   REM Print ship shape
100  PRINT @ (10,A +2), " "
110  PRINT @ (11,A +1), " "
120  PRINT @ (12,A), "    "
130  PRINT @ (13,A), "    "
140  REM Normal video
150  PRINT CHR$(25)
160  REM Print blackout border
170  PRINT @ (10,A +1), " "
180  PRINT @ (10,A +3), " "
190  PRINT @ (11,A), " "
200  PRINT @ (11,A +4), " "
210  PRINT @ (12,A −1), " "
220  PRINT @ (12,A +5), " "
230  PRINT @ (13,A −1), " "
240  PRINT @ (13,A +5), " "
250  REM Time delay
260  FOR N = 1 TO 50
270  NEXT N
280  REM Select next move at random ( +1. −1, 0)
290  LET A = A + (RND(3)−2)
300  REM Repeat random process if limits exceeded
310  IF A>0 AND A<75 THEN GOTO 80 ELSE GOTO 290
320  END
```

27. FORTRAN, COBOL and Other High-Level Languages

Now we know a little about one high-level language, BASIC, let us go on to look briefly at two others, and see how they differ from BASIC. We shall then outline some of the other languages in common use today. Why do such competing languages continue to be used, and what are their strengths and weaknesses?

FORTRAN

FORTRAN (which stands for FORmula TRANslator) was the earliest non-machine-specific high-level language to be specified, and it is still the most widely used language in scientific and engineering applications today. To understand why its dominance has persisted, we must go back in time to consider the conditions under which it was developed.

Before commercial data processing took off on a large scale in the 1960s, much of the early work on digital computers was concerned with performing scientific and engineering calculations of great magnitude and complexity. Computing was a costly resource, and it was best devoted to the type of problem that it was difficult and time-consuming to solve accurately in any other way.

For such large problems, the critical issue is the way data are handled: how they are input to the system, and how they are stored inside the available memory and processing space. To ensure that data are stored efficiently, it is desirable to distinguish between different *types* of data: not only between numbers and character strings, but between different types of numbers: integers, real numbers, numbers of different degrees of precision, and so on. There are then technical advantages in maintaining these distinctions from the input stage, through separate processing procedures, to the storage and output phases.

We saw how the version of BASIC we introduced had some rules for distinguishing between, for instance, integers and single- and double-precision numbers. However, these 'formatting' rules are comparatively simple. FORTRAN, by contrast, has very precise formatting control procedures covering the ways in which input and output data are organized. The data type of each variable that is designated has to be specified, including variables that are stored and displayed, but not manipulated at all. This emphasis upon efficient use of resources reflects the development of FORTRAN at a time when computer power was expensive. In consequence of it, FORTRAN programs run two or even three times more efficiently than BASIC programs.

A second major difference between the two languages lies in their input and output commands. FORTRAN 'READ' and 'WRITE' commands broadly correspond to BASIC 'READ' and 'PRINT' commands, but in addition they permit the user to select any one from a number of available input or output devices, and to handle its operation accordingly. This feature, again, reflects FORTRAN's uses for writing large application programs, and in particular as a language run on large and complex computer configurations.

FORTRAN has been designed to allow for greater flexibility than BASIC in the definition of functions and of subroutines. This capability was created as a result of the demand for highly optimized subroutines and procedures in FORTRAN, and it has been very effective in enabling the language to meet that demand. Today, large libraries of subroutines, operating procedures and prepared application packages are available for use by FORTRAN programmers; and they constitute a major investment in human development time, and a very important resource. Their existence will certainly ensure the continuation of FORTRAN as a major language for scientific and engineering purposes, for the foreseeable future.

Of course, a lot of BASIC programs have been written, too, as any reader of personal computer magazines knows! But relatively few of them deal with the scientific/engineering field in which FORTRAN remains pre-eminent.

It is important to realize that BASIC was originally conceived as a simplified version of FORTRAN: intended, not for use on large-scale commercial and scientific computers, but as a teaching tool for explaining the basics of programming. Simple FORTRAN programs are very like BASIC programs: that is one reason why we have not included any in this book. It is in more complex applications that the differences between the two languages are most apparent.

Ironically, the very simplicity of BASIC has made it so appealing to newcomers to computing (and especially to non-professional programmers) that additions and extensions to BASIC are now proliferating to grab the attention of the growing army of BASIC programmers who are eager to write more complex programs but do not wish, or indeed need, to learn FORTRAN. Many of these extensions do exactly what features of FORTRAN that were originally not included in the BASIC specification do. However, they do it less efficiently. Of course, computer power is cheap today, and in many circumstances user convenience is more important than efficient use of computer resources. Only the purist (ór the FORTRAN programmer!) grumbles at the technical inelegance of BASIC in these more complex applications.

A major difference between programs that make use of these extensions of BASIC, and comparable programs written in FORTRAN, lies in their appearance to the user. BASIC programs look more like statements in ordinary English to the layman, while FORTRAN programs are tightly structured and much less easy to follow for those without technical skills. As a result, BASIC is winning a great deal of ground in relatively simple commercial fields, and a little in scientific and technical fields.

It is still true, though, that FORTRAN is the best-defined and standardized high-level language. Its standards have not only been efficiently developed; they are also widely observed — a fact that is not true of many other so-called standardized high-level languages. Dialects of BASIC proliferate; even the simple programs we included in this book cannot all be run on machines other than the Tandy computer they were written for without modification. Proposals for standardizing BASIC come up all the time, but as the various dialects become increasingly entrenched, so their chances of success diminish rather than increase. As a result, the BASIC programmer who wants to experiment with different machines and transfer his programs from one machine to another has a hard time. And his need to document every detail of the machine environment for which his program was designed cannot be over-stressed. By contrast, adapting a FORTRAN program to run on a different computer is a comparatively trivial business. This vital feature of FORTRAN emphasizes its continuing importance, particularly in the professional programming environment.

COBOL

COBOL was developed a little later than FORTRAN, as we saw in Chapter 9; it reflected the growing swing away from scientific applications and towards large-volume data-processing applications in the commercial world. The differences between the two languages are more of emphasis than of basic conception.

To the inexperienced reader, a COBOL program appears abstruse and arcane. Its individual keywords reflect English words, but the program as a whole looks nothing like English: it is much too highly stylized and demands a great degree of precision in handling its syntax and grammar. (BASIC is free and easy by comparison: a comma here or a space there are rarely of great importance.) As a result, COBOL is not a particularly easy language to learn or to use; and COBOL compilers all too often contain bugs that reflect the difficulties of handling the language at this level, too.

Commercial applications of the type for which COBOL was primarily designed are characterized by a large volume of data and a low degree of processing complexity required by it. The main task of the system is to provide a variety of report formats and manipulate files that will be used for a number of different purposes. As a result, many COBOL commands are devoted to the description of data organization and manipulation, comparatively few to actual arithmetic and logical manipulation.

COBOL programs tend to be organized and laid out in a way that is very clear to the practised programmer: they are more 'visual' than FORTRAN and BASIC programs, which demand a mathematical eye for easy under-standing. This means that the language appeals to a different kind of cognitive psyche: one that responds to graphs rather than to tables, to use a broad analogy.

Other High-Level Languages

A large number of other high-level languages are also in common use today. We shall mention very briefly some features of some of the more common ones.

ADA: Designed by C.I.I.-Honeywell-Bull for the U.S. Department of Defense, and intended as a general-purpose language that would replace most others in use in the Department. Named after Lady Lovelace (see Chapter 4). Highly standardized, and hoped to be more portable between computers than current languages. Fully specified by 1980, but not yet popular, and criticized by some as unwieldy.

ALGOL: The two major incarnations of ALGOL, ALGOL 60 and ALGOL 68, are in fact quite different. ALGOL 60 was designed for use in handling scientific applications, and is particularly good on recursive techniques. It was widely used in Europe in the 1960s and early 1970s, but has now largely been superseded. ALGOL 68, its rejig, is also more popular in Europe than in the U.S. It is vast and comprehensive, but difficult to implement on any but large computers.

LISP (which stands for 'LISt Processor'): A list-processing language (see Chapter 32) that has become a staple tool of artificial-intelligence research. Good for creating complex chains of operations and data, and for manipulating data structures. Developed by John McCarthy at the Massachusetts Institute of Technology.

LOGO: Developed as part of the 'mathland' approach for introducing young people to mathematical concepts. LOGO is strong on list structures and graphics, and has a solid basic instruction set. The LOGO 'turtle', a turtle-shaped graphics plotter, has become widely known. It has also found uses in artificial-intelligence research.

PASCAL: Developed primarily from ALGOL, and designed as a teaching language. Good on structured programming techniques (see Chapter 28), a point at which BASIC, its main rival, is weak. Also good at handling complex data structures.

PL/1 (or 'Programming Language 1.'): Developed by I.B.M., and intended as a synthesis of the best features of COBOL, FORTRAN and ALGOL 60. Also available in a version for microcomputers, PL/M. Intended as a major general-purpose language, but has proved rather complicated to use, and has not caught on as widely as was first hoped.

SMALLTALK: Developed by Xerox Research as a strongly graphics-based language, with a wide range of symbol commands (smiling faces, pointing hands and so on). This has made it a good tool for children learning computing, as well as for developing high-resolution graphics. Much admired, but not widely available.

Table 26: How High-Level Language Formats Differ (some simple examples)

Language	Decision Format	Loop Format
BASIC	IF (condition) THEN (condition true sequence) ELSE (condition not true sequence)	FOR N = 1 TO 25 (loop statements) NEXT N
FORTRAN	IF (condition) GOTO (condition true sequence) ELSE (condition not true sequence)	DO 10 I = 1, N (loop statements) 10 CONTINUE
PASCAL	IF (condition) THEN (condition true sequence) ELSE (condition not true sequence)	I: = 1 WHILE I < = N DO BEGIN (loop operations) END

Mixing Languages

In an ideal world it would be possible to select any language at will: for use exclusively if it appeals, or at specific points in a program that also makes use of other languages. It would be nice if we could choose our own keywords, making use of logical connections that make intuitive sense to us, and of the specialized jargon of our own profession. Is this possible today, or might it come about in the future?

In theory, it is entirely feasible to move from language to language, not only on a single computer, but within a single program. We saw in Chapter 26 how, on the TRS-80 Model II, it is possible to switch from BASIC into TRSDOS routines, or even into machine code, and back again. However, the facility to enable programmers to switch from one high-level language to another is much less commonly available.

Why? Basically, because of the complexity of the operating procedures that would be needed to switch the different compilers and interpreters into and out of action, and to keep track of what the program is doing at each point in its execution. Few operating systems are up to the task, and only a few computer systems offer multi-language abilities as a real selling-point. However, the subtlety of software offerings is increasing all the time. Perhaps tomorrow, the programmer's dream of today will become a reality.

28. Program Writing in Practice: Techniques and Problems

Our brief look at program writing in machine code and in BASIC will, we hope, have served to show you some of the principles of writing a program. However, our examples were necessarily short; as a result, we have not looked at the rather different issues that can arise when writing a longer program. Nor have we considered some of the practical issues of actually getting a program to run on a particular computer.

This chapter is intended to fill some of those gaps. First we look at the dividing line between writing your own programs and purchasing ready-written programs. We consider program-writing programs, packages designed to simplify the task of writing more complex programs. Then we look at some aspects of practical program writing, including editing and debugging, and the thorny issue of documentation (which also affects bought programs). Finally, we look at the question of structuring longer programs.

Why Write Programs?

Doubtless some newcomers to computing assume that they can simply sit down at their new machine, slot in a program cartridge, and use the program on it with no difficulty. Others are convinced that they will never 'waste money' on buying ready-written programs: they are religiously determined to write every word themselves.

Most of those in both groups are mistaken. Why? Let us look in a little more depth at the practicalities of using a small computer system.

Ready-written software: As we explained earlier in this book, virtually every computer — even the most basic — comes with *some* ready-written software, even if it is no more extensive than a short monitor program containing a few simple subroutines (like those we described for EMMA in Chapter 24). Unless you are solely interested in learning to program the machine (and, indeed, even if that *is* your sole interest) you will certainly want to use these resources. The reason is obvious: the number and complexity of the programs you could write yourself, starting from the absolute scratch of the c.p.u.'s instruction set, is extremely limited.

Even a short program takes quite a while to write, check, and get running — though it is a fallacy to assume that the longer the program, the longer it took to write. Trying to write every piece of software you will need yourself would be like trying to re-invent the wheel. You would not get very far, you would not be able to offer the rest of the world anything it did not have already, and you would not even acquire a particularly balanced knowledge of the subject yourself.

What sort of ready-written software might you opt to use, then? It depends very much upon what you are using the computer for, and what you know about programming yourself.

The great majority of computer users (below the level of large firms with their own staff of programmers – but including many of those, too) will want to buy some application programs. These might be business-oriented programs like stock control or word processing packages; they might be games programs; they might be more specialized offerings. The computer press is full of advertisements for a wide range of programs tailored to run on different systems, and computer stores (and, indeed, computer manufacturers) offer them too. All these programs represent a considerable investment in programmer time; they are not the kind of programs you could dash off in an evening; and some of them have taken years to perfect. If you want to carry out any of the applications they cover, you will almost certainly be in the market for ready-written software.

If you look over the various offerings in the software market, you will also recognize many whose purpose would not have been at all clear to you before you began to read this book – and probably quite a few that are still beyond you. These might be classified under the general heading of systems software: they are not finished application programs but various types of utility program that make application programs easier to write, or otherwise extend the system's capabilities.

As your personal capability extends, so you will doubtless come to recognize your need for these more specialized offerings. They are *not* software designed for those who want to avoid program-writing entirely; they *are* designed to enable those who do program their computers to write better programs.

Many computer magazines also carry a number of program listings: literally lines and lines of program statements that you can type into your computer to make it perform the specified operations. Some are applications programs, including many simple games programs. Others are utility programs. For instance, a recent issue of *Byte* magazine (September 1982) contains listings for the following programs:

'Quinti-Maze', a game program written in BASIC for the Apple II;

'Three Dee Dee', a Rubik's-cube-like game for the TRS-80 Colour Computer, again written in BASIC;

a Pascal program, intended to be portable among different computers, for use in outputting braille on a lineprinter;

'Weave', a program to simulate woven-thread patterns, written in BASIC for NorthStar machines;

'Turn your Apple II into a storage oscilloscope' (another BASIC program).

As well as using these on your own system, you may aspire to produce similar programs yourself: most magazines accept, and pay for, similar offerings from their readers.

Mentioning these listings, however, brings us to our next point: the limitations of ready-written software.

Making ready-written software work : Just as the borderline between software and hardware is a vague one, so is the borderline between operating a computer and programming it. Operating today's computers is a far cry from simply feeding in a program: typing in a listing, slotting in a disc containing the program, or whatever. It is usually an interactive business, in which the user continually has to respond (and respond sensibly) to the computer while the program is running.

Application programs written for non-programmers try to make the business of responding as straightforward as possible, often by making a 'menu' of user choices appear on screen, to prompt the user to respond acceptably. But there is a limit to how straightforward that can be, and a much lower limit to how straightforward it normally is, today. As an example, let's look briefly at SCRIPSIT, the word processing package we use on our TRS-80.

SCRIPSIT comes, as we said in Chapter 23, in a package comprising the disc containing the program, a couple of manuals, and a teach-yourself course on cassettes. The course consists of eight lesson outlines on cassette; and Tandy recommend that the learner should spend from one to one and a half hours on each lesson . . . that means from eight to twelve hours spent before you understand the basics of operating the program.

Could you use the program without taking the course? Certainly, if you are an experienced computer and word-processor user, you could rip through it in a little less time, or pick up the basics from the manuals without bothering to listen to the cassettes; but it is difficult to imagine anyone getting away with much less than, say, four hours of experimenting before they can use the system reasonably effectively. And to make full use of the system demands *more* knowledge than the course contains. Most users will need to make themselves thoroughly familiar with the 78 pages (excluding index) of the reference manual . . . and by the time you have reached this stage, you will be performing operations that look suspiciously like programming.

What sort of operations? SCRIPSIT contains, for example, a facility for the user to 'define' keys on the keyboard. Up to twenty keys can be programmed to carry out special sequences of operations, selected by the user: this might be just entering in a frequently used address, or might be a more complex sequence including commands as well as data. At a more complex level, it is possible to change many of the system commands. You can edit the 'default' commands, which determine how the SCRIPSIT menus appear on the screen, to meet your special needs: for instance, entering into the program itself the number of lines you will normally want to print on a page, and the pitch of typeface you normally use. You can even change the printer control codes that determine how the printer responds to key input sequences. At a more complex level still, the program documentation includes instructions on how to 'patch' SCRIPSIT: in other words, to adapt the basic SCRIPSIT programs so that they better meet your own requirements. (You might opt to amend the program so that you get a larger shape of cursor, or a solid cursor that doesn't flash, for instance.) To do these last operations, you have to jump right outside the SCRIPSIT program, into TRSDOS (the disc operating system).

Even if you do not want to be bothered with these details (and you cannot get the best performance out of the program without considering them), you will need some specialist knowledge: for example, various kinds of operator error lead the system to come up with error messages that derive from its operating system, and not from the SCRIPSIT package. Hunting through the SCRIPSIT manuals will not tell you what 'System Error 48' stands for. (There are fifty system error codes in current use.) To get the system back to work requires familiarity with the TRS-80 owner's manual, which is much fatter (over 500 pages).

You might reasonably argue that learning to operate a program like SCRIPSIT is not quite the same as learning a programming language such as BASIC or FORTRAN. But the differences are not that great. SCRIPSIT has a language of its own, made up of the various commands that the user has to learn: and it is a sizeable task to master it.

In this, of course, SCRIPSIT does not differ from other complex application program packages. Learning to use any proprietary application program is a skill in its own right: you cannot just slot in VISICALC, or WORDSTAR, or any other such program, and expect it to do *all* the work for you. All these programs, even the best-written and documented, demand some work from the user. And the performance of that work is the equivalent of programming the system: both adapting the basic application program and providing input on a level one higher than that on which the basic application program is written.

Parameterized programs: In fact, to draw a hard-and-fast distinction between ready-written programs and home-produced efforts is itself misleading. Many commercially produced programs have been deliberately produced in an 'unfinished' way, waiting for the final user to finish them off by customizing them to his or her personal requirements.

Most computer programs are not unique in their general intent, although often they are unique, even in today's overcrowded software market, in their fine detail. Most commercial organizations have a similar range of basic administrative and control functions for which they require computer programs; for instance, payroll handling, sales ledger maintenance, stock control and so on are extremely common applications. And all payroll application packages (for example) have broad similarities. This is due not just to the underlying similarity of businesses working in superficially different fields, but also to standardized accounting practices and to common legislative or fiscal requirements (such as the necessity to keep track of Value Added Tax payments). Even in the personal or professional computing fields, where the range of common applications is still emerging from the general chaos, there are standard approaches to problems such as curve-fitting to data, discounted cash flow analyses, or critical path analysis techniques used by project managers.

However, individual users have requirements that differ in detail, even if they are the same in outline. Not all companies have the same size of payroll, even if almost all companies *have* a payroll. Therefore, the programs that different companies and individuals need differ in perhaps superficial, but nevertheless important, ways.

One result of this situation has been the development of a market in parameterized application packages. The package provides an outline algorithm: the basic features of a stock control application program, or whatever it is intended to do. The individual buyer then customizes the package by filling in the data applicable to his or her particular requirements, or by choosing between inbuilt alternatives. In effect, the buyer completes the programming task, even if he does so in a way that is simplified by the structure of the basic program.

Parameterized packages of this general type are available for just about every application that has reasonably close parallels with other users' applications. And whenever such a package is available, the user has to choose between adopting this pre-packaged approach and buying-in an 'off the peg' program, or programming from scratch (or hiring an outside agency to do so). The disadvantage with the packaged solution is that it is less efficient (in running on the computer; not necessarily in its user interface) than a custom-written program. The advantage, of course, is that it is a cheap solution and, often, a perfectly acceptable one.

Program-writing programs: A special type of 'parameterized' program has recently come on to the market for microcomputers and small business systems. This is the program-writing program: systems programs that claim they can generate endless application programs without the user having to do any actual programming work at all. (Similar tools have long been available for professional programmers working on larger computer systems.)

Two broad types of program-writing program are available. 'Program generators' produce programs in a high-level language, which can then be copied, listed, and run quite separately from the program generation package. 'Application generators' also produce application programs; but this time the programs they produce are dependent upon the software contained in the generator package, and they cannot be run separately from it. Apart from this basic difference, the two types operate in much the same way.

The simplicity of using the various proprietary offerings varies enormously, but basically the programs all aim to simplify the task of program writing by making it *more* like the task of, say, using an application program such as VISICALC or SCRIPSIT. They typically have a menu structure that takes the user step-by-step through the entire process of analysing his application, defining the parameters of his program (the size of files and file fields, for instance), specifying how input and output are to be handled (perhaps by designing screen formats that will prompt the application user for input), defining the arithmetical or logical manipulations to be carried out, and generating program statements that embody instructions for performing all these various operations.

A good program generation package, used for applications to which it is well fitted (most simple file-handling applications, for example, can be handled in this way), certainly cuts down the work of producing an application program. But it does *not* remove it entirely. The user still has to do *some* work — and probably a sizeable amount of it. He or she still has to learn the language of the program-generation program: a real one just like SCRIPSIT's language, even if not a recognized high-level language (and perhaps of less real value as knowledge to the programmer, simply because of its specificity). And he or she still has to know what is required of the program: often a much harder task than actually specifying the program in terms of program statements. As a result, few of those who have tried them believe that program-writing programs can realistically take the place of conventional programming experience.

Bugs in purchased programs: When your application program fails to work, or works in ways that the material in the package does not explain to you (as when SCRIPSIT comes up with error codes to which there is no reference in its manual), then there is, in a very general sense, a 'bug' in it. Some such bugs (like the error-code bug) are pretty easy to cure. Others can be extraordinarily resistant to treatment, even by skilled programmers.

And with this we come to one final reason why you are likely, whether you intended to or not, to need some familiarity with programming techniques: bought programs are not perfect. Even if they are ideally suited to your requirements and perfectly adapted for your system, you may need some specialist knowledge in order to make them work, and keep working. If they are *not* ideally suited to the application for which you intend them; if they are delivered to you with software bugs that the original programmer had not noticed, or had noticed but failed to cure; or if you want to adapt a program intended for some other machine; then you will have to provide programming input yourself, or find someone else to adapt the program for you.

Magazine listings are particularly susceptible to bugs. All too many computer magazines do *not* test the programs whose listings they run: and even if there are no typographical errors in the program listing, there may be bugs in the program itself. If you plan to obtain any program input from this source, then you will rapidly discover how very necessary a familiarity with programming techniques is.

With that dire warning, let us go on to look briefly at an aspect of programming we have not yet covered: editing and debugging programs.

Editing and Debugging Programs

There is no single right way to write any computer program. Even very simple programs can normally be written in a wide variety of ways: using different command sequences, ordering the program statements differently, handling the data input in different ways, and so on. In writing some very simple programs earlier in the book, we saw how much choice the programmer has in how he or she puts the system's resources to work in implementing an algorithm.

But if there are many 'right' ways to write a program, there are even more wrong ways. And the odds are that when you first draft a program, you will pick a wrong way. Try to run that first draft, and you will find, either that it won't work at all, or that it does something quite different from what you had intended.

The business of getting programs to work, and to work as the programmer intended, is known as 'debugging'. There are many tools used in debugging programs: we looked at some of them briefly in Chapter 9. Let us start by considering editing facilities: software tools that enable the programmer to adapt an incorrect program listing after it has been entered into the computer.

Editors: Word processing packages generally have very good editing facilities: if you type a wrong letter, or if you want to insert a new word or larger chunk of text, there are simple ways of accomplishing these tasks. Operating systems are not always so obliging. Sometimes you have to work through complex sequences of commands in order to effect the changes you need.

The ways in which editors work vary widely from computer to computer. The ideal is a full-screen editor: one that displays the whole program listing (or as much of it as will fit) on the video screen, and then enables the programmer to roam around with his cursor, adapting the listing at will. Much more common in microcomputers are line editors. With these, the programmer has to specify one line of his program at a time. The line is then made available for editing – perhaps by bringing it down to a specified area at the bottom of the video screen, or by repeating it in the next available screen position – and then the programmer uses 'edit' commands to adapt it.

This is the type of editor that is provided in our version of BASIC. As you may recall from Chapter 26, TRS-80 Model II BASIC includes an 'edit mode'. In order to adapt a line of program, the programmer goes into edit mode, by typing a statement like:

EDIT 100

The system then prepares the line for editing: and a special set of edit commands are used to adapt the line contents. These are quite different from either the commands used in programs themselves, or the editing commands used by SCRIPSIT.

Error messages: Editors are very useful when you know what is wrong with your program and simply want to change it. All too often, though, you *don't* know what you have done wrong. You could have sworn you wrote the program correctly; sadly, the system doesn't agree with you.

Very occasionally a bug in the system's hardware, or an anomaly in its intimate software, prevents the program from working as it should. Normally, though, the fault is the programmer's. Don't blame the machine until you are absolutely sure that the blame is not really yours!

One of the basic functions of systems software is to help the applications programmer to find errors; but the sophistication of the tools provided varies widely. So, come to that, do the kind of errors that might prevent a program from working correctly. We shall look first and briefly at some of the errors that might affect a program, then at some of the methods used to pinpoint them.

What might you get wrong, in writing a program for your machine in, say, BASIC? You might:

(1) enter an illegal program statement. You might try to use a command word that your dialect of BASIC does not contain. You might try to structure commands in a way which your dialect does not accept. You might use, as a variable name, a character sequence that is reserved for some other purpose. (Look back to our short interactive program on page 330. We originally thought of calling our variable 'NAME$'; but we rapidly discovered that the sequence 'NAME' is 'reserved' in our dialect, and that it cannot appear as a part or whole of variable names. So we called the variable 'N$' instead; and hey presto, the program ran.)

(2) include illegal data in a program: for instance, trying to enter a string into a variable that has been set up to receive numeric data only.

(3) structure your program incorrectly: muddling up your nested loops, say, so that they are tangled loops instead; or forgetting to provide an exit route from a loop, so that the program goes round and round in circles and never reaches the end.

(4) fail to fit your program into the machine's capacity. Small computers in particular can't always fit in complex programs: they literally run out of working memory. There is no use taking a listing intended to run on a machine with 32K of memory and hoping the program will fit into 16K.

It won't. Alternatively, you might make the result of an arithmetic operation overflow: and you would have to structure the operation differently, to avoid an incorrect result.

This is a basic list: it is by no means an exhaustive one. By the time you have tried to write a few programs yourself, you will have added many more types of error to it.

What might your system do, then, when you commit one of the cardinal sins listed above? If you are lucky, it will tell you what you have done, by means of an 'error message'. (If you have a very basic system, you may have to work out what went wrong with less help. If you are unlucky, the system might fail to trap the error, not because it is not there, but because it does not fit into any of the error patterns the systems software has been programmed to detect. The program will run . . . but it won't run correctly.)

Some computer systems check input for acceptability as it is being entered in 'program' mode. If an inadmissible sequence is entered, they produce an error message immediately. Others do not monitor input at all until the program is run. When it *is* run, some run it to the end, tagging all the errors they encounter on the way. Many, however, stop at the first error that is encountered, with an appropriate error message, rather than continuing right through the listing. Correcting that error, of course, will cause the machine to stop at the *next* error when you try to run the program again. If there are a number of errors, this can make trapping them all a time-consuming process.

What sort of error codes will you get? This varies widely from machine to machine. Helpful systems produce precise verbal messages like 'UNACCEPTABLE KEYWORD'. Less helpful systems produce less precise verbal messages that tell you that something is wrong, but do not give you much help in discovering exactly *what* is wrong. Many systems come up with numeric codes instead of verbal messages. Somewhere in the manual will be a master list that amplifies the codes. In any case, you will soon learn what the most common ones mean.

TRSDOS comes into the category of operating systems that check for errors only when programs are actually run, and that stop program running at the first error encountered. It generates a series of error codes that appear in numeric form on the display. To give you an idea of the kind of errors it can trap, we list these codes in Table 27. (*Overleaf*)

Table 27: TRSDOS Error Codes

Error codes in TRSDOS/BASIC are different from the normal operating system error codes. The first listing is the BASIC error codes; the second, the TRSDOS error codes.

(a)   in BASIC

Code	Abbreviation	
1	NF	NEXT used without FOR (e.g. in tangled loops)
2	SN	Syntax error: e.g.. incorrect punctuation, misspelled keyword
3	RG	RETURN statement encountered with no matching GOSUB before it
4	OD	Out of data. READ statement ran out of data to read
5	FC	Illegal function call. Various errors, e.g. negative array dimensioning
6	OV	Numerical overflow
7	OM	Out of RAM for program use
8	UL	Undefined line: reference in one program line made to another that was not entered
9	BS	Bad subscript in array
10	DD	Attempt to redimension array that has already been defined (must ERASE first)
11	/0	Division by zero
12	ID	Illegal direct. Program-only keyword in line for immediate execution
13	TM	Type mismatch: wrong kind of data assigned to variable
14	OS	Out of string space
15	LS	Long string (more than 255 characters)
16	ST	String too complex for system to handle
17	CN	Cannot execute CONTinue command
18	UF	Undefined user function
19	NR	No RESUME after error-trapping routine
20	RW	RESUME encountered with no error
22	MO	Missing operand
23	BO	Buffer overflow
50	FO	Field overflow
51	IE	Internal error
52	BN	Bad file number
53	FF	File not found
54	BM	Bad file mode
55	AO	File already open
56	IO	Disc input/output error
59	DF	Disc full
60	EF	Attempt to read past end of file
61	RN	Bad record number (in PUT or GET sequence)
63	MM	Mode mismatch
65	DS	Direct statement encountered during load of program

(no meaning attached to codes 21, 24–49, 58, 64; codes 57, 62, 66 refer to functions not defined in this version of BASIC)

(b)   Selected codes in TRSDOS
2   Character not available
3   Parameter error on call
5   Disc sector not found
6   Attempt to open file already open
7   Illegal disc change
8   Disc drive not ready
9   Invalid data provided by caller
10   Maximum of 16 files may be open at once
11   File already in directory
12   No drive available for opening a file
13   Write attempt to a read only file
14   Write fault on disc i/o
15   Disc is write protected (no writing possible)
17   Directory read error
18   Directory write error
19   Improper file name
24   File not found
25   File access denied due to password protection
26   Directory space full
27   Disc space full
28   Attempt to read past end of file
31   Program not found
34   Attempt to use a non-program file as a program
35   Memory fault during program load
42   Printer not ready
43   Printer out of paper
49   Hardware fault during disc i/o operations

Testing programs: As we have already hinted, the fact that your computer has *not* come up with an error message – or simply refused to run your program – does not necessarily mean that all is well. It is part of your job as programmer to make sure that all is well: and that means testing the program *after* you have first made it run.

Many programs have lurking bugs. The programs may work perfectly well with some input data, but inputting some other data will crash them, or cause them to come up with incorrect results. If you have forgotten to include a test for arithmetical overflow, it is no good assuming that the program will run correctly if the data on which you have tried it have not included any numbers that will overflow. This is an obvious example, but often the bugs are more subtle. The way to try and trap them is to run the program lots of times, doing all the *wrong* things you can think of. What happens when you do them? If the program asks for a number, and you give it a letter, does it go bananas, or does it politely tell you to try again? If it asks for a number between 1 and 50, and you enter '675', what happens? Making sure something sensible happens is part, not only of producing a bug-free program, but of producing a *good* program in the widest possible sense.

However, you can never assume that your program is totally free of bugs. There is no such thing as a perfect program. Decide for yourself when you are satisfied that the program will work acceptably for the purposes for which you intend it; then, if and when it fails to work acceptably, prepare to get back to work on it.

Of course, it may not be you who has to get back to work, if you are planning to sell the program, or let other people use it. And that is one reason why program documentation is so important. Good documentation makes it easier, not only for programs to be debugged, but for them to be maintained and adapted generally.

Documentation

Documentation is one of the most vital issues in writing good programs, and it is one that is very commonly overlooked. No error messages will come up on screen if you fail to document a program adequately. However, plenty of error messages will be generated by the hapless person (and it may be you!) who has the job of adapting the program later.

Of course, documentation is important to ready-written programs as well as to home-made ones. In fact, documentation is important to computer systems generally: to their hardware, as well as to their software. The more fully and clearly you know how the system works and what it is supposed to do, the more effectively you will be able to use it and the more easily you will be able to cure anything that goes wrong with it.

Failure to document adequately: Since documentation is so important, why is it so often carried out poorly and inadequately? Basically, there are two major reasons. One is happenstance and one is psychological.

The happenstance issue is that the world today is full of programmers who regret that, at the time they wrote a computer program, they failed to write down the detailed reasons why they chose certain values or procedures. There did not seem to be any pressing need to write them down at the time: nor was there any outside pressure on them to do so. Now, they can't fully remember the reasons: they know that the program ran at the time, even if they can't recall all the circumstances under which it ran (the system hardware and software set-up being the most important). That was all that mattered then; but now it may be necessary to modify the program to meet changed application requirements, or changes in hardware configuration. It will be extremely difficult even for them to do so; well nigh impossible for anybody else. And without knowing how the program works, how is anyone to document its working?

The psychological reason is that the activity of creating a computer program is still essentially an artistic rather than a scientific endeavour. It can indeed become an obsessive one, as many computer programmers will testify. The act of meticulously writing down the details of why and how the program works, on the other hand, is mundane, even banal. Since writing the program and documenting the program require different mental approaches, programmers often postpone the task of documentation until their creative fervour has worn off. Documentation gets to be regarded as a chore (it *is* a chore), and it is either skimped or neglected.

Standards for documentation: Standards for documentation, of varying degrees of authority, have indeed been drawn up; but it is a rare organization that can honestly say that they are fully observed. Practice among individual programmers varies. It is more than high time for it to be standardized at a top level, among both professional and amateur programmers. As a start, let us spell out the following basic principle:

Just as a program documents for the computer what it must do, so must the documentation of that program tell any user of that program what is being done, why it is being done that way, and how it is being done.

Let us go on from that principle to spell out just how we feel that documentation should be produced.

(1) Documentation should be physically associated with the program listing itself. The more closely the details on how the program works are tied in with the program statements, the less likely they are to be mislaid or simply never created.

We saw in Chapter 26 how the REM keyword in BASIC can be used to introduce details on program operation into a program listing. Similar methods can be adopted with other high-level languages. When the program listing is reproduced (on a video screen or on a printer), then the documentation will be reproduced too.

It used to be argued that the high cost of memory media made this method of documenting a program impracticable. However, that is no longer true. Documentation can realistically be included both on ROM chips and on floppy and hard discs.

(2) The program statements themselves should refer to the documentation wherever possible. Just as many word processor programs and other complex applications packages include default options to expand the brief menu prompts they offer, so that both regular and occasional users may make efficient use of them, so other types of program can include references that point the user who needs them to details on what is being done, and what the user needs to do.

(3) Not only should the documentation give reasons as to what data have been used, and why things are done in the way they are done; it should also include notes on any difficulties foreseen under exceptional circumstances, and a general description of how the program behaves.

(4) In these days of rapid hardware evolution and falling prices, it is likely that any well-used program will at some time have to be 'ported', or moved to a new machine or a new systems software environment. We have touched on the reasons why incompatibilities make this a difficult task. Some of these incompatibilities between established systems and their successors reflect genuine technical advance and innovation; some merely serve to protect the supplier's competitive situation in a fiercely competitive marketplace. Whatever the reason, the implications for documentation are the same. If you want to move an old program to an new environment, the first requirement is to know what the old environment was, in detail. The documentation must specify this.

We shall now build on these basic principles, to offer a short checklist of desirable features that should be found in good documentation.

Checklist of Documentation Needed: (You may regard some of the items on this checklist as unnecessary. Do not be tempted to miss them out: for example, you might think that because every program you have written so far has been for your machine only, and you have no intention of changing it, it is not necessary to note down what machine(s) the program will run on. But experience has shown that, in the long run, each item *is* necessary.)

(1) Details of machine and software environment and other general comments:
   (a) Summary of the program application.
   (b) Date when program first ran, as it is listed and specified.
   (c) Hardware equipment configuration on which it runs.
   (d) Systems software environment: operating system (and its version) plus language of program, plus compiler or interpreter details.
   (e) Specifications of any data files required.
   (f) Input and output specifications.
   (g) Data editing and checking procedures, security procedures.
   (h) Control procedures.
   (i) Typical timings for running the program.

(2) Details needed from a programming viewpoint (particularly if you intend to modify the program):
   (a) A description of the processing pattern, preferably with flowcharts.
   (b) Details of subroutines.
   (c) Details of any internal flags, checkpoints for intermediate outputs, trace routines.
   (d) Test data and test output.
   (e) Samples of input and output.
   (f) Sample of the complete input/output as it appears throughout the actual operation.

(g) Source listing, if the program has been run through a compiler, cross-references of variables and data types.

(3) Details needed from an operating viewpoint:

(a) Listing and comments on each error message and corrective action.

(b) Recovery procedures in the case of a software or hardware failure.

(4) Details needed from a development viewpoint:

(a) Relationship of this program to other programs.

(b) Where relevant (usually more often than is first thought), reference to the theory behind the program.

(c) If not developed by the user, who developed it, and contact point.

To some extent, the better systems software and the better processors provide some of the information we have listed automatically as the program runs, but usually only on the monitor display or on the program/output listings.

Documentation in practice: One practice we ourselves have found useful is to force self-discipline by building into the program a documentation check that operates each time the program is run, to see whether the documentation has been included to a pre-defined series of levels. System-generated messages can point out the need for documentation, and it is even possible to ensure that if the programmer repeatedly ignores warnings to document, the system will refuse to run the program!

There are many levels and approaches to documentation. You will have realized by now that it is much easier to find out what is going on (on an abstract, rather than a machine, level) in a high-level language program than in a machine-code program. Even assembly language can be a help. Many mnemonic codes such as LOAD or ADD are highly suggestive. Depending upon the level at which the program is written, different information will need to be added to the listing to make it fully explanatory to an outsider.

Other programming documentation aids exist, too. There are waves of interest in automatic flow-charting and, for those whose ability to visualize is particularly well-developed, such flowcharts are a powerful tool. Others who find tables easier to follow may find automatic indentation, highlighting and similar textual presentation techniques will help them. Other approaches cross-index variables to show where they were first defined, point out inconsistencies in use, and so on. A notable example is the PFORT (Portable Fortran) Analyser, that performs all these functions and effectively guarantees that the program will run if it is accepted totally by the analyser. And of course the diagnostic messages supplied by compilers and run-time routines are also in their way documentation aids.

When you are writing your own programs, you will naturally set your own standards — high ones, we hope — for documentation. Equally, any purchaser of packaged software has the right to expect a professional approach to documentation. It is regrettable that much of the software in current lists and catalogues falls far short of any reasonable standard. When it comes to scientific software, the standards of documentation insisted upon by the A.C.M. (Association of Computing Machinery) in the U.S. and N.A.G. (National Algorithmic Group) in the U.K. are extremely high. Standards for personal computing and microcomputer software are often extremely low, but it is likely that, as the importance of documentation comes to be recognized by users in this area, standards will rise.

As you begin to improve your own documentation practice, you will see that documentation proves very quickly to be time-saving rather than time-consuming. Above all, the need to document will contribute directly to an improvement in your general programming standards. Just as writing things down helps people remember in general, so the need to describe what you are doing sharpens the mind effectively and can help you to produce a neat, effective and elegant program that you can justifiably be proud of.

Writing Longer Programs

Writing very short programs, like those we have included in this book, is not a difficult job. You do not have to be too meticulous about matters such as documentation: it is quite an easy matter to glance over the listing and see what is going wrong. The longer the programs you write, though, the more important it becomes that you should adopt good programming practices.

Documenting a program fully is one such practice, but it is not the only one. Perhaps even more important is the business of structuring a program properly.

As we said earlier, there are many ways of writing a program that works, to fit an applications specification (an algorithm, that is). Some of the ways are comparatively brief and elegant; others are baroque and unwieldy. Unless space or run-time is at a premium, the computer will not mind too much whether you write a neat, logical program or an exotic monster of a program.

You will, though, when you come to amend the program later: so will anyone else who has the misfortune to work with a poorly structured program. From every possible angle, it makes sense to write programs in a tidy and structured way.

Structured programming: The term 'structured programming' has in fact been adopted to apply to a particular type of programming practice. In structured programs, for instance, it is normal to define all variables right at the start, and to write the program in self-contained 'modules' that are linked together in specific, defined ways. The result is certainly a tidy program: but critics of the 'structured programming' concept argue that it is *too* tight, *too* limited, and simply not well fitted to the shape of typical algorithms.

'Structured programming' in particular, then, may not altogether be a good thing. But structuring your program in the general sense certainly *is* a good thing. It does not matter all that much *what* the structure is: the important thing is that you should work out a structure (it might be modular or might be a 'layered' approach, with program sequences contained within program sequences, for instance), and stick to it – and, of course, describe it accurately in your documentation.

What sort of features make a well-structured program? Among the most important are the following:

(1) Writing a good algorithm, which you can implement effectively in the language you use. If you look at your flowchart and find that it is so complicated, with so many twists and turns, that it is impossible to tell how it works – then scrap it and try again. It will be much harder to tell what goes on in the program itself. And almost every problem can be summarized in a logical (if not a simple) algorithm. It just takes a bit more work.

(2) Handling data in a well-thought-out and consistent way: either grouping it all together at one point in the program, for instance, or including subsets of data at several natural and logical points.

(3) Defining and naming variables logically and sensibly.

(4) Handling subroutines in a logical way: perhaps grouping them all at the end of the program, or at any rate making it absolutely clear (to the reader, as well as to the computer) where they start and end.

It is often claimed – with some accuracy – that some programming languages lend themselves better to the creation of well-structured programs than others. So it is harder to write a poorly structured program in Pascal, say, than it is in BASIC, simply because of the types of Pascal commands and the logical constructions that are permitted in Pascal. That does not mean, however, that it is impossible to write a well-structured program in BASIC: simply that you have to choose your BASIC constructions with more care. Many people argue, for instance, that the use of a GOTO statement (which is permitted in most versions of BASIC) can make a program difficult to follow. Poorly written programs, making heavy use of GOTOs, seem to dash off all over the place: it is all but impossible to work out what happens where, and why. Others feel that GOTO constructions are too useful to discard; that if they are used carefully and logically, they need not confuse the program listing unduly. Perhaps the problem is that those least likely to write careful, logical programs are also those *most* likely to select programming languages in which it is easy to write sloppy, confused programs.

Similarly, specialist types of language – list-processing languages, for instance – undoubtedly affect the ways in which a program can be structured. Learning additional languages with specialist data-handling features is one step towards structuring programs as effectively as possible.

Fitting programs (and program modules) together: If you start writing simple programs for your own home computer, you will almost certainly do so in isolation. Most professional programmers, on the other hand, work co-operatively: for instance, a number of programmers might each write modules that are intended to be fitted together to make up one complex application program. This makes sense: when programming a large application, the logical way to do it is to take a broad overview of the structure, and then to take the elements that emerge and break them down into more detailed descriptions (which might in turn be broken down into even smaller parts, or might be directly transcribable into program statements). As a result, professional programming practice stresses the importance of writing program modules in ways that make them easy to fit together.

The same concepts are important to the individual amateur programmer too, though. As you come to write more programs, dealing with different but related aspects of your work and your life in general, so you will undoubtedly see the advantages in linking them together: using common data files for several purposes, as a very basic example. Consistency in your programming practice, yet again, is the key to not only writing a good program, but also programming an easy-to-operate and efficient computer system.

Few people buy computers so that they can run a single program on them. We almost all have a number of applications for which we use our system. Fitting them together in a well-structured way is just as important, on a large scale, as programming each application in a well-structured way is on the smaller scale.

Part Five: Some Applications of Larger-Scale Computer Systems

Our programming examples in Part Four will, we hope, have given you some indication of what small computer systems today can be used for. As well as writing some simple programs, in a number of places in this book we have described briefly a variety of commercially available software (and sometimes hardware) application products: from speech synthesizers to file-handling packages.

We have not yet looked, however, at larger computer systems. Why do some organizations still need to use larger computers? What can they offer that small ones cannot, and how do their applications differ?

Many minicomputers and mainframe computer systems simply do what smaller ones do, but on a more majestic scale. They handle greater volumes of data; they run longer programs and can interleave more programs; they cope with processing requests and collect data from many terminals. We hope our discussions of computer technology earlier in this book will have sufficed to make it clear that all these abilities really do require more processing capability, more complex operating systems, more memory space than a smaller computer can handle: in fact, that large computers – or at least, large computer systems (which might in fact contain not-so-large computers) – really *are* necessary today.

We shall not be looking in depth at any large-scale commercial data processing systems. Those who work with them will know far more about them than we could hope to put across in this book; and to the rest of the world, they are frankly not very interesting. What we *will* be doing, in this final Part, is looking at some more unusual applications of large-scale computer systems. We hope these will both add to our scope in exploring the vast range of modern computer applications and help to point out where large computers win out over the smaller versions.

First, we shall take a look at a bureau offering computer-aided design services: outlining some of the reasons why specialist bureaux offering computer-based services still have a role to play, and looking at the kind of advanced computer-aided design and computer-aided manufacturing applications that a powerful minicomputer can support. Then we shall be looking at a very large, very complex computer system: that at the U.K. Meteorological Office. This illustrates a typical application of the most powerful 'supercomputers', and also indicates how, today, smaller computers are appearing alongside the bigger versions in major computer installations. It will also give us an opportunity to look briefly at a system that deals heavily in data communications.

And finally, we shall look at the most demanding field of all for computer applications: research into 'artificial intelligence'. The last four chapters will introduce the field of artificial intelligence research, and look briefly at three important areas within it, that illustrate how the simple arithmetical and logical abilities of the computer are being turned to an even wider, more demanding — and more surprising — range of applications.

29. Computer-Aided Design

What *is* computer-aided design, and how does it compare with computer graphics of the type we have already talked about in this book? Basically, graphics is a tool: the ability to draw and manipulate graphics using the computer is something we can use for a wide variety of purposes, from art to engineering. Computer-aided design (C.A.D.) is one field of application of that tool: it covers the use of graphics to design things. What things? Just about anything, from a new building, or even a new town, to a precision piece of machinery, or even just a poster layout.

Of course, not all C.A.D. systems will be well adapted to the full potential range of C.A.D. applications. Specialist systems demand specialist software and hardware. We shall be looking at a specific C.A.D. system as an example of the uses of minicomputers (a step up from the microcomputers we have been looking at in detail) today, and as a result we shall be looking at a powerful system with a wide range of capabilities and potential uses.

First, then, we shall talk briefly about what C.A.D. systems actually do. Then we introduce the particular system we shall be describing. We go on to look at how it operates from a business angle; at the computer and peripheral hardware involved; and at the software that gives the system its capabilities. We shall be taking a look at some typical real-life uses of this specific system; and finally, we will see how it might be extended into the related field of C.A.M., computer-aided manufacturing.

Digitizing Drawings

A freehand drawing on a sheet of paper (or some other suitable medium) is basically an analog creation. There is no need to know, before drawing a straight line, exactly how long it is in digital terms; before drawing a curve, you don't need to calculate all the arcs and angles involved. And the same is true of many three-dimensional man-made objects. Their lines may be neither straight, nor easily describable in geometric terms. Basic digital data on their dimensions may not be known to their creators.

Of course, for many drafting purposes it *is* essential that some dimensions should approximate as closely as possible to predefined measurements. But not all: for instance, if you draw two lines whose dimensions and position on the paper you know precisely, you may then choose to add another line to join the ends of them, without knowing its length or angle in digital terms.

Computer-aided design systems of the general type we shall be describing are digital in their operation: it is essential to remember this. They hold digital data on a drawing or on an object that could be described at least partly by a drawing. They hold no analog data: everything they know about the drawing must be expressed in digital form. The drawing that appears on the screen may be created by the computer system, as a visual representation of the data it has on file. It may be created by the user: for example, using a light pen or moving a cursor to 'draw' by inducing a freehand line to appear. But even if it is not defined digitally by the user in inputting it, it *must* be defined digitally by the system before it can be stored or manipulated in any way. The system can *only* work in the digital mode.

The process of converting visual data that is to be stored by the computer into digital form is known as *digitizing* the data. All designs must be digitized if they are to be handled on a C.A.D. system. The user may himself or herself do some of this digitizing: for instance, telling the computer to store, and produce an image on screen of, a vertical line exactly 3.25 cm long. But the user need not do it all. If the user adds an element to the drawing that he describes without using digits, then the system will itself undertake the task of describing that element digitally, and storing and manipulating it accordingly.

Bear in mind that when we come to talk of the system manipulating a drawing, this is in fact a simplification. What the system manipulates is the file of digital data that it compiles on the drawing. And once it has manipulated this data appropriately, it can then generate another visual image on its display, that is a representation of a differently expressed set, or subset, of data.

The importance of the screen image — like the importance of the paper design it temporarily (or even permanently) replaces — is that it presents the data in a medium that is easily assimilated by human beings. The computer produces the visual display for the user's convenience: if the user could do without it, and simply input all the necessary data digitally, then the system itself could happily manipulate the digital data without ever coming up with a displayed image.

And in turn, it is entirely optional whether the C.A.D. system actually produces a finished drawing. The finished drawing does not add any *data* to those already in the system: it simply represents the data in the system to the human users of that system. If the data can be used directly, for instance by a machine tool which is to produce the part it describes — then there may be no need at all to produce a drawing.

Edenwade Ltd

Edenwade Limited are a small company who have recently (in 1982) set up what they describe as a 'Computer-Aided Design Centre' in Norwich,

England. Roger Mortimore and his colleagues aim to provide a bureau-type service in the broad field of C.A.D./C.A.M., primarily to local firms.

Computer bureaux sound outdated today: what can Mortimore and his colleagues offer that a company could not provide in-house, perhaps on dedicated microcomputers? True, there *are* microcomputer systems that can run C.A.D./C.A.M. software and perform some of the tasks that Edenwade's own system performs. But the company sees the major advantages of using a bureau service as being the following:

(1) Their system is more powerful and, hence, more flexible, than typical microcomputer software. The range of options they can offer simply could not fit on to a micro. And a firm that locates a microcomputer-based system that could perform the task they currently have in mind may find later that it is impossible to adapt the system or its software to perform some other related task.

(2) The bureau can provide a variety of 'user options'. They can take customers' design projects and carry out the design stage themselves, using their facilities and providing a finished design drawing as their output. Alternatively, they will train customers' own personnel to operate their terminals (in Edenwade's own offices, rather than by datalink, though the latter option may soon become available). Customers 'buy in' only as much expertise as they need and only as much computer time as they need.

(3) The bureau, not the customer, has to worry about the reliability of the hardware and software, and about the support aspects like the provision of adequate supplies of plotting pens and paper, and the all important organization of data and maintenance of files on designs created by the system.

Clearly, a bureau can provide a service to smaller firms that it would simply not be practicable for them to reproduce in-house. But Edenwade do find that a sizeable proportion of their work comes from larger firms that appreciate the wider advantages of using the bureau and its experts.

The Hardware

The system Edenwade use is a 'turnkey' system: their hardware and software are sold to them as a package on a 'turn it on and it will work' basis. Mortimore and his colleagues are not computer specialists: they are production engineers who happen to work with computers, and it is their system capability as a whole, rather than their computer time, that they in turn sell. Their knowledge of, and interest in, the nuts and bolts of the system hardware is strictly limited. If anything goes wrong, they call in the engineers to fix it!

The software system, McAuto's 'Unigraphics', can actually be supplied on a wide range of different computers of different sizes and capabilities.

Edenwade use a Data General Eclipse S/250, a standard minicomputer that other firms use for a wide variety of other applications completely unrelated to C.A.D./C.A.M.

The S/250 is a 16-bit minicomputer, with a 'flat' architecture: comparatively simple, that is, and not built up in a complex series of levels. It is designed for applications requiring a great deal of number-crunching, a requirement that is certainly true of C.A.D., and particularly of aspects such as stress analysis.

The use of graphics on an interactive basis means that the system needs to provide fast response to requests for screen changes. This demands the ability to provide rapid input/output access to a large disc store, and once again the S/250 can provide this. It is also very strong on communications: not only with the C.A.D. terminals, but with other computers with which information on the designs, or the data used in them, might need to be exchanged.

Finally, the system conforms to established industry interfacing standards. In consequence, a wide range of plotters and digitizers are available for use with it.

Edenwade divide their equipment into two rooms: end-user equipment, the terminals and related equipment; and system equipment. In the 'system' room, together with the computer itself, are:

a teleprinter, that provides the main form of communication with the computer itself. It is used for setting the system up each day, turning it off at the end of the day, for the transmission of system error messages, and so on. The volume of interaction with the system via this lineprinter is very low: on average, only around five lines of type (including input *and* output) are generated each day, unless any specific listings are required;

a standard Data General 'Zebra' hard disc unit, with a single hard disc pack with a data capacity of 96 megabytes. This contains all system software, as well as data generated during system operation. A backup disc duplicates the system programs, so that they can be reloaded rapidly in the event of system failure;

a magnetic tape drive, to hold a 1,200' (400 m) reel of tape. Medium format ½" (1 cm) magnetic tapes with a storage density of 6,250 bits per inch are used for holding and storing files of designs and other miscellaneous data. Daily tapes of system activity and customer tapes with customers' own design files are maintained and backed up on a regular basis, so that a minimal amount of work will be lost, should the system fail. The slow access time of this serial medium is no problem; the data on the tapes are loaded on to the disc for actual manipulation, and reloaded only for storage purposes;

a Calcomp 960 pen plotter, for outputting finished designs. This can take up to A0-size paper, and can plot in two colours, using coloured ball pens (which are typically used for checking plans before final versions are produced) or in two line thicknesses, using drawing inks in pens of two different nib thicknesses.

Figure 80: Edenwade Ltd's computer and related equipment

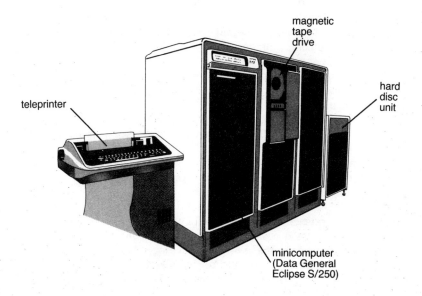

magnetic
tape
drive

hard
disc
unit

teleprinter

minicomputer
(Data General
Eclipse S/250)

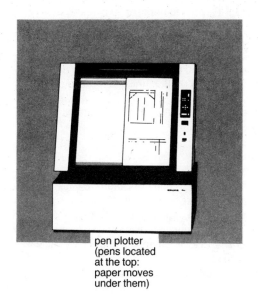

pen plotter
(pens located
at the top:
paper moves
under them)

Figure 80 gives an idea of what this equipment looks like.

What is in the 'end-user room'? Three terminals, that can be used quite independently, all run from the main computer. Each terminal work-station has:

a Textronix graphics terminal: again, a standard off-the-shelf terminal that fits the requirements of this system. It has a 14" (35 cm) green phosphor visual display screen, and a standard terminal keyboard: alpha/numeric, with some additional control keys. Next to the keyboard are two knurled wheels, for controlling the screen cursor: joysticks or graphic tablets (on which the user can directly induce drawings) can be provided as system alternatives, but Edenwade find that most users prefer the wheels. These control (one horizontally, and one vertically) a crossed-line cursor on the screen;

a small 'message monitor': a white-on-black video screen just 4" (10 cm) across, that sits on top of the terminal. All system messages and menus for choosing design options appear on this monitor, which means that the whole of the main screen is available for drawing purposes;

an additional keyboard, a large unit 12" × 12" (30 cm × 30 cm), with thirty-two control keys that light up when the functions they offer are available for choice by the user. These have legends written on them, and some of them are also numbered so that they can be used to designate menu choices not related to the written legends. Almost all system commands are entered via this secondary keyboard. The terminal's alpha/numeric keyboard is used for entering characters that are to appear on the display (plan headings or explanations, for instance) or data required for use in system analysis or calculations.

In addition, the terminal area boasts a 'hard copy' unit that can be used to draw off rapid copies (comparable to reasonable photocopier standard) of the information displayed on a screen at any time. This is used as a quick-reference aid, to augment the finished drawings produced on the pen plotter.

Figure 81 gives an idea of what the workstations look like.

The Software

What does the software actually do, then? Basically, it allows the user to specify the details of his design: indicating where features are to go (in a variety of ways) and then requesting straight lines, arcs, circles and so on to be drawn precisely in a specified place and to a specified size (which might be described, again, in a variety of ways: points a circle is to go through, its radius, points an arc is to join, the angle it is to describe, etc. As each new line or feature is added, it appears on the screen; if it is unwanted at a later stage (it might be a reference line only needed so that another line can be drawn accurately, for instance) it can be deleted from the drawing file and/or from the screen.

Figure 81: Edenwade Ltd's computer-aided design workstations

There is no need for the user to wield the cursor with uncanny accuracy: the system will 'find' lines or points the cursor is placed close to, and ensure that the drawing elements are perfectly aligned. If elements are added to the drawing sketchily (perhaps using a graphics tablet), then beginning with the fixed points already on screen, the system can digitize and then 'regularize' the connecting lines on screen.

The system will automatically calculate dimensions, and label designs with them, in ways that can be specified in great detail. It will calculate areas of specified shapes. It will infill shapes, drawing parallel lines (for example) at any specified distance from each other. It will enlarge part of the diagram, so that details can be added, or store the entire diagram on a different scale. It will even calculate what paper size is needed to reproduce the diagram, and add borders and legends, ready stored or entered in response to prompts. It has a wide variety (fourteen on this system) of stored fonts for adding alpha/numeric data, and can be 'taught' others if they are required.

Once part of a diagram (say, a single component that must be placed in a variety of different positions) is entered and specified, the system can 'copy' it as required. It can, for instance, calculate how to space spokes on a wheel so that exactly sixty-four of them are spread evenly around the circumference; if the number of spokes changes, it will recalculate the distances required, and 'repaint' the design accordingly. Elements that are frequently required in a design (special architectural or electrical symbols, for instance) can be designated as 'patterns', stored in a special pattern file, and recalled at will. Elements can be 'borrowed' from an existing design on file, to be incorporated into a new design.

The system will also work in three dimensions. Given sufficient data, and one perspective on a design, it will automatically calculate the data needed to display seven other perspectives; split the screen up into four, and display them four at a time (or a single view can be selected for whole-screen work). The user can add details to one perspective drawing, and they will automatically be added to the other views. The system will also calculate volumes and other data in the three dimensions.

Three-dimensional capability is undoubtedly a bonus; but it is not always needed, and some users find that they like the idea more than the reality of working in 3-D. To the inexperienced user, working in three dimensions can be thoroughly confusing: it is difficult to be sure that a new feature is being added to the right surface, and the resulting diagrams show little that an engineer could not deduce from a single set of drawings.

A particularly powerful feature of the Unigraphics system is the ability to 'layer' drawing files. Different elements of a drawing can be combined in different ways on different 'levels', which can then be overlaid rather like transparent overlays on a basic outline plan. Dimensions might be held on one layer, for instance, descriptions on another, special design details on another. The user then designates one layer as his 'work' layer, to which he adds new features; he need not see details of the drawing that he does not require and that would clutter the picture unnecessarily. Layers can also be combined in different ways in outputting the design, so that different features are included in different copies required for different purposes.

To the user, the Unigraphics capabilities are presented through menu trees: choice of an item from one menu displayed will often lead to the display of a further menu. No programming ability is required in order to use the system: it is very user-friendly, an aspect that makes it ideal for the bureau environment where many users work with it on an occasional basis. A special programming language *is* available, though: GRIP ('Graphics Interactive Programming Language'). This can be used to draw up, for instance, outline design procedures for the repetitive design of specific engineering parts with different dimensions. Programs written in GRIP can then be used with the basic Unigraphics menu-based system.

Clearly arithmetical operations are not the prime function of a system such as this, but it also contains calculator-type arithmetic functions: data can be stored in the course of specifying a design and later used in calculations that prove to be necessary.

Perhaps the simplest way to illustrate exactly how the system works is to use as examples some drawings produced on it. Every element in Figures 82 to 85, including the lettering, was produced on the Edenwade Unigraphics system and drawn out on their pen plotter specially for use in this book.

Figure 82 is a sample that illustrates some of the basic capabilities of the system: how lines can be constructed, how arcs are defined, and how curved shapes can be built up into complex sculptured surfaces.

Figure 82 :

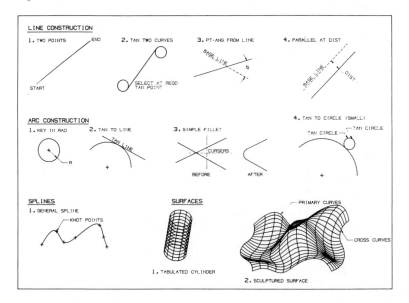

Figure 83 is an engineering drawing for the construction of a gear wheel. Note the multiple engineering aspects, each with its quantified data, which have to be taken into account to construct even such a simple object. The C.A.D. system will itself perform many of the necessary calculations.

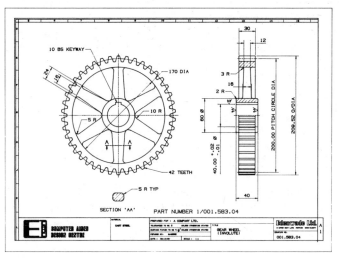

Figure 83 :

Figure 84 shows a simple architectural layout. Repetitive elements such as the lavatories and washbasins can be stored on file, ready for instant reproduction whenever and wherever they are needed.

Figure 84:

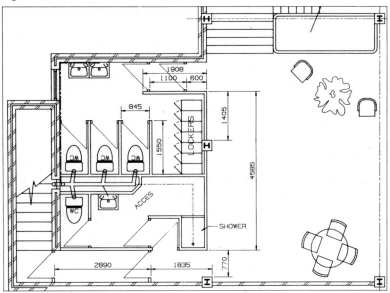

Figure 85 :

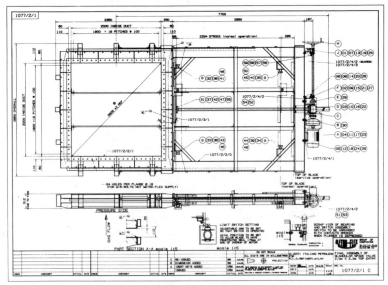

Finally, Figure 85 gives some indication of the complexity the system can handle. The system can automatically perform many of the functions involved in producing cross-sections and detail drawings of this valve assembly. The dimensioning is precisely accurate, and the labelling neatly aligned.

The Advantages of C.A.D.

But how does the time taken to produce a design on a system such as this actually compare with the time taken to produce the same design by hand?

It is impossible to give a general answer to this. For some purposes, it may take *longer* to design an item on the screen than it would to design it on paper. For others — and if you have done any drafting, you will recognize some such among our samples — it would take forever to produce a good drawing by hand, and hardly any time to produce it using the computer. But Edenwade — like suppliers of C.A.D. services — argue persuasively that comparing the time taken to produce a drawing is only a very crude measure of the worth of C.A.D. Among the other advantages they point out are the following:

(1) Revisions, adaptations or variations on a theme take much less time. It may take longer to produce an initial drawing, but the time saved on subsequent drawings will more than compensate for this.

(2) The system forces the user to specify all his data, and to *choose* as he does so. Delays further down the line are reduced.

(3) It is much easier to check how individual parts are assembled into a whole, and to discover — before they go into manufacture — any anomalies.

(4) The ease of checking out alternatives — and scrapping them if they do not work — means that more creative alternatives can be tried without fear of wasting undue time exploring blind alleys.

(5) Last but not least, the quality of the finished product is better than that of even a very good human draftsman. There is no illegible scrawl, no need for subsequent people working from the drawing to guess what it says, or to approximate measurements. And new *originals*, not poor-quality copies, can be produced as they are required.

Above all, it is important to remember that the system does not *do the design* for the engineer, architect or other user. It merely aids him in doing the design. He or she still has to do the work; but it can be done much better.

What is the System used for?

We would love to have taken some time on Edenwade's system to plan out all the drawings for this book ourselves. Alas, it was too expensive for us; anyway, book illustration hardly seems likely to be a major area of C.A.D. use in the near future. But who are Edenwade's typical customers and the customers of bureaux similar to theirs? What sort of companies buy this type of system for in-house use? Among the uses that Edenwade's system has found in recent months are:

a wide range of engineering applications, ranging from the mundane to the complex. They include designs for gear train complexes, rotors for pumps, and work connected with North Sea pipeline engineering. This last is particularly interesting, because the inaccessibility of the sites and the exacting specifications make engineering the parts a demanding job;

the design of car bodies, prior to testing in wind tunnels. If tests prove unsatisfactory, the designs can easily be modified, a process that is facilitated further by the use of single-mould glassfibre body manufacturing;

architectural work, primarily to date on a large scale: multiple-resident homes, estate developments and so on.

work for the shoe industry (strong in Norwich). This includes the actual design of new shoes, which has to be fixed before a heavy commitment is made to tooling; the economical laying-out of pieces on sheets of leather or of man-made material; and sizing up or down, which is not proportional for all components as the overall size of the shoe is changed.

Computer-Aided Manufacturing

Of course, a drawing is not a manufactured object; a plan is not the same as a house. It is easy to see how C.A.D. can *aid* the manufacturing process, but how does it actually make the transition into the related field of computer-aided manufacturing, C.A.M.?

Basically, computer-aided manufacturing means the use of computer power in drawing up specifications for the manufacturing process: calculating how tools need to be set, and what they must do. C.A.M. comes into play primarily in areas where tools themselves are computer-controlled, or at least numerically controlled; C.A.M. then becomes the process of drawing up programs for the control of these tools.

The Unigraphics system can itself be extended in this way, though this is not a field that Edenwade have yet been called upon to explore. The data generated through the design process can be used as input to a C.A.M. program, together with data on manufacturing variables such as tool dimensions, speeds, and tolerances required. The system can then draw up a program for the control of (for example) a lathe or a milling machine, and even simulate the machining of the object, displaying all the tool motions that would be generated, so that the process can be followed and checked out before it gets anywhere near the shop floor.

The advantages of C.A.M. are obvious. As well as cutting out a lengthy planning stage, it can point up any difficulties before production is started, and can ensure that no errors creep into the transition from drawing to object represented by the drawing. As computer-controlled tools become more common, so the pressure is likely to feed back *from* C.A.M., to generate even greater use of C.A.D.

30. Computers in the U.K. Meteorological Office

The United Kingdom Meteorological Office (Met. Office) was one of the first computer users in the U.K., and it is still an intensive user of computers and associated equipment. It makes use of a wide range of computers, including a 'supercomputer': a new, massive machine with enormous number-crunching abilities. In consequence, its computer system is a good example of the way in which very demanding and not-so-demanding applications mesh together, of the varying resources they require, and of how they have been developed over time as the capabilities of available computers have grown.

We shall look very briefly at the structure of the Met. Office's major computer resources; then at the pattern of its major activities; then, in more depth, at some of the computer applications themselves.

A Major Computer System Develops

Met. Office staff began to look at how computers might be applied to their work, and to experiment with some applications, back at the dawn of commercial computing: in 1951, to be exact. However, it was not until 1959 that the Office acquired its own computer: an early British model, the Ferranti Mercury. This was used until 1965 when it was replaced with an English Electric KDF9: a more powerful machine that also had the great advantages of being multiprogrammable and of using a high-level language, ALGOL.

The next machine to be acquired was an I.B.M., a Model 360/195. As we said on page 106 the I.B.M. 360s were general-purpose computers, in contrast to the 'scientific' computers the Office had earlier used. In consequence, this machine came to be used for a wide variety of general data processing work, as well as for the heavy number-crunching of the earlier machines. Three years later, a smaller I.B.M. machine, the 370/158, was added to the system as a 'front-end' processor: taking some smaller, less appropriate jobs from the main computer, and acting as a partial back-up to it.

The next major step forward came in 1981, when the Met. Office acquired the very first Cyber 205 to be delivered. This Control Data machine is the 'supercomputer' mentioned above; as such, it is a move away from general-purpose machines back to a 'scientific' computer. The Cyber is used primarily for the mathematical modelling work of the Office; the I.B.M.

machines and their eventual replacements will continue to handle the growing volume of general data processing.

Before we look at the system that has grown up around this hub of mainframe computers, let us compare their respective abilities. It is not easy to find a single measure that can indicate the relative power of very different machines: machines that perform very well according to one yardstick may perform much less impressively in another context. However, a rough guide is the number of floating-point multiplications the machine can perform in one second. On this basis, the power of the Met. Office's main computer resources shot up as follows:

Ferranti Mercury: 3,000
English Electric KDF9:   50,000
I.B.M. 360/195:   up to 5,000,000
Cyber 205:   up to 400,000,000

In practice on full-scale programs, the Cyber 205 has proved to perform at least thirty times better than the I.B.M. machines, for applications to which its abilities are well suited.

A Global Computer Network

The three mainframes that are currently in use — the two I.B.M. machines and the Cyber — are linked together, using a complicated mesh of operating systems, to form the hub of the Met. Office system. However, they by no means comprise the entire system. As well as them, the Office has the following major computer resources:

(1) a network of terminals (and, increasingly, mini- or microcomputers also acting as terminals) that link other U.K. Met. Offices to the headquarters installation at Bracknell, Berkshire;

(2) a wide variety of minicomputers and microcomputers that are used for separate specialist jobs, and are not permanently linked to the mainframe;

(3) and its own telecommunications-handling computers, which provide its link with a global telecommunications system collecting and disseminating meteorological information.

Let us look very briefly at the telecommunications computer system. This was initially based around a dual-processor: two Marconi Myriad II machines that went into action in 1972. Initially, their operation was quite independent from the data processing system; in 1975–6, however, the two systems were linked together, using an I.B.M. System 7 machine to handle the communications between them. In 1981, a pair of Ferranti Argus computers boosted the resources of the telecommunications system; and towards the end of 1981 the System 7 was itself superseded by a more standardized and flexible link.

Links from this telecommunications handling resource radiate out throughout the world: to other U.K. locations, to major European weather centres, and to one of the centres of the World Meteorological Organization in Washington, D.C. We shall look at one or two small aspects of the worldwide system operation, as it affects the U.K. Met. Office, later in this chapter.

Figure 86 summarizes the structure of this remarkable computer system.

Figure 86: Structure of the U.K. Meteorological Office's computer system

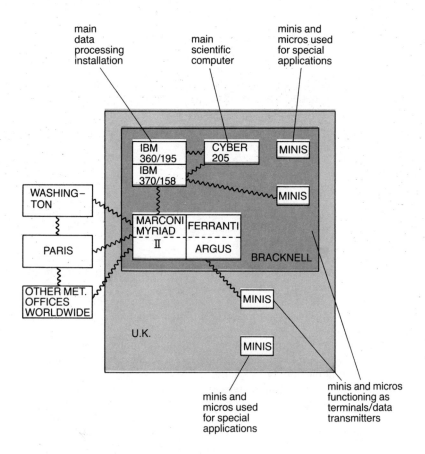

~~~   data transmission link

What Does the Met. Office Do?

We cannot do full justice to the range of Met. Office operations in a few lines. However, we shall outline the very major aspects of them.

To the general public, the Met. Office is known primarily as a provider of weather forecasts over the mass media (on television, on the radio, in daily papers). This is one of its major functions, of course, and it supplements the general-purpose forecasts by providing specialized weather-forecasting services to organizations and businesses that have need of them: to ships and aircraft, to farmers, to builders and other people working out of doors, for instance.

In order to make reasonably accurate forecasts, the Office has first to observe the weather; one of its prime functions is the recording of data on the state of the earth's atmosphere.

It is important to draw a distinction between atmospheric conditions – precisely measurable factors like temperature, humidity and pressure, not only on the ground but in the upper atmosphere as well – and the weather they cause at ground level, which cannot always be measured – or even described – with the same degree of precision. The Met. Office *does* provide actual data on atmospheric conditions as part of its service: on the amount of rainfall, for instance, or the daily hours of sunshine at holiday resorts. By and large, however, the atmospheric measurements are merely the raw materials from which the forecasters deduce elements of the weather as we know it: the winds, the rainfall, and so on. We shall see this distinction at work when we come to consider what part computers can play in weather forecasting.

The U.K. Met. Office plays a part in the worldwide exchange of weather information and monitoring of the climate: in obtaining data themselves, in receiving data from other met. offices, and in interpreting all these data on a world scale. And finally, it keeps an extensive databank, both of records of the climate in the past and of other information relevant to its functions. The specialized information in the databank is not only used by Met. Office personnel: it is also available for use by the general public.

With this very brief outline behind us, let us now go on to look at some aspects of the use of large and small computers in the Met. Office. First, we shall look at some of the varied application projects to which dedicated minicomputers are being applied. Then we shall look at computers at work in the main business of observing and predicting the weather: at how computers are used, first in connection with collecting observations, and second, in the preparation of mathematical models of atmospheric conditions. Finally, we shall comment very briefly about the ways in which meteorological information is transmitted worldwide.

Computers in Use

Small-scale automation: As with any large organization, the Met. Office has long been aware of a number of functional areas to which computers might theoretically have been applied with advantage, but which proved difficult to automate using the mainframe computer system. Some of them were geographically remote from the computer; some demanded real-time response in a way that simply did not fit in with the way the computer system was run. The advent of comparatively cheap mini- and microcomputers has made it possible to automate these areas. We list some of them below, to give an indication of the kind of varied applications computers have found in the Met. Office (many of these applications have obvious parallels in conventional business environments):

(1) the automation of central telecommunications at the Bracknell headquarters;
(2) the automation of satellite image preparation (that is, of preparing pictures from the data provided by satellites, by re-projecting them, adding coastlines, and merging pictures sent from different satellites);
(3) the automation of aspects of data preparation at regional centres, and the collection of data from them for transmission to Bracknell;
(4) a system to handle acquisitions in the Met. Office library, and to handle catalogue inquiries;
(5) word processing systems.

Observing atmospheric conditions: The Met. Office's weather forecasting system works with observations that are fitted on to a grid system: a three-dimensional array of points, on and above the earth's surface, from which can be built up an accurate picture of the pattern of atmospheric conditions over a specific area. The 'mesh' of the grid (the distance between points) varies, according to the scale of the forecast and the availability of observation resources: typically, the surface mesh has points at intervals of 100, 200 or 300 kilometres. Some weather 'models' (and this is essentially the framework for a weather model) work with fifteen upper layers, a number that allows for the increasing interest in upper layers of the earth's atmosphere (both by those who use it directly, for flight or for satellites, and because of the effect it has on activity in the lower layers). Other models use less, or even more.

It is relatively easy to adjust observations made at land-based observing stations (that are *not* located on the grid points of the weather models) so that acceptable figures can be obtained for all the points of the grid on land. It is much less easy, though, at sea or in the air, where there are no fixed observing stations and, as a result, less frequent observations can be made. The estimates that can be made from the available data are inevitably less accurate.

How are readings obtained? From the following main resources:

(1) from weather stations and observation points (airports, coastguard stations, lighthouses and so on) on land;
(2) from merchant ships at sea;
(3) readings of wind velocity and direction are made from aircraft and sent by radio to the land-based stations;
(4) from instruments carried by weather balloons;
(5) by deduction, from satellite information.

The use of satellites has not by any means ended the need to resort to weather balloons. Satellites certainly produce interesting pictures of the earth and its atmosphere, using either normal visible light, or in infra-red. But it is not easy to deduce from those pictures exactly what are the temperature, humidity and pressure (the readings that are of interest to the weatherman) at a fixed point some distance away from the satellite. The pictorial data are supplemented by rough temperature profiles through the atmosphere, obtained by observations made at several narrow bands of radiation. It is also possible to calculate, from the movement of clouds from one satellite picture to the next in time, what wind speeds and directions must be; but the technical and mathematical problems involved are formidable. (Obviously, computers play an essential part in this work.) For the foreseeable future, instruments borne aloft by balloon will play a part, too; and the use of computers in connection with them is particularly interesting to us.

Computers and the radiosonde: There are eight 'upper air stations' in the U.K.: weather stations from which balloons filled with hydrogen or helium are released, usually twice a day. Each balloon has attached to it a package of instruments known as a radiosonde: today's radiosondes typically contain a thermometer, a hygrometer (an instrument for measuring humidity), and a barometer. Together with these are electronic circuits that can translate the measurements made by the instruments into digital electronic form, and signalling devices to transmit the data back to earth – normally by radio.

As the balloon with its load ascends, its progress is carefully followed, either by radar (the balloon will have a radar reflector attached to it), or by tracking the radio waves it emits. The flight path of the balloon depends upon wind conditions, and this in itself provides valuable data. Finally, of course, the balloon bursts, and a parachute carries the instruments back to earth – where some are broken, others lost in remote locations or at sea, and still others are sent back to the met. offices (in return for a small finder's fee), where they can be re-used.

The monitoring of radiosonde data is a good example of the use of small computers in the Met. Office. Each tracking station has a minicomputer system, which handles the triple tasks of: receiving data from the radiosonde; processing that data, to produce temperature, pressure and humidity readings for the reference points on the forecasting grid; and transmitting the processed data to the main Met. Office, where it can be collated with data from other stations and used in the preparation of forecasts.

Processing the data is not a simple task. Each radiosonde has individually calibrated instruments, and the computer has to be fed with the data on the radiosonde's calibration before it can get to work on processing the output from the instruments. As the data are needed immediately, the processing task must be carried out in real time, as the data are received. And the actual conversion of the radiosonde data to the required likely gridpoint readings is mathematically complex. To handle the task as a whole requires a program which takes up 40K of internal memory capacity. This is not a convenient amount for mini- and microcomputers, that tend to come with 32K or 64K memory; fortunately, by doing some of the work when the balloon is launched, some while it is ascending, and some after it has burst, the memory requirement can be cut down to 32K.

Models of atmospheric conditions: In the early days of weather forecasting, it was regarded as more of an art than a science. Forecasters observed the weather regularly and learned to predict from early-warning signs and from general experience what it was likely to do in the immediate future.

The man who first showed how scientific principles could be applied to this hit-or-miss business was L. F. Richardson, a British mathematician who worked for the Met. Office for some years just after the First World War. Using the idea of the grid of points discussed above, he showed how the relationships between the temperature, pressure and humidity readings at different points at a fixed time, and the relationships between the readings at successive times, could be formulated in terms of the equations of classical physics: of motion, of thermodynamics and of conservation of matter. The relationships could then be manipulated mathematically and the readings projected forward, stepping them onwards by one small time-interval (half an hour, for instance) at once.

The calculations that Richardson's method demanded were laborious in the extreme. He worked for months on one single forecast, for the changes over six hours to be expected at a sole point on the earth's surface: and the results he came up with were depressingly unrealistic. However, the seed was sown; and when electronic computers were developed, John von Neumann (whose work we discussed on page 83) was among those who saw that they could be employed for this type of application.

Over the next decades, the problems of applying Richardson's highly theoretical methods to the practical business of predicting real-life weather were tackled by a number of meteorologists; and techniques were developed, for instance, to separate out purely local effects that distorted individual readings from large-scale effects that could reliably be used to predict the weather pattern over sizeable areas. By the 1960s, it had become clear that if suitable care were taken to monitor and correct the initial readings, a model very similar to Richardson's could indeed be used to provide useful projections of atmospheric conditions.

From the projection of atmospheric conditions, there is still a sizeable step to be taken to the projection of actual weather on the ground. This last step still depends mainly on human experience and judgement. The results of the modelling exercise are *not* used 'cold' in the weather forecasts that appear on television and elsewhere. Instead, they are passed on to professional forecasters who combine them with information from other sources (cloud pictures taken from satellites, for instance), and use their judgement to predict what the weather is likely to be. In predicting rainfall, the computer projections have proved to be more directly useful, but they are not of a high enough quality to use without review, and so they too are passed through a human forecaster.

Creating weather forecasts: And from this point, we can see how the Cyber 205 fits (as did its predecessors) into the sequence of operations that go to make up the production of a weather forecast.

First, observations on atmospheric conditions are obtained from the various sources mentioned above. Some local processing is done to convert the different observation formats from disparate types of observing equipment into a reasonably uniform format: this is essentially the function of the local computers handling the radiosondes, for instance. Then all the observations are transmitted to the mainframe computers.

Speed is of the essence in producing weather forecasts: it is of no practical use if working out the forecast takes so long that it is superseded by real events before it even appears. In the U.K., two different modelling runs are carried out to meet this requirement. A first run uses data from Europe and the Atlantic, together with any observations from further abroad to arrive by its cut-off time. It works with a relatively small grid mesh of 75 km, to produce a short-range local forecast for the British Isles and the surrounding area within three and a half hours of the time of the observations. A second run covers a larger area, and uses a larger mesh of 150 km points. It aims to produce forecasts that will be of an acceptable level of accuracy for several days ahead, for most of the northern hemisphere, within four and a half hours of the observation time. This large-scale model is also used directly to provide weather forecasts for the main aviation routes.

Work is going on continually to improve the accuracy and extend the range of the forecasts. The following enhancements were under discussion or had recently been made at the time of writing:
reducing the mesh size down to 50 km for the smaller-scale model;
developing a still more local model, covering just the British Isles, with a
  mesh size of 10 km, for forecasts for up to twenty-four hours ahead;
extending the useful range of the twice-daily forecasts from six days to ten
  or more.

Obviously, each improvement in the resolution of the model increases the demands upon the computer system that carries out the calculations. To reduce the mesh size by half increases the complexity of calculations required by a factor of eight! It is for this reason that the improvement in forecasts is so dependent upon the immense speed and capability of the Cyber machine. Models of the complexity of those used today simply could not be produced without the aid of a really large computer.

Disseminating data: Of course, the observations are not only used in the mathematical models. They are sent to the Met. Office's databank, which holds on-line (ready for immediate access by local or remote users of its facilities) data on the previous sixty hours' observations and, in archive form, the data on earlier observations. And they are transmitted, in various forms, worldwide.

The image of the 'weather map' – a map of our area, outlining the major geographical features and overlaying them with isobars and other details to help explain the recent and likely future weather pattern – is a familiar one to all of us. To the uninformed, it may be less easy to comprehend than the verbal forecast. But to the expert meteorologist, graphical data – in the form of maps, tables and satellite pictures – is of immense value. It simply cannot be replaced by a narrative description or by tables of figures.

As a result, the production and transmission of visual data are extremely important in the Met. Office system. The use of computer-controlled plotters, for producing charts and graphs directly from data held in (or produced by) the computer, has followed closely upon the technical state of the art. Automatic plotting began to replace manual plotting from the very early 1970s onwards. Today, graphical output is produced not only by the main computers in the system, but also with the aid of minicomputers in local forecasting offices. Figure 87 gives an indication of the type of graphical output that is produced directly by the computers in the Met. Office today.

The software required to handle graphics production is relatively complex, and this is one of the few types of computer program to be produced by specialist data processing staff, rather than by the meteorologists themselves. Maintaining the programs that control the databank is another such application, while most other programs are written (typically in FORTRAN or assembly language) by professional staff who are not full-time programmers.

Of course, the dissemination of visual data is also an extremely important aspect of the communications systems. Considerable use is made of facsimile transmitters to provide comparatively local communication links, while both analog data and digitized graphical information are transmitted using the 'trunk' lines of the main telecommunications network.

The importance of graphical data is illustrated in the current plans to enhance the quality of communication lines between the major centres to

Figure 87: A weather map produced on the U.K. Meteorological Office's computer system

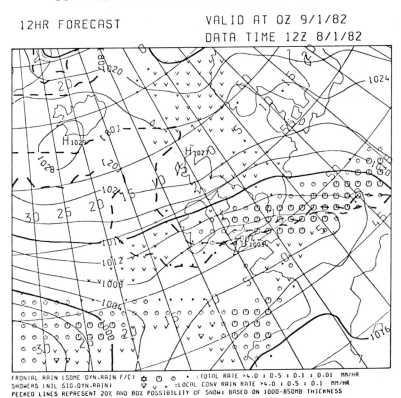

SURFACE PRESSURE AND PRECIPITATION

12HR FORECAST   VALID AT 0Z 9/1/82
                                 DATA TIME 12Z 8/1/82

FRONTAL RAIN (SOME DYN.RAIN F/C) ☼ ◐ ○ • =TOTAL RATE >4.0 : 0.5 : 0.1 : 0.01 MM/HR
SHOWERS (NIL SIG.DYN.RAIN)   ▽ ⌄ ⌄ =LOCAL CONV RAIN RATE >4.0 : 0.5 : 0.1 MM/HR
PECKED LINES REPRESENT 20% AND 80% POSSIBILITY OF SNOW: BASED ON 1000-850MB THICKNESS

Key/Explanation

⌒*1008*⌒   Isobars indicated at intervals of 4mb. Note the 'Low' across South-West England.

◐   Superimposed symbols indicating frontal rain. Note the belt running from Southern Ireland through Wales and Southern England into Germany.

v   Superimposed symbols indicating showers.

‒ ‒ ‒   Snow probability, indicating that most of the belt of frontal rain across the centre of the chart will in fact fall as snow.

This was a very good forecast!

which Bracknell is linked: Paris, the nearest European regional hub for meteorological communications, Washington, another major centre of the meteorological Global Telecommunication System, and a handful of other British and European meteorological offices. Most of the major lines today (1982) transmit at frequences of 2,400 bits per second: moderate, rather than exceptionally fast. The fastest lines have a transmission speed of 4,800 b.p.s. The latest plans to enhance these transmission lines further call for the introduction of a 9,600 b.p.s. link. This would then be divided by time division multiplexing into three separate channels. The main channel, operating at 4,800 b.p.s., would be used for the transmission of digital facsimile charts. Data transmissions would be carried on two lower speed lines, operating at 2,400 b.p.s.

Another interesting use of computer-generated graphics to illustrate weather patterns is the weather forecast on Prestel, the British Telecom databank service. Prestel is a particularly handy medium for issuing weather forecasts to the general public, since they can be updated frequently as more recent information adds to the overall picture. The Met. Office's offerings on the system include a weather map, land forecasts, forecasts for special events, and shipping forecasts.

The experimental service, started in Canada in 1980, of distributing a special service to farmers via the Telidon service (another viewdata service, a little more advanced than Prestel in its graphics capability) has proved both popular and effective, and further developments along these lines may well appear in the U.K.

31. The Coming of Artificial Intelligence

'Artificial intelligence' is a term that, it seems, nobody approves of. What *is* intelligence? *Why* artificial? Like it or not, though, it is here to stay; it is our subject in this and the following chapters.

First, 'artificial' in this context simply means as performed by a computer, and not by a living being. (We shall overlook the question we considered briefly on pages 247 to 248 as to whether computers might or might not become living beings.) And intelligence? It might be defined as the use of knowledge and of reasoning abilities in performing goal-directed activities: such as motion towards a fixed point, or communication of a set of ideas, or solving a problem.

According to Tesler's law, artificial intelligence is 'what machines cannot yet do'. By our definition, though, machines can already do much that must be classified as intelligent. Artificial-intelligence researchers are engaged primarily, however, in pushing outwards the boundaries of computer capability and increasing the breadth and depth of machine intelligence. It is these boundaries of capability — what machines might be able to do tomorrow — that we shall be exploring.

The Computer and its Programmer

The computer began as man's tool. Earlier in this book we saw how very simple computing devices like the abacus and the slide rule were developed into today's super-complex microelectronic computers; and we saw just how little their basic capabilities changed along the way.

Initially, the computer was used as a tool in intelligent action, but there was no doubt where the intelligence came from: it came from the user, the programmer. The programmer chose the goal, decided how the goal was to be reached, provided all the data required for the computation. The computer merely carried out the operations designated in its program. There was nothing unpredictable about its operation: given the same program and the same data, it would always come up with the same results, or with one of a specific set of results that might be chosen through the operation of a randomizing element. In this sense, the computer could no more be described as 'thinking', many would argue, than a spade could be described as digging. It is the human being who digs or thinks, using the tool *as* a tool in so doing.

What about a mechanical cultivator, though, that does dig by itself, without any more direct human involvement than is needed in switching it on and directing it to a field of rough ground? And what about an electronic computer that plays chess so well that it can beat its programmer? Just as there has to come a point where the digger ceases to be a tool and actually becomes that which digs, so we believe there must come a point where the computer ceases to be a tool and *becomes* that which thinks. If that point does not come before human beings cease to play an active part in the operation, then it must come at that very point.

Let us be more specific. We believe that *if* the computer is furnished with a set of tools — knowledge and reasoning tools — required for it to do its task, and is informed of its goal, *but* is not given specific (that is, task-related) instructions as to how it is to achieve that goal using those tools, *then* we must conclude that it provides thought in bridging the gap between means and end.

Many people find inherently repugnant the suggestion that a computer can think; thinking is, they claim, a specifically human activity, or at least an activity confined to living beings. By designating the computer as a thinking object, we must then be doing one of two things: either we are mistaking a model of thinking, an imitation of thinking that does not of itself actually demand any thought (all the thought was provided by its modeller) for the real thing; or we are demeaning human life and reducing our entire view of life, thought, consciousness and so on to that which can be captured by a crude mechanistic construction. Both these views demand careful consideration, which we shall now give them.

The Modeller and the Modelled

A model is a copy — let us be clear about that. A model of a series of events, of a ship or an aircraft, of a human being, is a copy of the original. It reproduces at least some aspects of the original, but maybe not all: the model aircraft may look perfect from the outside, but inside there are no engines and no cabin and, most importantly, it cannot fly.

However, that is of *no* importance if what we are modelling is not the aircraft, but merely the outside appearance of the aircraft; not the actual three-dimensional events that make up world economic activity, but merely some limited causal relationships between them. *Define* the boundaries of the model, and half the difficulties disappear.

We must be equally clear, then, about the relationship in modelling terms between computers and human beings. It may be true to say that the computer models human logical thought processes (or, again, it may not). But nobody is suggesting that the computer models human beings in their entirety. We certainly do not aspire to that at this moment, and perhaps we never will. Researchers are not, as far as we know, trying to induce computers to feel love, or fear, or awe. They are simply trying to get them to solve specific problems, or perform specific types of activity.

The boundary is not a clear one, though. What if a computer talks to us in English? English is a human language, a tool designed to convey human ideas and emotions. What does it mean if a computer says 'I love you'? Can we separate the words, which the computer may be able to use grammatically and in a context in which human beings might reasonably use them, from the feelings that those words are normally intended to convey? Even if we understand the distinction intellectually, can we emotionally sustain our awareness of it?

What if a computer plays chess against a human being? We see the moves of the game, not the processes that lead to the choice of those moves, just as we do with a human opponent. But, just as with the human opponent, we mentally link the moves together into a sequential plan, and we use linkages appropriate to human thought and motivation. Is the computer's motivation the same as a human player's motivation? Its logical processes may work entirely differently; but it is playing a game devised by, and for, human beings, and the humanly oriented goals of the game must shape its strategy.

Could it be argued that we should not model computers on any aspect of human behaviour or thought at all? This is hardly a feasible standpoint. There are already so many overlaps between human capabilities and machine capabilities. Where the two overlap, then there is a correspondence between them that we can hardly deny, even if we opt not to see it in terms of a model: And it is difficult not to continue the analogy into areas where the correspondence is much looser, or perhaps non-existent. As computer capability grows, so too, it seems, will this problem. Our only route towards making the computer do things we want and need it to do, and cannot do ourselves, lies through making it do things we can, and already do, do ourselves. But how are we to circumvent the problem, short of 'uninventing' the computer?

Of Life, Thought and Consciousness

The mysteries of human life are still just that: mysteries. Biologists, neurologists and other experts are clearing up more and more of them, but they have not explained everything, and perhaps never will. We have ideas about, models and theories about, how the human brain works, and how living things grow, learn and act. But they are still ideas and theories, and not the absolute truth, if there is any such thing.

Some similar ideas and theories are being applied in our attempts to impart intelligence to the computer: for instance, examination of how a child appears to develop conceptual awareness and language skills may give us ideas on how we might 'teach' a computer similar skills and abilities. But it need not be the case that the one is accurately modelled on the other. If the model works on a 'macro' level (the level of conversation, or of hand manipulation), that does not mean that the correspondence necessarily continues on the 'micro' level (the firing of neural cells, the pathways of electronic current on a silicon chip). The revelation that the foundations of the computer model are not the same as those of human thought may be disturbing. But it need not invalidate the model as a whole. The correspondence on a different level will remain as accurate, or inaccurate, as it ever was.

Certainly research into artificial intelligence may lead to some breakthroughs in research into 'natural' intelligence; and quite conceivably, at the end it will all turn out to be mechanistically explicable: we shall not be able to point to any fundamental difference between the computers of the future and human beings. Perhaps it is out of understandable fear of such an outcome, not out of conviction that it could never come about, that some people wish to limit research into artificial intelligence? These are reasons we (the authors) respect, but we cannot share them. We support the drive to know even if, in the process, what we discover changes our entire conception of human life. And we believe it may well do so. The diversity of human thought is truly awe-inspiring. But the simplicity of its basic building-blocks might be equally amazing. However, trying to impart intelligence to computers has already taught us one thing: it is an incredibly difficult process.

From Programming to Software

In Chapter 9 we took a look at the vast assortment of software that has already been developed. In different ways, all of it is helping to build up the 'intelligence' of the computer: all of it is providing tools to the computer in its thought-processing and controlling operations.

The trend towards systems software, in particular, exemplifies a movement that we see as fundamental to the imparting of intelligence to the computer. This is a movement *away* from one-off application programs and *towards* the acquisition of more broadly applicable tools.

Let us draw an analogy between this process and the acquisition of human intelligence. Human intelligence resides largely in our possession of, and the ability to apply, a wide range of background knowledge. Children acquire, and adults possess, a great deal of knowledge about their world and how it functions. Adults in particular acquire much more knowledge, in greater detail as well as depth, about their special fields of·expertise: their professions, their hobbies, their daily tasks. It is this knowledge, and the ability to bring it selectively to bear upon specific tasks and problems that arise, that enables human beings to function intelligently.

We do acquire specific data, or reasoning tools, that we may need in order to solve specific problems. But that is of relatively minor importance to us. Of much greater importance, we believe, is our acquisition of background knowledge and understanding.

Compare this with computer programs. Early computer programs concentrated on specific tasks. One problem, one task (or a small set of related tasks) was identified, and the computer was simply given the data and the techniques needed to tackle it. *All* software, originally, was applications software. Today, most software developed is not applications software, appropriate only to a single task. Rather, it is the equivalent of background 'knowledge': it is a step in imparting to the computer the ability to understand high-level languages, to schedule its own workload, to order its long-term data into bodies of knowledge.

In the chapters that follow, we shall be looking at the extension of this task in the field of artificial intelligence: away from giving the computer instructions on how to carry out one specific task, and towards giving it the ability to identify its own methods for reaching goals that are set before it. Even the goals are being specified in more and more general terms, and the computer acquires the ability to select its own sub-goals. In effect, we are giving the computer more responsibility, expecting it to act 'intelligently' within the broad guidelines we set out for it.

It is significant that not all software now consists of 'programs'. A program has a beginning and an end: the end defines its goal. When a program runs in isolation on a simple computer, the programmer knows what (at least in outline) the computer will do, and what (in general terms) its output will be. However, this is not true of, say, an interpreter or a resource scheduler. An interpreter is not a program: the computer does not simply follow a fixed path through a sequence of instructions. It is a general-purpose tool, to be brought into play when appropriate.

We can trace a similar blurring of the concept of the programmer's 'goal' in many other software developments. Interactive programming techniques, and programs that act on other programs (like, for instance, the program-writing programs we looked at in Chapter 28), are shifting the boundary between the program and the data (in the broadest sense) on which it operates. Heuristics and search techniques specify their ends in deliberately vague and general terms: they address complex problems for which the format of the solution cannot be so clearly spelled out. And databases and knowledge structures, which we shall be looking at shortly, pose yet other problems. In these, the distinction is blurred between *passive* data and *active* thought. Understanding (and that is the goal to which they reach) is neither simply active nor simply passive: it is both at once.

In summary, then, software has moved away from the stage at which the programmer always specified exactly how the computer was to use the data and manipulative tools he or she provided it with. Today, the programmer does not specify so closely: he/she often cannot predict when, or how, software tools or data will be employed. It is the computer that 'manages' its own resources: and as it comes to manage them with greater skill, and as those resources grow in richness and complexity, as well as quantity, so we believe the computer grows in intelligence.

We complete this argument by outlining the building blocks of computer 'intelligence', as we shall be exploring them in the rest of the chapter.

The Building Blocks of Intelligence

What makes up intelligent behaviour? We believe that it can be broken down, fundamentally, into three vital components:

(1) The ability to know what you are doing: or, if you like, the ability to display consciousness.

Instinctive behaviour, like much animal behaviour, does not imply self-awareness. Like the programmed computer blindly following instructions as it comes to them, the instinctive creature blindly follows cues that we do not yet fully understand. Consciousness, by contrast, implies an overview of one's actions: an awareness of where each individual action fits into a wider picture. In a sense, a conscious being holds in itself at one level a model of its behaviour on a different level. As a result, it can assess that behaviour; select between alternatives on the basis of criteria not included in the base 'program'; learn, in fact, from past experience. These are all activities that human beings carry out; there seems to be no reason why, at least in principle, they should not be activities that computers with several levels of interconnected programs could carry out.

(2) The ability to classify information; in other words, a method of concept formation.

Concepts are classes of objects, ideas, actions that we group together in an attempt to order our experiences and to generalize from them. Without such an ability, each new experience would be entirely new to us; we could not apply previous experiences to it and use them as a basis for handling it.

Together with concept formation, we must include an ability to fit information together into a coherent body of knowledge, and to identify both strictly logical linkages and looser, but still vital, associative linkages. It is an essential feature of our conceptual language structure that concepts have shared contents in a way that builds up, not into a neatly hierarchical knowledge structure, but into a tangled, heterarchical structure. Take a simple example: the desks in our office. We might conceptualize aspects of them as: desk, furniture, container, flat surface, wood, leather, glue, metal, brown . . . and so on. Each word, each conceptual label links them with a different cross-section of our total knowledge and experience.

Yet another concept must be included here, too. This is a method of drawing a boundary around 'sections' of our knowledge and experience, and thus designating 'worlds' within which our, or the computer's, knowledge can be considered as − if not complete − at least adequate as a basis for intelligent thought and action. Such 'worlds' might range from the rule basis of chess or draughts; to the perspectives and theories of the nuclear physicist or the biologist; to the geographic worlds of a room, a small town, a country.

(3) The ability to select: to find a route to the solution of a problem, unearth relevant information, assess and choose between alternatives.

'Brute force' is the simplest of all methods; and it was the first to be employed by the computer. But great though the computer's abilities are, and fast though its working speeds may be, brute force is not often applicable as a search technique, and can offer no help when it is unavoidably necessary to make choices. Random selection is self-evidently unsatisfactory except in very limited circumstances. But what other techniques have been developed? We shall need to look at some current alternatives.

Consciousness; the ability to classify, and to create bodies of knowledge; the ability to make choices. These are, we believe, the fundamentals of intelligent behaviour. And researchers into artificial intelligence are making great strides in improving computer capabilities in each of these three areas. Their successes are as yet strictly limited: though the computer has greater ability than man in some fields, in many it has barely begun even to emulate a child. But that they should succeed at all suggests to us that computer intelligence is a reality, and a growing one.

The Turing Test

Alan Turing, whom we have met earlier in this book (and shall meet again), proposed perhaps the most famous of all 'tests' for assessing computer intelligence. It has become known as the 'Turing Test'. It is a rough guide, but an interesting one, and you may like to ponder its effectiveness and its limitations.

Turing's suggestion (outlined in a paper first published in 1950, 'Computing Machinery and Intelligence') was that an interrogation session might be set up, in which an interrogator asks questions of two entities, A and B, one of which is a person and one a computer, and which he cannot see. The interrogator can specify *which* entity should answer which question; but he/she cannot expect the entity to tell the truth all the time; playing 'the imitation game' and pretending to be what you are not is part of the essence of the game. So it is no good asking A, 'Are you the computer?'.

The aim of the game is for the interrogator to decide, upon the basis of the input he receives from the entities, whether B is the person or the computer. B can do his/her/its best to help the interrogator in this endeavour, but clearly the value of B's help is limited by the fact that A may not be telling the truth.

Could a computer fool the interrogator into believing it was a human being? People have certainly been fooled by computers when they were not expecting a computer to talk to them; but would they still be fooled if they were trying their best to catch the computer out? And if they *could* be fooled, would that prove that the computer was as intelligent as a human being? It is worth thinking about.

32. Knowledge Structures and Expert Systems

With a brief introduction to the idea of artificial intelligence behind us, we shall now go on to look briefly at the three aspects of intelligence we identified at the end of the last chapter: consciousness, the ability to classify and to create bodies of knowledge, and the ability to make choices. We shall be changing that order slightly, though. This chapter is concerned with knowledge structures, and with the 'expert systems' that make use of them. Chapter 33 will look at search techniques, an aspect of the computer's growing ability to 'choose' for itself how to solve the problems set to it. And a final chapter (Chapter 34) will look at some aspects of how the computer is 'escaping' from its programmer and developing something that just might be interpreted as consciousness.

Data Structures and Knowledge Structures

In Chapter 27 we looked at ways of structuring data; and we ended up with a brief examination of databases, a term applied equally to the structures into which the data are fitted, and to the contents of those structures. In this chapter, we shall be going on from that point, looking at structures, not of *data*, but of *knowledge*.

What is the difference? In data structures, the structure is a convenient way of storing and retrieving pieces of data that are more or less self-contained. The data are normally arranged logically, to be sure, but the structure is primarily a way of getting *at* the data, not an extension *of* the data. Once we have found, say, a particular address, or a list of train times, we don't care just how it fits in with the rest of the database contents. By locating the timetable (or whatever), the database has done its job for us.

In a knowledge structure, by contrast, the way in which the datum fits into the structure is at least as important as the actual datum itself, considered in isolation.

Let us take a very simple example. Consider the equation
$$4 = 3 + 1$$
Is this one or more pieces of data, or is it a structure? Really, it is both. '4', '3' and '1' are all data: they are numbers that exist in their own right, or that can be used to represent actual qualities of real-life objects or situations. The equation '$4 = 3 + 1$' is also a datum, on a larger scale. But from another angle, the construction of this equation (the general form, '$x = y + z$', into which the numbers 4, 3 and 1 have been fitted) is a structure. It is more than

just a datum: it is a statement of the relationship between the different pieces of data that fit into the slots 'x', 'y' and 'z'.

And this structure *adds* something to our knowledge, as provided by the individual, smaller-scale pieces of data. The person who is aware that '4 = 3 + 1' has *more* knowledge than the person who simply possesses the three unrelated data, '4', '3' and '1'.

Of course, the same is true if we use, not numbers or arithmetical symbols, but more concrete statements. 'Mrs Jones' and 'Mrs Smith' might be our two data. 'Mrs Jones is a neighbour of Mrs Smith' is a knowledge structure that adds something to them, and on a larger scale turns them into a single, more complex datum.

The dividing line between data structures and knowledge structures is not a clear one. Any databank or other data structure that orders the data in a meaningful way (even just listing items alphabetically) contains elements of a knowledge structure. But the structures we think of as knowledge structures are structures in which the structure is at least as important (in adding to our knowledge) as the data it contains. To consider the data in isolation from the structure is to lose a very real aspect of their significance.

As a result, the development of knowledge structures has concentrated upon the implementation of new ways of expressing relationships between data. Not all the relationships between disparate data items can be expressed easily and efficiently by fitting them into a simple array structure. The more dimensions the array has, the harder it is to order data meaningfully along each of them. If the ordering is to have a meaning of its own, rather than being an arbitrary by-product of our ways of storing the data, then we must find more complex ways of handling it.

Let us extend our second example to illustrate this. Suppose that we have *three* women to consider: Mrs Jones, Mrs Smith, and Mrs Robinson. And we know that:

All three women work as teachers.
Mrs Jones and Mrs Smith are neighbours.
Mrs Robinson is *not* a neighbour of either of the other two women.
Mrs Jones and Mrs Robinson both belong to the bridge club.
Mrs Smith and Mrs Robinson both belong to the sewing circle.
Mrs Jones is thirty-five; Mrs Smith is forty; Mrs Robinson is forty-five.
To express those relationships in array form would be a horrendous task. But they *can* be expressed simply and efficiently in some of the other knowledge structures we shall be looking at.

Frames

The 'frame' is a concept often used as a building block when a 'loose' data structure is being built up: one intended to express not merely formal, logical relationships (like those expressible in Boolean algebra) but other types of meaningful but informal relationship (like, for instance, 'is a neighbour of'). The frame might be thought of as a boundary within which a coherent group of data are linked together, in a variety of ways that can be tailored to the qualities of the relationships between the pieces of data. Frames, in turn, can be linked with one another; but (in contrast to the idea of adding another dimension to an array structure) linking the frames might not produce analogical links between the contents of different frames.

We shall try to exemplify this, too. The set of data and relationships we have just offered (Mrs Jones, Mrs Smith, Mrs Robinson and their inter-involvement) might be enclosed within a single frame that contains all this information. Let's call it 'Teachers'. 'Mrs Jones' might also appear as an element in another frame — as, say, 'the wife of Mr Jones' in a frame called 'Mr Jones' — and a cue will point from the 'Mrs Jones' in the 'Mr Jones' frame to the 'Mrs Jones' in the 'Teachers' frame. But there need not be any connection (except the very indirect one implied by this cue) between Mrs Robinson and Mr Jones, or Mrs Robinson and other aspects of the 'Mr Jones' frame (the golf club, say).

Figure 88 is a pictorial representation of this simple knowledge structure.

Figure 88: Example of a 'frame' structure

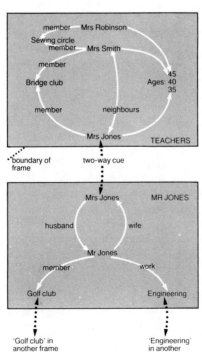

By working through the cues to look at all the frames in which Mrs Jones appears, we can build up an idea of Mrs Jones and her life as a whole: an entity that has a very real existence, even if not all aspects of it fit logically together.

Lists

List processing has obvious relevance to the 'frame' concept. Basically, the list-processing idea is a way of expressing relationships — between the items within a frame, say, or between frames, on a larger scale — between the pieces of data held in a computer system's memory.

The 'relationships' and 'cues' we discussed above are exemplified in list processing by a system of 'pointers' or 'links'. List-processing links (the term we shall use) are in effect links between data storage locations that express relationships between the contents of those locations.

What exactly is the link? Basically, it consists simply of a datum (or several data), permanently associated by the computer system with another datum (just as the second word of a program statement is firmly associated with the first word). It comprises the address of yet another datum with which the first is also associated (in a logical, or looser-than-logical, sense, but not necessarily in the physical storage structure within the computer). It may also contain some indication of the relationship between the two data: varying from the precise (address of the person whose name is stored in the original location) to the vague (this frame and that have an associative link of an unspecified kind). One datum may have more than one link pointing to other data; and links may be two-way (the datum pointed to points back to the original datum) or only one-way.

Sometimes links are further distinguished by whether they point to a single location in memory or to a string of data held in sequential locations. The latter type are called 'string pointers'.

A series of pieces of data with links pointing to each other in a continuing sequence is called a 'threaded list'. Perhaps because of this, the handling of knowledge structures based on links of this general type, whether they consist of threaded lists or not, is called list processing.

We describe some high-level languages such as LISP (page 344) as being list-processing languages. These languages use this method of structuring data. Figure 89 gives an impression of how knowledge structures based on list-processing techniques are put together. One of the great strengths of the list-processing idea is that the links can be used on so many different levels: between single data; between lists of data; even between programs (which are themselves lists of data). As a result, the idea of list processing paves the way to the use of the recursive techniques that we shall look at in Chapter 34.

Figure 89: List processing knowledge structures

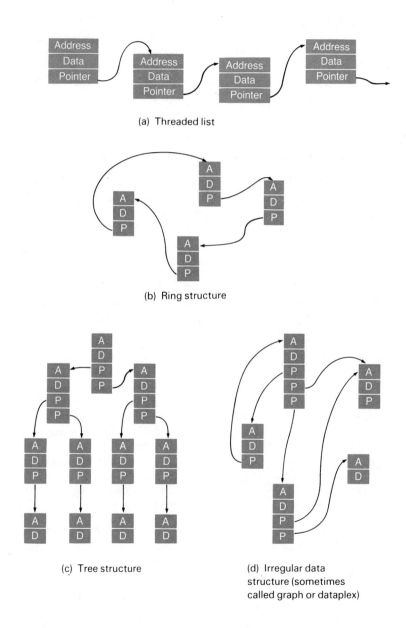

(a) Threaded list

(b) Ring structure

(c) Tree structure

(d) Irregular data structure (sometimes called graph or dataplex)

Worlds of Knowledge

Let us go on to look at a knowledge-structuring concept on a different level of generality: that of the 'world' of knowledge.

Of course, when we talk of levels we are being shamelessly imprecise: because the whole point of complex knowledge structures such as those we are describing is that, instead of building up a neat, hierarchical structure, they build up an anarchical (but effective) structure that muddles levels and makes it impossible to talk about them precisely. (We can and will, for instance, refer back to our discussion of 'frames' to illustrate the concept of worlds of knowledge, even though the frames we earlier discussed were much more localized than the worlds we will now discuss.) But from a non-logical viewpoint, the idea of levels is intuitively helpful.

And it is in fact an idea that can be applied to worlds of knowledge. Take, for example, the specialized knowledge possessed by a nuclear physicist, a geologist, and a civil engineer. Each of these three professionals works with a body of knowledge that is centred in general ideas, and theories, and expressions of those ideas and theories in the form of formulae that work. The nuclear physicist works with our currently accepted theories (or his/her newer, tentative theories) about how matter and energy are related on a sub-nuclear scale. The geologist is not interested in the sub-nuclear: he is interested in the properties of different natural materials on a larger scale. And the civil engineer works on a similar scale, but with a quite different set of theories and formulae from those of the geologist.

The bodies of knowledge that these three professionals possess (and, of course, the same is true of professionals in other fields) are not easily meshed together. What the nuclear physicist discovers, for instance, proves daily how utterly wrong Newton was — on the subatomic level. The relationship between energy and matter is far more complex than Newton ever dreamed. But at the same time, new theories about the subatomic world are all but totally irrelevant to the geologist or the civil engineer. *They* know that on their scale of interest, Newton's laws provide an extremely good prediction of how matter will behave. Discarding 'laws' that still work for them is out of the question.

Meshing the nuclear physicist's 'truth' and the geologist's 'truth' together to produce a coherent picture of the world that will be acceptable to both would be an immensely difficult task: infinitely more difficult than the not inconsiderable task of providing a comprehensible set of linkages between all the data in the frames 'Teachers' and 'Mr Jones' that we looked at earlier. However, in fact, for many purposes there is no *need* to mesh them together. The geologist's world of knowledge is complete and coherent (by and large) in itself; so is the nuclear physicist's. If we keep within one of those worlds of knowledge, and frame it around as we framed the 'Teachers' data, then we can concentrate upon learning about it and temporarily (or even permanently) ignore the vast volume of knowledge that it does *not* encompass.

What makes up the 'frame'? Simply the boundary of coherence, or an arbitrary cut-off point at which we stop trying to relate more data comprehensively to our existing body of knowledge. Outside the frame (whether the boundary comes on a physical 'level', or at a mental change of perspective on the same physical level), things still make sense, but they make a *different* sense; and not all cross-connections still hold true.

Let us give some more examples of 'worlds' of knowledge, that have proved useful boundary-providers in tackling the task of setting up knowledge structures within computers:

the world of formal mathematics;

the world of three-dimensional geometry;

the world of medicine (and within that, the sub-worlds of different disease syndromes);

the world of the Rogerian psycho-analyst;

the world of microelectronic engineering.

The Development of Expert Systems

Each of the 'worlds' we mentioned above (and, as you will appreciate, most of them can be defined on many different 'levels', or with very widely differing degrees of precision) has been the subject of an attempt to impart both a body of knowledge, and the ability to use it 'intelligently', to a computer. This is the field known as expert systems research.

This sub-set of artificial-intelligence research works with the assumption (borne out by experience) that it is much easier to create a working knowledge structure within a tightly defined 'world', such as those we have just mentioned, than it is to give the computer a modest degree of common sense in general. Obviously, much of the emphasis has been on 'worlds' in which it is relatively easy to codify and express (in logical, or looser-than-logical, ways) our knowledge. In many other 'worlds' that we might nominate, the task would be far harder.

An expert system, then, is a computer system which has been given:

(1) the software ability to set up and maintain a knowledge structure;

(2) data from a particular, well-defined 'world' of knowledge, that is fitted into that structure in such a way that the data and the structure are inseparably linked;

(3) the ability to manipulate the knowledge in that structure, in order to solve real-life problems that arise in the 'world' in question.

How successful has such research been? Clearly, the successes there have been are only a small step towards the larger-scale goal of making computers as 'intelligent' (in a general sense) as human beings. But successes there have been. Expert systems in many areas have succeeded in solving problems human beings could not solve, simply by making good use of their ability to manipulate large volumes of data and to draw conclusions from those data in ways defined by their knowledge structure and by their programming in general. Such systems have very real uses: for instance, in helping to diagnose diseases (a very data-intensive task), or in predicting where mineral deposits might be located. Their consistency means that already they can outperform leading human experts in these limited ways.

Limiting the field of endeavour in this way has also led to some successes in more general directions. Programs like Terry Winograd's SHRDLU, which deals with the manipulation of three-dimensional objects on a video screen, and Joseph Weizenbaum's much-imitated ELIZA, which parrots the conversation of a Rogerian psychotherapist, have succeeded in giving the computer at least the superficial ability to hold a conversation, responding in an acceptable (if limited) way to natural language input. Of course, the input has to be of a type the system is expecting: it is no use trying to slip in a totally unpredictable, sarcastic or ironic comment!

Below we list some expert systems under development, or in use, today. As you can see, the range of systems developed is remarkably wide.

Dendral: Developed at Stanford University, California. Handles mass-spectrographic analysis and prediction. Now widely available worldwide.

Digitalis Advisor: Developed at the Massachusetts Institute of Technology, to advise on the application of digitalis in treating heart disease.

Ladder: A Stanford Research Institute program, to help Navy personnel identify ship silhouettes and similar patterns.

Macsyma: A mathematical system, developed at the Massachusetts Institute of Technology.

Prospector: A geological analysis program, evaluating sites for potential mineral deposits. Developed by Stanford Research Insititute, now in commercial use.

Puff: Analyses patient data to help in the diagnosis of lung diseases. Another Stanford development.

Sacon: A program acting as a structural analysis consultant, assisting structural engineers in identifying the best analysis strategy for problems in their field. Developed at Stanford.

Xsel: Developed at Carnegie-Mellon, a system that assists computer salesmen to recommend appropriate systems to their customers.

From Expert Systems to Intelligent Computers

Expert systems can be very impressive in performance. Their abilities are strictly limited, though. Ask SHRDLU what the weather is like, or try to talk to ELIZA about astrophysics, and it will take no more than a couple of exchanges before the systems fail the Turing Test, without a shadow of a doubt.

But in spite of their limitations, we believe that expert systems are a very real step towards the achievement of more generalized artificial-intelligence ability. Slowly the systems are coming to perform acceptably in wider and wider fields of knowledge. Within limited fields, they already outperform human experts. How long before they succeed in outperforming us on every front?

33. Search Techniques

The game of chess has long had a peculiar fascination for researchers in artificial intelligence. Few of them actually play good chess, but perhaps that is no disadvantage: they gain an extra thrill when their programs beat them! (Chess programs are not yet at the stage when they can beat the very best human players.) And many expert chess players have returned the compliment by showing a fascination with artificial intelligence and its application to their game.

Chess is not a highly commercial field for research, but the development of chess-playing programs has been supported by commercial organizations as well as academic institutions, largely because chess covers such a wide and interesting spectrum of intelligent behaviour. And, of course, several chess-playing computers are now on the market.

In this chapter we shall look at chess as an intelligent activity, with a particular emphasis on 'search' techniques: finding suitable criteria for selecting a course of play. Chess can be used to introduce many of the major search techniques currently employed by computers, not only in chess-playing programs (which are themselves a form of expert system, of the type we looked at in Chapter 32), but in many other expert systems.

The Solution Space

First, we must introduce the concept of the 'solution space'. This is the theoretical 'world' of alternatives within which the solution to a problem (here, selecting a move, and ultimately winning the game) is to be found. In a sense, every legal move in a game of chess is a solution to the player's problem of how to move his pieces. Intelligent behaviour, though, demands not only that the player should identify the possible solutions, but also that he (or it) should select the best, or — at the very least — a good, solution. In other words, the task of the human player or of the chess-playing program is: to first, identify all the legal moves available, and thus map out the solution space; second, to identify from within the solution space the optimum move, according to intelligently developed criteria.

The solution space in a game of chess is tree-shaped: a quality shared by many games, and by many, but by no means all, other problem situations. Each choice of move at a specific stage in the game opens up a different series of choices to the opponent at his next move, and so on. Figure 90 sketches out part of the tree structure of a game — not the whole structure,

Figure 90: Tree structure of part of a chess game

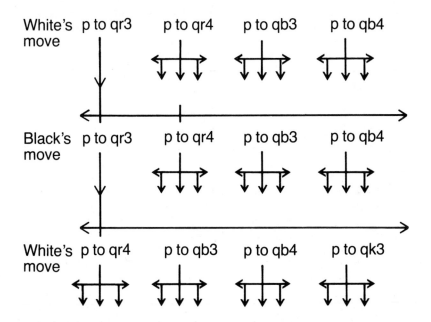

for that is incredibly large. Claud Shannon calculated that the solution space of a chess game contains around 10^{120} alternatives. For even the fastest modern computer to explore all those alternatives would take millennia. Hence, brute force is not a feasible way of selecting moves, and more sophisticated methods are necessary.

Selection Criteria

What methods have been developed, then? And what are their strengths and weaknesses, as compared with those of a human player?

Human players do not, in fact, look very far down the tree of solutions in selecting a move. Depending on the stage of the game, they will consider the implications of a move perhaps only three or four moves forward; more in the end game, and fewer (perhaps none at all) in the opening phase. Nor do they examine all legal moves. A good player tends to select only a very few moves to explore in depth; many he or she dismisses without any conscious thought at all. The main criterion is not an easily evaluated one. It is an intuitive insight into the 'state of the game': the strengths and weaknesses of his/her and the opponent's position, and the developing pattern of the play.

For intuitive insight, the computer must substitute pragmatic selection of criteria that can be numerically evaluated. It cannot dismiss any legal moves as obviously inferior: it must examine even the least promising in some way, or risk missing an obvious winning move. It has little flair; and much of its superior processing power is wasted in performing evaluations with which the human player does not consciously bother. However, it is learning, or its programmers are: and its criteria are becoming ever more subtle and complex. Among those considered by at least some programmers have been:

the number of pieces retained by each player at the start of a move, and thus their need to attack from a strong position, or defend a weak one;

the area 'controlled' by each player; this can be estimated mathematically. Sometimes particular emphasis is placed on control of the centre of the board;

pieces that are directly threatened by one of the opponent's pieces, or that are in a position to take an opposing piece;

the quality of pieces. Each piece can be weighted in value, so that a queen 'scores' higher than a bishop, a knight than a pawn;

the safety of the king, according to the number of pieces protecting it, or the area controlled around it;

the mobility of pieces. Obviously, a mobile position scores more highly than a cramped one.

These are all factors that any player would agree are of some importance in assessing the state of a game. However, few of them directly contribute to winning the game by achieving checkmate. Clearly they must be interleaved with a consideration of the possibility of checking the opponent, or being placed in check. In the endgame in particular, checking becomes of overriding importance: and here there could be a case for working, not *down* the solution tree from possible moves to their outcomes, but *up* it, from a winning position to sequences of moves likely to lead to it.

Evaluating alternative moves: Using a series of criteria like these, the program can evaluate each move numerically, in an alternating cycle: one move according to its value to the player, and the options it opens up according to their potential value to his, her or its opponent. The further down the tree the computer looks for each move, the more precise the evaluation will be. In chess, of course, the evaluation may change dramatically from one look-ahead phase to the next, as winning strategies for one side or the other are unfurled. Needless to say, the computer must assume that its opponent will use some comparable method of evaluating moves; for simplicity, it is normally (if somewhat unrealistically) assumed that the opponent will actually make what the computer calculates to be his 'best' move.

The technique that results is known as 'minimaxing': the calculation gives equal weight to maximizing the player's advantage and minimizing his (her, its) opponent's potential advantage. Figure 91 shows a simple example:

Figure 91 : The technique of minimaxing

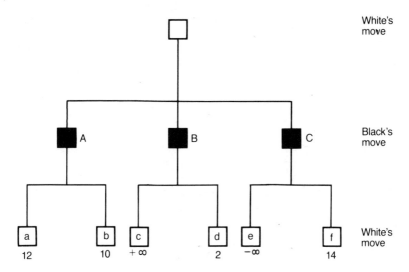

(a) An evaluation two layers deep is made of the value
of the potential positions for Black and White.

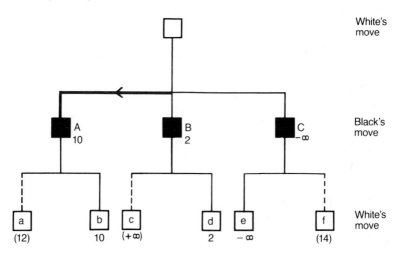

(b) Black would reject the dotted-line alternatives (best for
White) and select the solid-line alternatives. White's
best choice from between A, B and C then becomes
the heavy line, A.

White has a choice of three moves, each of which will leave Black with a choice of two moves. The positions that would result after Black's move are evaluated on a scale that ranges from minus infinity (Black win) to plus infinity (White win).

It is assumed that Black will always make his best move, which will be the one that scores lowest: b if he is choosing between a and b, d from c and d, and e from e and f. As a result, White's alternative moves, A, B and C, can be re-evaluated (lower diagram) as scoring 10, 2 and minus infinity respectively. The potential win for White from move B is no longer taken into account, since good play by Black would negate it. Instead, White's best choice becomes move A.

All this numerical assessment, though, adds up to nothing more than a method for evaluating moves. In a solution space too large for all moves to be evaluated exhaustively, how is the computer to decide which moves to evaluate at all, and in what depth? Still other techniques must be employed here.

Figure 92: Breadth first and depth first search sequences

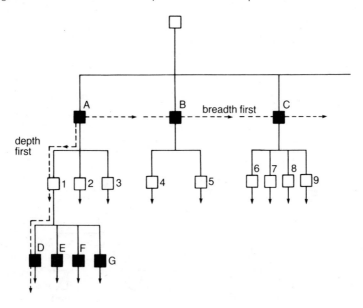

In a tree-shaped solution space, two different basic search techniques have been identified: breadth first, and depth first. 'Breadth first' assumes that all the solutions will first be examined on a basic level; then that some, or all, will be examined in greater depth; and so on to greater and greater depths, until a fixed cut-off point is reached (a limitation on the search time, say, or the discovery of a move with a suitably high rating). In Figure 92, the breadth-first search technique would involve examining and evaluating moves in the following order: A, B, C (and other moves immediately open), then 1, 2, 3, 4, 5, 6, 7, 8, then D, E, F, G, and so on.

Depth-first searching concentrates on exploring one branch of the solution tree exhaustively, then going on to explore other branches in equal depth. The depth-first sequence in Figure 92 would comprise A, 1, D, and subsequent moves, E, F, G, then 2, 3, B, 4, and so on.

Each technique has obvious strengths and limitations, and the choice of one or the other will depend largely on the nature of the solution space. Is it a question of getting progressively nearer and nearer to one 'right' answer, or are acceptable answers randomly distributed across the space? Are the lower branches of the tree as important as the upper ones to the discovery of a solution, or do they merely provide corroborative evidence? Is there a risk, in pursuing a depth-first search, of getting lost down an infinite blind alley? It has to be borne in mind, too, that the computer must use memory space to 'remember' where it has already looked. Depth-first searches are generally more efficient in their use of memory than the breadth-first type.

In practice, of course, there are often suitable ways of combining the two techniques. In evaluating a chess move, one method might be to give a first-level evaluation to every possible legal move, and then to select a relatively small number of higher-scoring moves for further evaluation to a pre-defined depth. Another method that is widely used is the alpha-beta technique for 'pruning' the solution tree.

Alpha-beta pruning works on the simple basis of not carrying out further evaluation on parts of the tree that will have no effect upon the ultimate decision. It can be combined with the minimax method for alternately evaluating minimum risk, and maximum advantage: the alternate phases are designated as the alpha phase and the beta phase. Figure 93 (*over*) indicates very simply how it works.

It is White's move, and move A has already been valued at 1 (a slight advantage to White). Move B by White would give Black four alternatives, a, b, c and d; and the computer goes on to evaluate them in order. Move a has a value of 2 (a marginally greater advantage to White). However, b proves to have a value of −5 (advantage to Black). Black must be expected to choose move b or any better move that turns up, and this means that the choice of move B by White will lead (by minimax evaluation) to an advantage for Black. This is not the case for move A. Therefore, White will not choose move B over move A, and further investigation of move B is pointless. Alternatives c and d are 'pruned' from the tree, and go unexplored.

Alpha-beta pruning has wide applications in artificial intelligence search techniques, but still other selection methods are unique to the game of chess — though analogies to them can be found elsewhere in search theory. For instance, the classic openings in chess have been extensively documented and discussed in chess literature. There is no need for the computer to evaluate every move when opening a game: at the present state of our knowledge, it is quite sufficient for it to select one of the relatively small number of standard 'preferred' openings. Human players know by long

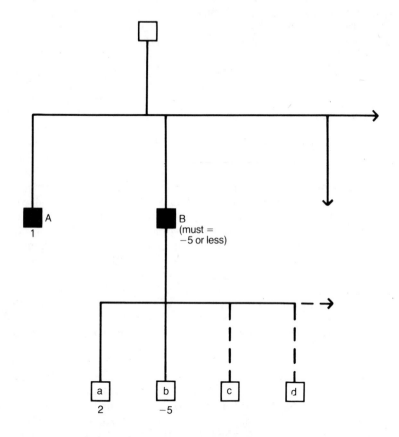

Move A is evaluated first, then move B as far as option b. Minimax evaluation means the assumption that Black would choose move b or any more advantageous move. Move B for White will thus be less advantageous than move A, whatever the value of c, d and other alternatives. Moves c and d are 'pruned', and no further evaluation of them is carried out.

Figure 93: The technique of alpha/beta pruning

experience that P–K4 is a reliable opening move, and it would be pointless for the computer to waste clock time exploring a dozen other legal opening moves, and to fail to consider this one.

Similarly, suitable responses to such openings are widely recognized. Even grand masters use them: why shouldn't a computer?

Heuristic techniques: Even the earliest researchers who concentrated on chess programs took account of such simple non-numeric techniques. Alex Bernstein, who worked on chess programs for I.B.M. in the late 1950s, studied *Modern Chess Openings* in detail and used the information he gleaned from it in developing his numerical evaluations as well. Alan Turing, back in 1950, introduced the idea of 'dead' positions, drawing a distinction between moves that introduce specific strategic plans and moves that merely continue them: for instance, a sequence of 'exchanges' of pieces, once begun, must be considered as a whole: the state of the game cannot be evaluated accurately in the middle of it. Only when the sequence ends and there results a relatively stable situation, should an evaluation be made, and a new strategy instigated, Turing argued.

Techniques like these are leading to the use of a quite different overall method: the heuristic method. An heuristic approach is a trial-and-error approach: or a short-term plan that may not lead to a final solution (a win, in chess) but that will have results that can be evaluated and used as a basis for developing a subsequent heuristic. In chess, the heuristic might be a fixed sequence of moves (including, not just a first move, but subsequent moves that are likely to be available to the player as a result of the opponent's predicted responses), which the computer selects after evaluation of the state of play. The computer will not then re-evaluate the position until the entire sequence has been completed, or unless it has been interrupted by unpredictable play on the opponent's behalf.

In a broader sense, the word 'heuristic' can be used to describe any search strategy that (unlike an algorithm) is not certain to culminate in success or in the certainty that there is no acceptable solution. So, on one level, any general plan for conducting a non-exhaustive search of the solution space is a form of heuristic. On another level, the solution that is chosen as a result of that heuristic search may itself be an heuristic, if it comprises not just one move but a planned sequence of moves.

Heuristics can, of course, be developed for situations where the solution space is not tree-shaped at all: for multi-dimensional solution spaces, for instance. And different heuristics will be suitable in situations where the solution or solutions are randomly distributed, and in situations where it is possible to tell when you are getting close to a solution. The heuristic may lead to a zig-zag search right across the solution space, following 'clues' that appear, or it may simply comprise a pragmatic plan of search like the minimax method outlined earlier.

Combinatorial factors: Elaborate heuristics are necessary if a well-planned search is to be carried out in a solution space with a complex structure. We end this chapter by looking briefly at one of these aspects of complexity: the problem of combinatorial factors.

Combinatorial factors are factors that cannot be evaluated in isolation, but only in relation to the presence or absence of other factors. This is clearly true of some of the factors we described for evaluating the state of a chess game. The position of a specific piece has some relevance of itself: how near White's queen, say, is to White's end of the board, or to the centre. However, much more important is the position of other pieces: is Black's bishop in a position to threaten White's queen, or could White's queen make a single move to check Black's king? As a result, it is not sufficient simply to give a numerical value to the position of each piece, and then sum them. It is essential, in finding a good solution, to make a combinatorial evaluation of the positions of all the pieces in relation to one another. And this evaluation must itself be combined with, rather than simply added to, the results of other evaluations: the number of pieces left to each side, and so on. Indeed, this is a major reason why it is so difficult to evaluate the position in a chess game, and why good moves are so widely distributed across the solution space.

Similar combinatorial factors appear in many other fields of artificial intelligence research. Take, for instance, the problem of diagnosing a disease from a list of symptoms. The knowledge that a child has a headache means little of itself: it could be a symptom of dozens of different maladies, some very serious and some not serious at all. However, the combination of the headache and a rash, together with some other minor symptoms, might enable a positive diagnosis of, say, chickenpox or german measles to be made. The headache cannot be dismissed as a symptom simply because it is such a mild and general one: in the second instance, it plays a vital role in confirming the tentative diagnosis.

From Complexity to Intelligence

By spelling out these complexities, we are coming right back to our initial point: that for an accurate evaluation of such complex situations to be made, far more than simple undirected number-crunching power is needed. What is needed is intelligence: the ability to direct the computer's manipulative power to where it can do most good. And the development of techniques like the search techniques we have outlined is giving the computer that intelligence.

Man no longer has to intervene directly in the problem-solving process: the general-purpose tools with which the computer is being equipped enable it to direct its own abilities purposefully. Given a chess-playing program making use of search and evaluatory techniques, the computer itself approaches the problem posed by each new move and directs its abilities towards solving it. Given a diagnostic program, it can do the same for disease; with appropriate programming, it can and does do the same in many other 'worlds'. Is this not a very real step towards making the computer 'intelligent'?

34. Beyond Understanding

In this chapter, we shall be looking at one final aspect of artificial intelligence. How is a computer to 'understand' how the programs it is running work, and thus to approach a form of consciousness? And, as something of an introduction to this topic, what are the implications when we, as users or programmers, do *not* understand what the system is doing, or how it is doing it?

When we deal with complex programs — or, more properly, with computers programmed in a complex way, perhaps with many different programs running on different levels — then inevitably there are occasions when it becomes difficult or impossible for a user who is not aware of how the system is programmed to understand how it works. On such occasions, it is easy to imagine that the computer is behaving 'intelligently': displaying real understanding of a subject, for instance. However, most systems sooner or later betray their limitations and fail the Turing Test!

On a more profound level, there are also times when we must conclude that a programmed computer has 'escaped' from the understanding of its programmer(s), as well as of its users. The computer might, for instance, be able to outperform the human beings who fed programs and data into it (as do many expert systems; as do some chess-playing programs). Or it might simply be the case that, for one reason or another, the programmer is unable to predict how the computer will react to input, or run a particular program.

Of course, we frequently use computers to solve problems — highly complex mathematical problems, for instance — that we could not solve ourselves in the same space of time. The very fact that computer abilities to solve problems are better than human abilities in some directions lies behind the development of computing machines. But often when the computer does such number-crunching, though its manipulations may be complex, its program (and the way the program runs) is *comprehensible* to the programmer. The programmer can follow the steps the computer takes: literally so, if he or she chooses to single-step through the program, peeking at registers and memory locations. He/she can tell how far the computer has got in running the program, and what it is going to do next. The operations of some other types of computer program are *not* comprehensible to the programmer in the same way. It is with these latter programs that we shall be concerned in this chapter.

This lack of comprehensibility is a fact that some people find very difficult to grasp. The programmer *wrote* the program, they argue, so how can its operation possibly be incomprehensible?

In fact, there are a number of ways in which it might be so. We shall enumerate some of them briefly.

(1) Some programs make heavy use of randomizing techniques. In these cases, the programmer knows what *type* of choice the computer is going to make: but he/she cannot predict exactly what the choice will be. If such a program is complex enough, it may give users (though not the programmer) the impression that the computer is 'intelligent', or is understanding them, or is using initiative; even though, to the programmer, nothing mysterious is happening. We will look at one such program, which might be said to imitate rather than emulate some aspects of intelligent behaviour, in a moment.

(2) Some programs are simply too long or too complex for the programmer to be able to grasp exactly what is going on, at the statement/instruction level, at any moment.

How could the programmer have written the program, in that case? Simply by adopting a structured approach and tackling it by writing one self-contained module, or one 'layer', at a time. When working on the individual section at a detailed level, the programmer does not need to keep in his/her head how that section will interrelate with other sections. All the program will be comprehensible at one time or another, but only part of it is comprehensible at any particular time. And as the program execution swaps around from module to module and back again, so the programmer is simply unable mentally to swap around and follow it.

You may find it easier to grasp this if we offer the analogy of a sentence that, though correct grammatically, is so elaborately constructed that we have to read it two or three times to discover what on earth is being said. Take the first sentence of Thomas Love Peacock's novel *Headlong Hall*, for instance:

> The ambiguous light of a December morning, peering through the windows of the Holyhead mail, dispelled the soft visions of the four inside, who had slept, or seemed to sleep, through the first seventy miles of the road, with as much comfort as may be supposed consistent with the jolting of the vehicle, and an occasional admonition to 'remember the coachman', thundered through the open door, accompanied by the gentle breath of Boreas, into the ears of the drowsy traveller.

A book full of such sentences might tell a comprehensible story, or build up a perfectly legitimate argument, but the reader has to work so hard to unravel each individual sentence that he or she may never succeed in fitting them together in his or her own mind, and making sense of the whole. Nothing is *wrong*, except about the style, but the result is confusion.

Of course, a well-written program of a given level of complexity is easier to follow than a poorly structured, confused program. And it is easier to 'get lost' in a lengthy program than in a short one consisting of only a few statements (though it is by no means impossible with the latter!). But there comes a point of complexity at which even a highly intelligent person cannot grasp every detail of even a very well-written program. The program may be quite simply *too* complex for the human mind to hold.

(3) The program may have been written with the help of software tools that the programmer does not fully understand. We have already considered how the use of 'layers' of software inside a computer helps to build up its capabilities. For instance, if the programmer invokes a subroutine that he understands only on a high level (that is, he knows what it does, but not how it does it), then he may 'get lost' if he tries to keep track of program operation on a lower level. If the program has been written with the aid of a program-writing package of the kind we looked at in Chapter 28, the same may be true of the entire listing.

(4) Similarly, the program may have been designed to incorporate 'learning' techniques. An expert system, for instance, is often designed so that it can 'learn' how to add to its knowledge structure and to apply the knowledge fed into it to new situations. Such a system may easily outstrip the ability of its programmer to apply such knowledge: so that a medical system can diagnose diseases with more consistency than the doctor whose knowledge it encompasses, for instance. Is the performance of such a program comprehensible to its programmer? On some levels maybe, but not on all.

In the rest of this chapter, we shall be looking primarily at ways in which the program structure may become too complex to follow: with particular reference to programs and sets of programs that are relatively short but are elaborately constructed. We shall start, though, with a look at a program that uses some simple techniques to give the unwary user the impression that it shows more 'understanding' than it actually possesses.

Programs that Appear to Understand Us

Perhaps, to the layman, the most impressive of the programs that 'simulate' intelligent behaviour are the interactive programs that appear to converse in natural language. And indeed, they do represent an exciting development in programming capability. But it is important to distinguish between programmed computers that 'understand' what we input to them, and programmed computers that merely produce appropriate responses.

We mentioned two programs that concentrate on natural language response – Terry Winograd's SHRDLU, and Joseph Weizenbaum's ELIZA – in Chapter 32. They are examples of these two classes – programs that understand, and programs that simply appear to understand – respectively. Let us now spell out the difference between them.

SHRDLU is a program that handles the manipulation of shapes – in fact, two-dimensional lines on a visual display screen, though the user (and the computer, in some ways) takes them to represent three-dimensional shapes – of fixed dimensions in a special sub-world. Within limits, SHRDLU can 'hold a conversation' with the user about how the shapes are to be manipulated: so the user might enter, for instance, a command like 'Find a block that is bigger than the last one you moved, and put it in the box', and SHRDLU will make sense of it (working out what 'it' must stand for, for example), and act accordingly. When SHRDLU is given a natural-language command like this that it succeeds in interpreting, then it quite literally *understands* it. The system knows what it is intended to do, and proves it by doing it.

True, SHRDLU's 'world' is a very simple and limited one, but within that world the computer's 'understanding' is real. We might say that the program acts on two different levels: on one level, it handles the nuts and bolts of making conversation (constructing grammatically acceptable responses, and so on); and on another level, it handles the business of working out what the input *means*, and devising a response (in action, as well as in words) that reflects that meaning. The same is not true, however, for ELIZA.

ELIZA was designed to hold conversations (via a keyboard and screen) in which the computer plays the role of a Rogerian psychotherapist (the kind of psychotherapist who specializes in 'non-directional' feedback in response to his/her patient's conversation) and the user the role of the patient. So long as the user keeps to conversational exchanges that fit inside this 'world', ELIZA is normally able to respond reasonably appropriately.

But what *is* ELIZA's world? And what does ELIZA do within it? ELIZA is not a 'real' psychotherapist: the computer running the ELIZA program knows nothing about real people's problems and how to cure them. So we cannot say that ELIZA 'understands' the world of psychotherapy in the same way that SHRDLU 'understands' a world of simple geometric shapes. ELIZA is simply that which can imitate human conversational responses, within certain defined limits.

How does ELIZA work? There are many versions of ELIZA. We have a version in BASIC (not as elaborate as the original, but fun to play with) on our TRS-80 Model II: in Table 28, we reproduce a sample run from it.

Table 28: A Sample Run of the ELIZA Program

(ELIZA's dialogue on the left; human input on the right)

HI! I AM ELIZA. WHAT'S YOUR PROBLEM?

I THINK I AM A COMPUTER

ARE YOU SURE?

YES, I AM VERY SURE

I SEE

HOW CAN YOU SEE?

DO YOU WANT ME TO BE ABLE TO SEE?

I THINK SO

COME, COME, ELUCIDATE YOUR THOUGHTS

I'M FRIGHTENED OF COMPUTERS

ARE YOU TALKING ABOUT ME IN PARTICULAR?

YES

I UNDERSTAND

HOW CAN YOU UNDERSTAND?

YOU WANT ME TO BE ABLE TO UNDERSTAND?

WHY SHOULD I?

WHAT ANSWER PLEASES YOU THE MOST?

COMPUTERS AND PEOPLE ARE NICE

WHY DO YOU MENTION COMPUTERS?

I DREAM ABOUT COMPUTERS

DO YOU DREAM OFTEN?

I CAN'T HELP IT

How long a program does it take to produce this level of output? Our version consists of just 49 BASIC lines containing program statements; another 150 lines or so containing data; and (inevitably) a few lines of REMarks, to show subsequent users how the program is constructed.

Basically, the program does four things:

(1) it asks for a string of input from the user, and prepares it for processing (using some simple tricks like removing apostrophes, to make the task easier);

(2) it looks through the input for keywords or short word sequences (thirty-six of them: some general, like 'I'; some more specific, like 'dream' or 'computer') that it can use in constructing a reply;

(3) it performs some simple grammatical inversions as a first stage in constructing a reply: turning 'I am' into 'are you', for instance;

(4) and for every keyword or sequence of keywords (there are rules of

precedence, so it prefers the more precise keywords to the vaguer ones if both are present) it has a selection of outline responses from which it can select one. (The responses to 'dream', for instance, include 'Are you disturbed by your dreams?' and 'What does that dream suggest to you?' Those to 'I feel' include 'Do you often feel [a section of input is repeated here]?' and 'Do you enjoy feeling [input]?') Our version simply works down these, tagging the next one when the first has been used, and so on; other versions might use a randomizing technique for selecting one. If no keyword is found, the system produces one of a separate sequence' of 'temporizing' responses (like 'Tell me more').

ELIZA is a cleverly constructed program: and it has been known to fool people that it 'understands' them and their problems. But as our brief description of it will have shown, in fact it does not even *try* to understand them. Its techniques have nothing to do with natural language understanding, as Weizenbaum was at pains to make clear; it is simply concerned with some simple aspects of how grammatical responses that can at least occasionally 'echo' input are put together.

Is the computer running ELIZA acting 'intelligently'? It is very much a matter of definition, as we have tried to show. It is an impressive program in its limited way, though it has been much criticized, both by people who wish it were less limited and by people who fail to understand exactly what it does. But nobody would suggest that the computer running ELIZA (in the way we have outlined) is *conscious*. It is just a normal computer running a very normal type of program.

Programs that Program

If we are to succeed in our search for a conscious computer, then, we must look elsewhere. Let us resume our search with a look at complex structures: at ways in which programs might act upon other programs.

We have already mentioned program-writing programs: utility programs that enable the programmer to specify his requirements on a higher level of abstraction than that which he would normally use. Though limited in some ways, they are indeed very useful tools. But what exactly do they do?

We might think, in fact, in terms of a hierarchy of software inside the machine. On the lowest level are basic operations: the operations that the c.p.u. can perform as the result of a single instruction. Slightly higher up, as we have seen, come subroutines and other system utilities that can be 'called up' by programs and literally incorporated into them. Higher still come program packages, programs on the borderline between applications and system functions, like word processing and financial forecasting packages. These make use of system utilities, but in turn they are the subject of more specific programming activities: they are 'tailored' on a higher level to fit them for specific uses, as we saw in Chapter 28. And almost as a reverse of these come the program-writing programs: utility programs that 'write' specific programs.

These alternative hierarchies of low-level and high-level software tools are illustrated in Figure 94.

Figure 94: Hierarchies of software tools

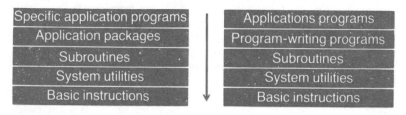

Put baldly, the idea of programs that write programs may seem to be a strange one. But if you think back to Chapter 4, when we considered just what the stored-program concept meant, you will realize that it is at the very heart of computing power. The whole importance of microelectronic technology rests on the fact that solid-state devices make it possible for programs (and data) to be modified by other programs, or other parts of the same program, without human intervention. And the more modification there is without human intervention, the harder it becomes for the human being, eavesdropping at a later stage in the proceedings, to be sure exactly *what* is going on.

Recursion: If it is difficult to think of a program writing or modifying another program, it is much harder still to think of a program modifying itself. But this can happen, too.

You may recall from Chapter 4 that Boolean algebra — the logical system on which computer logical manipulations have been based — depends heavily on the idea of sets; and from set theory, we can come naturally to the idea of recursion.

What is recursion? It is, fundamentally, when something refers to itself. So the archetypal recursive set is the set of all sets —a paradox, you may feel, because the set of all sets must be defined on a level higher than that of its contents; and yet it must contain itself, or it would not be the set of all sets. Playing with the idea of recursion turns up endless paradoxes when levels get mixed in this way: Douglas Hofstadter, whose book *Gödel, Escher, Bach: An Eternal Golden Braid* centres on this idea, has explored many of them. (Try the famous recursive sentence, 'This sentence is false', for instance.) But at the same time, recursion provides a route for 'bootstrapping' a system into higher and higher levels of complexity and power.

Let us look at another recursive building block: the loops and nested loops with which we build compact power into computer programs. Every time we loop around, we make the loop change itself, often with a statement like:

$N = N + 1$.

What a peculiar statement, when you come to think about it. $N = N$; so how can $N = N + 1$? Indeed, to make N equal $N + 1$ we have to overlook the normal rules of logic for a moment, and pretend that the equals sign means something quite different from what it normally means. We call the first 'N' the name of our variable, and tell ourselves that the second 'N' refers to part of its contents, for instance. From a different angle, what we are doing, though, is to have the statement 'rewrite itself' — redefine itself *in terms of* itself. There is a massive difference, in logical terms, between

$N = 30$

and

$N = N + 1$

The first of these is a straightforward definition: the second is recursive. Got it?

Of course, the same principles can be applied on any level of the programming hierarchy. There is no conceptual difference between having a variable redefine itself in terms of itself, and having a program redefine itself in terms of itself (rewrite itself, in other words).

When we come to have a program that contains itself, in this way, then it no longer becomes feasible (if it ever was, except in a very simplistic way) to produce a neat hierarchy of programming levels. We end up with 'tangled hierarchies', in Hofstadter's phrase, in which we have no idea any more which units include which others, and which are included *by* them.

Tangled hierarchies: As well as having an entity modify an entity further down the hierarchy, and having an entity modify itself, we can have an entity modify an entity further *up* the hierarchy. Let us briefly illustrate this, too.

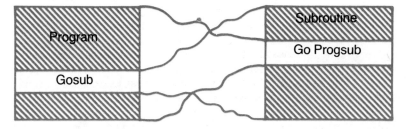

Figure 95: Tangled hierarchies: programs and subroutines

Imagine we have a program, A, and a subroutine, B. At a fixed point in A, we call up the subroutine: so that we can think of A as encompassing B (Figure 95). But there might conceivably be an instruction in B which says simply: call up program A. So we can also think of B as encompassing A. Or rather, A contains B, which contains A, which contains B . . . shall we go on?

Towards Consciousness

We have one last step to make: from tangled hierarchies to consciousness.

What exactly *is* consciousness? As we suggested in Chapter 31, to many people it is the ability to know what you are doing: to encompass yourself. You both *are* yourself, and at the same time you hold within yourself an awareness of what yourself is up to. In other words, your mind is a recursive system with gloriously tangled hierarchies of thoughts. No wonder you have difficulty working out what you are thinking!

People used to argue, with varying degrees of conviction, that computers could not be conscious (could not be intelligent, some went on to say) because they did not have this ability to know what they were doing. Certainly, you could introduce a program on one level that 'monitored' events at a lower level, or even changed programs at a lower level. You could develop a program that 'understood' aspects of itself, in the sense in which SHRDLU understands what its exchanges with its users are all about. But there would always be a topmost level of programming that *didn't* know what it was doing. The human brain (the argument went) did not suffer from this limitation: so it had an advantage over the computer, which could never be taken away.

Introduce the idea of tangled hierarchies, though, and this argument falls to pieces. What topmost layer? Why not set a program on a different layer to monitor it? Or why not make it monitor itself? In fact, why not introduce into computer programming the same glorious confusion that we suspect reigns in the brain?

We already use the idea of layered programs, with programs or data on one level 'running' or adapting programs or data on another, to build up the computer's manipulative and problem-solving abilities. We use knowledge structures to add to their own knowledge (indeed, the whole power of list-processing languages like LISP lies in their recursive abilities). Why not use thinking structures to add to their own intelligence, and bootstrap the computer up into consciousness?

The wary will add that we should be stopped by the fear that the computer will escape our control. But there are already, as we have seen, so many ways in which today's computers are not in our control. We do not fully understand what they do, or why they do it. And we could not understand, without reducing the complexity of what they do: our minds cannot manage it. Is reducing the computer's power what we want? Or do we want to extend the power of this 'artificial brain' as far as it will go?

That is perhaps the best of all questions with which to close this examination of what computing is all about. We have taken a very simple set of building blocks — the basic arithmetic and logic operations we outlined in Chapter 1 — and tried to show how they can be combined in more and more complex ways, to enable them to carry out more and more complex operations. Today's computer applications are amazing. Perhaps tomorrow's will be quite literally beyond understanding.

Glossary

(This glossary includes a number of words, phrases and alternative spellings, that are in common use but that are not used elsewhere in the book.)

access time The time required to send signals to a given memory location, and retrieve its contents.

accumulator Register holding data on which arithmetic/logic operations can be carried out.

a/d conversion See **analog to digital conversion.**

adder Circuit that enables two numbers to be added together (usually includes carry in and carry forward).

address Character code that identifies a specific location (or series of locations) in memory.

address bus Bus that conveys address data from one system component to another.

address decoder Circuitry that enables data to be obtained from a particular location when its character code is provided.

addressing Techniques for locating a required piece of data. See Chapter 10.

algorithm Set of step-by-step procedures used in solving a problem. See also **flowchart, heuristic**.

a.l.u. See **arithmetic/logic unit.**

analog(ue) Term used to describe properties (e.g. temperature, pressure, voltage) that vary continuously (not in fixed 'steps') over time.

analog(ue) computer Computer that operates at least partly with analog properties. See also **digital**.

analog(ue) to digital conversion The process of producing digital approximations to analog readings.

AND gate Logic circuit that will output a 1 only when all inputs are equal to 1. (In all other circumstances, output is 0.)

applications program(me) Computer program that performs an end-user function, rather than a system-oriented function.

architecture The way in which the circuit pattern of a chip, or a computer or part of a computer not on a chip, is laid out.

arithmetic/logic unit (a.l.u.) Part of the computer's central processing unit that can perform arithmetical and logical operations on data sent to it.

array An orderly set of data, or of locations for the storage of data, referenced by dimension (one, two, or more).

artificial intelligence The development of computer applications in which the computer performs functions that cause it to act, or appear to act, intelligently.

ASCII American Standard Code for Information Interchange (several successive versions). Widely used code that converts alpha/numeric and other common characters and control instructions into a seven-bit binary code. Often an eighth bit is used as a parity check.

assembler Computer program that prepares a machine-code program from a mnemonic (assembly-language) program.

assembly language Low-level computer-programming language that makes use of mnemonic codes.

asynchronous Not synchronized; not controlled by time signals. A form of data communication (see Chapter 15).

band Range of frequencies used to transmit a single signal.

bandwidth Width of a band used in a communications system (as measured by its frequency range).

base (of numbering system) The number that is taken to increasing powers as one moves from right to left in the positional notation.

BASIC Beginners' All-Purpose Symbolic Instruction Code. Widely used high-level computer-programming language.

batch processing Form of processing data that involves grouping input data, or tasks, before inputting them. See also **real time**.

baud Unit of signalling speed, approximately equal to one bit per second.

BCD See **binary-coded decimal**.

binary Numbering system with base 2: only the two digits 0 and 1 are used.

binary code Coding system that uses the digits 0 and 1.

binary-coded decimal Either (a) number-coding system in which four binary digits represent one decimal digit; or (b) character-coding system in which six or eight (Extended Binary-Coded Decimal, or EBCDIC) digits are used to code alpha/numeric and associated characters.

bipolar transistor Particular type of transistor more usually found in large computers.

bit Binary digit. The smallest possible unit of data: a two-state, yes/no, 0/1 alternative. The building block of binary coding and numbering systems.

board computer Computer in which all electronic components are laid out on a single circuit board.

Boolean logic Type of mathematical logic used in computer programming, and echoed in the design of logic circuits.

bootstrap (boot) To enter systems software into a computer system (sometimes using special operating routines).

bootstrap program(me) Program that performs the bootstrapping function.

b.p.i. Bits per inch. Measure of density with which data can be stored on tape or cassette.

branch Point in a computer program at which the sequence of instructions followed may deviate from the program sequence.

bubble memory Form of magnetic memory medium making use of small magnetic domains, or 'bubbles'.

buffer (a) Temporary memory/storage locations, e.g. for holding information before it can be transmitted to a peripheral device; (b) (more generally) an electronic isolator.

bug Error in a computer's hardware configuration, or in its software. See also **debug**.

bus (or buss) Two or more conductors, running in parallel, used for carrying information from one component to another.

byte Sequence of adjacent binary digits, operated upon by the central processing unit as a whole. Normally consists of eight bits.

calculator Calculating device that does not embody the variable stored-program concept.

cassette (tape) A form of serial access-memory medium. See Chapter 7.

central processing unit (c.p.u.) Part of a computer system comprising the control and arithmetic/logic units, together with some associated storage registers.

character A symbol that conveys a piece of information.

chip (a) piece of silicon or similar material on which an integrated circuit is manufactured; (b) the entire circuit so formed.

COBOL COmmon Business-Oriented Language. A high-level computer language.

command Either (a) a program instruction; or (b) a single word (perhaps one of a fixed set) used within a high-level language instruction.

compiler Computer program that prepares a machine language program from input in a high-level language.

computer Device that stores and manipulates data, which can control other devices as a result of its manipulation and storage of data, and which can communicate with other computers, with other types of device, and with human beings.

control bus Bus that conveys control signals from one component of a computer system to another.

controller Circuitry that handles the operation of a peripheral device.

control unit That part of the central processing unit that handles control operations.

c.p.u. See **central processing unit**.

cursor Small luminous square, rectangle, etc., on a visual display screen, indicating where the next input will appear.

cycle (a) the undulation of a waveform from positive to negative and back. In communications, measured in Hertz (Hz) = cycles per second; (b) set of procedures involved in performing a program instruction; (c) set of procedures involved in accessing a memory location, reading its contents, and restoring them if necessary.

cycle time Time taken for any of the operations detailed under **cycle**.

d/a conversion See **digital to analog conversion**.

daisy wheel Print head. See Chapter 16.

data Known facts (for storage and/or manipulation by a computer system) expressed in character form.

databank Database system, often structured in menu form, designed for storage and retrieval of data rather than for intensive processing.

database (or data base) System of arranging data in a structured way in a computer system, for user access or for processing by application programs.

data bus Group of conductors, operating in parallel, that transfer data from one part of a computer system to another.

data processing Computer applications that place a heavy stress upon the manipulation of large quantities of data.

debug To remove inaccuracies from a computer program (or from its circuitry).

decimal Numbering system based upon the ten digits, 0 to 9.

decoder Circuit that transforms designated groups of input signals into designated patterns of output signals. Used to 'decode' program instructions or addresses, and initiate the operations (or obtain the data) they specify. Found in the c.p.u.

dialect Specific version of a high-level language that runs on a particular computer system.

digital Describes the measurement of properties in discrete steps. See also **analog**.

digital to analog(ue) conversion The transformation of digital data into an analog equivalent.

digital computer Computer that works in a digital fashion.

diode Electronic device that controls the direction of current flow in a circuit.

direct access Equivalent to **random access**.

direct addressing Method of indicating where data are located in the computer's memory. See Chapter 10.

disc (disk) Flat circular disc, coated with magnetic material, that acts as a memory medium. See Chapter 7.

disc cartridge Hard disc unit.

disc drive Unit on which discs are run.

disc operating system Suite of computer programs that handle the transfer of data between a computer system and disc storage (and usually other operating functions).

disc pack Stack of hard discs. See also **floppy disc**, **hard disc**.

diskette Term sometimes used for floppy discs.

documentation Description of hardware and/or software, designed to facilitate use and adaptation of the system.

dopant Substance added in process described under **dope**.

dope Add another substance to an element (e.g. phosphor to silicon) to change its electrical characteristics.

D.O.S. See **disc operating system**.

dot matrix Printing technology that builds up characters out of discrete dots. See Chapter 16.

dynamic memory Form of data storage circuitry that steadily loses its charge and has to have information rewritten into it at regular intervals.

EBCDIC See **binary-coded decimal**.

edit Modify the form or format of data; amend or correct a computer program.

editor Computer program used as a tool in modifying other programs.

electronics Technology in which the movement of electrons in circuits is controlled.

EPROM Erasable Programmable Read Only Memory. Form of read only memory that can be reprogrammed in certain circumstances.

error code Code that a computer system uses to inform the user of errors found in a program or in general system operation.

error message Message about errors found in programs or in system operation, that may be conveyed in an error code.

exclusive OR Logic circuit with two inputs. Outputs a 1 only if exactly one input is a 1 (otherwise outputs a 0).

execute (a) portion of a computer's operating cycle, during which a particular operation is accomplished; (b) mode in which a computer runs a program.

executive program(me) Systems software program that controls the running of a compiled program.

expert system A computer system that contains, and is able to use, data on a specific 'expert' field of knowledge.

fetch Portion of a computer's operating cycle during which the central processing unit obtains the next instruction it is to perform.

fibre optics Technology based upon **optical fibre**.

firmware Computer programs embodied in read only memory circuits.

flag Data storage location in the arithmetic/logic unit that indicates whether a certain condition exists after an arithmetic/logic operation has been performed (e.g. whether the operation resulted in a zero, positive or negative accumulator content).

flag register Register containing a number of flags.

flip-flop Circuit that can be used to store data. A read/write memory medium.

floating-point number A number expressed in exponential form, i.e. with the decimal point in a fixed position (e.g. following the first digit) and with a suffixed number indicating the significant position of the decimal point, e.g. $1.23E + 3 = 1.23 \times 10^3 = 1230$.

floppy disc (disk) Secondary computer data storage medium. Flexible magnetic oxide-coated, plastic-based discs, usually 3–8″ (7.5–20 cm) in diameter. Random access.

flowchart (or flow chart) Method of representing the analysis or solution of a problem graphically, in which the sequence in which operations are to be carried out is designated.

format The way in which data are arranged.

format a disc (disk) To organize a pattern of data storage sectors on a disc.

FORTRAN FORmula TRANslator. A high-level computer language.

frame A knowledge-structuring device used in artificial intelligence research. See Chapter 32.

frequency How often regular waves or pulses occur (e.g. in a circuit). Normally measured in Hertz (Hz) = cycles per second.

function The capability to perform a mathematical operation such as obtaining a square root or generating a random number.

gate A circuit with two or more inputs and one output.

gate transistor Particular type of transistor technology normally found in microcomputers.

general-purpose computer Computer that can be programmed to handle a wide variety of tasks. See also **special-purpose computer**.

handshaking Control signal sequence that makes it possible for two electronic devices to synchronize their operation.

hard disc (disk) Secondary computer data storage medium. Random access.

hard sectoring Fixed pattern of data storage sectors on a disc.

hardware The physical components of a computer system. See also **software**.

Hertz (Hz) Measure of cycles per second.

heuristic Set of procedures used in attempting to solve a problem. Less definite (and less sure of success) than an **algorithm** (which see also).

hex(adecimal) Numbering system with base 16, using the digits 0 to 9 and letters A to F.

high-level language Computer-programming language that uses succinct codes (which must be translated into the computer's machine code before the program is run) to convey instructions.

immediate addressing; indexed addressing; indirect addressing Methods of indicating where required information is located in the computer. See Chapter 10.

information Data that are communicated.

input Data entered into a computer system.

input device Hardware device used to handle the input of data to the system.

instruction (a) any data sequence that the computer takes as a directive (that causes a particular operation, or series of operations, to be carried out); (b) computer program statement that specifies an operation to be carried out, and the values or locations of the operands.

instruction cycle The period of time that the central processing unit takes to fetch and then execute an instruction.

instruction set The set of basic instructions, any of which a central processing unit can carry out in one operation.

integer A number without a fractional or decimal part; a whole number.

integrated circuit Electronic circuit containing a number of components and connecting wires, manufactured as one unit.

intelligent device (a) any device with arithmetic/logic or control circuitry that enables it to carry out some computer applications; (b) device that performs in a way that can generally be described as intelligent. See also **artificial intelligence**.

interface (Verb) To enable two pieces of equipment to communicate with each other.

(Noun) (a) the point at which two devices are connected; (b) hardware device that accomplishes the interfacing procedures.

interpreter Computer program that 'interprets' high-level instructions by translating them into machine code. Each instruction is executed as it is interpreted.

interrupt System that the computer uses to halt an operation in progress, in order to carry out some other operation.

intimate software Programs that are incorporated in a marketed computer system, and are specific to the control of that system.

inverter Circuit whose output inverts its input, turning a 1 into a 0 and vice versa.

joystick Computer input device consisting of a small stick which can be used to control the movements of a cursor on a visual display screen.

jump Point in a computer program at which there is, or may be (conditional jump), a deviation from the normal sequence of executing instructions.

K (a) 1,024 (usual in describing computer memory); (b) 1,000.

keyword (or key word) Single word used to designate a command or instruction in a high-level language.

language Set of representation conventions and rules used to convey information. See **high-level language**.

large-scale integration Method of producing a large number (from 100 to 1,000) of electronic components (and connectors) as a single unit.

laser Device that emits a beam of coherent light.

L.C.D. See **liquid crystal display**.

L.E.D. See **light-emitting diode**.

light-emitting diode Semiconductor device that emits light when current is passed through it in a particular direction. Used in data displays.

light pen Computer input device. Pen shaped, works by (a) sensing patterns of light and dark and inputting data on them to the system, or (b) 'drawing' on a visual display screen and thus inducing signals that the system can pick up.

line printer Printer that produces a line of type, not merely a character or part of a character, effectively at once, rather than in character sequence.

liquid crystal Substance that is under certain electrical conditions transparent to light. Used in data displays.

liquid crystal display (L.C.D.) Display that uses liquid crystal.

list A knowledge-structuring device used in artificial intelligence research. See Chapter 32.

listing List of program statements (e.g. written or displayed on a visual display screen).

list processing Processing methods that use the list device.

load (a) enter data into computer storage locations; (b) transfer a program from a secondary storage medium to a computer's internal storage circuits.

logic gate Circuit (in microelectronic or comparable hardware form) that controls the passage of electronic pulses in a way that can be interpreted as representing logical manipulations. See **AND gate, OR gate, exclusive OR gate, NOT gate**.

L.S.I. See **large-scale integration**.

machine code Operation code (in binary form) that will trigger a set sequence of instructions in a particular computer system.

machine language Synonym for 'machine code'.

magnetic tape A form of serial access memory medium. See Chapter 7.

mainframe Large computer, originally manufactured in a modular fashion. Sometimes used to refer to the computer's c.p.u. and internal memory, excluding peripheral devices.

matrix A two-dimensional array, or ordered set of data (or of locations for storing data). See also **dot matrix**.

matrix printer Printer that uses dot-matrix technology.

mega- One million – as in MByte, one million bytes. When referring to memory capacity, equals $1,024^2$, or K^2.

memory That part of a computer's circuits in which data are stored. See also **secondary memory**.

memory map An indication of what type of data are stored where in a computer's memory.

menu List of user options, usually displayed on a visual display screen, that correspond to potential branches in a program.

micro- One millionth – as in 1 microsecond, a millionth of a second.

microcomputer (a) computer whose central processing unit is contained on a single silicon chip; (b) entire computer's circuitry contained on a single silicon chip.

microelectronics Branch of electronics concerned with large-scale, very large scale and ultra large scale integration of components.

micron A millionth of a metre (measure used to describe chip components).

microprocessor Central processing unit contained on a single chip.

minicomputer Computer of moderate size: larger than a microcomputer, smaller than a mainframe.

modem MOdulator/DEModulator. Device that handles analog/digital signal conversion in data communications.

modulation Method of varying waveforms in order to convey information.

monitor (a) set of systems software programs concerned with basic system operation (see Chapter 9); (b) visual display unit.

MOS Metal Oxide Silicon. Technology used in the manufacture of silicon chips.

multiplexing Technique for transmitting more than one sequence of signals down the same channel.

multiprocessing The running of more than one program simultaneously on the same computer system.

NAND gate Logic circuit that will output a 0 only when all inputs are equal to 1. Otherwise, outputs a 1.

nano- One thousand-millionth: as in one nanosecond, a thousand-millionth of a second.

network A system in which a number of computers and peripheral devices are linked together.

NOR gate Logic circuit that will output a binary 0 if any of its inputs is equal to 1; and a binary 1 if none of them are.

NOT gate Logic circuit that acts as an inverter: outputs a 1 if input was 0, and vice versa.

octal Numbering system using base 8.

on-line (a) control system whereby one unit is controlled by another without manual intervention; (b) immediately available for use by the computer system.

operating code Code for a computer instruction.

operating cycle The fetch/execute/store sequence by which the central processing unit obtains and performs a program instruction.

operating system Set of systems software programs that facilitates system operation.

optical fibre Fibre that can be used to transmit coded light signals.

optics Technology concerned with the manipulation of light signals.

opto-electronics Technology concerned with the integration of optics and electronics.

OR gate Logic circuit that will output a 1 if any input is 1; otherwise, outputs 0.

output Data signal emitted from a system, or part of a system.

output device Hardware device that handles output operations.

package (a) a set of computer programs sold together; (b) the program listing, together with supporting documentation and possibly training manuals.

paging Technique for dividing up the computer's memory into blocks. See Chapter 10.

parallel processing Method of data processing in which more than one bit is handled at a time.

parallel transmission Method of data transmission in which more than one bit is sent at a time.

parameterized program(me) Program written in such a way that some of its aspects can be defined by the user, thus enabling it to be fitted to a wide range of specific applications.

parity check Error-checking method that uses an extra digit (e.g. eighth digit added to seven-digit codes) to ensure an even number of 1s and 0s are transmitted.

peripheral Hardware device that can be attached to, and used in conjunction with, a computer system.

pin Device by which a chip circuit is connected to adjoining circuitry.

pixel Tiny portion of a video screen.

plug-compatible Refers to a device supplied by one manufacturer that interfaces to another manufacturer's system.

port Connection point for input/output to a computer system.

portability The ability of software designed for one computer system to be used on other systems.

precision The number of significant figures that can be expressed in a given number — e.g. double-precision arithmetic works with twice as many significant figures as single-precision arithmetic.

processor Synonym for **central processing unit**.

program(me) A sequence of instructions that is determined before the start of an operation, and that is translated into a series of actions performed by the computer system hardware.

program(me) counter Register that holds the address of the next program instruction to be implemented (unless implementation deviates from the program sequence).

program(me) statement Section of a program that the central processing unit treats as one unit.

PROM Programmable Read Only Memory. Memory device containing fixed data that can be read but not altered. Entering of the data is performed after the device is manufactured.

pulse Single burst of electrical current that is treated as a unit.

RAM Random Access Memory. A memory device in which data can be written or read in any order. Often used to refer to the computer system's internal memory circuits with this ability. See **read only memory**; **read/write memory**; **serial memory**.

random access Ability to access circuits (e.g. memory circuits) in a random fashion: i.e. going directly to the required portion, without accessing a fixed sequence of prior circuitry first. Often used of technology that is in fact only pseudorandom in access.

raster (a) repetitive pattern generated on a visual display screen; (b) visual display system that generates pictures in a systematic, line-by-line way.

read only memory Memory device from which unchanging data can be read, but into which no new data can be written.

read/write memory A memory device into which data can be written, or from which data can be read. See **RAM**; **read only memory**.

real time Interaction with the computer in which instructions are performed as they are entered; generally, an interactive mode of user/computer relation. Often used when computer response time is insignificant to the human user.

refresh circuitry Circuitry that is necessary to restore (a) the data stored in dynamic cells, which steadily lose their charge; (b) the data displayed on a visual display screen.

register Set of temporary storage locations for digital information, handled as a unit. Usually found in the computer's central processing unit. May enable some arithmetical/logical manipulations to be performed.

register addressing; register indirect addressing; relative addressing Methods of indicating where required data are located in the computer. See Chapter 10.

ROM See **read only memory**.

run Execute a computer program.

run-time The time a computer program takes to run.

run-time routines Specialized subroutines that help to minimize run-time.

secondary memory Hardware devices that can act as computer peripherals, and can store information. See **disc**; **cassette**; **magnetic tape**.

sector Part of a disc used for the storage of data.

semiconductor Material (such as doped silicon) that acts as a conductor of electricity under some circumstances, and a resistor to current flow under others.

sequential access Access to data in a set sequence (see also **random access**).

serial memory Memory medium to which access is in a set sequence, and not at random.

serial processing Method of data processing in which only one bit is handled at a time.

serial transmission Method of data transmission in which only one bit is sent at a time.

silicon chip Sliver of silicon upon which a microelectronic circuit is built up.

soft sectoring Applies to a type of data storage disc in which division of the space into sectors is performed by the disc operating system.

software (a) any computer programs; (b) systems, rather than applications, computer programs (precise definitions vary); (c) man's interpretation of the actual or potential activities of a computer system, in terms of arithmetic, logic and control operations (or combinations of these on a higher level).

solid state Device with no moving parts.

special-purpose computer A computer whose hardware is designed to make it specially applicable to a single use, or a limited range of uses (e.g. word processing).

stack Set of data storage locations that are accessed (and from which data are retrieved) in a fixed sequence.

stack pointer Register that holds the address of the next available location in the stack.

standard Widely observed set of rules governing an aspect of computer system operation. May be laid down by a statutory body, or simply created by a major manufacturer's practice. See Chapter 14.

statement A fixed portion of a computer program. See Chapter 10.

static memory Memory circuitry that does not require refreshing.

string A sequence of characters that is handled as a unit by the computer.

subroutine Part of a larger program that can be called up as a unit and repeated as and when necessary.

supercomputer Extremely large and powerful computer.

synchronous Controlled by common timing signals. A form of data communication (see Chapter 15).

synthesis Process of creating or re-combining components to make a new whole — as in speech synthesis, music synthesis.

system (a) a network of individual devices or activities in which overall behaviour is determined by the pattern of the network; (b) a computer and its peripheral devices, working together.

systems analysis The analysis of a system that is to be the subject of a computer application, with a view to drawing up an algorithm for its computerization.

systems software Computer programs concerned with the operation of the computer system, and not with the performance of applications.

teletype A comparatively cheap, basic printer/keyboard. See Chapter 16.

terminal Computer input and/or output device that can be operated remotely from the main computer system.

time sharing The use of a single computer system by many programmers/operators at the same time. The system interleaves the operations connected with different programs.

transistor Solid-state electronic component.

truth table A table showing the outcome of passing various sets of input through a logic circuit. Sometimes generally to show the simple consequences of different combinations of events.

T.T.L. Transistor-transistor-logic. A type of integrated circuit construction used in computers.

U.L.A. See **uncommitted logic array**.

ULSI Ultra Large Scale Integration. Manufacture of over 1 million electronic components as an unit.

uncommitted logic array Logic chip that has not yet been completed. The user 'programs' it with a final circuit pattern.

user friendly Applied to techniques for making the computer easy to use (especially by non-professionals).

utility program(me) Systems software program that facilitates the running and testing of application programs, particularly in relation to input/output. Often part of an operating system.

variable (a) location in memory that can contain variable information; (b) information contained in such a location; (c) name given to such a location.

V.D.U. See **visual display unit**; **video**.

video A specific technology used for the production of on-screen images.

videodisc (disk) Disc that stores coded visual data; or on which data is recorded by an optical system.

visual display unit Hardware device incorporating a visual display screen (not necessarily a video screen).

VLSI Very Large Scale Integration. Manufacture of between 1,000 and 1 million electronic components as a single unit.

Winchester disc (disk) Synonym for **hard disc**.

word Group of bits handled as a unit, and usually stored in locations designated by a single address, in the computer.

word processing Application of a general-purpose or special-purpose computer system to textual manipulations.

Selected Bibliography

General

David H. Ahl (ed.), *The Best of Creative Computing*, 3 vols. (Vol. 3 co-ed. by Burchenal Green). Creative Computing Press, U.S.A., 1976/1977/1980. Wide range of articles, reviews, progams, etc. Our ELIZA program (see Chapter 34) was adapted from one by Steve North/Jeff Shrager, listed in Vol. 3.

Don L. Cannon and Gerrald Luecke, *Understanding Microprocessors*, Texas Instruments/Radio Shack, 1979. Very clear introduction to the basic technology.

H. Dominic Covvey and Neil Harding McAlister, *Computer Consciousness: Surviving The Automated 80s*, Addison-Wesley, U.S.A./Canada, 1980. Clear general introduction with a stress on commercial data processing.

Michael L. Dertouzos and Joel Moses (eds.), *The Computer Age: A Twenty-Year View*, M.I.T. Press, U.S.A., 1979. Good essays on computer applications, socio-economic implications, technological trends.

Charles P. Lecht, *The Waves of Change: A Techno-Economic Analysis of the Data Processing Industry*, McGraw-Hill, U.S.A., 1979. Full of figures, good summaries of technical trends.

A. J. Meadows, M. Gordon and A. Singleton, *Dictionary of New Information Technology*, Kogan Page/Century, U.K., 1982. Thorough and well-illustrated.

Eric Morgan, *Microprocessors: A Short Introduction*, U.K. Dept. of Industry, 1980. Clearly written and extremely well illustrated.

Ted Nelson, *Computer Lib*, pub. Ted Nelson, 1974. Now ageing on the technology, but still an excellent introduction to the wilder shores of computing.

Gordon Pask and Susan Curran, *Micro Man*, Macmillan, U.S.A.; Century U.K., 1982.

Nat Wadsworth, *Understanding Microcomputers and Small Computer Systems*, Scelbi Computer Consulting Inc., U.S.A., 1977. Good on basic technology: addresses, registers, etc.

Susan Wooldridge, *Software Selection*, Auerback, U.S.A./U.K., 1973. Commercially oriented, good on software history.

On Electronics in General

F. R. Connor, *Electronic Devices*, Edward Arnold, U.K., 1980.

Edward V. Ramirez and Melvyn Weiss, *Microprocessing Fundamentals: Hardware and Software*, McGraw-Hill, U.S.A., 1980.

On the History of Computing

B. V. Bowden (ed.), *Faster Than Thought*, Pitman, London, 1953. A classic, still unbeatable on the early history of computing. Narrative, not a collection of essays, but includes Menabrea's paper and Lady Lovelace's notes as an appendix.

Herman H. Goldstine, *The Computer from Pascal to von Neumann*, Princeton University Press, U.S.A., 1972.

S. H. Hollingdale and G. C. Toothill, *Electronic Computers*, Penguin Books, U.K., 1965. Not written as a history, but now valuable as a basic introduction to contemporary technology.

N. Metropolis, J. Howlett and Gian-Carlo Rota (eds.), *A History of Computing in the Twentieth Century*, Academic Press, U.S.A., 1980. Exceptionally thorough, occasionally technically demanding collection of essays. Includes the best article we know on the development of languages (Donald E. Knuth and Luis Trabb Pardo, 'The Early Development of Programming Languages').

Brian Randell (ed.), *The Origins of Digital Computers: Selected Papers*, Springer-Verlag, West Germany/U.S.A., 1973. Includes papers by Babbage, von Neumann, Mauchly, Wilkes.

Sigvard Strandh. *A History of the Machine*, A&W Pubs., U.S.A., 1979. Contains brief but well-illustrated section on early calculators and computers.

On Home/Personal Computing

Robin Bradbeer, *The Personal Computer Book*, Input Two-Nine, 1980. Contains a good rundown of available machines, user groups, magazines, etc., at the time of publication.

David Bunnell, *Personal Computing: A Beginner's Guide*, Hawthorn, U.S.A., 1978. Generalist, but sound.

Ted Nelson, *The Home Computer Revolution*, pub. Ted Nelson, U.S.A., 1977. Lively general introduction (no programming), good on the birth of home computers.

Mark Sawusch, *1001 Things to Do with your Personal Computer*, T.A.B., U.S.A., 1981. Only a slight exaggeration; includes some interesting programs.

Also recommended:

Byte magazine, U.S.A. Can be over-technical, but still the best available.

Personal Computer World magazine, U.K. Overall, best of the U.K. computer magazines.

On Specialist Aspects of Technology

John Eargle, *Sound Recording*, 2nd edn, Van Nostrand Reinhold, U.S.A., 1980. Good section on digital recording techniques.

Jerry FitzGerald and Tom S. Eason, *Fundamentals of Data Communications*, John Wiley, U.S.A., 1978. Very clear.

H. W. Franke, *Computer Graphics — Computer Art*, Verlag F. Bruckmann

KG, Munich; Phaidon, U.S.A./U.K., 1971. Brief and now outdated on technology, but contains a good selection of illustrations.

Harry F. Olson, *Music, Physics and Engineering*, Dover, U.S.A., 1967. Outdated technically, but excellent on the physical properties of music.

On Computer Programming

Andrew Colin, *Programming for Microprocessors*, Newnes-Butterworths, U.K./U.S.A., 1979.

Van Court Hare, Jr, *Introduction to Programming: A BASIC Approach*, Harcourt, Brace & World, U.S.A., 1970. Contains a brief but valuable historical section. Emphasis on commercial data processing, but still a good general introduction.

Clive Prigmore, *30 Hour BASIC*. National Extension College, U.K., 1981. Based around the B.B.C.'s 'The Computer Programme', and aimed primarily at the B.B.C. Computer (alternative edition for the ZX81).

Ian Stewart and Robin Jones, *Peek Poke Byte & RAM!*, Shiva, U.K., 1982. Cheerful, informative introduction to practical BASIC programming for the Sinclair ZX81.

Mainly on Computer/Microprocessor Applications

Iann Barron and Ray Curnow, *The Future with Microelectronics*, Frances Pinter, U.K., 1979. Report to the U.K. Government, solid in projections, but not easy reading.

Alan Burkitt and Elaine Williams, *The Silicon Civilization*, W. H. Allen, U.K., 1980.

Ray Curnow and Susan Curran. *The Silicon Factor: Living with the Microprocessor*, National Extension College, U.K., 1979. Brief general introduction that looks at computers in education, in the home, etc.

Susan Curran and Horace Mitchell, *Office Automation*, Macmillan, U.K., 1982.

Peter Large, *The Micro Revolution*, Fontana, U.K., 1980. Readable general introduction.

Simon Nora and Alain Minc, *The Computerisation of Society*, La Documentation Française, France, M.I.T. Press, U.S.A./U.K., 1978. Thorough look at the impact of information technology, prepared for the French Government.

G. L. Simons, *The Uses of Microprocessors*, National Computing Centre, U.K., 1980. Brief descriptions of a wide range of actual applications.

On the U.K. Meteorological Office and its Work

R. E. W. Pettifer, 'A Brief Introduction to the United Kingdom Mark 3 Radiosonde System', Met. Office, 1978.

'Computers in Weather Forecasting', Met. Office internal paper, *c.* 1979.

'The Development of the Meteorological Office New Operational Forecasting System', *Meteorological Magazine*, H.M.S.O., July 1982.

Meteorological Office Annual Report 1981, H.M.S.O., 1982.

On Artificial Intelligence

Avron Barr and Edward A. Feigenbaum (eds.), *The Handbook of Artificial Intelligence*, Vol. 1, Pitman, U.S.A., 1981. Highly recommended.

Margaret Boden, *Artificial Intelligence and Natural Man*, Harvester Press, U.S.A., 1977. Solid, slightly indigestible classic.

Ray Curnow, 'Artificial Intelligence Today', Science Council of Canada, 1982.

Edward A. Feigenbaum and Julian Feldman (eds.), *Computers and Thought*, McGraw-Hill, U.S.A., 1963. Classic collection of essays. Includes Alan Turing's 'Computing Machinery and Intelligence'.

Douglas R. Hofstadter, *Gödel, Escher, Bach: An Eternal Golden Braid*, Basic Books, U.S.A.; Harvester Press/Penguin Books, U.K., 1979. Lengthy, eccentric, but contains some valuable insights.

H. A. Stein, 'A Study of Artificial Intelligence', Science Council of Canada, 1982.

Deborah L. S. Sweitzer and Paul-André Schabracq, 'Artificial Intelligence: The State of the Art', Science Council of Canada, 1982.

Index